Software
Inspection

Software
Inspection

Tom Gilb
Dorothy Graham

Edited by Susannah Finzi

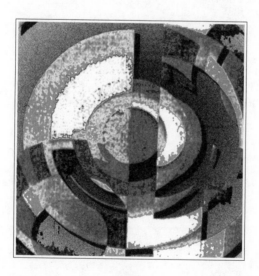

Addison-Wesley Publishing Company

Wokingham, England • Reading, Massachusetts • Menlo Park, California • New York
Don Mills, Ontario • Amsterdam • Bonn • Sydney • Singapore
Tokyo • Madrid • San Juan • Milan • Paris • Mexico City • Seoul • Taipei

Cover designed and illustrated by Arthur op den Brouw, Reading,
incorporating photograph by Norman Hollands
and printed by The Riverside Printing Co. (Reading) Ltd.
Typeset by Columns Design & Production Services Ltd, Reading.
Printed in Great Britain by TJ Press (Padstow) Ltd, Cornwall.

First printed 1993. Reprinted 1994.

British Library Cataloguing in Publication Data
A catalogue record for this book is available from the British Library

Library of Congress Cataloging in Publication Data
Gilb, Tom.
    Software inspection / Tom Gilb, Dorothy Graham ; edited by
Susannah Finzi.
        p.   cm.
    Includes bibliographical references and index.
    ISBN 0-201-63181-4
    1. Computer software—Quality control.   I. Graham, Dorothy.
II. Finzi, Susannah.   III. Title.
QA76.76.Q35G48   1993
005.1'4—dc20   93–1151
                                                              CIP

Authors' Addresses
Tom Gilb, Iver Holtersvei 2, N-1410, Kolbotn, Norway
Tel. (+47) 66 801697

Dorothy Graham, Grove Consultants, Grove House, 40 Ryles Park Road, Macclesfield,
Cheshire SK11 8AH, UK
Tel. (+44) 625 616279
Fax (+44) 625 619979

Editor/Agent: Susannah Finzi, 14A Junction Road, London W5 4XL.
Tel./Fax: (+44) 81 847 0471

The Authors dedicate this book to their families and their colleagues. Dorothy would like to thank her husband Roger for his continual encouragement, helpful suggestions and support, and her children Sarah and James for their patience and understanding. Tom would like to thank his family, especially his son Kai Thomas who was of so much practical help in the final stages of Tom's authorship. But authoring is also 'family'. The book is definitely a 'child' and the community of colleagues is very much our professional family.

Foreword

Since you picked up this book, you probably have a few questions about inspections. For example:

What are inspections?
Would they help me do a better job?
Would they help my organization?
How do I do them?

If this is what you want to know, you are looking in the right place. Tom Gilb and Dorothy Graham have done a masterful job of answering these questions, as well as a lot of others that may not have occurred to you.

As they point out, if there were a Nobel prize for software, Mike Fagan would deserve it for introducing formal inspections. IBM gave him its highest technical award for this work, its Outstanding Contribution Award; and he was given a cash prize of $50,000. This is because properly run inspections both cut development costs and improve quality by an order of magnitude.

The inspection method is not intuitively obvious. It takes up-front investment, it is often hard to sell to a skeptical organization, and it requires skill. One of the reasons this book is important is that it captures the logic for doing inspections in straightforward and forceful terms. It should thus convince you of their importance and then help you to convince others.

That, however, is not the principal value of this book. Inspections have now been practiced for many years, and a great deal has been learned about how to introduce them and how to do them. To be most effective, you should build on this experience. This is where the authors make their primary contribution. Tom has lectured and taught this subject since 1975 and has a wealth of knowledge on the hows and whys of inspections. The authors have captured this knowledge in clear and compelling language. They use many examples, simple everyday terms, and a pleasant conversational style.

You will find the book both easy and fun to read.

In sum, if you are not now doing inspections, you must read this book and apply its lessons. If you are doing inspections, this book has many hints and ideas that will help you to do them better.

January 1993   *Watts S. Humphrey*
SEI Fellow
The Software Engineering Institute
Carnegie Mellon University
Pittsburgh PA

Watts Humphrey is author of *Managing the Software Process*, and formerly a director at IBM, instrumental in supporting the development of inspections.

Preface

The word 'inspect' is an ordinary English verb meaning 'to look at or examine.' Software Inspection (with a capital 'I'), as described in this book, is an extra-ordinary technique which has been proved successful again and again – in so far as it is properly applied.

In the software engineering world, there is now quite a lot of Inspection going on. But there is strong evidence to suggest that much of this Inspection is not correctly done, and many practitioners do not realize it (see the Self-Assessment Test at the end of this Preface to assess your own review process).

There was (until now) no definitive book which described the Inspection process clearly and in its most advanced, complete and productive form.

The authors have extensive experience in many and varied software engineering quality improvement techniques, and in particular in Inspections, and a particular feature of this book is the numerous small tricks, insights and practical observations gathered since we began to spread this method to our international clients in 1975.

What is This Book Based On?

This book will probably be the first published textbook primarily treating Michael E. Fagan's Inspection method, developed for IBM and first published by him in a Technical Report dated December 1974. It will include the extensions to Inspection which our clients have found that they have needed to make it work in their culture and for their purposes in doing serious industrial software engineering. These include the excellent work done since 1983 for process improvement by Carole Jones and Robert Mays and colleagues at IBM.

None of this should hide the fact that the software engineering community owes a great debt to Michael Fagan for bringing us this great gift, just as we and Mike recognize our common debt to

Shewhart, Deming and Juran for laying the basis upon which Mike built. If there were a Nobel Prize for Software Engineering, Michael Fagan should get it!

Who Helped us Write the Book?

This book is a product of teamwork and of many voluntary contributions. The 'official' authors want to thank the many colleagues and friends who have contributed.

The following people made serious detailed constructive criticism after reading early draft manuscripts which has impacted the book in major ways: Barbara Spencer, Ed Barnard, Lindsey Brodie, Jacqueline Holdsworth, Trevor Reeve, Denise Leigh, Graham Terry, Suzanne Garcia and Michael Wearing. We are particularly grateful to our case study authors (of Chapters 12 to 17), who have each taken the trouble to write extensive accounts of their experiences in installing Inspection in their very different organizational environments.

Our clients and students have been a major source of inspiration at all times in the development of the method. We have named many of them within the book, but there are far more who are not specifically named. They have shared their experiences, their personal tricks and inventions with the method, and their serious concerns with us, and we are keenly aware of the debt we owe to dozens of friends from our practical teaching and implementation work.

We want to thank the many professional colleagues, most of whom appear in the bibliography or other literature references, for the useful insights they have provided. The greatest debt goes to Michael Fagan and Carole Jones and their respective colleagues for their landmark contributions.

Certain companies have been particularly helpful in letting constructive people work with the method together with us extensively, thus contributing experiences and ideas to this book. They include IBM, Hewlett Packard, Texas Instruments, Cray Research, Philips, ICL, Douglas Aircraft, Boeing, and Shell.

Very special thanks goes to our editor and agent, Susannah Finzi, who got the authors' intention to write this book translated into an actual product, by setting schedules and keeping the flow of communication going between a number of very busy people. Her clearer way of expressing an idea, a simpler sentence construction, and a cleaner layout has added a great deal to the readability of the book.

How To Navigate Around This Book

This book aims to provide a comprehensive description and guidelines for installing Inspection. A reasonable management overview could be obtained by reading Chapters 1, 2, 3 and 10 only. Chapters 4 to 7 provide a detailed exposition of the method, and Chapters 8 to 11 some specialist viewpoints including 'everything you need to know' for Inspection leaders. Chapters 12 to 17 are case studies, each written by a professional software engineer about their experiences in installing Inspection. The appendices provide all reference material including a glossary.

The terms used in this book for the various elements in the Inspection process are not all the same as those used by other and earlier practitioners of the method, and in the interests of accurate reporting of the events in question, there has been little or no attempt to achieve perfect conformity of terminology between the case studies and the rest of the material in the book.

This book has not been Inspected. As such it is no more defect-free than any other, and the authors would appreciate any constructive comments from readers. We also apologize to any other author on the Inspection process if we have not included a specific reference to their work. We would be delighted to receive copies for future reference.

Where Are You Today?

You may believe that you are already performing Inspections reasonably well or even very well, because you are getting noticeable improvements in your software engineering products. However, there is a danger of being satisfied with a process which is far less effective than it could be, precisely because of this. Inspection is so powerful, that even applying it poorly gives quite good results!

If you would like to get an idea of how your current process compares with its full potential, audit your own process using the questions below.

A Self-Assessment Audit of Your Inspection/Review Process

Inspection Audit Questions

These questions should be used for a relatively mature review or Inspection process which has been in use for some months at least.

(1) Do you prohibit entry to the Inspection process when the source documents for the product to be Inspected have not exited a previous Inspection? If the answer is no, do you first carry out a mini-Inspection on those documents or at least on a sample of them? Do you prohibit Inspection if the source documents are not of adequate quality as a result of your miniInspection or sample?

Always   Usually   Sometimes   Never

(2) Does the kickoff meeting set Inspection goals numerically, and establish corresponding strategies for reaching them?

Always   Usually   Sometimes   Never

(3) Are special roles assigned and defined in role checklists? Is there a library of such role checklists available for all Inspection leaders?

Always   Usually   Sometimes   Never

(4) Does the Inspection leader check that every issue logged has had some action taken by the editor?

Always   Usually   Sometimes   Never

(5) Are the rates for both individual checking and the logging meeting updated, compared to the optimum rates, and used to plan the next Inspection cycle?

Always   Usually   Sometimes   Never

(6) Is an acceptable logging rate used as an exit criteria?

Always   Usually   Sometimes   Never

(7) Is the number of remaining defects after edit predicted? If this number is too high for the type of document, does the document fail exit? In other words, is the estimated number of remaining defects an exit criterion?

Always   Usually   Sometimes   Never

(8) Is defect-finding effectiveness computed, based on test and field data? Is the current known effectiveness used to estimate defects remaining at the end of the Inspection cycle?

Always   Usually   Sometimes   Never

(9) Do you log substantial quantities of issues in your source documents? (for example, on average between 10% and 25% of reported issues resulting in a change request)

Always   Usually   Sometimes   Never

(10) Are Inspection leaders formally certified according to written criteria? Is there an up-to-date list of certified leaders? Are non-certified leaders prohibited from running software Inspection (unless under adequate supervision)?

        Always   Usually   Sometimes   Never

(11) Are rules, procedures and checklists improved to some degree on a regular basis (for example, weekly)?

        Always   Usually   Sometimes   Never

(12) Are the results of Inspection standards improvements shared among all Inspection leaders and Inspectors?

        Always   Usually   Sometimes   Never

(13) Is there a library of Inspection material (for example, forms, checklists, rules) which is well-organized and known, and used by all Inspection leaders?

        Always   Usually   Sometimes   Never

(14) Is a process brainstorming meeting held to analyze the root causes of the defects found in the product Inspection? Are small-scale local individual improvements implemented immediately? Are all improvement suggestions formally logged?

        Always   Usually   Sometimes   Never

(15) Does someone or some group of people (for example, the Process Change Management Team) follow up and implement process improvements using the Inspection database?

        Always   Usually   Sometimes   Never

Scoring Your Self-assessment

Score the following points for your answers:

Always	3 points
Usually	2 points
Sometimes	1 point
Never	0 points

If your total score was:

A Total of 45: (Perfection)

You have not been honest with yourself. No one in the real world achieves perfection! Go back and recompute your real score.

Between 0 and 7 points: (Nowhere)

You may occasionally do one or two things correctly with regard to the product documents which you are reviewing, but you are certainly not doing them all or doing them consistently.

Whatever you are calling your current process, you are not doing Inspection as described in this book. You are only misleading yourself and your organization if you do call your process 'inspection'.

You should read and study this book thoroughly. You should identify the priorities for how to get started in doing Inspections properly.

You have the greatest potential for improvement.

Between 8 and 15 points: (Beginning)

You probably have a good start in Inspecting products, but you do not do all of the things you should, and those which you do, you do not carry out consistently.

You may have enthusiastic followers of Inspection who are doing their best to use what they can of the Inspection techniques, but they are probably not being given adequate support to do it properly.

You are unlikely to be doing any of the process improvement part of the Inspection process as described in this book.

You should read this book thoroughly, identifying the areas which you need to change, starting with the product Inspection cycles. Begin to think about the process improvement ideas, but make sure that the product Inspection is well established first.

You have made a start, but have a long way to go.

Between 16 and 23 points: (Competent)

You probably have the Inspection of product documents fairly well under control, and are experiencing improved quality of software deliverables.

However, you do not yet have a good process improvement process in place, so although you are getting good at detecting defects, you keep finding the same ones cropping up over and over again.

Continue to keep your product Inspection working well, and improve those areas which still need attention, but begin to put in place the process improvement part of the Inspection process to realize the real power of the technique.

You should read this book from two viewpoints: to ensure that your product Inspection technique is as good as possible, and to learn about the process improvement side.

Between 24 and 31 points: (Experienced)

Your Inspection of products is well-established and mature, and you have made a good start on implementing the process improvement side of Inspection. You may still be feeling your way in terms of finding the best way to follow through the improvement suggestions and actually change the software development process, but you are certainly going in the right direction. Keep up the good work and continue your progress.

You should read this book to check that you are exploiting all aspects of both product Inspection and process improvement; you will probably find a lot of useful ideas.

Between 32 and 38 points: (Established)

You are consistently performing product Inspections extremely well, and your process improvement mechanism is now well established and beginning to show real benefits.

Although there is still room for some improvement, particularly in the consistent implementation of process improvements, you are basically doing the right things.

You should read this book for any ideas or tips you may not yet be aware of. You should be involved in giving presentations based on your experiences at seminars and conferences, and should be in touch with other like-minded people at the leading edge of Inspection technology.

Between 39 and 45 points: (Trailblazer)

You are doing very well, and are probably in the forefront of the software development industry in terms of the quality of your software products and the productivity of your organization. (If you really scored 45, congratulations!)

You should read this book to identify any areas where you may differ from the processes described, for reasons which you have discovered and proved in practice to be superior.

You should be involved in presenting papers at conferences and sharing your experience on a global level, and helping to push forward the frontiers of the Inspection technique itself.

Contents: an Overview

Contents

1

The Historical Background of Inspection and Comparison with Other Methods

1.1 The Historical Roots

1.1.1 Michael Fagan at IBM

The Inspection technique was developed by Michael E. Fagan at IBM Kingston NY Laboratories. Fagan, a certified quality control engineer, was a student of the methods of the quality gurus W. Edwards Deming and J. M. Juran. (See Figures 1.1 and 1.2).

Fagan decided, on his own initiative, to use industrial hardware statistical quality methods on a software project he was managing in 1972–74. The project consisted of the translation of IBM's software from Assembler Language to PLS, a high-level programming language assembler. Fagan's achievement was to make statistical quality and process control methods work on 'ideas on paper'. In 1976 he reported his results outside IBM in a now famous paper (Fagan, 1976).

Due to its substantial results, the method spread widely within IBM, but not without some resistance. As initially applied it was used for computer source code and pseudo-code, but was quickly spread to all aspects of software engineering by Fagan and his colleagues. By 1979–81 both IBM and Fagan himself became interested in improvements to requirements, architecture and logic specification (pseudocode) languages, and this enabled the effective spread of Inspection 'upstream', where IBM had determined that the really high payoff in using the technique was to be found.

Fagan called his method 'Inspection' and it is still often called

1

Figure 1.1   W. Edwards Deming. Photograph by © Helaine Messer.

'Fagan's Inspection'. With hindsight this was inappropriate for software professionals, since the term inspection can mean 'finished goods checking'. Software people would call 'finished goods checking' test, or systems test, but Fagan's Inspection is a very early upstream development and maintenance process which aims at both document quality improvement and work process improvement.

1.1.2   AT&T Bell Labs

AT&T Bell Labs started using Fagan's Method in 1977, and reported their history in an entire Issue of *AT&T Technical Journal* (Godfrey, 1986). AT&T is the site of the initial development of statistical quality improvement by Walter Shewhart (assisted by Deming and Juran)

Figure 1.2   J. M. Juran.

at Western Electric Co., AT&T's manufacturing subsidiary in the 1920s.

One of Bell Labs major software development organizations with 200 staff reported the following experiences with Inspection in 1986:

- 14% productivity increase (for a single release);
- better tracking and phasing;
- early defect density data improved by ten times;
- staff credit Inspection as an 'important influence on quality and productivity'.

1.1.3   Subsequent Improvement and Extension of Inspection

Defect Prevention

The Inspection technique was built on by Carole L. Jones and Robert Mays at IBM (Jones, 1985) who created a number of useful enhancements (see Figure 1.3):

- the kickoff meeting, for training, goal setting, and setting a strategy for the current Inspection cycle;
- the causal analysis meeting;
- the action database;
- the action team.

IBM fulfilled Fagan's original intention of process improvement by turning Inspection from predominantly a defect *correction* process into also being an effective defect *prevention* process (Mays, 1990).

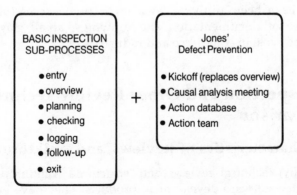

Figure 1.3   Carole Jones' defect prevention as part of the Inspection Technique.

> **The Prevention Principle:**
> Prevention is better than cure.
> or
> An ounce of prevention is worth a pound of cure.

The IEEE Definition of Inspection

The ANSI/IEEE Std. 729-1983 IEEE Standard Glossary of Software Engineering Terminology defines inspection as

'...a formal evaluation technique in which software requirements, design, or code are examined in detail by a person or group other than the author to detect faults, violations of development standards, and other problems...'

It also defines the objective of software inspection as

'to detect and identify software elements defects. This is a rigorous, formal peer examination that does the following:

(1) Verifies that the software element(s) satisfy its specifications.
(2) Verifies that the software element(s) conform to applicable standards.
(3) Identifies deviation from standards and specifications.
(4) Collects software engineering data (for example, defect and effort data).
(5) Does not examine alternatives or stylistic Issues.'

(reference: ANSI/IEEE Std. 1028-1988,
IEEE Standard for Software Reviews and Audits)

Felix Redmill (Redmill, 1988), Trevor Reeve (Reeve, 1991) and others report that work processes, other than those involved in software, have been applying 'idea Inspection' successfully over a wide range of documentation and drawings, at all stages of the product life cycle in commerce and industry.

1.2 Inspection and Other Review Techniques – a Comparison

1.2.1 Characteristics of Reviews and Walkthroughs

Traditionally, technical reviews and 'structured walkthroughs' have been held for software development products. They have been found to be 'helpful' in finding problems and improving the quality of software, but there is almost no substantial documentation on how cost-effective these older methods are. However, these techniques are much less formal than Inspection, and are much less effective at identifying defects. They have gradually been replaced by formal Inspection, for example at IBM Rochester, Minnesota Labs (Lindner, 1992).

The Horses for Courses Principle:
Use walkthroughs for training, reviews for consensus, but use Inspections to improve the quality of the document and its process.

Reviews and walkthroughs are typically peer group discussion activities – without much focus on defect identification and correction. They are usually without the statistical quality improvement which is an essential part of Inspection. Walkthroughs are generally a training process, and focus on learning about a single document. Reviews focus more on consensus and buy-in to a particular document.

It may be wasteful to do walkthroughs or consensus reviews unless a document has successfully exited from Inspection. Otherwise you may be wasting people's time by giving them documents of unknown quality, which probably contain far too many opportunities for misunderstanding, learning the wrong thing and agreement about the wrong things.

Inspection is not an alternative to walkthroughs for training, or to reviews for consensus. In some cases it is a pre-requisite. The different processes have different purposes. You cannot expect to remove defects effectively with walkthroughs, reviews or distribution of documents for comment. However, in other cases it may be wasteful to Inspect documents which have not yet 'settled down' technically. Spending time searching for and removing defects in large chunks which are later discarded is not a good idea. In this case it may be better to aim for approximate consensus on technical issues first, and then Inspect the consensus documents. The educational walkthrough could occur either before or after Inspection (see Figure 1.5).

The description of 'Inspection' in other literature can be very misleading. For example, in the otherwise excellent Freedman and Weinberg (Freedman, 1982), no mention of metrics is made in the description of Inspection. They claim that Inspection differs from walkthroughs and other types of formal review by 'confining attention to a few selected aspects, one at a time.'

Other sources describe Inspection, or more accurately 'inspection', though in considerably less detail than in this book (Hollocker, 1990).

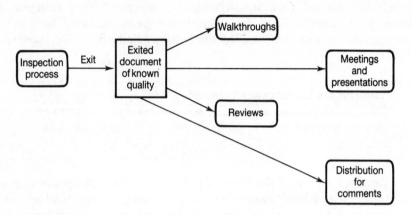

Figure 1.4   Inspection is not an 'alternative': Inspection first.

In other cases, some of the characteristics of Inspection are called by a different name. For example, Yourdon's 'Structured Walkthrough' emphasizes the purpose of detecting rather than correcting defects. It discourages managers from participation, and assigns similar roles and stages to the review process (Yourdon, 1989).

Definition, however, is not the only problem. The *IEEE Transactions on Software Engineering*, 1989 reports a recent industrial study in which it was found that 84% of organizations performed reviews or inspections, but 0% performed inspections entirely correctly.†

A detailed description of inspection is found in Humphrey (Humphrey, 1989) which describes a good inspection process for products, and which distinguishes inspections from management reviews, technical reviews and walkthroughs. Unfortunately, this book mistakenly believes that inspections are more relevant to detailed design and code, and so misses the most effective use of the technique. Otherwise, the rest of the description of the inspection process is well worth reading.

Humphrey places the use of inspection at Level 3 of the SEI process maturity framework, as a technique used by organizations with a defined (as well as repeatable) process. Garcia (Garcia, 1991) also makes the point that Inspections can be set up at the start of a measurement programme.

Expected benefits of Inspection, when compared with reviews, walkthroughs or other types of inspection (with a small 'i') are:

† D.B. Bisant and J.R. Lyle, A Two-Person Inspection Method to Improve Programming Productivity, *IEEE Transactions on Software Engineering*, **15** (10), Oct 89, 1294–1304.

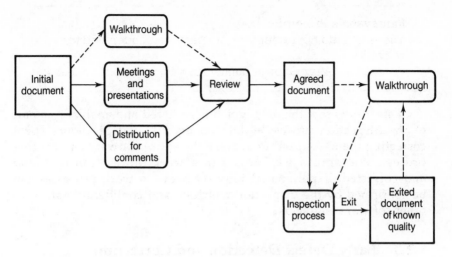

Figure 1.5   Inspection is not an 'alternative': Inspection last.

- measurably higher product *quality*;
- greater *productivity* from people in development and maintenance;
- shorter and more predictable *development times*.

A paradoxical problem with Inspection is that even a pale imitation of the 'real thing', such as a walkthrough, can be quite effective at improving software quality by finding some important defects. Even doing Inspections badly can give quite good results. This is particularly evident when no type of review at all has been performed to date. However, the 'good' really does work against the 'best' in this case, as the benefits from doing real Inspection properly would be far greater. The tragedy is that many people are satisfied with the 10% improvement, and never explore the potential for 100% or more improvement.

Trevor Reeve in Chapter 14 (Case Studies) of this book discusses more of the differences between the various 'cousins' of review techniques.

1.2.2   Statistical Quality Improvement

The fundamental difference between Inspection and other review methods is that Inspection provides a tool to help improve the entire development process, through a well-known quality engineering method, 'statistical process control' (Godfrey, 1986).

> **Santayana's Principle:**
> Those who do not remember the past are condemned to
> relive it.
> (After George Santayana, 1905, *The Life of Reason*)

This means that the data which is gathered and analyzed as part of the Inspection process – data on defects, and the hours spent correcting them – is used to analyze the entire software engineering process. Widespread weaknesses in a work process can be found and corrected. Experimental improvements to work processes can be confirmed by the Inspection metrics – and confidently spread to other software engineers.

1.2.3 Early Defect Detection and Correction

A second important difference between Inspection and other forms of review is the emphasis on the formal written logging of potential defects in the software task document (requirements, design, test plans, test cases, source code, for example) at the earliest possible moment. This is followed by equally formal emphasis on the correction of defects before the documents in question can pollute further development or production and test efforts.

Experience has shown that the cost of executing software tests to catch and correct problems is at least an order of magnitude greater than if such items are found and corrected earlier by using Inspection (see Figure 1.6).

> **The Sewing Principle:**
> A stitch in time saves nine.

1.3 Inspection Compared with Testing

1.3.1 What Inspection and Testing have in Common

Inspection and testing both aim at evaluating and improving the quality of the software engineering product before it reaches the customers. The purpose of both is to find and then fix errors, defects and other potential problems.

Inspection and testing can both be applied early in software development, although Inspection can be applied earlier than test.

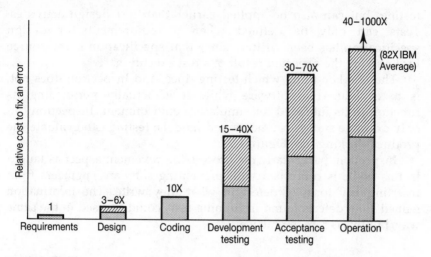

Figure 1.6 The cost of fixing errors escalates as we move the project towards field use. From an analysis of sixty-three projects cited in Boehm: *Software Engineering Economics* (Boehm, 1981).

Both Inspection and test, applied early, can identify defects which can then be fixed when it is still much cheaper to do so.

Inspection and testing can be done well or badly. If they are done poorly, they will not be effective at finding defects, and this causes problems at later stages, test execution, and operational use.

We need to learn from both Inspection and test experiences. Inspection and testing should both ideally (but all too rarely in practice) produce product-defect metrics and process-improvement metrics, which can be used to evaluate the software development process. Data should be kept on defects found in Inspection, defects found in testing, and defects which escaped both Inspection and test, and were only discovered in the field. This data would reflect frequency, document location, severity, cost of finding, and cost of fixing.

There is a trade-off between fixing and preventing. The metrics should be used to fine-tune the balance between the investment in the defect detection and defect prevention techniques used. The cost of Inspection, test design, and test running should be compared with the cost of fixing the defects at the time they were found, in order to arrive at the most cost-effective software development process.

1.3.2　Differences between Inspection and Testing

Inspection can be used long before executable code is available to run tests. Inspection can be applied much earlier than dynamic testing, but can also be applied earlier than test design activities. Tests can only be defined when a requirements or design specification has been written, since that specification is the source for knowing the expected result of a test execution.

The one key thing which testing does, and Inspection does not, is to evaluate the software while it is actually performing its function in its intended (or simulated) environment. Inspection can only examine static documents and models; testing can evaluate the product working (see Figure 1.7).

Inspection, particularly the process improvement aspect as taught in this book, is concerned with preventing software engineers from inserting any form of defect in what they write. The information gained from defects found in running tests could be used in the same way, but this is rare in practice.

1.3.3   The Relationship between Inspection and Testing

Testing and Inspection are not mutually exclusive alternatives. Both have a role, and the best of both worlds is achieved using each where it is most appropriate. Test documentation is just as prone to defects as any other document, so it is essential that test documents are Inspected.

Defining tests early means Inspecting test plans early. Professional software testing practices include:

- the planning and design of testing from the beginning of the software development life cycle;
- acceptance tests defined by users at the same time as user requirements are defined;
- system tests defined during requirements analysis – integration tests defined during architectural design;
- unit tests defined during detailed design;
- execution of unit tests;
- execution of integration tests;
- execution of system tests;
- execution of acceptance tests;
- evaluation of test effectiveness.

In fact, it is even more effective to define tests *before developing* the life cycle deliverable, as argued by Bill Hetzel (Hetzel, 1984).

The consequence of early test planning is that Inspection can be effectively used to improve the quality of the test planning documents and the test planning process at early stages of a project. This will help avoid 'last minute before deadline' problems in getting projects successfully out of the door.

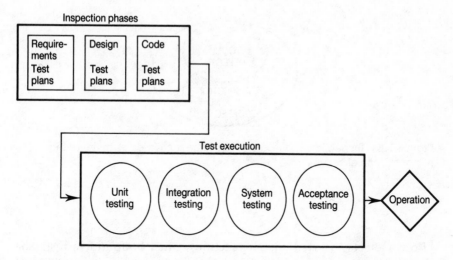

Figure 1.7 Inspection can only examine static documents. Testing can look at the end product.

Inspecting tests can save a lot of time (85% at IBM for example) in the test running phases of the development (Larson, 1975). Test documents are also used in Inspection. For example, requirements-based test cases or plans would be a source document for the Inspection of a design implementing those requirements. Does the design correspond to the planned tests?

Experience data:
Unisys Inspection Experience
One organization (Unisys) which implemented better testing practices found that the number of defects was reduced by 50% by introducing five levels of testing. Their next step was to implement Inspection, which gave them an eventual result of a four-fold improvement in four years (Ulmer, 1991).

Inspection does not replace testing. They both perform some unique functions, which neither can replace for the other (see Figure 1.8). Inspection finds defects not found in testing, and testing finds problems not found in Inspection (Sutton, 1992). What testing *could* find, but Inspection finds *first*, probably gives a saving in correction

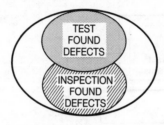

Figure 1.8   Inspection and testing complement each other in the defect removal business.

effort. Defects inserted *after* Inspections, must be found in test. The defect insertion rate during Inspection corrections was reported at IBM by Fagan (Fagan, 1986) as one out of six correction attempts.

AT&T (1986, *op cit.*) correctly classified Inspection as a form of testing. The mechanics are the same, but Inspection does not use a machine to work out what the result of an input (source) and a rule (program) would be in terms of expected 'output' (or 'task product'). This human effort is more costly than if a computer did it, but for many kinds of Inspection no computer is yet capable of making the necessary judgments.

It should be noted that the first of *either* of these two techniques which is actually applied always seems more effective, simply because there are, at the earlier stage, more defects available to find.

1.3.4   Inspection and Defect-finding Tools

Static analysis tools can find some types of defects, such as data-flow or control-flow errors and anomalies. Control-flow problems include unreachable code or infinite loops. Data-flow errors include variables declared and not used, or variables with a value stored twice without being referenced in between.

Software tools are very effective at finding certain types of defects. People are good at making trivial errors such as misspellings or punctuation errors, but are very poor at finding them. Software tools are much faster and more accurate in identifying these, but they cannot find all types of defect. Do not Inspect for things which can more easily be found at the stage you are at by automated tools. Inspect for those things which the tools can't detect at that stage.

> **The Tools for Fools Principle:**
> Automated tools *should* be used to find problems, but not if
> you must delay detection until the fixing costs outweigh the
> advantage of automation.

The notion of which stage you are at is important. This is
because although we can automatically detect some errors at later
stages, the cost of fixing the defects might be so high as to easily
justify using people to Inspect and find the same error at an earlier
stage of the development process.

2

The Benefits and Costs of Inspection

Before introducing any new method into an organization, it must be clear that the eventual savings and benefits will outweigh the costs incurred, including not only the ongoing running costs, but also the start-up costs.

This chapter gives an idea of the overall benefits which some organizations have achieved by using Inspections, and the costs of Inspections.

Inspections are one of the easiest methods to cost-justify because the benefits which can be achieved are considerable and well-documented. However, short-cutting the essential implementation tasks will reduce the benefits which you can expect to get. The short-term investment is essential to achieve the long-term savings.

If you don't really care how cost-effective Inspection is, and if you simply need to learn how to do it, then you might like to skip this chapter entirely. Later, when you discover that you need specific arguments to convince other people of what you already believe about Inspection, you can return to this chapter for data or give them the chapter to read.

Estimating costs without estimating benefits will not give a balanced view.

Experience data:
One project manager showed me a print-out of time sheet effort for 'quality control reviews.' It amounted to 20% of effort.
'Is this reasonable?' he asked.
'I don't know,' I replied, 'how many severe defects did they find?'

> *Continues*
> 'No idea,' he replied.
> 'Then it is not reasonable.'
> He had actually attended one review which reportedly went
> on for two hours and was an in-depth discussion of problems
> with a software development methodology.
> *Source*: Jacqueline Holdsworth (UK, 1992)

2.1   What do Defects Cost Now?

The computer press carries many stories of software systems which
are delivered full of errors, often with serious financial and other
consequences. Purchasers and users are no longer willing to accept
'bugs' as part of the price to pay for having the software delivered at
all. They now expect quality software products delivered on time
within strict budgets. The number of related court cases, both in the
USA and elsewhere, is growing rapidly. Software developers who
have not used the industry's best known techniques for ensuring
quality are beginning to be seen as negligent.

2.1.1   Published Examples

'A UK bank has accidentally transferred £2 billion to UK and US
companies because a software design flaw allowed payment
instructions to be duplicated.'
Computer Weekly (UK), 19 October 1989

'Hundreds of automated bank teller machines . . . went on the
fritz this week, . . . traced to a computer software glitch.'
UPI, 22 August 1990

'A British Steel subsidiary is issuing a writ for £500,000
compensation against a . . . software house which allegedly
corrupted data.'
Computing (UK), 24 October 1991

'London Ambulance Service [lost] four emergency calls. . . . [For
one case,] the details were eventually found and an ambulance
despatched but the patient later died.'
Computing (UK), 20 February 1992

'American Airlines reckons it has lost $50m in passenger
bookings due to a software design error in its own computer
reservation system.'
Computer Weekly (UK), 22 September 1988

A 1991 Survey by the National Computing Centre (UK), found that the two joint highest significant logical security breaches over the last five years were: 'deliberate disruptive or fraudulent software (for example, viruses)' and equally as damaging: 'introduction of unchecked or incorrect software.'

PC User, 25 February 1992

'A marine surveying and salvage company which claims a £300,000 computerized accounting system was plagued by hundreds of faults and unusable from day one has begun a high court claim for almost £1 million in compensation.'

Computer Weekly (UK), 10 October 1991

'The . . . Bank's five million credit card customers were yesterday urged to check their statements for mistakes caused by a computer bug.'

The Times (UK), 11 August 1992

'[A] local government ombudsman . . . found that the housing benefit software from . . . had been delivered late . . . and was riddled with errors.'

Computing (UK), 25 June 1992

'On 1 July [1991] there was a 6-hour [telephone system] outage affecting over 1 million customers in the Pittsburgh area. . . . [It] had finally been attributed to a hitherto undetected but reproducible software fault.'

Risks Forum, *ACM Software Engineering Notes*, July 1991

There are hundreds of other stories, particularly in the Risks Forum of the *ACM Software Engineering Notes*, which tell of hospital radiation systems killing patients through overdoses (and under-dosing), the implication of software faults in fly-by-wire systems for aircraft (nothing proven as yet), financial problems, security breaches, and others from virtually every area of modern life.

The stories which reach the ears of the press probably represent only a small percentage of the problems which are caused by defects in software which never get reported, and yet have a significant impact.

However, there is another iceberg. The waste of resources within an organization due to poor quality software often goes unnoticed and unrecorded, and can involve significant direct and consequential costs, many of which are never even brought to the attention of managers (Hankinson, 1991).

'The cost of non-quality software typically accounts for 30% of development costs and 50–60% of the lifecycle costs.'

IT-Start's Developers Guide,
The National Computing Centre (UK), 1989, p. 2.41

The costs incurred as a result of the production and use of poor quality software are always unjustifiably high when there are known and unexploited ways of producing better quality software.

2.1.2   Defects and the Drive for Quality

Software developers are very concerned to produce quality products. The international standards such as ISO 9000, and quality awards such as the Baldridge Award, are providing the impetus and rewards to those organizations who take quality seriously. The process maturity model, developed by IBM (Radice, 1985) and the Software Engineering Institute (Humphrey, 1989), makes it painfully evident that many organizations are still at the 'chaos' maturity level in software development.

Inspection applied to all software in the widest sense (including all levels of documents from proposals to data-flow diagrams) is now well established as the prime technique to reduce defect levels (in some cases virtually to zero defects), and to provide an increased maturity level through the use of Inspection metrics. If Inspection is implemented as described in this book, it provides within the quality plan the required mechanisms for verification and review activities, as well as higher level quality improvement activities.

2.2   Direct Savings

2.2.1   Development Productivity Improvements

Fagan, in his original article, reported a 23% increase in 'coding productivity alone' using Inspection (Fagan, 1976, *IBM Systems Journal*, page 187). He later reports productivity gains of a 10% productivity increase with informal moderator training, 25% increase with formal moderator training and design change control, and 40% by adding code change control, Inspection of tests and fixes, and test defect tracking ('Defect-free software development – an overview', Lecture Slides by M. Fagan, handed out 24 January 1989, California).

Experience data:
IBM Federal Systems Division (FSD) collects 14 pages of parameters after each project. In one published report 30 projects using Inspection (Fagan's Inspection, FSD Dialect) were compared to about 30 similar projects at FSD using the older 'Structured Walkthrough' (see Figure 2.1). The net delivered lines of non-commentary source code productivity rate per work-month median was:

> *Continues*
> - 300 for the 30 Inspection-managed (Fagan's Inspection) projects
> - 144 for the 30 Structured Walkthrough projects (see Figure 2.1).
>
> *Source*: Walston and Felix, *IBM Systems Journal*, No. One, 1977 and supplementary data in private communication to us

2.2.2   Reducing the Development Timescale

Considering only the development timescales, typical *net* savings for project development are 35% to 50%. Fagan reported 25% reduction of schedule plans in 1976 from a predicted 62 programmer days to 46.5 programmer days actually taken including Inspection (Fagan, 1976, *IBM Systems Journal*, page 189).

> **Experience data:**
> One Inspection user, with a very large systems programming project, had finished three weeks before the official deadline. They didn't believe it themselves. So, they spent two and a half weeks checking to see what they had missed. After all, nobody had ever finished anything on time. They found no defects (indeed there were virtually none, as it turned out) and handed over officially three days early.
> *Source*: IBM, personal communication

2.2.3   Testing Cost and Time Reductions

Inspection reduces the number of defects which are still in place when testing starts because it has removed them at an earlier stage. IBM and others report removal of well over 80% of defects at a single Inspection, and more by accumulation of Inspections before testing (Remus, 1978). This means that testing after Inspection runs much more smoothly because there are fewer defects to find. This in turn leads to less debugging and rework, which shortens the testing phase.

At most sites, Inspection reduces total dependency on testing for quality improvement. In fact it eliminates about 50% to 90% of all the defects that get into the development process before test execution even starts.

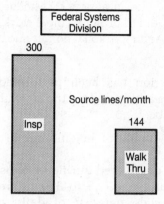

Figure 2.1   IBM FSD data showing that Inspection apparently doubles net software engineering productivity compared to structured walkthroughs.

Experience data:
Some advanced users (for example IBM) manage by a series of Inspections to remove over 82% of all defects *before* testing. They set targets (1992) to achieve 85% to 90% of all defects removed before testing. Defect removal rate at IBM FSD had (1991) *goal* 85% (actually done 82–83%).
Source: Paul N Hutchings, IBM Santa Teresa Labs, November 1991, personal communication

---

The early detection of defects by Inspection:

- reduces the downstream test and field costs for those defects by a factor of ten to twenty (compared to costs when found by conventional testing);
- gives reliable prognosis data about the defect density that can be expected at test and field stages;
- tackles problems early in the project, not at the last minute.

Experience data:
When test plans, test designs and test cases are Inspected, as much as '85%' of work-hours normally needed for unit testing may be saved (on a system with 20 000 lines of code).
Source: Rodney Larson, IBM TR 21.586, 1975

> *Continues*
> Confirmed as a long-term benefit by Michael Fagan 'because
> it forces test planners to organize their work so much better.'
> *Source*: Michael Fagan, personal communication, 1982

If proper Inspection has been performed on most upstream documents leading to and including the code and test cases, then the typical result would be:

- a sharp reduction (order of magnitude) in defects remaining at unit test time;
- close to no defects discovered during systems test;
- no worse than about one (0.5 to 3.0) failures observed per ten-thousand lines-of-code per-year of daily operation, and much better (0.1 to zero) if you have really well-organized Inspection and test.

> **Experience data:**
> An eight work-year development, delivered in five
> increments over nine months for SEMA Group found 3512
> defects in Inspection, 90 in testing, and 35 (including
> enhancements) in the field. After two evolutionary deliveries,
> unit testing was dropped because it was no longer cost-
> effective. System testing was completed a day early.
> *Source*: Denise Leigh, presented at British Computer Society
> (BCS), 1992

It follows from these observations that the actual burden of time taken in the test phases to get to the same level of quality as before is sharply reduced.

However, at least one very large industrial user (IBM Santa Teresa Labs, 1979) has ploughed all Inspection savings (15% yearly cumulative savings) back into increased test work, because they had such a large worldwide user community that this seemed a reasonable reinvestment for them at that time.

As a rule of thumb, each major defect found at Inspection will save about nine hours of downstream correction effort (Reeve, 1991).

Experience data:
Barbara Kitchenham reports on experience at ICL, where
57.7% of defects were found in Inspection, and only 4.1%
found in in-house use. The normal rates at the time were
11.2% of defects found in use. The cost of finding one defect
in design Inspections was 1.58 work-hours; the cost of finding
one defect without Inspection was more than five times more,
at 8.47 work-hours. Yet the total proportion of development
effort devoted to Inspections was only 6%. These figures
would have been improved if better training in Inspection
had been given, and the Inspection process had been
applied as rigorously as it should have been.
Source: B.A.Kitchenham (Kitchenham, 1986)

Experience data:
The reported range is from four (ICL ref.: Gilb, 1988) to thirty
hours (Shell ref.: Doolan, 1992) average effort downstream
(test or field) cost to fix defects which could otherwise have
been identified by Inspection. 9.3 Hours average for Thorn
EMI, Crawley (Reeve ref.: Chapter 14 in this book) for all
types of Inspection, including software.

2.2.4   Lifetime Cost Reductions

The savings achieved using Inspection are even greater when you
account for the lifetime of the system. Inspection can be expected to
reduce total system maintenance costs dramatically (at least ten to
one, according to several experiences). About two thirds of this
reduction will be due to failure reduction, the remainder due to
improvement in documentation intelligibility. Fewer defects in the
field will result in a more competitive product, which in turn leads to
more business at less cost.

Experience data:
In a United Kingdom production planning system, around 800
computer programs were generated. In the middle of the
project, after about 400 programs had been Inspected,
Inspection was dropped because people could not see the
effect (because they did not have Inspection metrics). One

Continues
year later, the maintenance and development project
manager, on our advice, measured the maintenance cost of
the two groups of programs. The Inspection-managed
program's total maintenance phase cost was '0.6 to 0.7
minutes per line of code per year,' while the uninspected
programs cost 'seven minutes per line of code per year.'
Result: 10 times cheaper maintenance on Inspected software.
Source: Imperial Chemical Industries (ICI), Fine Chemical
Manufacturing, Manchester, personal communication from
project manager, about 1982

Experience data:
Standard Bank reported 28 times less maintenance cost for
several Inspected projects. They compared the maintenance
costs of 88 000 lines of Inspected COBOL code against 900
000 lines of uninspected code.
Source: Trevor Crossman, Monterey Guide-Share
Symposium, 1979

2.2.5   Towards Zero Defects

Inspection can be expected to reduce defects found in field use by
one or two orders of magnitude. The reliability of the software
system is greatly increased, as the number of problems experienced
in the field are significantly reduced.

Experience data:
In one large IBM project, one half million lines of networked
operating system, there were 11 development stages
(document types: logic, test, user documentation) being
Inspected. The normal expectation at IBM at that time (1980)
was that they would be happy only to experience about eight
hundred bugs in trial site operation. They did in fact
experience only eight field trial bugs.
Source: IBM Quality Manager, personal communication

Experience data:
The Space Shuttle software made by IBM Federal Systems
Division had zero mission defects for onboard software
during the last six (of nine) missions in 1985. The software
contains approximately 500 000 lines of code and is modified
(tailored to mission) between each flight. Substantial and
specific credit was given to Fagan Inspections and to a
process improvement method.
Source: 'Shuttle Code Achieves Very Low Error Rate,' *IEEE
Software*, 1988, pp 93–95. Also reported in Quality Progress
Sept. 1988, *ACM Software Engineering Notes* (1988), and
various conferences (JPL/NASA, June 1988)

Experience data:
IBM Rochester (Minnesota) Labs
Effectiveness of defect removal using Inspection (1991–2):
• in Source code 60% for single Inspection pass
• in pseudocode 80%
• in module and interface specification 88%
Source: Lindeman slides and oral updates

Experience data:
It has been reported for several smaller (10 thousand lines of
code) projects that they have had one to three years of
failure-free operation from Day One.
Source: several written internal studies given by the Authors
to Gilb from such diverse places as UK, Finland, Hungary and
South Africa

In addition, IBM experience with the 'defect prevention' mode
of Inspection indicates at least 50% reduction in errors during
development and test in addition to the earlier cited figures for
defect detection and correction using Fagan's Inspection (Mays,
1990). The present book 'spells out' the Inspection process in its
fullest form, including the additional features of defect prevention
and quality improvement.

2.2.6 Sources of Inspection Savings

Inspection savings are achieved by reducing and eventually virtually eliminating defects in all parts of the software product. The savings from the lack of defects is due in the long term to avoiding costs in the following areas;

- defect detection costs downstream from Inspection – mainly testing costs in various forms;
- defect correction costs downstream (at test, in field);
- overtime costs, caused by last-minute defect handling, immediately prior to deadlines;
- test running activities, particularly extra bug-fix testing required due to defects found in testing;
- field service to deal with the defects in the systems you supply to others;
- recruitment costs, due to high turnover – often due in its turn to heavily overworked professionals;
- increased marketing efforts to compensate for poor product quality.

The eventual savings to be achieved using Inspection should be calculated on the basis of what would really have happened without Inspection, not on an optimistic estimation of what *might* have happened.

Results will partly reflect what kind of technical reviews the organization used prior to the introduction of Inspection. Naturally, a smaller productivity gain will be achieved when moving from walkthroughs to Inspection than when moving from no reviews of any kind whatsoever to Inspection.

2.2.7 Summary of Direct Inspection Savings

This is a summary of typical results from organizations which have introduced Inspection.

- net productivity increases of 30% to 100%;
- net timescale reductions of 10% to 30%;
- reduction in test execution costs and timescales of 5 to 10 times since there are fewer defects to find;
- reduction in maintenance costs (2/3 due to defect elimination) by one order of magnitude;
- near 'automatic' improvement in software engineering work quality and consequent work product quality;
- early or on-time delivery of systems (no defect-correction backlash at systems integration time, since most defects are treated earlier).

2.3   Indirect Benefits

2.3.1   Management Benefits

'Management gets what it Inspects, not what it expects.'

When Inspection is fully up and running, managers can expect to get access to the relevant facts and figures about their software engineering environment. This means they will be able to identify problems earlier, and to understand the payoff for dealing with those problems.

They will also be able to see the immediate effects of change, and to correct the poor implementation of new ideas when necessary. Inspection can help a manager get away from 'managing by the fingernails.'

The project manager gets a more successful project. The manager of the project manager gets a better organization and more successful projects.

Inspection does not solve all your problems, but it is a strong technique applicable to software engineering work products of all kinds, for which there seems to be no competitor in sight.

Implementing Inspections will impress the quality audit function. In fact current quality standards such as ISO 9000 (MSQH, 1991) demand something very much like Inspection, and Inspection certainly does satisfy the Quality System requirements for verification and review.

Inspection enables managers to encourage developers to take over more responsibility for the quality of their own work.

2.3.2   Deadline Benefits

Inspection cannot in itself guarantee that a thoroughly unreasonable deadline will be met. It will, however, through its quality and cost metrics, give early warning of impending problems. It will also give early danger signals by providing quality milestones (exit approval), and these are far more reliable than hurried managerial sign-offs.

Inspection will also substantially reduce the shock which so many of us experience after integration testing. Usually too many defects are discovered too late, and the costs of fixing defects after testing exceed expectations.

Predictable delays follow from this late discovery of defects. All too often we are tempted to meet the deadline by inadequate correction and inadequate checking of correction. It is not uncommon to find mention of 'the several hundred defects we knew about when we shipped the release.'

2.3.3   Organizational and People Benefits

The benefit of Inspection for most software professionals is that their work is of better quality and is more maintainable. Furthermore, they can expect to live under less intense deadline pressure. Their work should be better appreciated by management, and their company's products will gain a quantifiable competitive edge.

It is important that the individual software professional be made fully aware of these benefits. Otherwise they may take the short-term view that Inspection is just an extra task which interferes with their already high-pressure schedule.

Inspection also tends radically to improve the quality of the documentation standards and source documents, thus having a greater effect than a review or walkthrough on the total development activity across all areas of the organization (see Figure 2.2).

Inspection has particular benefits for all professionals on the team. In picking up the culture of the organization, in being exposed to the best of other people's ideas, but also becoming aware of their own and others' weaknesses, professionals are given strong positive motivation to change for the better. The Inspection process has a formal training value which complements other forms of training.

It also reduces 'single point failure' where all knowledge in a given area is invested in a single individual, and provides senior software engineers with a vehicle for passing on their knowledge.

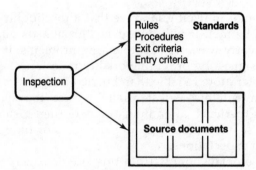

Figure 2.2   Inspection impacts and changes process standards and source documents.

Experience data:
One Inspector put it this way. 'An hour of doing Inspection is worth ten hours of company classroom training for me.'

Later, a director of the same company said that 'Even if Inspection did not have all the other measurable quality and cost benefits which we are finding, then it would still pay off for the training value alone.'

Source: Douglas Aircraft Co, 1988, personal communication

The Inspection meeting-culture provides a successful example of a well-disciplined and focused meeting. This has a tendency to spread to other types of meetings. People arrive on time and insist on a clear focus (what are we to do at this meeting?) and productivity (let's do it, and not waste time on something else!).

2.4   Costs of Inspection

2.4.1   Ongoing Inspection Costs

The cost of running Inspection is approximately 10–15% of the development budget (not including start-up costs). This is about the same cost as other walkthrough and review methods. However, Inspection finds far more defects for the time spent, and the upstream costs are made up for by the benefits of early detection and therefore less costly defect-fixing later, in testing or in the field. An even greater pay-back for the investment comes when the maintenance of software systems is taken into account.

More effort is required 'upstream' (before test) to do Inspection than other review methods, whereas the benefits will arrive 'downstream' (largely from test and later). It is critical to use the known optimum checking rate when doing Inspection – about one hour per product document page intensively studied, because this will enable you to discover the major defects and other items which other methods miss.

2.4.2   Short-term Costs: Budgeting for Inspection

Inspection takes additional 'up-front' time which people are not accustomed to using. This is not only true for the Inspection process itself, but people will be doing a more thorough job of writing any documentation which is a candidate for Inspection. It will seem that Inspection takes more time. Indeed it does – but only to begin with.

An additional short-term budget must be created which gives people permission to take the time to do Inspection properly. If this is not done, they will feel that the organization is not serious about improving things and doing Inspection.

Experience data:
One computer manufacturer project manager pulled off a neat trick to encourage sufficient use of time for Inspection. He simply declared all deadlines extended by 15% for those who used Inspection. This was simply the historical gross cost of doing Inspection at IBM (according to Fagan) when it was in full swing. The 'deal' was accepted, and it instantly defused potential arguments that people were not being given adequate time to get Inspection started. Of course he expected to win far more than he was giving away, and in fact eventual measures of the real initial total cost of all Inspection activities at this site showed that they were using only 4% to 5% of total resources.
Source: (Gilb, 1988)

The cost of implementing the Inspection process within an organization is a separate topic in its own right, and is covered in Chapter 10 of this book.

The Pay now or Suffer later Principle:
Inspection is one of the best investments you can make. If you can't make it, you will end up paying more, but later.

2.4.3   Long-term Costs

Implementing and running Inspection will involve long-term costs in new areas. Here is a list of those things you will probably spend money and time on, which in turn gives a picture of your changed long-term expenditure profile:

• Inspection leader training (minimum three to five days, half theory and half practical exercises);
• management training (one-day appreciation of Inspection, half theory, half experience);
• management of the Inspection leaders (by professional Inspection specialists, not their line manager);
• metrics analysis: what do the costs and defects mean?

- experimentation with new techniques to try to improve the Inspection results;
- planning, checking and meeting activity: the entire Inspection process itself;
- quality improvements: the work of the process improvement teams.

You may also find it effective to consider computerized tools for improving development documentation and consistency checking (particularly tags and cross-references). These may include text processors with indexing, data dictionaries, configuration management tools, logic and module-interconnection documentation and analysis tools, and static analysis tools for software code.

Tools to help plan and control the Inspection process can be as simple as a word processor or spreadsheet. A spreadsheet is ideal, for instance, for recording and analyzing the statistical data.

Another good investment may be for more and better meeting rooms or even better sound insulation so people can concentrate during individual checking. The whole Issue of better working environments for computer professionals is well handled by DeMarco and Lister in their book *Peopleware* (DeMarco, 1987).

2.5 Distribution of Activities within the Inspection Process

Table 2.1 shows roughly how much effort the various Inspection sub-tasks take of the total Inspection effort:

Table 2.1   Distribution of sub-tasks within the Inspection effort.

Phase	Range	Typical
Planning	3–5%	4%
Kickoff	4–7%	6%
Checking	20–30%	25%
Logging	20–30%	25%
Editing	15–30%	20%
Process brainstorming	15–30%	16%
Leader overheads, follow-up, entry, exit, release	3–5%	4%

2.6   Side-effect Costs

Side-effect costs must not be ignored when budgeting for implementing Inspection:

- a heavy increase in activity to improve the software engineering process in general (documentation, rules, testing, automated tool support, training in new methods);
- the cost of collecting data outside Inspection, in areas where reviews and walkthroughs remain, in testing activity and field service.

It is important not to feel swamped with the enormity of these tasks. Prioritizing them helps keep them in perspective, so that improvements can be implemented in a rational order (see also Chapter 10).

3
Overview of Software Inspection

Inspection is described in this book as it applies to software development, but the Inspection techniques themselves are equally applicable to any discipline which produces documents. Since 1988, in fact, they have been applied with excellent results to all manner of hardware engineering (aircraft, electronics), management and meeting documents.

The Inspection process can be thought of as two parts: product Inspection and process improvement. This book examines both aspects and shows how they fit together.

3.1 Product Inspection

Figure 3.1 shows product Inspections taking place between development cycle stages. One effect of the product Inspection is to give feedback to the 'development' process.

3.1.1 Product Inspection and Software Development Stages

Inspection may, for example, take place between requirements and architectural design, between architectural and detailed design, and between detailed design and coding. Figure 3.2 shows how one product Inspection fits with its preceding and following software development stages.

The document produced by a software development stage is shown as being 'infected' with various defects as it enters the product Inspection (1) (see Figure 3.2). The purpose of Inspecting the product is to look at it 'through a microscope' so that the defects can be discovered. Although some defects, like some bacterial infections,

31

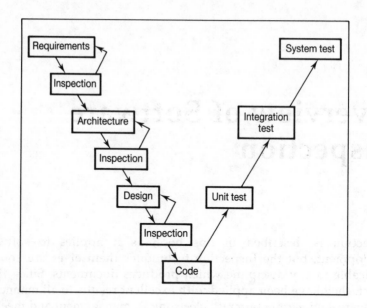

Figure 3.1   The V-model.

may be visible at a glance or to the naked eye, examining the product in detail under the microscope will find far more, and may identify the more dangerous bugs.

The arrow (2) returning to the preceding software development stage reflects the changes which are made to the product Inspected as a result of correcting defects found in it. Thus it recycles the development stage activities for selected parts of the product.

Change requests (3) refer to upstream, source document stages (see Figure 3.3). For example, if a design is being Inspected, any changes to that design would be done by the Inspection 'edit' process, but any changes required in the requirements specification would be the subject of a change request.

The improvements (4) on Figure 3.2 are the suggestions for improvements to rules, procedures or checklists which are recorded in the logging meeting as well as potential defects (issues) and questions of intent to the author. The improvement suggestions go towards the process improvement part of Inspection, described in Section 3.2 and Chapter 7.

The product exits from Inspection (5) and is passed on to the next software development stage.

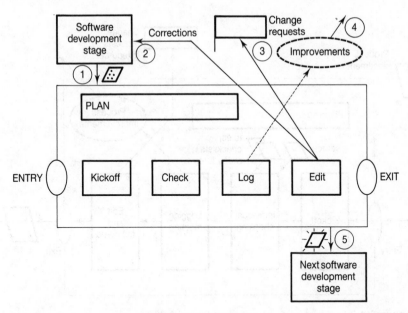

Figure 3.2   Inspection and development stages.

3.1.2   Product Inspection Steps

Each stage of the Inspection is described briefly in the following section (see Figure 3.4). More detail is given in the exposition of the method in Chapters 4 to 7.

Request: Initiating the Inspection Process

The Inspection process begins with a 'request for Inspection' by the author(s) or owner of a task product document. This is given to the responsible quality authority who finds a suitable Inspection leader, or directly to the Inspection leader if one is already determined.

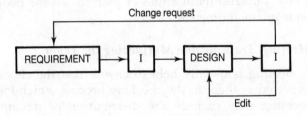

Figure 3.3   Change request to previous stage from Inspection (I).

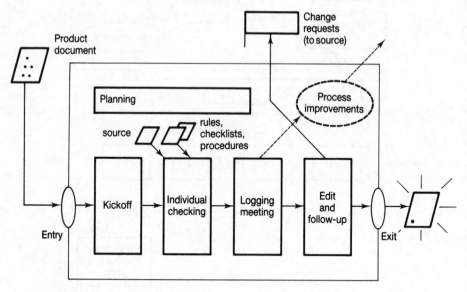

Figure 3.4   Product Inspection steps (simplified).

Entry: Making Sure 'Loser' Inspections don't Start

As part of Inspection planning, the Leader checks the product and its source documents against relevant (generic and specific) entry criteria. The purpose of entry criteria is to reduce the probability that the team will waste scarce resources, only to discover that product approval ('exit') is impossible or uneconomic, due to some factor which should have been corrected before the Inspection began.

Planning: Determining the Present Inspection's Objectives and Tactics

The Inspection leader determines how many cycles will be necessary, who should participate, and other practical details. This is the planning task, and results in a master plan for all the people on the Inspection team, including the author.

Kickoff Meeting: Training and Motivating the Team

A kickoff meeting is usually held to ensure that the checkers know what is expected of them in the checking process which follows. The kickoff meeting may include the distribution of documents, role assignments, feedback on process changes, training in Inspection procedures, and the setting of targets and corresponding strategies for Inspection productivity goals.

Individual Checking: The Search for Potential Defects

The checkers then work alone on the product document using the source documents, and the rules, procedures and checklists provided. The aim of each checker is to find the maximum number of unique major potential defects, mainly by looking for discrepancies between a source document (source) and the document generated from it (product). The issues are identified as objectively as possible according to the rules, the checklists, and the understanding of the participants, and are recorded for later personal reference in any way which the checker wishes.

Logging Meeting: Log Issues Found Earlier and Check for More Potential Defects

A logging meeting is convened for three purposes. Firstly, to log the issues which have already been identified by each checker in individual checking. Note that the lack of ability of even a single participant to understand the document constitutes an issue worth logging.

Issues are not recorded as 'defects' at this point because they may not *be* defects. They are simply 'matters requiring attention'. At this stage, no discussion is allowed.

Anything logged at the meeting is an 'item'. An item can be an 'issue' (an assertion about a potential defect), which may be evaluated as a real defect when the editor investigates it. An item can also be a 'question of intent' to the author, or a process improvement suggestion. Questions of intent are answered at the conclusion of the meeting. Answers may immediately lead to the logging of related issues.

The second purpose of the meeting is to discover *more* major issues during the meeting. This is stimulated by peer pressure, and by giving enough time to permit more checking to take place during the 'logging' meeting.

The third purpose is to identify and log ways of improving the development of the Inspection process. This may include improvement suggestions to procedures, rules or checklists. Such improvement items will be sent to the appropriate process owner for consideration.

The person who controls the logging meeting is a 'moderator'. The Inspection leader is usually the moderator.

Edit: Improving the Product

Someone, usually the author, is given the log of issues (and improvement suggestions) to resolve. This person (author or otherwise) is known as the editor. The real issue may be judged to be quite different from the perceived issue as logged by checkers. If the issue is a defect, it is now classified as a defect, usually determined by the current rules, sources and procedures. If an issue is not a defect, an ordinary comment or footnote may be added to avoid future misinterpretations. A defect in a source document cannot be directly corrected by the editor, so a change request to its owner is made. The editor may also make further process improvement suggestions, and may also make other improvements or corrections to the document they 'own'.

Follow up: Checking the Editing

The Inspection leader checks that satisfactory editor action has been taken on all logged issues. Change requests to correct defects in any source document must have been sent to the owner of the document. Follow up is completed successfully if these issues have been dealt with by being sent elsewhere, and are under some form of configuration management.

The issues classified as 'defects' in the product document must have been corrected by the editor. The Inspection leader checks to make sure that the editor has taken action to correct *all* known defects, although the leader does not have to check the corrections themselves. Process improvement suggestions should be sent to the process owner in question.

Exit: Making Sure the Product is Economic to Release

The exit process is performed by the Inspection leader, using applicable generic and specific exit criteria. For example, follow up must be complete, the checking rates must be within acceptable limits, metrics must be recorded, and the number of errors left in the document should be below a numerically prescribed quality threshold. If a document has been divided up to be Inspected in separate Inspection cycles, all chunks must have exited before the document as a whole can exit Inspection.

Release: The Close of the Inspection Process (for Products)

The product is made available, as officially 'exited', with an estimate of the remaining major defects in a 'warning label'.

3.2   Process Improvement

3.2.1   Process Improvement and How it Relates to Product Inspection

Defect detection Inspections are one of the components of Inspection as taught in this book. The other component uses the results of product Inspections to institute continuous process improvement of the entire software development process. The elements of this process improvement include the logging of improvements within product Inspection, Process Change Management Teams (PCMT), and a separate 'process brainstorming meeting' held as a spin-off of the Inspection process. The process improvements are 'outside' the software product development model, but are used to improve the whole development process.

Figure 3.6 gives a detailed view of the process improvement box in Figure 3.5. It shows the product Inspection as 'defect detection'. One of the outputs of the product Inspection is a list of suggestions for process improvements. It is these which are the raw material of the process improvement part of Inspection.

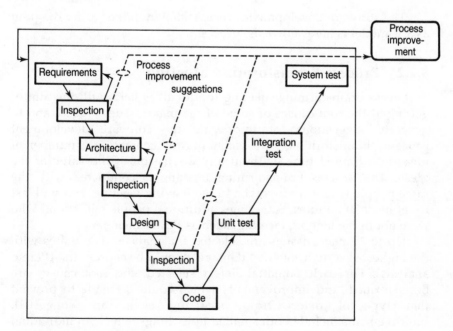

Figure 3.5   The V-model.

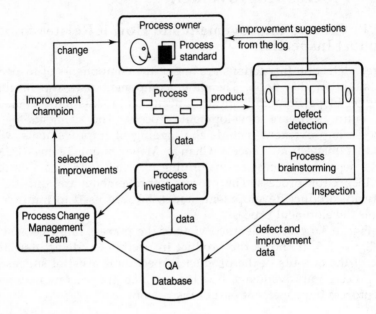

Figure 3.6   The 'process improvement' process.

The software development process, shown in the earlier diagram as a V-model is here shown as 'process'.

3.2.2   Process Brainstorming Meeting

A process brainstorming meeting (optional) is held with the aim of getting at the root causes of some of the major issues logged, and to generate suggestions for improving the software development process. 'Brainstorming' is a technique for generating a number of ideas in a limited time, without any discussion of the value of the ideas. The process brainstorming meeting is conducted with the same people who were involved in the logging meeting, and will last for at most 30 minutes. Sometimes additional people will attend who were not in the logging meeting, such as PCMT members.

Up to 10 major issues are selected for analysis. The issues with the highest severity (potential damage) should be chosen first (Pareto analysis). For each potential defect selected, the root causes are brainstormed, and improvements which could be made to prevent that type of defect from occurring again are suggested. Improvements include both small simple things, which an individual could begin doing immediately, as well as major investments. The meeting-scribe records causes and improvement suggestions in the process brainstorm log, which is incorporated into the QA database.

3.2.3   Process Change Management Teams (PCMT)

The process brainstorm log, stored in a QA database, is used by a team of people who are charged with managing improvements in the software development process. The PCMT may delegate specific changes to an individual champion. The Process Change Management Team determines which changes are most valuable, and implements the changes according to their plans.

3.3   Summary

Inspection finds and corrects defects by checking the product document against its sources, and the rules for producing it. Meetings are controlled by a trained Inspection leader. Entry and exit criteria ensure that time spent in Inspection is effective.

The most powerful element in Inspection is in improving the process which produced the products Inspected, since this means that defects are prevented from occurring in the future. The logging meeting and the process brainstorming meeting generate process improvement suggestions which are further analyzed by the Process Change Management Team or process owners.

4

The Inspection Process (Part 1) – Initiation and Documents

The next four chapters (4 to 7) give the detail of the activities which make up the Inspection process. The first three of these cover Inspection as applied to defect detection and removal. The process improvement aspect of Inspection is covered in Chapter 7.

This chapter covers items to the left of the broken line in Figure 4.1.

4.1 Request for Inspection

4.1.1 The Product is Volunteered

The starting point for any Inspection is a request from the author of a document that the document be Inspected. Inspection is always voluntary, and authors must not be coerced into 'volunteering' documents against their will.

Authors are motivated to request Inspection for two reasons:

- they will get help to upgrade their document before official release;
- they must achieve exit status in order to claim that they have met a deadline, and that the quality of their work is really good enough.

4.1.2 Inspection Leader Selected

Choice of Leader

The next step in the Inspection process is that an inspection leader is selected to manage the Inspection. In a large organization there may be a pool of Inspection leaders which a quality authority or overall Inspection coordinator can choose from. In a small organization there

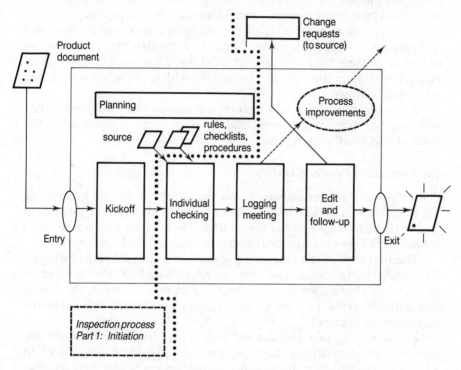

Figure 4.1   The Inspection process (simplified).

may be only a few, or even only one person, so the choice of leader is fairly simple. Leaders can be drawn from a quality assurance department or, more often, from within the development teams. Each organization needs to make their own practical decision as to how to do this.

Should Managers Lead the Team?

The Inspection leader should not normally be the line manager of the people whose work will be Inspected. Line managers may be Inspection leaders for other technical areas or for the Inspection of management documents such as budgets, schedules, plans, and so on. Managers should be directly involved in Inspection in their peer groups.

Who Chooses the Inspection Leader?

The Inspection leader must be properly trained (about five days of theory and exercises) and 'certified'. Certification means the leader has been judged as a qualified leader. This 'trained and certified' notion is a customary generic 'entry criterion' for Inspection.

An Inspection leader may be chosen from a roster of trained, and still certified, Inspection leaders, based on availability, and whether or not it is time they did a tour of duty. They will register their Inspection leader time on the project to which the document being inspected belongs.

Allowing untrained and uncertified persons to lead Inspections is a practice which can only lead to poor implementation of the method and finally its demise.

The Inspection Leader's Duties

The Inspection leader attends to all the practical details of running the Inspection. Leaders have a specific set of duties and powers to enable them to organize the Inspection. These tasks are explained in greater detail specifically for Inspection leaders in Chapter 8.

The first task of the Inspection leader, on being asked to Inspect a document, is to check that the entry criteria for the Inspection process have been met (as described in Figure 4.2). If not, the leader will actively work to remove failed entry conditions to enable the Inspection to proceed.

For example, this is what the leader would do to evaluate the generic entry criterion of checking input quality. If, in a brief look at a page of the product document, the Inspection leader can see that there are a large number of minor defects, or even a small number of major defects, the entry fails. It is not worth wasting the time of the Inspection group when the defects can more efficiently be dealt with by the author before continuing into Inspection.

4.2 The Planning Process

4.2.1 Planning Activity

If the document passes its entry criteria, then the Inspection leader will continue with the formal planning of the Inspection process.

This planning includes:

- deciding who to invite to Inspect the documents, and inviting them to participate;
- identifying all necessary supporting documents (sources, rules, checklists);
- continuing to check entry criteria, for example for acceptability of additional source documents identified;
- identifying other tools such as Inspection procedures for individual team member activity;

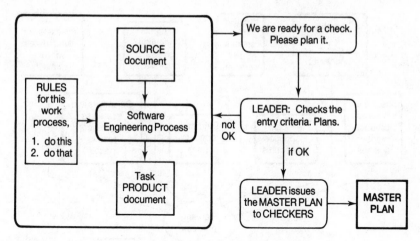

Figure 4.2   Initiation of the Inspection process.

- defining one or more specialist defect checking roles for each checker;
- dividing the material into chunks;
- establishing average optimum checking rates for checking work;
- establishing mutually convenient times for team meetings (kickoff, logging, process brainstorming);
- preparing suggestions for kickoff improvement objectives, and strategies for meeting them.

As a result of the planning process (see Figure 4.3), the leader must attend to some practical details such as:

- ensuring that selected documents are clearly marked, lines numbered, and copied;
- ensuring that team members get copies, or access to electronic copies of all relevant documents;
- booking suitable meeting space.

4.3   Documents needed for the Inspection of the Product

4.3.1   Summary of Input Documents for the Inspection Process

These are the input documents which are used in Inspection by checkers:

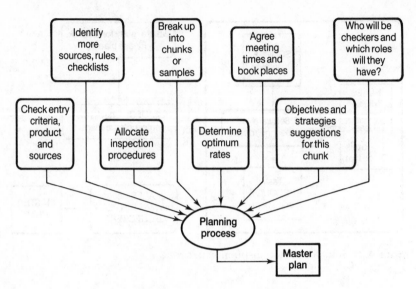

Figure 4.3 Components of the planning process which lead to the master plan.

- Product document (or documents or part of a document) – the entire document is normally available even though the focus is on one chunk or sample;
- Source document (or documents or parts of documents from which the product document should have been derived according to the 'rules');
- Rules: a 'writing' standard (which should have directed the software engineering task which produced the product document from the source document);
- Checklists: interpretations of rules which help checkers find more defects;
- Procedures: a 'doing' standard – teach participants what the expected behavior and activity is during an Inspection sub-process;
- Master plan (a table of contents of all participating documents, roles, meeting sites, times and people) – see the Inspection leader chapter (8) for details of the master plan.

The six basic document types used by checkers are listed in Figure 4.4. All five document types except the plan are subject to logging of issues (in sources and product, rules, procedures and checklists) and improvements (in rules, procedures and checklists). Specific rules and checklist questions are normally referenced in the log as the reason why an issue is logged.

The Inspection master plan is not itself the subject of logging, but it may contain errors or ambiguities which need to be taken up

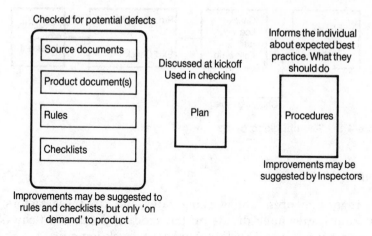

Figure 4.4   Documents handed out to checkers.

at kickoff and during checking. Procedures help teach expected Inspection behavior. Improvements to procedures may be logged by checkers during issue logging or process brainstorming as suggestions to procedure owners.

4.3.2   The Product Document to be Inspected

The main document which is being Inspected is referred to as the product document. This document could be a design, a requirements specification, a code listing, a test plan, a contract, a rule set, and so on. The main focus of the Inspection activity is concentrated on the product document, although defects or issues are also sought in the other documents.

> **The Multiple Target Principle**
> The product document is the primary focus of Inspection, but not the sole target of checking.

The product document is usually the primary target for checking, as it is the one we are trying to 'exit'. It is, therefore, usually the document on the basis of which the workload is calculated and determined. An exception to this would be when a checker was assigned a special role to (primarily) focus attention on source documents, rules or checklists. The rates and workload planned should then reflect the actual materials to be studied.

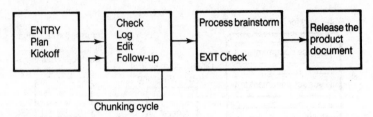

Figure 4.5   The chunking cycle.

Chunking

With regard to optimum working rates and tiredness factors, the Inspection leader must divide up the product document ('chunk' it) for treatment in several cycles (chunks) of check-log-edit.

A chunking cycle (see Figure 4.5) is repeated as often as necessary to get through documentation at the optimum rate of checking, without over-tiring checkers with more than two hours of logging meetings. It provides early experience with the document which can be used to adjust the checking process or to abort the entire thing.

4.3.3   Source Document(s)

Source Document Characteristics

The source document (source) is the primary document which the product document is checked against. Types of source document include ideas, memos, contracts, policies, requirements, plans, and so on. It is the document which was, or should have been, used as a source for the work process which produced the product document. Part of the reason for doing Inspections is to ensure that the source documents which should have been used were in fact used.

In some cases, not all of a source document will be applicable to the Inspection of a product document. In this case, the Inspection leader must select the particular source documents or parts of those documents which should have been used, and make sure that the relevant checkers have access to them.

What if Sources (or Rules) are not Available in Writing?

If the sources or rules are not yet written down, it is impossible for a checker to check for potential defects against them. This means that even oral knowledge must be converted into a written format, by the leader if necessary, so that it may be objectively shared by a team of checkers (see Figure 4.6).

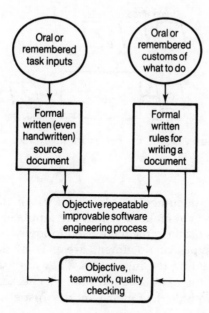

Figure 4.6   Recording of oral sources and rules.

Inspection Checks the Process as well as the Product

It is not merely the product document which is checked, but also the process of producing that document (that is, the task just submitted for Inspection). The transformation process is evaluated partly by its inputs ('source input documents'), its rules, and finally (in greatest detail and focus) its output documentation (the product document). This is shown in Figure 4.7.

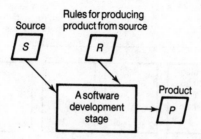

Figure 4.7   The software development task uses source and rules to produce the product.

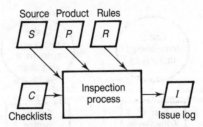

Source Product Rules

S   P   R

C → Inspection process → I

Checklists   Issue log

Figure 4.8   Software Inspection uses source, product, rules, and checklists to produce the issue log.

The 'product' document is the result of all those inputs. The goal of Inspection is to make sure that the inputs have been heeded, and that the rules of the game have been followed.

These three types of document are part of the work process immediately preceding the Inspection. They are used twice, first in the software development task and then by checkers (including the author of the product document) in the Inspection process (see Figure 4.8).

Checked and Exited does not Mean Defect-free

Even when sources have 'exited' (formally finished their own earlier Inspection process successfully), the exited source documents are not expected to be totally defect-free. Even in the best of worlds, about one major defect per four pages, and three minor defects per four pages, might be found in the source document during the Inspection of the product document (see Figure 4.9). This implies that there may be an exit criterion which accepts that no more than one defect remains per four pages even after successful exit from an Inspection.

The difference is that we will have some idea of how many, and that we will not find it economic to continue removing them at this

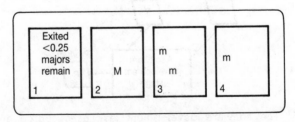

Exited <0.25 majors remain

1   2 M   3 m m   4 m

Figure 4.9   Even exited documents will contain some defects.

stage. The remaining defects are probably one or two orders of magnitude less than you are currently finding at this stage. So the Inspection process will require at least some of the checkers to recheck the source document in all cases, and to report any potential defects found in it.

4.3.4 Rules

The Relationship between Standards, Procedures and Rules

A standard gives guidance for performing some activity in a particular way. Within Inspection, standards include forms, entry and exit criteria, issue logging codes, and checking rates, to give a few examples. There are also standards which prescribe what to do in step by step detail to perform a particular task. These are called procedures.

Procedures must be written down so that best-known practices are shared by the team, and to serve as a baseline for continuous improvement. A result may have been produced using the right procedure or it may not; whether the right procedure has been used is not necessarily evident in the final result (but the result is more likely to be satisfactory if the correct procedure was followed).

Procedures can apply to producing written documents or to other tasks. For example, in Inspection there are procedures (by definition, 'standard' procedures, since procedures are a sub-set of standards) for meeting-etiquette, including how to report issues at the logging meeting.

Procedures for writing documents are called 'rules' in this book. A rule specifies the content and format of a software development task deliverable, and also prescribes how the deliverable should be written, using the source document(s). Rules are the key to finding defects since they alone officially define what is required in a written product. Rules can be thought of as a 'program for a person', telling the person how to convert the source document information into the product document. They serve a wide variety of functions, as illustrated in Figure 4.10.

The relationship between standards, procedures, and rules is shown in Figure 4.11.

Rules

Every work process has some rules by which it is undertaken. Sometimes these rules are arbitrary and random – in the head of someone doing the work. ('This is a good way to do it.') However it would be unreasonable to check a document for conformance to some set of rules, without having informed the document author in advance of writing the document what those rules were.

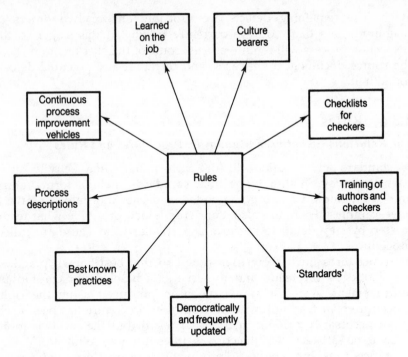

Figure 4.10 Rules serve a wide variety of functions.

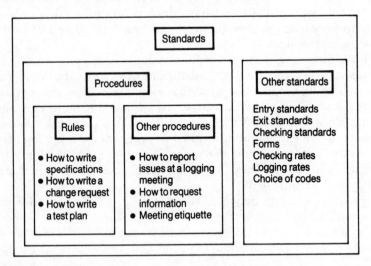

Figure 4.11 Relationship of standards, procedures, and rules.

For this reason, the work of producing or modifying any document must be undertaken by adhering to a set of task rules, called rule sets. A rule reflects the 'official' view of the group about the best-known way to write things. When the group for some reason

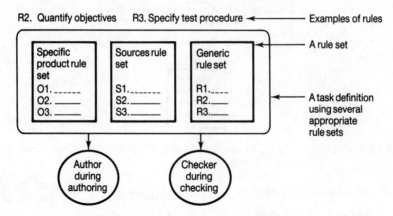

Figure 4.12 Rules are grouped into related rule sets.

doesn't like that rule, they may change it, but the present accepted rule set represents the written, documented, 'correct' way to work.

A rule is a single statement directing an author to read sources, interpret them and/or write product documents during a task in a particular way. Related rules make up a rule set.

A rule set is a group of related rules, which rarely exceed a single page, usually relating to a particular task, for example 'test planning' or 'coding' (see Figure 4.12). Several rule sets will probably be necessary to write or check a single document.

Objectivity Tools

Rules help increase the objectivity of the Inspection process. There is objectivity in Inspection, in that it concentrates on identifying discrepancies between two (or more) documents, usually a source and a product, according to applicable rules.

The objectivity in a rule set, as opposed to 'this is a good way to do it,' has the advantage that it allows professionals to remove the ego factor from disagreements arising from assertions of a potential defect. Instead of the exchange being along the lines of 'this is a good way to do it' and 'I disagree,' the exchange can be along the lines of 'this appears to conflict with rule G2 as follows' and 'I see what you mean.' We can explicitly focus on the product, not the person.

The rules define the way in which the product document should have been produced (see Figure 4.13). Rules define the notion of an 'issue' as an apparent violation of the rules, and therefore a potential defect.

Another type of objectivity is given by the checklists, described below, which define the notion of a defect even more precisely than a

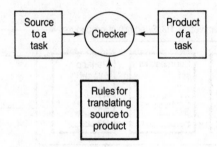

Figure 4.13   Rules tell the checker how to analyze documents when checking.

Example of a rule set
RULES for document type: Test Plan Document tag: 'TP'
Owner: DG Exited (Max. Mj=1/pg).

TP1:   Specify test plan identifier as SYS.TP.n, where SYS is
the system name, and n is the sequential test plan number.

TP2:   Introduction: summarize software items to be tested
with references to project plan, quality plan, and test design
documents.

TP3:   Identify test items including version level, hardware
and software requirements, and references to requirements
specifications and design documentation.

TP4:   List features to be tested and features not to be tested
(with reasons).

TP5:   Describe test approach to be used, including
techniques and level of comprehensiveness.

TP6:   Specify item pass/fail criteria, and person responsible
for the decision.

TP7:   Specify test suspension and resumption criteria.

TP8:   Specify test environment, including tools required,
user involvement, and special equipment.

TP9:   Specify schedule, resources required, responsibilities,
and contingencies.

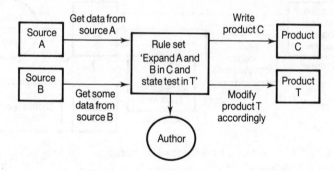

Figure 4.14   Rules tell document authors where to get certain data, what to do with it, and where to put their translations, design, code, tests.

rule, for participants in the Inspection process. Checklists are refinements of rules, not separate opinions!

Contents of Rules

A work process rule set will define:

- which source documents or which parts of them should be read;
- how to translate the information in the source documents into the language of the product document;
- how to format and structure the product document;
- the best-known working practices for producing the product document.

The rules should be improved as often as is necessary to upgrade the quality of the work produced (see Figure 4.14). Insights for improved rules will be recorded in the process brainstorming meetings where improvement ideas for the rules may be raised as 'improvement suggestions' by checkers. Improvements can be logged at any time during the Inspection process – as well as outside it. When issues of taste crop up during a meeting, then the Inspection leader should have them logged on the item log, as an 'improvement suggestion' for a new rule or other change.

Suggestions for improvements in the author's formal technical process, defined by process standards (entry criteria, rules, procedures and exit criteria) can be made by the software developer in these ways:

- logging a formal 'improvement suggestion' at the logging meeting (only for rules, procedures or checklists);
- suggesting an improvement, a change in the rules, checklists or procedures at a process brainstorming meeting;

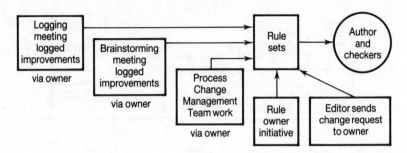

Figure 4.15 Rule sets can be upgraded continuously as a result of input from several sources.

- raising a change request to the rules, with their owner, in writing during editing, because the logged issue seems to be the result of defects in the rules themselves;
- sending the process owner some improvement suggestions at any time.

In addition, changes to the rule sets can be initiated by the owner of the rule, or by the PCMT (Process Change Management Team) as part of their general management of changes to the software development process as shown in Figure 4.15.

Note that suggestions for improvements to the source and product documents are *not* normally permitted – because this is the owner/editor's 'right'. The editor and owner of a document have full responsibility for figuring out how to improve their document. An author or editor who is present at a logging meeting may request improvement suggestions to their own documents. Answers to this should be short (15 seconds, keywords or references only), and not the subject of discussions or consensus. Any longer discussions should normally take place outside the meeting between the interested parties.

How to Tell When the Rules are or are not Working

Here are some remarks made during an Inspection meeting which are issues of taste and which therefore ideally should already have been resolved by the rules:

- 'We think all headings ought to be in italics for clarity.'
- 'Why does this specification have to ramble on for 10 pages when what needs saying could be said in one paragraph?'
- 'The estimates should be better justified.'

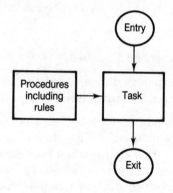

Figure 4.16 Procedures describe how we probably best do a task. Rules are a special kind of procedure limited to the writing task.

The following, by contrast, are signs that the rules *are* working (issues are usually stated more briefly than this, during an Inspection logging meeting):

- 'The date and responsibility are not established as per the rules, point 16.'
- 'Line 25 does not contain a source reference, as required by the rules. Item R23.'
- 'The estimate does not have supporting evidence as required by the rules. Item R33.'

Procedures Define What to Do – and Best Practice

Procedures give process participants their basic training in how the organization wants work done. A procedure should be continuously updated to include the best-known practices for efficiency, effectiveness and quality (see Figure 4.16).

Whenever any user of a procedure has any problems with it or has any constructive suggestion, there should be an immediate and natural path of communication to the owner of the process which the procedure describes. If not, many useful insights will be lost. People will begin to ignore procedures and productivity will decline.

A procedure is not an iron law. It represents the best-known documented practice. An exception to the use of a procedure should be made only rarely and with good reason. If exceptions are regular, then perhaps it is time to change the procedure to reflect real practice.

A single procedure should never exceed one page of description. This forces conciseness. People have time to read and deal with procedures if they are brief. Larger complex processes such as

Inspection can be divided up into sub-procedures for individual participants as is illustrated in the Inspection procedures in Appendix C of this book.

When should Procedures be Modified?

There are several occasions when Inspection encourages logging of improvement ideas to procedures (see Figure 4.16):

- At the kickoff meeting when it is clear that a suggested procedure is unclear or inadequate. The Inspection leader can take responsibility for noting changes to a procedure as an improvement suggestion.
- At any sub-process of Inspection when a procedure is being used, the user should be able to direct a comment to the owner directly. The owner's name and contact address must therefore always be on the document describing the procedure.
- During the Inspection logging meeting. The improvement to the procedure is shared with others, logged formally, and the editor must send the suggestion to the owner and put it in a tracking system for process improvement.
- During process brainstorming, suggesting procedure improvements is quite natural.
- Process Change Management Teams and their sub-teams can suggest and experiment with procedure changes.

4.3.5 Checklists

Characteristics of Checklists

Checklists are a fundamental part of the Inspection process. There are individual checklists for each type of documentation in Inspection. Sometimes individual checker specialist roles are defined by means of a special set of checklist questions. More detail is given in Chapter 8. Checklists are built to the following rules (see Figure 4.17):

- checklists must ultimately be derived from the rules of the process which itself is being checked by Inspection;
- checklists should include a reference to the rule tag which they are interpreting (using the format 'checklist question?←rule tag');
- checklists should be kept updated to reflect experience of frequent defects;
- a set of questions for one document type should never exceed one single physical page (about 25 items);
- checklists may contain suggestions for probable defect severity (for example, major, minor);
- checklists are usually, though not always, stated in a question

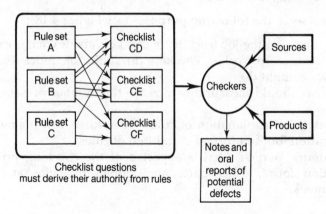

Figure 4.17 Checklists are extensions and interpretations of rules. They help checkers see how to spot a potential issue better than the rules alone.

form, so that a negative answer means you have found an issue – for example, '23. Are all pages numbered?' (if not, it is an issue to be logged);
- the checklist does not need to contain every possible question;
- a checklist should concentrate on questions which will turn up major defects;
- checklists should not be misused to 'define' a new rule;
- checklists are part of the on-the-job training of a checker.

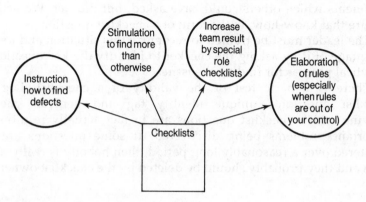

Figure 4.18 Some aspects of checklists.

Purpose of using a Checklist

Checklists serve the following purposes (see Figure 4.18):

- instruction – on-the-job teaching of checkers about what is expected;
- stimulation – provokes checkers to look for more than they otherwise might do;
- checklists should measurably increase the number of issues found by a team;
- more detailed explanation of rules – checklists can play a role as elaboration (but not formal definition) of rules;
- they define part of what is expected of the checking process, in 'question form'; other parts are defined by rules and source documents.

Building Checklists Based on Experience

Checklists should not be copied from other environments. Experience has shown that such copied checklists do not actually contribute to the identification of major defects. They are often either obvious or irrelevant, and are usually an attempt to formulate rules which should properly be in the rules themselves. They tend to be brainstormed quickly by one person, and they do not reflect a significant contribution in addition to the rules, which function as checklists in the hands of checkers. This means that no further progress is made with seeking out powerful and effective new checklist questions, and the checklists themselves lose credibility.

Checklists should be based on 'hard experience' developed locally, and be based on one powerful useful question at a time. The need for particular questions should be logged as potential checklist improvements, during a logging meeting.

The specific stimulus for this is when it is clear that a major issue has been identified by a checker who has asked a question of the documents which others could have asked, but did *not*. We need to capture that know-how, in the form of a checklist question.

The leader must be trained to recognize this situation and to take advantage of it by asking the checker to identify the key question or analytical process for finding the issue.

There is a basic test of the validity of a checklist. Log the checklist question's unique identity tag and generate metrics showing which checklist questions are in fact actually resulting in important problems being discovered. If some questions are not registered over a reasonably long period, then nobody is really using them and they probably should be deleted by the checklist owner.

Updating Checklists

A checklist may be updated by means of:

- an 'improvement' suggestion at the logging meeting;
- the identification of a useful question asked by a checker in individual checking or in the logging meeting, which is logged in the logging meeting as an improvement suggestion to the checklist;
- the initiative of the Inspection leader or other checklist 'owner' (see discussion below);
- a suggestion from a process brainstorming meeting;
- the result of the Process Change Management Team work;
- anybody who is unhappy with the present checklist may submit their proposals, in writing, directly to the checklist owner.

In principle each checklist has an owner, named on the checklist (see Figure 4.19). Only this owner makes official changes to the checklist. Everything else is a suggestion to the owner. The owner can be anybody who will take the responsibility, including the leader, senior leader, quality assurance manager, or a special discipline manager (like testing manager).

Checklists must not be misused to state official rules for document authors. The reason for this is that checklists cannot and

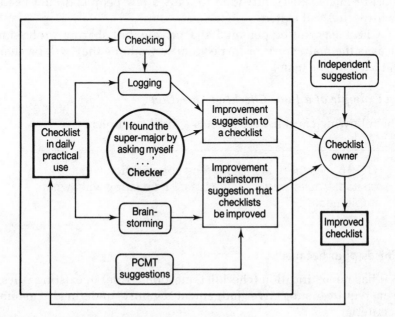

Figure 4.19 How checklists develop.

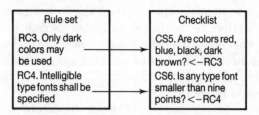

Figure 4.20 Checklist questions must get their authority from rules, and document it.

should not be used to direct the author. They should only be used analytically to trigger the identification of issues.

Checklists should contain questions which 'illuminate' rules (see Figure 4.20). They should directly refer to the rule they illuminate (in the format 'question←rule'). Checklist questions must not be used to 'make' new rules. Only legislative debate can make a law. The rule owner must be a part of any real rule change process.

But there are rules for checklists too – at least for the more critical ones. Even checklists should ideally be checked and exited before passing them out to many people in an organization. Less formal, short-term checklists, intended for only a few people, do not need to be inspected and exited.

Checklists can be personal and private, but sharing professional ideas is the main spirit of Inspection, so we hope they will be shared – at least by the team.

An Example of a Poor Checklist Question

The following checklist question is a 'bad' example:

CTP10: Is there any part of the specification which a customer/user might be the least bit unhappy with, when implemented?

This is poor because:

- it has no justification (checklist question<–rule) in existing rules;
- it requires subjective judgement against undefined customer criteria;

- it poses the question so that a positive answer indicates discovery of an issue (negative answers should consistently indicate issues);
- it should pose such questions only in relation to a checked and exited set of written sources which officially stand for the 'customer' view.

Neither checklists nor rules should contain information relating specifically to minor issues, since these on their own are not economically justified as an object of the Inspection process. Rules and checklists should be strongly focused on helping checkers to identify major defects. These are the ones which, by definition, cause the most loss later if they escape our clutches now.

4.3.6 Summary of Rules and Checklists

Rule sets are directives for authors, but in the hands of checkers, they are only used as if they were checklists (see Figure 4.21). The only real purpose of checklists is to permit and encourage interpretation of rules which would probably not be made by some checkers, but which will lead to uncovering major issues.

Rules are:

- instructions to the author and editor of a document about necessary practices;
- a summary of known best practices;
- a way of transferring know-how to other people;
- a checklist when used by checkers (they must ask if rules have been followed);
- formally approved and hopefully checked and exited;
- formally 'owned';
- formally updated and distributed;
- updated by the owner reacting to logged improvement suggestions during the logging meeting;
- updated as a result of process brainstorming suggestions;
- updated as a result of Process Change Management Team activity;
- selected for use in checking by the leader during planning, as applicable;
- taught during kickoff, as necessary;
- learned by practical daily author and checking use;
- re-enforced by daily peer use during Inspection and when producing documents;
- continuous improvement vehicles;
- one type of 'standard' for a work process (they 'define how to check' and thus are also a standard for the checking activity).

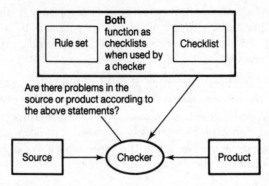

Figure 4.21 Rules function exclusively as checklists when used by checkers.

Rules are not:

- to exceed a single page per document type (to prevent creeping bureaucracy);
- to be used blindly (regardless of formal requirements for this particular system, and so on);

Checklists (see Figure 4.22) are:

- analytical checking tools;
- less formal than rules (less dangerous if 'bad');
- not necessarily 'owned' by anyone (but *should* be for continuous improvement);
- created on the spot, if this is useful;
- possibly special purpose, as 'role' checklists are;
- derived from existing written rules (the appropriate rule identity tag, like 'GE2' should be included);
- on-the-job training in checking work;
- a way of spreading know-how, helping organizations to learn;
- continuous improvement vehicles;
- only as valid as the major defects they help us find in practice.

Checklists are not:

- rules for document authors (they should not be used by authors at all during the writing task);
- a standard for authors – they are advice to checkers;
- to exceed a single page per document type (prevent creeping bureaucracy!);
- to be misused to sneak rules into checking without formal approval;
- independent of rules, they are interpretations;
- to be used to define and find minor defects and trivia.

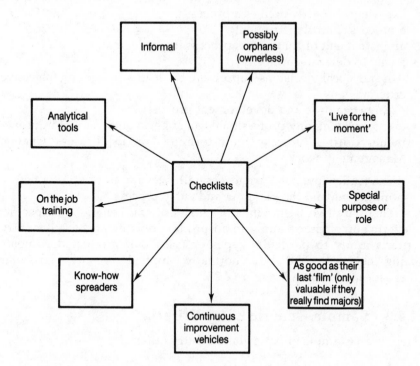

Figure 4.22   Checklists are less formal than rules.

4.4   The Entry Process

4.4.1   Entry Criteria

The purpose of having entry criteria to the Inspection process is to ensure that the time spent in Inspecting the product and associated documents is not wasted, but is well spent. If the product document is of obviously very poor quality, then the checkers will find a large number of defects which can be found very easily by one individual alone, even the author. Inspections are cost-effective when the combined skills of a number of checkers are concentrated on a document which seems superficially to be all right, but actually has a number of major defects in it which will only be found by the intensive Inspection process, not by the author checking the product.

The purposes of entry (and exit) criteria:

• to kill error spreading at the earliest point in time;

- a formal way to accumulate and teach your organization's experience – partly defines a process;
- a process control instrument;
- an instrument of continuous process improvement;
- a way to delegate authority
  - faster local decisions (approval by leader based on objective criteria)
  - faster response and development process;
- empowerment: any professional can suggest entry or exit improvements during 'process brainstorming' or in 'Process Change Management' work.

The leader must check and pass all relevant entry criteria before continuing beyond the planning and entry process.

There are two basic kinds of entry criteria; generic and specific. Generic entry criteria apply to all product documents. Specific entry criteria apply to particular types or classes of product documents being checked. Both are normally applied to any particular Inspection, as shown in Figure 4.23.

4.4.2 Sample Generic Entry Criteria

Here is an example of basic generic entry criteria:

Generic entry criteria   Tag=GE

GE1:   The author can veto (decide not to enter) any sub-stage of Inspection.

GE2:   The leader can veto (decide not to enter) any sub-stage of Inspection.

GE3:   All source documents are in writing and have successfully exited with a known level of maximum remaining defects. Failing this, they will be mini-checked or sampled to determine their defect level before proceeding, and this will be noted on the document. Failing this, they will be clearly marked as NOT EXITED on all pages.

GE4:   The applicable set of generic and specific rules for the task which produced the product is available in writing.

GE5:   A formal master plan has been made for the rest of the checking task where the optimum recommended checking rate has been established and it is not faster than about one full page per checking-hour.

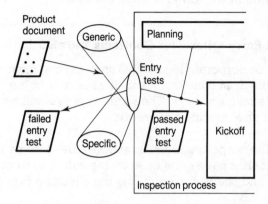

Figure 4.23 The product document must pass both generic and specific entry criteria tests before it is allowed to begin the Inspection process.

GE6:   The leader has been trained for several days (three theory, two practice) and is officially certified as an able practitioner.

GE7:   A cursory examination (<5 minutes) of a sample (page or so) of the product document shows less than one major per page findable. (Otherwise the author cleans up.)

GE8:   Ordinary text documentation shall have been cleaned up by a spelling checker before submission. Other possible machine checks or diagnostics have been done (clean compile, cross referencing, indexing, grammar check).

GE9:   The author (or editor) agrees to participate as a checker.

Any violation of these basic criteria is asking for trouble! If your long-term experience says that you need to add additional generic entry criteria, then you should do so. When you do, you will be improving your process.

4.4.3   Specific Entry Criteria

In addition you must expect to develop specific criteria for individual document types. It is important that these are built slowly, based on real need and experience. To help you understand the nature of them we will give some examples.

Specific Entry criteria for Contracts Tag=EC

EC1:   The corporate legal office shall have at most one week to view the draft contract and shall initial it as being within the correct legal framework. Their final approval will be given after edit as a specific exit criteria.

EC2:   The corporate rules for software development contracts shall have been used by the author to draft the contract and shall be used during the checking process.

EC3:   The purchasing manager shall also initial the draft contract as a valid draft (and will have exit control over the final version).

As a further example:

Entry criteria for Software Integration Test Plan TAG=ITPE

ITPE1:   The following source documents must have exited their own Inspection process: quality plan, integration test standards, requirement specification, system test plan, architectural design.

ITPE2:   The software test manager has initialled the draft copy as being reasonable for going to checking.

ITPE3:   The test planning rules have been applied and are made available for checking.

4.5   Kickoff Meeting

A 'kickoff' meeting can be held, if desired, but is not compulsory for every Inspection cycle. For example, a kickoff may be held before only the first chunk of a longer document Inspection. Whether or not to hold a kickoff meeting depends on whether the Inspection handbook guidelines require such a meeting, or if the Inspection leader judges that it is necessary or advisable due to the special nature of the material, or the special nature of the participants (for example, new checkers or outside guest checkers).

4.5.1 Kickoff Meeting Objectives

The purpose of the kickoff is to save time by disseminating information which everyone needs at the same time, and clarifying the task.

The kickoff meeting may be held for the following specific purposes:

- familiarize checkers with their tasks;
- agree on their individual special defect-searching 'role assignments' which were suggested by the planner of the Inspection in the master plan (done initially by the Inspection leader);
- hand out the recently produced materials ('product'), as well as their source materials ('source documentation'), relevant rules and checklists;
- ask any general questions about the documents being checked;
- obtain group or individual instruction on how to do the Inspection work;
- obtain group or individual instruction from the leader on how to interpret any document;
- inform team about current logging rates and effectiveness;
- attempt to set numeric team improvement targets ('more than 70% of issues logged to be majors');
- identify and agree to use suitable new tactics for meeting their improvement targets ('slow down from last time to achieve the optimal rate of checking').

The leader and the team can discuss anything they need to discuss in order to be ready for a successful individual checking effort.

IBM in some reports[†] uses the kickoff meeting to feed back 'hot news' from the Inspection database, from the Process Change Management Team and from immediately preceding Inspections. Here the kickoff is used less to familiarize checkers with the material at hand, but rather to try to improve their performance by the latest experience and advice at the beginning of a software development stage.

† Jones C.L. (1985), *IBM Systems Journal*, **2**.

4.6 Summary

In this chapter, we have looked at the initial stage of the Inspection process for products, and we have discussed in detail the documents which are used in product Inspection.

The initial stage is critical to the success of Inspection. One way to fail to achieve good results in Inspection is to dive straight into the checking process, without planning and without strict entry criteria.

4.6.1 Inspection Activities

A number of Inspection activities are covered by the initial stage. Inspection begins with a request for a product document to be Inspected. This request comes from the person who produced that document (the author). An Inspection leader is then appointed who takes charge of the Inspection process for that product.

The Inspection leader plans the Inspection, including chunking the document if it is too large to be Inspected at once, and also organizes the involvement of the individual checkers and the administrative details. (More details of the Inspection leader's job are given in Chapter 8.)

A major task for the Inspection leader at this stage is to check that the product passes the entry criteria for Inspection. A document which fails the entry criteria may be returned to the author for further work. Otherwise, appropriate action to fix the entry conditions will be initiated by the leader.

A kickoff meeting may be organized by the Inspection leader to distribute documents, make sure that everyone understands what they are to do and set improved targets for the Inspection process itself.

4.6.2 Inspection Documents

The main focus of Inspection is on the product, which has been produced by a software development task or process. This is the document which is used as the basis of Inspection rates and which the Inspection leader uses to chunk the task into reasonable length parts.

The source document (or set of documents) is what was (or should have been) used by the author in producing the product. Ideally, the source should also have exited Inspection, but this is not always achievable in practice, for example in the very first Inspection. Suggestions are given in Chapter 8 for dealing with un-Inspected source documents.

Standards, procedures and rules are defined ways of carrying out tasks within the software development process. Rules are standard procedures for writing documents. The rules should have been used in creating the product document; they are used again in Inspection to check that the product document has been created correctly.

Checklists are interpretations of rules and other guidelines which are provided for the purpose of assisting the Inspection checkers to do the checking process in the most effective way.

5

The Inspection Process (Part 2) – Checking

This chapter looks at the checking part of the Inspection process, which takes place in two stages: first the individual checking (called 'preparation' in some versions of Inspection), and secondly the group checking, which takes place at the logging meeting.

5.1 Individual Checking

5.1.1 The Purpose and Process of Individual Checking

Each checker will be assigned one or more specific roles, so that they focus on the identification of a particular type of defect which others (with a different focus) might miss. This maximizes the chances of as many 'unique issues' as possible being found, which in turn makes for a better total team result.

How Individual Checkers do their Checking

The checking work is done by the individual checkers (see Figure 5.1). They find their own time and place and their own working style. This means they can use any set of documents as tools, any search sequence, any advice from anybody, any sequence of working times and any geographical location. The only central requirements are that they:

- complete their checking by the time their team has agreed to hold a logging meeting;
- make use of the recommended optimum working rate, or one that they can show is even more productive for them personally;
- perform their assigned specialist roles fully, and do not let their

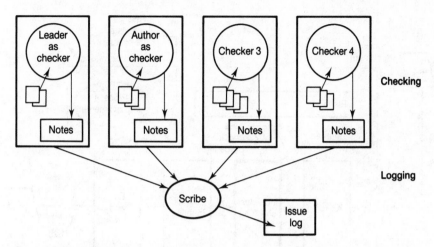

Figure 5.1 Individual checking prepares checkers for reporting their potential defects as issues to the scribe at the logging meeting.

team down by failing to cover their expected territory as specified in the Inspection master plan;
- contact their Inspection leader early if they encounter any difficulties, or suspect that the team's time might somehow be wasted on these documents;
- make every effort to follow the defined checking procedure for the checking process.

The reason for these requirements is that there should be systematic control over the checking process, even though a wide degree of latitude in the manner of doing it is permitted and encouraged at the same time. The aim is (Deming, 1986) the systematic improvement of the Inspection process as the organization learns about better ways of practicing it. If a procedure is not built upon the best practices (and not followed by team members), then it is not possible to improve productivity systematically.

Checking is not all of Inspection!

The individual checking phase as it fits in with the Inspection process considered so far is shown in Figure 5.2.

Are all Inspectors Checkers and are all Checkers Inspectors?

It has been traditional to call anyone on the Inspection team an 'Inspector'. We will continue with this, but it is useful to distinguish

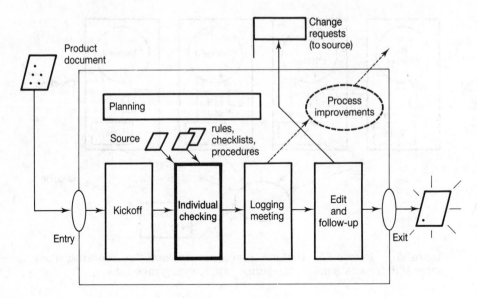

Figure 5.2 Inspection process showing where individual checking fits.

between the various types of Inspection activity as shown in Figure 5.3:

- A person who is actively checking for issues, using rules, checklists and sources, and who reports issues to the scribe at the logging meeting will be called a 'checker', as well as an 'Inspector'.
- A person who is doing any other activity will also be called an 'Inspector', but will also be called by a more specialized descriptive term, as follows:
  – The scribe writes the issues and other items during the logging meeting or the process brainstorming meeting (also there called 'scribe'). A scribe is probably also a checker.
  – The author is the person who produced the product document. The author checks that logging is intelligible during the logging meeting, and answers questions of intent at the end of the logging meeting. The author is also a checker.
  – The meeting moderator is usually the Inspection leader. In any case the moderator is the person 'running' the kickoff, logging or brainstorming meeting, and could well also be a checker.
  – The role specialist is a checker, who has undertaken specific checking tasks.

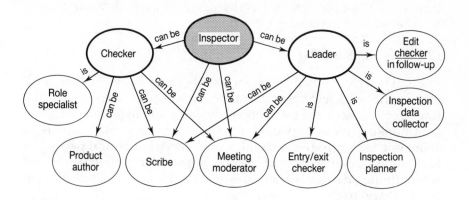

Figure 5.3   Some general and related specific functions of Inspectors.

5.1.2   Checking Large Documents

The Speed Limit

Checkers should never attempt checking large documents in one cycle. Typical optimum checking rates of one page per hour per checker are necessary to permit checkers to really find the defects which ordinary reviews and walkthroughs usually miss. An order of magnitude reduction in defects per page identified would probably result from the common practice of trying to check dozens of pages in a few hours.

The speed at which checking is done is like the optical power of a magnifying glass. Inspection is a way of looking at documents under a magnifier or microscope. If you put ordinary clear glass in your magnifier, you will still find some bacteria (defects) – but you will find far more, and far more deeply embedded ones, if you use a magnifier of a high power. There is a limit to this analogy, because there is an optimum rate which you should find through experimentation. In general, the slower the Inspection rate, the higher the power of magnification to examine the document.

A checker may refer to and scan sources, rules and checklists fairly rapidly but the core product document in particular must be worked on at the optimum rate by most participants. An exception would be when a checker is assigned a special role of studying another document, such as a source which we suspect has too many defects in it. Checkers must go at optimum rates for their 'source' document role, but can go at scanning speed for documents outside their role. The optimum rate is discussed in more detail in Section 5.1.5 below, and in Chapter 8 (Section 8.5).

Chunking and Sampling

The intensively studied long documents must either be 'chunked' into a series of a few pages at a time, or 'sampled' a few pages at a time, depending on the instructions given by the Inspection leader.

Chunking means dividing up the documents into sections of about one to four pages. A chunk would consist of critical pages (not background commentary or headings for example), but sections where finding defects is really worthwhile. We could call them 'non-commentary' pages.

A chunk is equivalent to what a team can log and continue checking during the logging meeting, at the optimum rate for the logging meeting. This could work out at about one page per hour if you want to find about 15–20% additional issues to those identified in individual checking.[†]

When a chunk is studied, a break must be made (hours rather than minutes), before attempting to do a new cycle of checking.[‡]

Sampling selected portions of a document is an excellent practical alternative to complete checking. It can be used to estimate the issue density per page in the unchecked pages. This can lead to a determination of the value of checking other pages. Sampling can lead to exiting the document based on its sampled quality. It can give the author as editor enough samples of issues to permit some systematic correction of defects in pages not actually checked.

Sampling cannot identify specific issues in unchecked pages, but that may not be the current purpose of the Inspection. If the purpose is the measurement of quality, or deciding on the value of doing further Inspection, or teaching the author, or helping the author upgrade the document, or gaining insights about defects which will help in process improvement, then sampling is an economic and viable thing to do.

Sampling is an important alternative in non-software environments,[*] although these tend to be samples of mass-produced identical components. However, the sampling technique is valid for software documents because the process used to produce a large document would have been the same for the whole document.

---

† *Source:* Cindy Arksey, Boeing Seattle 1989. Report on her experiences with Software Inspections (Arksey, 1989).
‡ *Source:* Frank Buck, IBM Technical Report, Kingston NY (Buck, 1980).
* See Juran and Gynna, *Quality Control Handbook*, McGraw-Hill (Juran, 1988).

Hence, mistakes made on one page will often recur on many other pages of the document as well.

5.1.3 Checking for Major or Minor Defects

The basic definition of a major defect is one which will probably have order of magnitude or larger costs for fixing if it is not dealt with now, but is allowed to get through to testing or operational stages. The identification and repair of major defects is thus a primary reason for software Inspection at stages upstream of test execution.

If you do not follow certain basic principles outlined below, there is a danger that checkers will use too much of their time searching for, identifying, reporting and editing economically unimportant defects. These are formally called 'minor defects'.

You might then wonder why we bother to log and edit minor defects at all. The reason is that an issue initially classified as 'minor' may be classified in error, and may indeed be major. Carole Jones of IBM observes this in her paper on defect prevention (Jones, 1985). She points out that apparently trivial defects are often the source of really big problems later. Another reason for bothering to log minor issues at this stage is simply to clean things up and emphasize quality. Fixing minors is not especially profitable. It is no justification for the Inspection process. But it is a side benefit, and it does not cost *more* to correct minor defects at this stage than later.

It is easy to make the point that major defects should be looked for, but it is difficult to put this into practice. It is always easier to find minor defects and get carried away with identifying many similar types of minor defect. However, it is essential that this is not allowed to happen if Inspection is to fulfill its potential as the most cost-effective defect detection and defect prevention technique. Here are some tricks to achieve this:

- Give checkers special roles with special role checklists, which only ask questions directed at major defects.
- Teach at kickoff meeting that the search for majors is primary.
- Hand out checker procedures which define the fact that majors are the primary concern.
- Use rule sets which for approximately 19 of 20 rules identify major defects.
- Limit rule sets and checklists to a maximum of one physical page. This has the effect of squeezing trivial ideas 'off the page', as soon as higher priority major defect identification rules, task activities and checklist questions are gradually identified.
- Identify the probable classification of an issue identified in a checklist question next to the question itself as M (major), m (minor).

- Ask checkers to do their own personal classification of major/minor during the checking activity.
- Ask checkers to report (initially noted at the bottom of the Inspection master plan form) how many issues they found during checking in the various severity categories. This is done orally with the team. Those who report too many trivial issues compared to the others will feel motivated to do better next time.
- Have checkers always state orally 'major' or 'minor' when they report an issue to be logged, at the 'public' logging meeting. It gets embarrassing to constantly cite 'minor' when all others around you are stating 'major'.
- Calculate Inspection 'return on time invested' based on major defects found, never on minors.
- State numeric Inspection team process improvement objectives in terms of major defects per page and per hour. Never have it as a team objective to get better at finding minor defects!
- Never discuss the root causes of minor defects at the process brainstorming meeting. Only majors are worthy of discussion.
- When time for logging is particularly short, report only major defects. Only if time permits, allow the reporting of minors and formally log them.
- Report only a symbolic sample of minors, for example on a single page. The rest, if checkers have notes of them, can be handed informally to the editor. They are simply not worth more formal treatment or priority!
- If editing time is under pressure, only major defects may actually be fixed.
- If follow-up has an overwhelming number of things to check, then the leader would take majors seriously and skim over the minors, perhaps looking at a sample only.
- Report Inspection metrics to management based on major defects.
- Determine optimum rates of checking which ignore minors and use only majors found per hour per page as the basis for calculation of rates.

This list is not necessarily complete. But it does show how pervasive the 'small tricks' of Inspection are for making sure that minor defect finding is not overdone.

5.1.4 Checking Roles

Checkers should be assigned a particular role which ensures that they have a unique viewpoint. This role should be assigned with a view to their special interests and talents.

It is important to note that 'roles' encourage and permit

individuals to do a particular defect-searching task better than their colleagues. It does not give them exclusive territory over that defect type, and any defect is fair game for all checkers. Nor is the Inspection leader limited to suggesting only one single role to one person. Multiple and overlapping roles may be assigned.

The whole situation is very much like a ball team coach assigning players special roles in an effort to compete better against opposing teams, and setting up a team for defensive play where every player guards a different member of the opposition.

If individuals have a warm feeling about a favorite role, they should get it. If the Inspection leader refuses to formally assign it – they can do it anyway! The Inspection master plan form and the kickoff meeting should make all checkers aware of the special roles of the other checkers.

You can use your imagination, knowledge of the application, your company, and the individuals concerned to select appropriate roles. The important thing for the final results is that the duplication of potential defect assertions is minimized, and unique issue contributions maximized.

Here are some examples of roles:

User: concentrate on the user or customer point of view (checklist or viewpoint role).

Tester: Concentrate on test considerations (testability, test requirements, order of testing and order of development for parallel testing, and so on).

System: Concentrate on the wider system implications (hardware, documentation, selling, timing of delivery).

Financial: Concentrate on cost and revenue implications, estimates, uncertainty, dates, quantities.

Quality: Concentrate on all aspects of quality attributes directly and indirectly.

Service: Concentrate on field service, maintenance, supply, installation.

Backwards: Concentrate on the material from the back pages first (procedural role).

Rules: Pay special attention to the rules for this product (document role).

This list is intended to be illustrative, not exhaustive. There are dozens of other roles which an imaginative Inspection leader can suggest. More detail about roles is given in Chapter 8.

5.1.5 Rate of Checking

The Optimum Checking Rate

During individual checking there is a known optimum rate of work, which is calculated from the Inspection experience metrics. The rate of work is the speed needed to check a document thoroughly against all related documents – the 'power of the magnifying glass'.

There could well be many sources, many rules and many checklists which need to be applied for the checking of a single page of a product document.

We are typically concerned with the product documents when calculating rates. But, in some circumstances a checker may be assigned a special role of checking a source document thoroughly. This could be because it has suspect, or low, quality. In this case the optimum rate would apply to that checker, for that role, on that source document. The rate would ideally be one which was known to apply to that particular document.

The optimum rates, which are found by practical experience, have a strong tendency to be in the range of about one full page (plus or minus 0.5 page) per hour of individual checking activity. This fact comes as quite a shock to most people. We typically review documents at five to twenty pages per hour, when systematic calculation and application of optimum rates are not applied. The optimum checking rate seems to be a function of:

- human ability to absorb ideas;
- the complexity of the ideas in the documents;
- the personal qualifications of the checker;
- the number and complexity of related documents used as checking tools (sources, rules, checklists);
- the probability that defects still exist;
- the cost of *not* finding defects now, and alternatively of suffering their downstream costs (20 to 80 times higher in test and field use phases according to IBM experience).

The optimum checking rate is also a function of whether you want to find a maximum number of major issues per work-hour or a maximum number of issues per page, irrespective of hours used. This is a choice between efficiency and effectiveness.

The Inspection leader is trained to determine how much time people need, at the optimum rate of checking, for the particular material supplied, and to inform them in advance of how much time they are expected to use on the assigned material. If they fail to put in the time specified, it will quickly become apparent because they will arrive at the meeting with fewer Issues in hand to report than those who have given sufficient time to individual checking.

The things to take into account in determining the optimum rate are:

(1) How many full non-commentary pages will the checker study intensively?
(2) What type of pages will be studied by the checker intensively? (code? requirements?)
(3) What is the optimum rate for such types of pages, according to historical data?
(4) Variation from the average rate, but keeping within boundaries indicated by a scatter diagram of rate versus defects-per-page found:
   (a) variation due to individual involved (ability and experience);
   (b) variation due to quality of document;
   (c) variation due to actual total load of pages of sources, rules, checklists and specialist roles of the checker;
   (d) variation due to environment (noise, heat, interruption);
   (e) variation due to personal fatigue at time of checking;
   (f) any other factor which the leader or the checker thinks might impact the rate.

Individual Variation in Checking Rates

In spite of the statistical average checking rates, the individual checkers will vary by as much as ten to one in the time they need to do an optimum job personally. Individual checkers should consider the recommended checking time as 'permission' to use at least that amount of time. They should not feel they should speed up because of deadline pressure. If there is time pressure, they should consider doing smaller chunks of work or sampling, usually by agreement with the Inspection leader.

In practice, if checkers have 'run dry' (can't find more major issues after a period of checking), but have already found many issues in a shorter period of time, they should stop checking and use the time for better purposes.

On the other hand if after most of the time has been used up, they have finally 'got their minds around the material', and the issues are flowing freely, then they should continue to find as many issues as they can until they too 'run dry'.

This is not easy in the typical working environment with the usual deadline pressures. However the value of finding a single defect is so high, in terms of time saved later, that this practice must be encouraged.

One client found, for example, that the average defect found in their environment saved an average of five hours of time[†] which the project team would have to spend later. Another company found that they saved 30 hours software engineer time per hour of Inspection time.[‡] Obviously, if such issues are rolling in for the individual every fifteen minutes, it will pay to continue – even if some issues are found by others simultaneously.

Obviously, a perfectly correct and stable rate cannot come into play in the early months of Inspection. But it is quite critical. At the very least, until your own rate data is available, you should avoid rates above two pages per hour and preferably keep to no more than a page per hour.

5.1.6   Checking Method

We recommend that people mark potential defects, that is, issues, in writing, or highlight them with markers, circling the appropriate locations in the texts. A checker should be completely free to choose any personal checking method which succeeds in making them a valuable player on the team. The aim of Inspection, and indeed of individual checking, is not actually the volume of issues which are found by an individual. The ultimate judgement of the individual's contribution is how many defects they find (especially major ones) which nobody else on the team found, though the fact that some checking roles may be more naturally productive than others should be taken into account. You should also judge whether the issues found are major or minor (according to the definition which your group has adopted). The final verdict on the severity classification of each individual issue (major/minor) is with the editor.

During checking an individual checker may use the checklists as a guide to finding issues. Alternatively the checker may choose to leave a checklist to others and go for defects which are not findable by means of the checklist. The checker should not merely read the product document, but carefully compare it to the rules and the source documents.

[†] ICL Bracknell, UK, 1984. See details in *Principles of Software Engineering Management*, Chapter 21, Addison-Wesley (Gilb, 1988).
[‡] Shell Research, Ryswyk, The Netherlands, report, 1991, in *Information and Management* (Doolan, 1991).

5.1.7 Summary: The Cost and Benefit of Individual Checking

We have looked at the individual checking part of the Inspection process. The time spent in individual checking is a key and critical part of the Inspection process described in this book. Without individual checking, you will end up with merely a group review which will probably only find 10% of the defects which could have been found by applying Inspection rigorously.

The individual checking process is optimized when each individual finds the maximum number of unique issues, that is, issues that are found by that individual and not by anyone else. This gives maximum benefit from the time invested by the team as a whole.

In order to make the individual checking effective, roles are assigned, with associated checklists, which help to focus the individual checking process in different directions for each individual checker. It would be wasteful for all checkers to check for the same thing; they should all be checking for different things.

Individual checking consumes about 20–30% of all Inspection time. This may seem expensive, but if you drop it or cut corners on it, you will be able to measure (using Inspection metrics) that you are losing heavily. You will be missing major defects and incurring higher costs than any 'saved' in checking. This is something anyone can test by using their own Inspection data.

5.2   The Logging Meeting

The logging meeting has three purposes:

- to record all potential defects identified during individual checking, as issues in the issue log;
- to perform the checking process in a group environment to identify additional issues, which had not been found during individual checking, so that they are also logged as issues;
- to record other items, that is, improvement suggestions and questions of intent to the author.

The logging meeting is shown in Figure 5.4 in relationship to the other parts of the Inspection process which have been discussed so far.

5.2.1   Guidelines for the Logging Meeting

The logging meeting is a group activity. It is very much like brainstorming, and a high rate of flow of activity is strongly

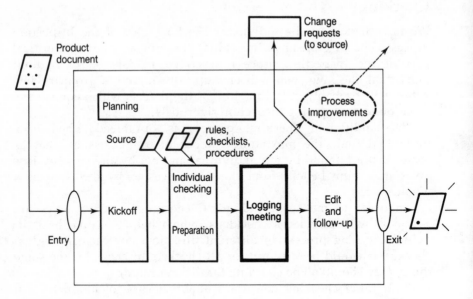

Figure 5.4 Logging relative to other activities.

encouraged. Issue identification replaces the 'ideas' of brainstorming. Anything like debate, defensiveness, rejection, or criticism which might threaten this flow of issue identification is consciously excluded from the meeting. The Inspection leader is trained to remind participants diplomatically of this agreed meeting discipline.

The overt activity of the meeting is identifying issues aloud to a scribe. But there is an important 'quiet' continued checking activity by all participants, in order to find even more issues than those found during the individual checking process.

The meeting starts with an entry process of collecting checking data (time, majors, pages studied and scanned) from each checker, recorded anonymously.

The checkers who attend the logging meeting must have spent the right amount of time in individual checking, so that they have a reasonable number of issues to contribute to the meeting. Any checker who has not adequately prepared by doing the individual checking is either dismissed from the meeting, or could be the scribe for this meeting. If more than one checker has not completed individual checking, the logging meeting is postponed.

Inspection is led by a trained Inspection leader, who acts to ensure the greatest possible productivity, measured in issues identified for the hours of team time used.

The person who controls the logging meeting is called the moderator. This may be the Inspection leader, or someone whom the leader appoints to control the meeting. The moderator must be trained in techniques for controlling the meeting both in terms of time discipline and discipline in issue reporting by the participants. The certified leader takes responsibility for managing the process, even when delegating tasks to others such as leading a meeting.

Meetings start on time (like football games and orchestral performances) and end not more than two hours later. This is for human tiredness reasons only. You must not, as some have attempted, squeeze an arbitrarily large document into these two hours! You must 'chunk' or sample the material so that you can check and log at the optimum rates. Some practice a short break mid-way between two full hours. This is intuitively a sound practice, but no measures have proven it yet.

The meeting consumes only 20–30% of all the time used in the Inspection process. This may surprise people who assume that the meeting is the dominant activity.

There will be strong tendencies, especially with inexperienced checkers, towards extraneous activity like explaining, defending, suggesting fixes and asking questions. There is a time and place for all this, but it is not the logging meeting. If the moderator cannot suppress this extra activity, then the meeting will be ineffective, and the moderator or Inspection leader needs retraining or replacing. The result of an unfocused meeting will show up quickly in the Inspection metrics, and these can be used to remind the Inspection leader what is being lost in time and money by 'being too nice'.

It does not matter, for the moment, whether the documents which we have reported and logged issues in, are 'logically correct' or 'really defective'. We have, after all, intentionally put novice employees into the Inspection teams in order to see whether they easily understand the material. When they report something as an issue, that is, a potential defect, in spite of its real 'logical correctness' (or its perceived correctness by the authors), then this is a sign that the documentation has not managed to make the 'logically correct' statement clear to the novices. This is the situation which needs correcting. Therefore,

Unintelligible to novices is a potential defect.

5.2.2   Discussion of Issues is not Allowed

The Inspection logging meeting-culture largely prohibits discussion and comment other than identifying potential defects and logging them as issues. If this procedure is not followed, much of the power of Inspection is lost, and there is a lack of productivity focus in the Inspection process.

There are good reasons for this rule being imposed. People will happily discuss a single issue for 10 or 20 minutes. Yet in this same time, the group is normally capable of logging 20 to 40 other issues (perhaps more), most of which may be 'major'! It is not difficult to calculate which is the more valuable use of time.

As a rough estimate we can assume that five hours are lost for the team for every major defect not logged. If people discuss each issue this could mean fifty hours lost every 10 minutes because people enjoy discussing issues!

There are two areas that people love to discuss: is it really an issue, and how would I solve this issue? Discussion about whether or not it is an issue is not allowed. It is much more efficient simply to log it and get on to the next one. Discussion about how to solve the issue is also not allowed; it is the editor's job to fix defects and resolve issues later. If editors wish they can set up a time to discuss how to fix the defect with the interested individual, but this is outside the Inspection process, and outside the logging meeting.

5.2.3 The Scribe

The person who records the issues has traditionally been referred to as the scribe. Ideally, the moderator will find someone else, who is not a checker, to be the scribe, so that the checkers and the moderator can concentrate their attention on generating a maximum flow of issues per minute (about two per minute, for example) without being distracted with note-taking. It is, however, the responsibility of the moderator either to be the scribe or to get the job done by someone else.

One might be forgiven for assuming that the editor should be the scribe, as that would ensure legible notes for later use. However, the editor is usually also the author, and we need authors to be active in the defect-finding role, both because they are qualified to find issues, and because of the psychological need to participate. Sometimes a secretary is used to log issues.

Some users have collected issues during logging meetings, using computers such as an unobtrusive laptop. This has a number of advantages, though it is still uncommon:

- avoiding handwriting legibility problems;
- capturing the details in machine-readable form for later analysis;
- making metrics more quickly available on an internal network in a confidential way;
- making it possible to display and print the issue-list for participants, as you go, or immediately afterwards.

It is important that the editor understands the issues recorded, that is, what is wrong, since it is the editor who must read the issue log and take action on every issue logged.

It is useful for the checkers to be aware of the issues logged by the group during the logging meeting. If an issue which a checker is about to report has just been logged by someone else, then they should remain silent about it to avoid duplication. However, if they have identified a different issue which is in the same part of the document where someone else has just logged an issue, it is important they do report it. Otherwise, due to a misunderstanding about the previously reported issue, they may fail to report what might be judged an important major defect.

5.2.4   Logging Meeting Rate

Like the checking rate, there is a calculable optimum rate of holding a meeting for each type of documentation. These rates are quite sensitive to variation. For example IBM (Frank Buck, an internal Technical Report, 1980, IBM Kingston NY Labs) found that a 35% (to 130 lines per hour) deviation from the optimum rate (95 lines of structured COBOL per hour) led to a predictable fall of 30% in defects found amongst those available (seven not found of 21 possible). This is quite a penalty to pay for operating at other than the optimum rate.

How fast should we log items? One possibility is simply to say the faster the better. The limiting factor will then be the speed at which the scribe can write down what the checkers report. However, this is not the best way because it would be quicker to simply give the individual issue lists to the editor to get on with fixing them, and this means there is no real purpose for the meeting.

A purpose of the meeting is to find new issues which were not found in the individual checking (and if the logging-meeting checking-rate is too fast, this will not happen). The logging-meeting checking-rate needs to be slow enough to allow new issues to be found. The word 'synergy' means an effect which happens when different things or people are together which would not have happened otherwise. The logging meeting should stimulate synergy in issue finding.

Figure 5.5 illustrates an example of the percentage of total issues found during the logging meeting that leaders report. It is essential that we monitor the percentage of new issues found so we can find the best logging-meeting checking-rate. Cindy Arksey writes: 'The category called synergy is in effect one measurement of the benefit of team members coming together in the logging meeting, versus

Fagan inspection teams statistics

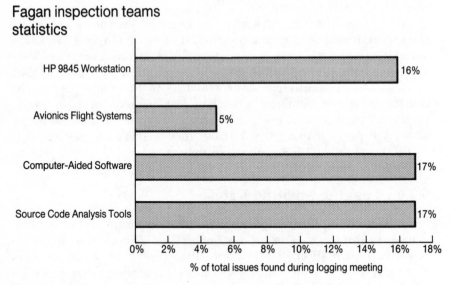

% of total issues found during logging meeting

Figure 5.5 1989 Boeing Computer Services Technical Report, *Fagan method pilot*, by Cindy Arksey, metrics from four inspection teams.

handing off their marked-up documents to the author. (Which, by the way, some checkers wanted to do at the beginning of the inspection process but soon realized – *as they found defects in the meeting they likely would not have found on their own* – was not the best way to go.) Frankly, I'm not sure why some leaders (and teams) found more additional defects in the logging meeting than others. I am sure that the *leaders need to remind checkers at the beginning of every logging meeting that they are expected to be on the lookout for more issues,* not just to log the ones they've already found.' (Arksey, 1989).

These 'checking time at the logging meeting' rates will vary as the quality of the documentation increases, and as the learning curve for checkers improves, and both of these factors must be expected to go through dramatic change in the first months after installing Inspection. This means that the early numbers for rates of checking for logging meetings cannot be relied upon to serve as a long-term guide.

The quality assurance function or chief Inspection leader (or whoever is looking after the successful implementation of Inspection) must track the numbers for the results. They must inform Inspection leaders and moderators of the optimal rates, and they must tell them when it is suspected that their performance is poor due to poor rates.

5.2.5   Issue Logs

An issue log is the primary output of an Inspection meeting. Although it is referred to as the 'issue log', meaning a list of potential defects, it is more accurately an 'item log', because the things which are logged are not just issues, but also include improvement suggestions (see Figure 5.6). Questions to the author are also logged during the meeting and are answered at the end of the meeting. (See also Chapter 8.)

Most organizations will use a logging form which they have designed locally. A log can be a fairly simple blank-page list, as long as you get the essential items. This is an example of a very simple item log:

Item Log
   for Inspection 97-0023,
      Design Solution Module DEEP.SHOOT

m   1. No tag on line 234.<-GE8

M   2. Insufficient detail in solution specification line 23 page 1.<-RS13

?   3. Don't understand DEEP.SHOOT.AMMO (question to author)

M   4. AMMO is inconsistent with SHOOT.CANNON.<-GE2

NM 5. CANNON is inconsistent with Source-LEV.MAX-SIZE.<-GE2 (new in the meeting)

I   6. Procedure could include consistency check step (improvement suggestion)

A complete detailed suggestion for a logging form is in Appendix C of this book.

What Should the Item or Issue Log Contain?

The log will contain three types of items: issues, improvement suggestions, and questions to the author.

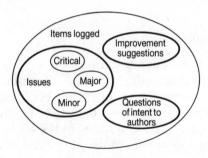

Figure 5.6   'Items' is a term covering all those things which are written in the log.

The logging of the improvement suggestions and questions to the author are not classified into major or minor severity, and may or may not have a specific reference to the product document being inspected, so are slightly simpler to log.

When logging issues, you must identify:

- exactly where the issue is located on one or more documents;
- the nature of your assertion – cite the exact rule or checklist reference code;
- suggested severity of issue (M or m);
- whether the issue was found in individual checking or was 'new' – that is, first identified in the logging meeting.

You should have a line reference number (saves counting later). A goal to pace a logging meeting may have been set, such as 'at least one issue recorded every 30 seconds'. If after half an hour the moderator reports the result that 'only 20 issues have been logged in the first 30 minutes', it brings home the fact that time is being wasted, and helps to keep the meeting moving. However, the actual logging rate may be acceptable if new major issues are being found.

You can include as headings:

- date of Inspection;
- name of Inspection leader or moderator;
- document references: product (chunk), sources, rules and so on.

Issues can be logged against the product document, but can also be logged against the source document(s). If an error is noticed in a rule, procedure or checklist, it is usually logged as a process improvement suggestion rather than an issue.

How to Report Issues for Logging

The moderator or Inspection leader should specify how issues should be reported in the logging meeting. The verbal logging should be as concise as possible. One suggestion is to keep every issue to no more than seven words. A useful principle here is to agree to the following:

- the required content of the logging;
- the codes to be used;
- the sequence of reporting.

A card 'tent' (printed on both sides) which has this agreed logging sequence and content can be brought to a meeting and put on the table to remind people of the agreement. It is important that the item log does *not* include information on *who* suggested the issue, as explained below.

Real Time Log Validation

The procedure below devised by Mary Apt of Douglas Aircraft in 1988 is recommended to avoid the need to get back to participants during the editing process.

The author/editor is a team member – an entry requirement. The editor is charged by the leader with monitoring the scribe as the log is written. If there is any problem with handwriting or content, the editor must stop the logging process and get that issue satisfactorily clarified before proceeding. In other words, we emphasize the need to check logging quality in real time.

Remaining difficulties with the log will later have to be solved without the help of identification of who said what at the logging meeting.

Why not record who raised each issue? Wouldn't this help the editor later? NO, it wouldn't, for the following reasons:

Even if there was a note about who had reported an issue, if the editor were to go back to that person during editing, they may not remember what it was about, always assuming that the person was available to answer the question when the editor wanted to find them!

The effort of recording who the reporter was would have to be done for every issue, thus adding significantly to the overhead of issue logging, and only sometimes (in a very few cases) would the information be helpful. This is not an efficient approach.

The psychological consequences of noting exactly who logged an issue are also negative. Checkers may begin to compete for getting the 'credit' for reporting issues, again leading to inefficiency.

It is far better to use the process of validating the log during the meeting by assigning the editor to read the log as it is written, and stop to clarify things immediately if there is a lack of clarity.

An Alternative Approach to Logging Issues

Barbara Spencer of Schlumberger reports (1991) that her teams reported orally, but there was no scribe function. Instead, those who had noted the issue, but did not report it, crossed out their note, thus saving the editor the bother of discovering the duplication. The set of checking notes from all the checkers was then used as the log at the end of the logging meeting. This avoided the boredom experienced when checkers had to wait for the scribe to write things down. (See Barbara Spencer's case study in Chapter 12.)

Issue Classification, Comments and Clarification

The severity logged is what the person reporting the issue *thinks* the classification is at the time, major or minor, and any other classification codes which are in use. It does not matter whether the reported classification is absolutely correct or not, because it is not the full and final classification at this point.

When the editor deals with each issue in the log during editing, they will resolve each one. If the issue is a defect, it will then be classified as major or minor. This is the full and final classification. The editor is free to change the logged severity in any way.

This is why classification is not discussed at the meeting. It is simply not worth spending any time on something which may well be changed anyway. However, we do want to capture the asserted severity from whoever submits the issue, so that the editor has a starting point, and for other reasons mentioned earlier (emphasizing 'major defects').

You need to give the necessary analytical minimum for the editor to understand your assertion. The editor, who will be at the logging meeting as a checker, should verify as the logging is done that this minimum need is satisfied.

For the sake of efficiency, anything more than the minimum necessary for the editor is time wasted, not just the editor's time but that of every participant.

The vast majority of issues logged will be simple to fix once they are identified. It is the identification of these 'simple to fix now' issues which is the reason for Inspection at this stage, rather than at test or in the field.

The editor (who is normally also the author) is responsible for finally classifying all issues, and for dealing with all issues which are not classified as defects. Taking time out of the logging meeting to discuss solutions is very wasteful and inefficient. Although everyone will have ideas about solutions, so will the editor. The editor's solutions are the ones which will be implemented, so the others are hardly worth discussing. If the editor wishes to seek advice on solutions after the logging meeting, then that is an editor prerogative, but it should be done one-on-one after the logging meeting.

Information Collected from Item Logs

The following defect log parameters are collected by IBM for their computer database of defects. This level of data is useful when the process has matured and there are fewer defects than most people experience in early stages. The defect volume goes down from an initial high, due to rapid personal learning, and due to effective defect prevention action.

Defect entry number.

Product name.

Release identifier.

Driver identifier.

Functional line item.

Process stage where defect detected.

Process stage where defect created.

Quality Improvement Team (QIT) department (for suggestions).

Defect report number for miscellaneous defect suggestions.

Date defect entered into the system.

Person who should be contacted for questions (author).

Analysis type (Inspection, test, field, QIT, miscellaneous).

Review type (group, peer, team leader, other).

Current status (being investigated, closed).

Closing reason codes, answer text, author identification, date closed.

Continues

Category of cause (communications, education new function, education base function, other, oversight, transcription problem, mistake).

Abstract of defect (short description).

Defect cause description.

Assigned process improvement suggestion list.

Defect description.

Suggested improvements.

Log of all activities against this defect.

Source: Jones C. (1985). *IBM Systems Journal*, (2) 163–4 (Jones, 1985)

Note that these parameters are not all collected during the Inspection logging process. Most are added during later stages of work on the defects.

5.2.6   Issue and Defect Classification Codes

Early Inspection recommended classification of issues or defects into two additional dimensions in addition to severity (major/minor). The reason for these classification schemes was to get information which would help to analyze faulty work processes and to improve them. This concept has now been superseded by the work of Carole Jones and her colleagues on process improvement, which started in 1983.

They have shown that the process is best improved by analyzing issues one at a time, shortly after logging them, in what we call a 'process brainstorming meeting'. This insight as to root causes and process improvement ideas is then followed up by Process Change Management Team activity. Both of these processes will be described in detail in Chapter 7 on process improvement.

In addition Jones makes use of goals and strategies at the kickoff meeting to encourage process improvement of the Inspection process itself. Further, the extended use of a QA database, including the 'process brainstorming' logs contributes to an improved result.

It seems that detailed classification into various categories was mainly irritating to the checkers and did not result in as great an insight into the real root causes as the Jones process does. Some parts of Hewlett Packard (HP) reported substantial resistance among software engineers to various classification schemes introduced in the 1980s. The schemes were constantly changed in response to the negative reaction. Jones' process is reported (Mays, 1990) to reduce injection of defects in all phases by 50% initially compared to the old method.

The completion of the Inspection process for software development products (described below) is very important to ensure that the potential quality improvements actually happen.

The editor classifies all issues logged into their final severity (major or minor), and identifies them as actual defects or not. The editor must deal with every issue logged. The editor corrects all defects in the product document. Issues which apply to source documents have a change request raised which is sent to that document owner. Cross-references to the change request are inserted in both the source and product documents. Improvement suggestions are sent to the process owner. Editors are free to correct defects at their discretion, and may also take the initiative to correct unlogged defects or defects noticed during editing.

The Inspection leader performs the follow-up phase, which includes checking that the editing has been completed and that every issue has had some action taken. The leader is not responsible for ensuring the correctness of the actions taken – only that everything has been acted on.

Follow-up also includes the compilation of the final Inspection metrics.

The Exit process of Inspection ensures that the product Inspected is acceptable to be released to the next software development stage. The Inspection leader must complete follow-up, and must also check other exit criteria, both generic and specific for the product or Inspection. Exit criteria include checking and logging rates being within prescribed limits, the estimation of remaining defects in the product and the recording of the metrics in the QA database. All chunks of a long document must exit before the whole document can exit.

The metrics are the most important component of Inspection. They provide the means for actually seeing what is happening in the whole software development process. Without metrics, you are working 'blind' (as many review techniques do). Inspection (and other) metrics are used to monitor not only the Inspection process, but also the effect of introducing changes to the software development process. It is essential that test and field metrics are linked to Inspection metrics, so that the benefits from the Inspection process can be properly traced.

Figure 5.7 shows some possible outputs which result from the issue log data. They use the issue log as a source for their task. All of these outputs come from the editing process.

5.2.7   Summary of the Logging Meeting

The logging meeting is held for the purpose of recording three types of items: issues (potential defects), questions of intent to the author, and improvement suggestions.

The checkers must have done their individual checking before the logging meeting, or they should be disqualified from attending the meeting, or could become the scribe for that meeting.

The meeting is very strictly controlled by the Inspection leader or the moderator, who has been trained in the control of the logging meetings. The items are reported and logged in a steady but rather fast pace throughout the meeting, which lasts a maximum of two hours per chunk.

The correct optimal rate for product pages per meeting hour at the logging meeting is found when approximately 20% of issues of the total found are discovered within the logging meeting (that is, issues that had not been discovered in individual checking by the checkers).

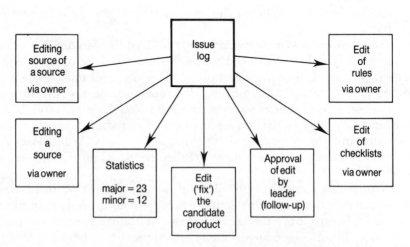

Figure 5.7   Some of the written outputs as a result of the Inspection process (not including process brainstorming logs and so on).

The issues logged give sufficient (but no more) information for the editor to classify and correct the issues raised. The editor is responsible within the logging meeting for ensuring that what is logged will be understandable later on.

A number of things are intentionally not included in the issue log, such as who reported which item, full and final classifications, full details and explanation, and any solutions to the issues logged.

Rather than log extensive classification codes, a better approach is that described in this book of holding a process brainstorming meeting after the logging meeting, to analyze root causes of issues immediately, and to begin working to improve the process as soon as possible.

6

The Inspection Process (Part 3) – Completion

This chapter looks at the final stages of the Inspection process as applied to products, and covers everything to the right of the broken line in Figure 6.1.

6.1   Edit

6.1.1   The Importance of the Edit Phase

One of the main purposes of the checking part of Inspection, both the individual checking and the logging meeting, is to produce a list of issues which may potentially be defects in the product document. The whole point of finding the defects is not only to identify them, but to have an opportunity to fix them. There would be little point in having a process which only tells us with great confidence that we have lots of defects. The only way in which the quality of the Inspected product can be improved is by removing those defects.

> Don't call them 'bugs', call them 'quality improvement opportunities'.[†]

Inspection without the correction process would simply tell you how bad you were. It is essential that the correction process be done at least as well as the other parts of the Inspection technique. If not, then the benefits will not be there.

The word 'issues' was used when potential defects were identified in checking, and logged, because it was not yet certain

---

[†] Graham Babel, UK Inland Revenue, at National Computer Centre (NCC) Seminar, 1990.

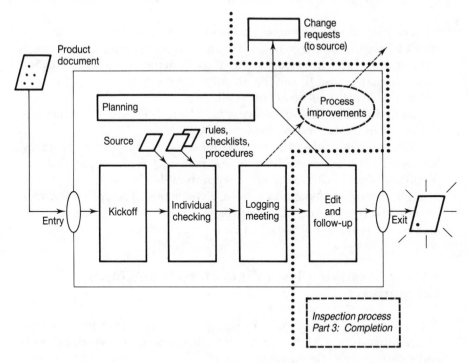

Figure 6.1   The Inspection process – completion.

whether they were 'real' defects or not. Calling something a defect, when it isn't, can lead to misunderstandings and antagonism. However, the point of product Inspection is to remove defects from the product, and this is done in the 'edit' phase. Again, because we do not want to use language which will unnecessarily antagonize anyone, the person who looks at and resolves all the issues logged is called an 'editor' rather than a 'corrector', 'fixer' or 'reworker'. This is a more accurate term because the editor does more than correct defects. The editor is the first person to acknowledge that an issue is really a 'defect'. The editor also deals with non-defects, defects in other documents, and improvement suggestions.

6.1.2   The Edit Process

Editing is a process carried out by a single individual, the editor, who 'edits' the issues logged. It includes both changes to the product document and requests for changes to other people's documents, as well as the logging of further improvement suggestions.

The edit is checked for completeness, not necessarily correctness, by the Inspection leader, during the next Inspection stage 'follow-up'.

The central idea of the edit process is that something is done as a result of each issue logged. The action may be a correction, a change request, or an inserted written comment to avoid further misunderstandings. It can be in any appropriate form. The only unforgivable action is no action at all.

The edit and follow-up process is shown in Figure 6.2 in relation to the rest of the Inspection process so far.

Edit activity during the logging meeting is consciously avoided, because it can be unproductive. As many as five people may be involved, often with divergent viewpoints. What is usually needed is a single person to make a satisfactory correction. The correction will be effectively checked in later Inspection and tests. We are not looking for perfect solutions, but cost-effective ones.

6.1.3   Classifying Issues into Defects and other Categories

The first step of the editor is to classify the issues into those which are genuine defects and require correction, and those which are not, and require some other action.

The editor determines final classification, severity and action for each issue, and has considerable power to reclassify, after doing a responsible analysis of the reality behind the item.

For defects in the product document, the correction is finally the choice of the editor, based on the current rules and sources. No checker can tell the editor what they 'should' do. The editor is the best person to do this job, since they are probably the responsible author and current owner of the product document. If the documentation has to be beefed up with comments to explain things for the novice, then they should be added. If the source materials are in need of fixing, then a change request is the appropriate action. If the rules are inadequate, then an 'improvement suggestion' is required. If a 'kickoff' briefing, before the checking, was in need of more detail, then make a note to include it in the next kickoff meeting.

Any logged issue can be re-classified to a 'defect' or an 'improvement suggestion'. Any defect can be either corrected in the product, or treated as an issue for other owners (of sources, checklists and rules). This then becomes a change request. Any defect can be re-classified in severity (minor, major).

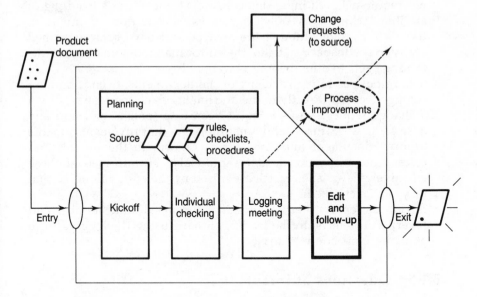

Figure 6.2   The Edit process.

6.1.4   Appropriate Edit Actions

The following are appropriate actions for the editor to take during editing:

- assign final severity (major, minor) classification of defect, whenever in the editor's judgement the initially logged classification was incorrect;
- correct the product document (according to sources and rules);
- send a change request to the source document owner when an issue has been raised in the source which cannot be resolved by the editor directly;
- note in the issue log that an appropriate change has in fact been made earlier in this edit or elsewhere;
- the editor may fix something logged as a major issue, when it is really *not* a major defect, by adding comment to the product, to explain why it is not a defect – this would then be considered a 'minor defect';
- send a request for improvement to the owner of rules or checklists – this may result from a direct improvement logged by a checker, or by a decision of the editor as to how to treat anything logged, or by a new initiative by the editor during editing;
- voluntarily improve the product document for future product

'customers', even though reaction to logged questions of intent is not required in editing – this is based on the editor's handling of an item which was only logged as a 'question of intent to the author', and although the answer will have been explained orally to the Inspection team, the editor may like to make sure the message gets to other people as well;

- take initiatives to improve any of the documents, even if nothing is logged, either directly to the document which they 'own', or via a change request – this is not a license to 'polish' and add any desired new features, and unauthorized 'improvements' to the product document must of course conform to the sources and rules – the Inspection leader should also be informed of these effectively new issues which are raised by the editor alone, so that they can be checked;
- the editor reports metrics on 'edit hours used' and 'number and severity of defects' to the leader, perhaps using the logging form or a joint Inspection database.

6.1.5   Questions of Intent

Any logged question of intent to the author can, at the complete discretion of the editor, be reclassified and counted as a defect. In other words, the editor can choose to modify the candidate product as a result of the question, giving them an insight into possibly beneficial improvements. However, this is entirely voluntary, while dealing appropriately with other items is not. This is one reason why the questions are logged in writing. The other reason is to keep up the pace of logging, undistracted by digressions.

6.1.6   Edits in the Product Document

Some action to each issue and each improvement suggestion must be taken in written form, and duly noted on the item log. It would be useful if the editor were to make some note of what action was taken on the log itself, otherwise, unless it is perfectly obvious, the Inspection leader will have to search for it in the documentation when they come to check the editing actions taken, in follow-up. If the action taken is noted directly beside each item listed on the log, this makes it easy for both the editor and the leader to check.

6.1.7   Edits in other Documents

What is a Change Request?

Ideally, the source documentation (the source used both in Inspection and to produce the product document) is 'exit' clean, due to previous Inspection. In practice, upstream Inspection can find only about 80% of the defects, and the rest filter through to the next level. We expect to find that a substantial number (15–30% of all issues logged in an Inspection) are not themselves in the product document. Logged items may turn into potential improvements in the rules and checklists, as well as point to potential defects in the sources.

When found, these issues typically need dealing with by people outside the editor's immediate responsibility. The editor cannot and should not normally attempt to fix them. Other parts of the organization and process may be more capable, and may have a better overview of the consequences of change.

The editor must, as part of the action on issues logged, generate a request to another department or to the person responsible for that document. This request for a change to a document not under the requester's control is called a 'change request'.

When a change request is received, it can and probably will have an impact on the present work on the document affected. In the meantime it is vital that we keep track of the fact that we have requested a change and that we document exactly where one is pending. We can use cross-reference markers for this purpose.

We should also mark, or get others to mark, the source document which is 'under change request' immediately, so that other teams using it are immediately aware of the issue.[†] These markers are illustrated in Figure 6.3.

See Appendix C for an example of a change request and a sample from a client's handbook.

Who Follows up a Change Request?

It is not practical for a change request to be followed up by the Inspection leader, since it might well take longer than the time for which the leader has formal responsibility. The Inspection leader ensures, in the follow-up process, that the change request has been sent by the editor, and that appropriate cross-references to the request are inserted into the product documentation.

The formal responsibility for following through the change request is with the manager of the work process being Inspected which resulted in the change request being issued. In practice, the local quality improvement person might actually follow up in detail and make sure the change comes back in time to avoid their team's commitment in a wrong direction.

---

† One early example of 'being analyzed' markers is found in TRW Systems' 'Requirements Properties Matrix' (*Characteristics of Software Quality*, North-Holland); Gilb: *Software Metrics*, page 71.

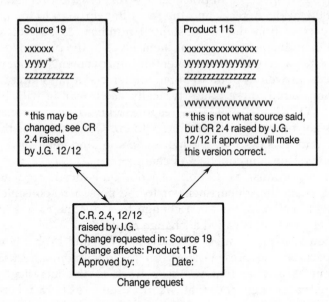

Figure 6.3   Embedding cross-reference pending change requests.

Even if the follow-up process is via a log record in a computerized database, it is still necessary to mark it as such on the product documentation, so that people reading it know that the issue is not yet resolved.

What Do You Do if You Get No Reply to a Change Request?

The situation may arise where colleagues in another department will not service the change requests at all. There may be good reasons for failing to reply from their point of view, such as lack of resources, relevant people now moved on to other work, or it may simply be seen as unimportant or irrelevant.

What should be done? One alternative is to treat such change requests as having been turned down, that is, to continue to work with the source documents as they are, with known defects. This approach may conform to the 'letter of the law', but does not have the improved quality of either this product or the whole organization at heart. It may in any case be impossible to accept the source document as it is, for example if it is inconsistent with itself.

Another alternative is simply to undertake to clarify or rewrite the source documentation yourself, and send a copy of your 'working assumptions' to those who *should* have taken the responsibility for making the changes. In some cases this may involve considerable hours of effort to do somebody else's job, like clarifying the required system quality attributes. But it may be necessary to have some reasonable source assumptions to work on, in order to make any progress at all. Make the changes which will be most effective at making your own work easier and of better quality.

This approach may be perceived as being helpful to the other parties, if they were too resource-constrained to be able to make changes which needed to be done. On the other hand, it may be seen as obstructive or 'empire-building'. It is the job of the quality manager to sort out disagreements about quality between departments, and not the job of the person who raised the technical change request.

6.1.8   Re-calculating Metrics after Editing

The editor must give the Inspection leader all edit data required by the Data Summary Form. This is the first time we have a reliable picture of the *real* number of defects which this Inspection cycle has found.

6.2   Follow-up

Just as errors are made in developing software, and in the checking process, so the editing process is not immune from errors either. When the editor has completed the editing task, the thoroughness of that completion is checked by the Inspection leader. This phase is called 'follow-up', and is done by checking that *some* due consideration has been made regarding all items in the issue log, and that appropriate responsible action has actually been taken in writing.

It would be unreasonable to ask the leader to guarantee perfect editing. The practice is to concentrate on making sure it is complete, looks reasonable, and to take a calculated chance on missing some errors in editing. Fagan (1986) reports that one of six edit changes are incorrect or incomplete. These poor fixes are simply added to the burden of the defects not even identified by a single Inspection pass (between 12% and 40% of existing defects are not caught by a single Inspection alone in mature Inspection processes[†]).

Successful edit completion, as judged by the leader in the follow-up process, is one pre-requisite for Inspection 'exit', and thus for the

---

† IBM Rochester Labs reports in 1992 60% defect finding effectiveness in Code Inspections, 80% in Pseudocode Inspection and 88% in Module and Interface specification. Source R. Lindner, presentation slides and personal visit.

further use of the product material as an input to other work processes.

6.2.1   The Follow-up Tasks and Responsibilities

The Inspection leader is responsible for follow-up. The following tasks are essential, and when successfully completed, are the basis for a formal exit from the Inspection process:

- Check that all listed issues are acted on in writing.
- Check that improvement suggestions are sent to appropriate process owners.
- Report final Inspection metrics for defects by severity and hours used for all tasks, including edit and follow-up.

6.2.2   Checking that Issues are Acted Upon

The editor is not permitted to decide that no action is required on a logged issue. Some action must be taken on whatever caused the checker to assert that there was an issue. This may simply take the form of additional documentation to prevent a possible misunderstanding or misinterpretation. The Inspection leader in follow-up ensures that all issues have had some action taken on them.

Any unresolvable issues at this level of work, or at this time, must be documented by an explicit cross-reference embedded in the documentation to show the existence of an unresolved item, and to point, via a tag or other device, to the change request or to other action requested.

6.2.3   Reporting Final Inspection Metrics

Initial determination of the issue severity classification (major, minor) is made by the checker who reports the issue. However, the final determination of severity is made by the editor, who probably is the only one who studies the matter in depth. This means that follow-up is the first opportunity to add up correct totals for severity of defects.

Metrics often do not seem to be important to the individuals concerned with a single document, but they are vital for productive control over the entire software engineering process. Not delivering Inspection metrics is the equivalent of spending money, but never giving receipts to your department, and never doing any bookkeeping. We would all like to avoid these things, but there is a penalty to pay if we fail to do them.

6.3 Exit

6.3.1 The Exit Process

The follow-up process described above validates one of a number of exit criteria which are used as the final gate in the Inspection process for products. Products are not allowed to enter the Inspection process unless they are of a certain minimum initial quality, so that Inspectors' time is not wasted in Inspecting them. It is even more important that the product when exited is of the quality which is required, so that the software development process which will take place next on this product will not waste developers' time. The exit process is shown in Figure 6.4.

The Inspection leader is responsible for checking that all exit criteria have been met. The exit criteria are set by the organization. Most criteria are generally applicable to all software Inspections. However, special criteria can be set for particular software Inspections and particular document types.

The whole point of formal exit criteria is to ensure that 'exit' is truly a reliable management indication that the product can now safely be passed on to others in the organization without intolerable or unanticipated consequences.

No doubt, hard-won experience will teach you that you need different and better exit criteria than those we suggest here. That is what the exit condition process control point is for. It is a place to put hard-won experience to work for you, so that you do not continue to repeat the mistakes of the past. A true sign of wisdom is

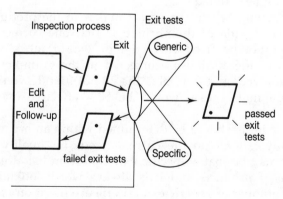

Figure 6.4 Exit process.

not 'never making a mistake', but not making the same mistakes over and over again.

Having formal written exit criteria is a basis for systematic upgrading of the process, which is defined partly by exit criteria (but also by rules, procedures and entry criteria).

If current exit criteria are allowing too many serious defects to escape downstream, then the logical step is to tighten the exit criteria so as to win economically. We trade more effort during the Inspection process for less effort afterwards.

The exit process is the fishing net and we need to decide how small a fish we are going to let escape, by adjusting the net mesh size (see Figure 6.5).

6.3.2   Exit Criteria

One of the most fundamental checks for exit is the quality level of the edited product. This is expressed in the maximum number of major defects estimated as remaining per page.

A good rule of thumb for the number of defects *remaining* is that it is roughly equal to the number of defects *found* per page. For example, if you found fifty defects in ten pages, you probably have five per page left, *after* edit.

However, this is primarily a function of the defect-finding effectiveness of your Inspection process. Effectiveness is highly variable depending on document type and process maturity. It is calculated based on historical data of the percentage of defects found in Inspection, in test execution, and in the field.

If effectiveness is historically 60% for the Inspection process on code, then if you found 30 defects in one Inspection, there would be approximately 20 (40%) defects remaining after Inspection. Some of these may be found spontaneously by the editor during editing, but this should not be counted on.

The corrections which the editor makes to the product are not perfect either. A rule of thumb here is that one correction in six would either not be fixed correctly, or would introduce a new defect. Thus of the 30 defects corrected in the example above, 25 would be removed, and five, plus the 20 not found, would remain. So Inspection in this case would be 50% effective overall, after editing.

The exit criteria should be determined within an organization to be specifically tailored to the current needs for quality of exited products. It may be that a specific exit condition list already exists for the type of products and it is always worth looking for one. However, a number of generic exit criteria are listed on page 202, as a starting point for defining your own.

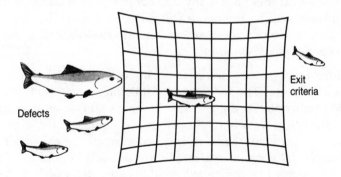

Figure 6.5   The fishing net model of Inspection.

It is vital that all generic exit criteria (Section 8.16.1) and those on the relevant specific exit criteria list have been met before approving exit and enabling release.

6.3.3   If a Document Fails Exit

The exit process is intended as a quality check on the entire Inspection process. Most of the time, if Inspections are working properly, candidate products will successfully pass the exit criteria (when Inspection is 'mature'). However, if the exit checking is working properly, it will not be a 'rubber stamp'. Sometimes, a product will fail to exit. This is due to one or more of the exit criteria not being met.

If a document fails to exit because of too many estimated defects remaining, then there are the following alternative courses of action.

(1) Get the author to do a massive cleanup or re-write – beyond the logged issues, and re-submit to Inspection.

(2) 'Burn' the document and produce a fresh one. Fagan calls this identification of error-prone modules. This approach is often far more cost-effective than is realized, because of the paradoxical (but well-supported) fact that products which start defective tend to stay defective. One of the strengths of Inspection is the ability to identify error-prone products early enough to completely re-create them. Error-prone areas of software systems are not only a problem during Inspection, but fail many other tests, and use an inordinate amount of maintenance effort. That is why it is generally more cost-effective to re-write them as early as possible.

(3) Repeat the Inspection after edit. You can expect to find the same

percentage of defects remaining as you did in the initial Inspection. If there are many defects per page remaining initially then there will be too many *still* remaining after the next edit to permit exit. So this is not an efficient alternative if there are many defects per page remaining.

Failure to exit does not necessarily involve redoing the entire Inspection process. The leader and colleagues must simply remove the failed exit criteria. Sometimes this is as simple as making sure that the statistical data is really put in the database. If the optimum rate was not observed, then a re-Inspection would be called for.

If metrics delivery, or proper edit are the only conditions stopping exit, then they must be completed. If other exit criteria such as 'too high defect rate' or 'too high checking rate or logging rate' are stopping exit, then a re-inspection may be called for.

When the leader signs off on successful exit, the work is officially releasable to the next software development phase, the 'customers' of the authors of this product. Authors can then, and only then, claim to have met their deadlines. The product is now no longer a 'candidate' for Inspection approval, but a fully approved 'exited product'.

Determining Whether Repeated Inspection is Necessary

The Inspection leader determines whether or not another Inspection is necessary. If it meets all the formal exit criteria then no repeat is necessary. There are usually no exit criteria which in themselves demand an immediate and simple repeat of the checking process.

However, if, for example, the failed exit criterion is that the checking process went faster than the optimum rate, one possibility is to rerun the checking at the optimal rate. Even this decision needs to be taken in the light of how issues have turned up. Even at a less than optimum rate, the existing issue log should form the basis for the first edit and follow-up, followed by a further Inspection, this time at the correct rate.

Re-cycling the Inspection, after editing the product using the issue log is not normally necessary because it is not normally cost-effective. Most of the product documentation will, after all, be subject to either a new Inspection in its role as source input to the next development process, or be validated by means of testing. However, the decision to re-cycle or not should be made on the basis of the type and number of defects found, and the defects per page to be expected for this type of document, taking into consideration the costs of the repeat and the risks in not doing it.

A repeat Inspection is not needed to check the quality of the editing of logged issues. Remember that we do not expect to log more than about 60–80% of the available defects at one Inspection pass. The fact that one sixth of the defects might have been edited incorrectly, and these errors have slipped by the leader's follow-up process, is not considered worth worrying about.

6.3.4   The Exited Product

Exited work is deemed to be of a standard that is economically acceptable for processing by other people in the 'downstream' work processes. Note that successful exit is an entry condition for the next work process, and for the next Inspection where this product document is the source (input) document.

Since the exit will still permit some defects to remain, and since the remaining number of defects can vary depending on the exit criteria, we recommend that you include an estimate of remaining defects together with the exit notification. People will then not be shocked to discover more defects. A possible format would be:

Document Title.   **Page 1**
Exited on 3 Feb. By TsG. Est. maximum remaining major defects per page = 2.5

Managers do not give any separate approval to a product which has exited Inspection. Management has already participated in setting up the entire process, including the exit criteria, and it is important that they delegate and trust the process.

6.3.5   Metrics
The Importance of Metrics in Inspection

Inspection metrics are far more important than most people think. Inspection metrics are, if anything, one of the most important differences between Inspection and other similar processes such as reviews and walkthroughs.

Inspection metrics give you a much more reliable picture of what is happening in the software engineering environment than unaided intuition. Inspection metrics allow you to sense trends in time earlier than otherwise. They allow you to argue for change, armed with facts about productivity and costs. You are more certain both to sense the need for change, and to argue its case successfully when you have Inspection metrics to back you up.

Inspection is based on the engineering process known as statistical quality improvement,[†] which is derived directly from methods preached by Deming (born 1900), Juran (born 1904) and their mentor Shewhart.[‡] The process we are interested in getting under control is our own software engineering process. Statistical quality improvement is driven primarily by numbers. There are targets to be met and there is the flow of statistical information to inform people reliably whether those targets are really being met.

Metrics as Applied to the Inspection Process

The metrics in Inspection can be compared to financial accounting systems for general management. The software engineering process has its own values and economics, and it needs a specialized accounting system. Inspection data provides one important class of data for the software engineer. Other data is collected from test metrics and field experience metrics. Only by gathering reliable and complete data about software engineering activities can we hope to understand them well enough to exercise the control we need.

It is through the regular detailed metrics that we can see the economics of the process; what things are costing us in terms of time and money. With metrics in front of us we can see subtle negative trends early, and argue for making changes before a problem becomes a crisis.

Management can see the arguments clearly in terms of how much will be lost if action is delayed, and how much will be saved by acting now. Later, when improvements in work process are in place, the metrics can defend the decisions as the right ones. If the implementation is poor, action can be taken to correct it in time. If an idea is a failure, the initiative to kill it can be taken before it does much damage.

Metrics on defect density and severity, as well as on the time needed to find and remove defects, are captured for both same-day and later analysis. Metrics on corrective actions are also kept.

Metrics as Applied to the Bigger Picture

Inspection metrics measure all aspects of Inspection itself directly. They also measure, indirectly, the effect on cost and quality of every mechanism you have in the software engineering process. The metrics give you information on the successful workings of

---

[†] See for example Juran, ed. *Quality Control Handbook*, McGraw-Hill, or Deming, *Out of the Crisis*, MIT Press.

[‡] The best proof and history of this is to be found in the *AT&T Technical Journal* March/April 1986, a special issue on quality including Fagan's Inspection.

languages, structures, organizational forms, software tools, better physical working conditions and other items of interest.

For example, if you had just implemented a new software tool, such as a diagramming tool for design documentation, you might compare the rate of defects found by those people Inspecting designs created using the new tool and those not. Table 6.1 is an example of the kind of report you might get:

Table 6.1

Method	Defects found in Inspection	Modules	Lines	Inspection effectiveness (Acceptance test)
New tool	3.3 Def./module	250	35 KLOC	66%
Old manual method	1.2 Def./module	3000	400 KLOC	24%

The conclusion is that more defects will be found earlier (at design time) by Inspecting designs created using the new tool. This will result in downstream savings (at Acceptance test). Such savings would not be calculated on Inspection metrics alone. Similar metrics from testing and field usage are vital for understanding the full economic and practical significance of Inspection metrics.

Another example might be assessing whether to run a static analysis tool on code before or after Inspection, or whether Inspections are cost-effective after static analysis. By collecting metrics about actual defects found in a number of cases where both alternatives were tried, you will now have solid facts on which to base a decision about what the most cost-effective approach is.

The Role of Test Metrics and Field Metrics

It is essential that test and field metrics are also collected and collated with the Inspection metrics, so that the effects of Inspection and other techniques can be assessed across the whole of the development process. If Inspection metrics only are kept, and not compared to test and field data, then you will not know how effective the Inspections really are. The real payback comes in the savings in testing and field operation.

Keeping track only of your costs (Inspection) and not your benefits (in test and field use) is not going to give a balanced cost-benefit analysis (see Figure 6.6).

Most people find that defects in the field are by far the most expensive to fix (even when you don't include consequential costs to customers or the business). Catching the defects when tests are run is

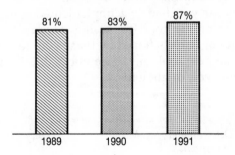

Figure 6.6   Percent defects removed before test (that is, using Inspections) at IBM Rochester Minnesota Labs. The developers track the unit test defects found. Notice that the process seems to be getting more effective every year (Lindner, 1992).

ten times cheaper, but catching them in Inspection is in the order of 80[†] times cheaper than catching those same defects in the field.

Figure 6.7 shows how the metrics act to affect all aspects of the software development process.

Inspection and other Improvement Approaches

A large number of technologies and organizational ideas may be tracked by the metrics (Inspection and others). Improvements in these other technologies, such as testing and development areas, may all contribute to an improvement. Although it can be difficult, if not impossible, to isolate the effects of one technique such as Inspection from the other solutions, it really doesn't matter which particular technique is most responsible for improvements, as long as improvements are clearly happening. If the stopping of one technique leads to degradation in quality, then metrics will make it evident.

Inspection metrics are particularly vital because they give us insights into areas of requirements planning, architecture, design engineering and documentation which conventional field and test data cannot provide with sufficient sensitivity at an early stage. Inspection can tackle the vital upstream part of the process, which is low in volume but high in criticality.

Mere defect-finding and repair are good for the short-term economics and health of the individual products and project, but the statistical data which Inspection provides, together with other data

† based on IBM Santa Teresa Labs data 1980 (factor 82), Remus.

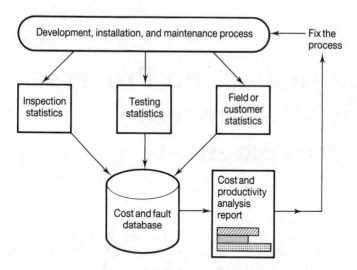

Figure 6.7   The use of metrics in the software development process.

(test, field, reviews) allows management, aided by local Process Change Management Teams, to make systematic improvements in the entire software engineering process. This includes languages, structures, tools, metrics, motivation, hardware access and capacity and any other device which might influence productivity.

6.4   Summary

Identifying defects does not improve the quality of the product document. Fixing defects does. The editor is responsible for classifying issues into defects (major and minor). The editor also writes change requests and sends improvement suggestions to the process owner. The editor must take some action on every item logged.

The inspection leader checks that the editing has been completed, but does not check the actual edit actions. The final metrics, as classified by the editor, are stored in the Inspection database. This is called follow-up.

The Inspection leader authorizes exit from the Inspection process if the exit criteria have been met. This ensures that the exited product is now fit for use in a 'downstream' software development process.

This is why Inspection as taught in this book does not stop with exited products, but goes on to process improvement, which is described in the next chapter.

7

The Inspection Process (Part 4) – Process Improvement

In the previous chapters, Inspection as it applied to software development products was discussed. Product Inspection is primarily a *defect detection* and removal method.

The other aspect of Inspection is primarily a *defect prevention* method, and is ultimately far more powerful and effective than product-based Inspection alone.

7.1   Problem Removal Contrasted with Problem Prevention

Product-based Inspection is mainly a potential defect-finding technique for products, documents, code, and so on. A summary of this part of the Inspection process is shown on the left in Figure 7.1. The problem prevention aspects of Inspection as a process improvement technique are shown on the right in Figure 7.1.

The process improvement part of Inspection takes the wider view based on the Shewhart cycle described below. This view incorporates what is learned in the checking phase of Inspection to translate these lessons into process improvements, which can then be fed back into the planning and management of the whole process of software development. Figure 7.2 shows how the process improvement suggestions, which are collected as part of the logging-meeting in product Inspection, are gathered together to form part of the process improvement process, which then feeds back into the software development process as a whole.

Undoubtedly, Inspections are successful in finding faults, and improve the quality of the Inspected product. But the larger, long-term

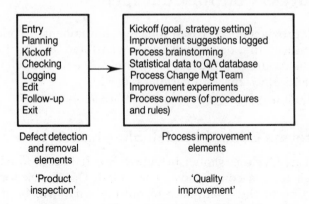

Figure 7.1   The Inspection defect detection and removal process compared with the process improvement elements.

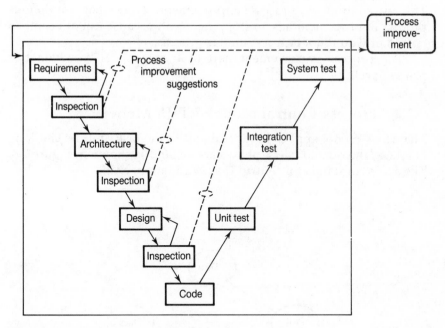

Figure 7.2   The V model of development.

payoff is not in merely getting better at finding the types of faults that Inspections do so well, but in identifying the process error that generated the fault in the first place.

7.2   Process Control Concepts

Process improvement is based on the fundamental concepts of 'process control', first developed by Shewhart and later by Juran and Deming. The nature of a process is dynamic. Events happen in a time sequence, and 'flow' through various stages.

Some famous process control models are shown below.

7.2.1   Process Control Model: Shewhart Cycle

The Shewhart Cycle is shown in Figure 7.3. It is composed of four steps which form a continuous cycle: 'Plan, Do, Check (or Study), Act'. Starting at the 'Plan' step to outline what will be done, the carrying out of the main task is the 'Do' step. The task is then checked (this is also called 'study'), and action is taken as a result, which results in further plans. Thus the basic process which is carried out (the 'Do') is being continuously improved through what is learned in checking the task, and in the actions taken as a result. This is continuous process improvement. Note that continuous process improvement has no stopping point, because if it did come to an end, it would not be a continuous process.

The process improvement part of Inspection is based on this process cycle.

7.2.2   Process Control Model: ETVX Model

The ETVX model applies in more detail to the task and the checking of a task, the do and check phases above, and is shown in Figure 7.4. The acronym stands for 'Entry, Task, Validation, eXit'.

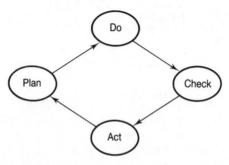

Figure 7.3   The Shewhart Cycle.

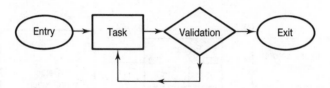

Figure 7.4   ETVX Process control model.

This is a 'process control' concept which says: 'Check it before you let it pollute the downstream part of the process. Re-do it if necessary, before letting something suspicious out – which might damage other work processes.'

The Inspection of products is based on the ETVX model.

7.3   Process Brainstorming (Root Cause Analysis)

The distinguishing feature of Inspection as inspired by Carole Jones and developed in this book is the inclusion of a process brainstorming phase in the total Inspection process, giving continuous process improvement. The process brainstorming phase is shown in Figure 7.5 in relation to the defect detection part of the Inspection process which has been described in the preceding chapters (product-based). Inspection as taught in this book is concerned not only with the quality of the products which are checked, but also with the quality of the software development process *and* the means to achieve process quality improvements.

7.3.1   Process Brainstorming Meeting

The Purpose of the Process Brainstorming Meeting

The purpose of the process brainstorming meeting is to brainstorm the process-based causes for selected issues or defects which were found in the Inspection logging meeting. The causes for the defects could include technical, organizational and political causes. The emphasis is on positive recommendations for curing the causes of the defects so that they will not happen again. The suggested process improvements which are logged aim to address the roots of the

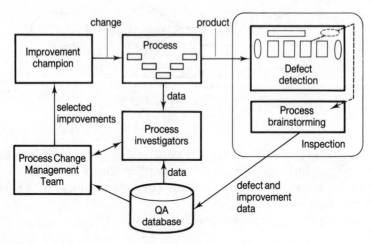

Figure 7.5. The Process Brainstorming Phase.

defects. The suggestions do not attack authors, who are not responsible for the process environment within which they work.

The output of the process brainstorming meeting is a log of improvement suggestions to the software development process, which are passed to the Process Change Management Team (PCMT) via the QA database.

The purpose of the process brainstorming meeting is *not* to deal with the document and its defects. It is to deal with the *causes* of those defects. Changing the way an organization performs its major work processes is a major undertaking, but like a major journey, begins with a single step. This meeting empowers people to take small steps on their own, and also records and initiates the larger steps towards process improvements.

It is recommended that the process brainstorming meeting carries straight on after the Inspection logging meeting, in the same room and with the same people. There are practical reasons for this: the difficulty of mounting a new meeting, and the advantage of keeping the issues fresh in peoples' minds. IBM holds separate meetings, hours or days after an issue logging meeting, for process brainstorming. But we recommend that it be held immediately. Additional interested parties may be invited in for the process brainstorming meeting who were not involved in the logging meeting, if they can attend at that time.

What Issues are Discussed at the Process Brainstorming Meetings

It is not essential or desirable to discuss all logged items from the logging meeting. It is not even essential to discuss all major issues or defects. Strictly speaking, they should still be called 'issues' at this point, because the editor has not yet classified them as defects. However, in practice, those issues which are reasonably certain to be real defects, and are the most important, are the ones which would be selected for process brainstorming.

In deciding what the most important defects are, the principle to use is known as 'Pareto Analysis'[†] and is shown in Figure 7.6. The defects which have the greatest impact and will give the greatest pay-back when they are fixed are addressed first. When they have been dealt with, we can address the next most important defect causes. Curing the source of a defect with little impact will not make much difference to our process; curing the source of a defect with a large impact will significantly improve the process.

This principle was well understood and documented by Fagan, as he was a student of Deming and Juran. The major innovation in Inspection by Jones *et al.* of IBM was to encourage the practice of causal analysis using Pareto Analysis at the grass roots level by every software professional who participates in Inspection.

What is Discussed on Each Issue?

Each issue is presented within the space of one minute, to remind all brainstorming attendees exactly where and what the potential defect is.

Next the possible root causes for the defect are explored in a 'brainstorming' manner. The essential idea of brainstorming is that any and all ideas are welcomed uncritically and logged. No evaluation of an idea is allowed. That means that no one is permitted to say why this idea might be good or bad, workable or impractical, or which is the best idea so far. The aim of brainstorming is to log the maximum number of ideas, no matter how outlandish they may be. In fact often the crazier ideas are far more fruitful in sparking off other ideas than more usual traditional ideas (de Bono, 1971).

A defect may be caused by a number of different factors, but it is the underlying root causes which are sought at this meeting. For example, an interface definition may have been omitted from a design. The cause might be because the author simply forgot to specify it, but the root cause could be because designers are not given an adequate overview of the whole system and how it fits in

---

† Dr Juran's term, discussed in his various books.

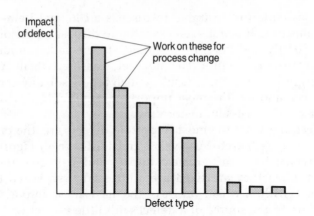

Figure 7.6   Pareto Analysis principle.

with other systems. Other possible root causes may have been because the ventilation system has been poor lately, giving people headaches, or the designer may have been frequently called away to 'fire-fight' in the middle of the design task, or perhaps the designer was getting married next week and was not concentrating as normal on the work in hand. The latter is not a systematic cause, unless you ask why there was no backup person.

The cause might have been that the author didn't think that they were supposed to specify these interfaces. The root cause of that could be that the description of the design process didn't mention interfaces of this type, or that the author had not been trained in the design methodology which included guidance on what interfaces to design. The brainstormed root causes are recorded in the process brainstorming log (described below).

The classification of the cause of the error is the probable *basic* process reason why the error was made. A defect in a product (which we call issues until the editor has confirmed them as defects) is caused by some human being making an error or mistake. It is perfectly normal and natural for people to make mistakes; we make them all the time. However, when errors are made in the documentation for software systems, a simple and trivial error from a human point of view can be extremely serious in effect when a computer executes it. This is why it is important to realize and identify the human causes of errors.

The classifications in the Mays and Jones paper (Mays, 1990) are a useful starting point for channeling the discussion about the immediate causes of such human errors (see also Chapter 17):

- communications failure (information required not received, incorrect information received);
- oversight (didn't include something, not enough time to do the job thoroughly, or simply forgot something);
- transcription error (knew and understood what to do, but a 'slip of the finger' resulted in an unintended outcome);
- education (didn't realize that something else or something different should have been done, didn't understand the problem, the solution, the context, the job).

Some errors may have multiple causes, such as a communication failure due to lack of education about what should be communicated. More than one classification may be noted, or the most fundamental one. The improvement suggestions may also address more than one classification, and so will attack the whole problem in any case. It may also be helpful to ask exactly what the nature of the error in this particular instance was. For example, exactly what was not understood, what particular item was forgotten, which aspect of information was not communicated, and what were the circumstances when the error occurred. This then leads into the consideration of the root causes for the error.

The root cause is our first guess about the specific process-related reason why a particular error was made. For example, transcription errors may be more frequent in a noisy environment, or a communication failure may occur between analysts and programmers because the analysts assume knowledge which the programmers have not yet been given in their training program.

The root causes for oversights may include a lack of guidance in a methodical way to perform a task; there may be rules but no procedures for example. There may be ways of automatically checking for oversights which were not used; this may be caused by a lack of education in the use of static analysis tools, for example, or by the lack of availability of such tools. The root cause of a communication failure may be a poor or non-existent mechanism for notifying people of changes made in one area which affects another area. The brainstorm log should contain simple keywords which identify the root causes, not lengthy explanations.

In some cases improvements will be fairly obvious, and may in fact already have been suggested in the logging meeting. It is important to note them so that the obvious things are not overlooked.

In other cases, it may be difficult to find ways of improving to prevent such defects, but there will always be something which can be done which will help in some way. The improvements suggested do not have to completely solve the whole problem in order to be useful. Simply making a start can often open the way for improvements which may not be capable of being envisaged now. The point of this process is not to 'solve' process problems, but to initiate process improvement effort and give grass roots feedback to process analysts.

Process Improvement Suggestions

After the root causes have been brainstormed for a minute, then process improvements are brainstormed. An improvement is any process change which someone could make which would help to address the root cause and make this particular defect less likely to occur next time under similar circumstances.

For example, the author could be sent on a design training course, or an overview meeting could be held with all designers of the system and related systems. An item describing this type of interface could be added to the rule set describing the design process, and to the checklist for Inspecting design documents. If too much 'fire-fighting' is disrupting the design flow, then a reallocation of emergency work assignments to those not currently engaged on critical design could be recommended. Or the whole organization could move to a different building where the ventilation is better. (The impending marriage would not require any corrective action, as the preoccupation with wedding details will have disappeared after the wedding anyway.) The suggested potential actions are also recorded in the log (described below).

For each defect, the improvements should include at least one suggestion which can be easily accomplished by one or more people in the process brainstorming meeting. For example, adding an interface item to a checklist, or simply becoming aware of where the system overview documentation is kept so that it could be referenced next time. The 'big' solutions can also be logged, such as moving the whole company to a different building, because small solutions may only be treating the symptoms and not the disease. If possible there should always be something which someone can do right away, without much effort, which will help to make a start towards eliminating the cause of the defect.

The process improvement suggestions from the preceding issue logging meeting will be directly forwarded to process owners by the editor during editing.

The Organization of Process Brainstorming Meetings

In our first experiments with process brainstorming meetings, we just let people discuss defect causes freely, not unlike third hour[†] meetings, but we soon observed that people happily discussed a single issue for 30 to 120 minutes, usually only limited by the need to move on to other activities. We also observed that most of their time was spent discussing minor issues, and that several important issues went undiscussed. If this was allowed to continue, this new meeting would soon be killed by a manager trying to improve productivity. The solution is to sharply limit meeting time, and thus to force recognition of the need for discussing high priority items.

It is now recommended that no process brainstorming meeting should exceed 30 minutes. Further, that it should not exceed the time spent in the logging meeting, so a 20-minute logging meeting would permit only 20 minutes of process brainstorming.

The Inspection leader needs to use a couple of minutes, after ending the logging meeting, to identify the number and location (on the log) of major issues. If there are few issues (under 10) then each one can be discussed for a limited time (three minutes). If there are more than this, or if the defects are obviously of the same general type, then the Inspection leader will need to suggest that the type or group be discussed. It is most practical to take a single defect and use it as a representative of its defect type.

If for example there are eight major issues and about 24 minutes left for a process brainstorming meeting, the discussion must be sharply limited to three minutes for each issue. That means approximately one minute for understanding the defect, one minute to brainstorm root causes, and one minute to suggest possible improvements.

It is important that each person is very brief and gives the others a chance to express an opinion. What we want to hear is some key words about what each person thinks is the cause, and if possible a quick suggestion about what can be done about it. There should be strong encouragement to suggest things that can be done locally and can be quickly proven to work.

The brainstormed causes and process improvements will be logged to the QA database and from there will be followed up by the Process Change Management Team (PCMT). If anyone is particularly interested in working on one particular improvement idea, they will be formally encouraged to accept an assignment to take deeper analytical and corrective action by the Process Change Management Team (see Section 7.5).

---

† Because Inspection logging meetings are limited to two hours, if attendees were desperate to discuss solution ideas which are forbidden during the logging meeting, some variants of Inspection have allowed post-logging meeting time to discuss solutions. Since this took place after the two-hour logging meeting, it is sometimes called the 'third hour'.

7.3.2   Process Brainstorm Log

The process brainstorm log records the causes and improvements which have been suggested at the process brainstorming meeting. This data goes to the QA database and is then updated as the Process Change Management Team analyze the suggested improvements and implement them.

It is very important that the actual improvements are recorded so they can be monitored and followed up. It is demotivating for someone to suggest a quality improvement and then for it just to be forgotten about. The process brainstorm data is used by the Process Change Management Team to keep track of the progress of individual process improvement suggestions (see Figure 7.7).

7.4   Comparison with IBM's Method

7.4.1   Innovations to the Inspection Process

Figure 7.8 shows IBM's innovations (underlined) to the Inspection process to make systematic process improvement a practical reality. Further details are given in Robert Mays' Chapter 17.

The IBM method, developed by Mays, Jones, Holloway, and Studinski (Mays, 1990) is called the 'defect prevention process'. Although the defect prevention process can be applied using Inspections, it also has wider applicability, but Inspections in this area of IBM are only done for the design and code stages. This book regards Inspection of the 'upstream' stages as far more important, and least important for code. Both recommend that test and field metrics are used for the process improvement activities.

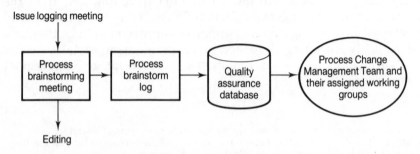

Figure 7.7   Tracking improvement suggestions.

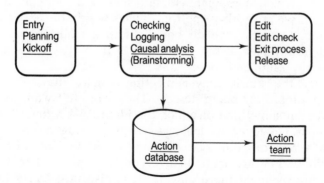

Figure 7.8   The Inspection process with the addition of the Kickoff, Causal Analysis Meeting, Action Team, and Action Database.

7.4.2   Causal Analysis versus Process Brainstorming Meeting

The IBM causal analysis meeting would typically last for two hours. The leader of the causal analysis meeting is trained in the running of such a meeting. The causal analysis is described as a mini-post mortem of each software development stage. The last half hour of the meeting is general analysis which concentrates on the wider implications of the defects discussed, such as error trends, what was successful and should be preserved, and how similar defects can be prevented. The aim of the whole process is 'defect extinction'.

IBM recommend that the causal analysis meeting should not be held immediately after the Inspection meeting, for a number of reasons.

First, an additional two-hour causal analysis meeting after a two-hour logging meeting will lead to exhaustion. Since IBM's meeting is two hours, this would certainly be the case, and is one of the reasons why the method described in this book restricts the process brainstorming meeting to a maximum of 30 minutes.

Second, the logging meeting people may be the wrong people to analyze root causes, so a separate meeting is called. Additional people may be called in, or if there is someone from the logging meeting who does not want to stay or would be inappropriate, a change of personnel is permissible. Because the process brainstorming meeting is shorter, it necessarily goes into less depth. Further analysis is carried out by the Process Change Management Team, which would be done by a larger meeting in the IBM method.

The IBM causal analysis meeting excludes (or sees as unnecessary) some of those who would naturally be at the logging meeting, such as testers, planners, information developers and so on. However, if we are addressing root causes within the entire software development process, we do not want to exclude anyone who is involved in any part of the process. IBM Inspections are concerned mainly with design and code.

Thirdly, the causal analysis meeting is held after the defects are verified as definitely being defects. They wouldn't want to spend a lot of time on something of which the identity as a defect was open to argument. However, we feel it is worth 'wasting' a few minutes of everyone's time on some occasions to get the benefits of analyzing issues while they are fresh in everyone's mind, and to begin the process improvement more quickly. It is also possible to introduce additional defects in the interval between one logging meeting and a causal analysis meeting, which could have been prevented by earlier attention to fixing the process.

Fourthly, because of the sensitivity of the author in the logging meeting, it is better to collect together a number of instances of a defect type before analyzing them, and to take some of the pressure off the individual (who may not relish being in the 'hot seat' for a further two hours immediately). Again the 30-minute meeting addresses this problem to some extent, but we also recommend that similar past defects and issues are considered together, and the Inspection leader should be aware of past defects which would also be relevant in the present brainstorming meeting. However, because of the time lag between the logging meeting and the causal analysis meeting, authors can be given a list of defects to be considered and have time to reflect on them before the causal analysis. The Inspection leader in this book's method is advised to consider adopting this for selected defects if he thinks that similar ones may be raised at the logging meeting, as it may lead to the causes being analyzed more deeply. Otherwise the Process Change Management Team will do the deeper analysis, and may consult the author about their thoughts on any particular defect type.

A broad perspective on the defect causes and how to prevent them is encouraged at the process brainstorming meeting, as at the causal analysis meeting. Looking for trends in defects and underlying process failures is done by the Process Change Management Team.

The fifth reason to hold the causal analysis meeting later is to allow time to screen and select the defects to be analyzed, from a variety of sources. However, we believe that a single Inspection does provide sufficient results to perform meaningful analysis of root causes and an opportunity to suggest process improvements,

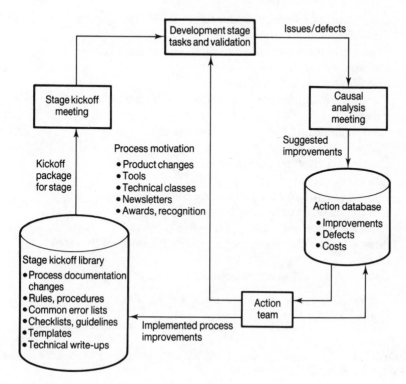

Figure 7.9   The IBM defect prevention process.

particularly in the time-limited and structured context of the process brainstorming meeting. The Inspection leader must make some decisions about which the highest priority issues are, and select a maximum of ten to discuss, but this can normally be done in a minute or two between the two meetings.

7.4.3   Other Aspects of the Defect Prevention Process

A 'stage' kickoff meeting is held to launch a software development stage, and is a process review to prepare the developers for the stage (see Figure 7.9). Kickoff may also still be held for Inspections.

Figure 7.10 shows the contents of the IBM computer-based causal analysis database – a result of process brainstorming and Action Team (Process Change Management Team) meetings.

Purpose: to track each improvement that is recommended.
Product name identifier.
Person submitting the improvement.
Date improvement entered into the database system.
Priority (scale of one to four).
Area code where implementation was done (process, tools
and so on).
Specific item within the area.
Current status (attentioned, screened, being investigated,
closed).
Cost estimate (days for implementation).
Target date completed.
Close data (reason codes, who, date).
Final cost (actual days).
Short description of the improvement.
Full description of the improvement.
Associated defects (all linked to this action).
Answer text: full description of the improvement that took
place.
Log of all activities checkpointed against the improvement.

Source: C.L. Jones in *IBM Systems Journal*, 2/85, page 164,
(Jones, 1985)

Figure 7.10   The causal analysis database parameters, and later related
data captured by IBM development labs.

The IBM view of the action team concept is shown in Figure 7.11.
An action team is charged with making use of defect data to
initiate and manage process improvements. The job is to find
changes which measurably improve productivity or quality. When a
change has been proven locally the action team is responsible for
spreading the news to other parts of the company.
The action team is described by IBM as being outside of current
product development projects. This avoids conflict of priority with
project deadlines over process improvement. The action team is led
by an independent manager, has a separate budget, and members
are especially trained for their work. The Process Change
Management Team described in this book is patterned on the action
team idea, but is perhaps less formal.

Purpose: To avoid discouragement due to ideas not implemented
- Size depends on number of suggestions.
- Make a manager responsible for a team.
- Action Team manager's job to see that work gets done and is visible.
- Consists of one or more people who can handle suggestions in areas of process and tools.
- Other actions (outside the normal support areas) can be sent to appropriate people.
- Final resolutions will still be team responsibility.

Action team costs:
- For small group: one part-time person + manager involvement.
- For 100–150 people: four or five full time members with a dedicated manager.[†]

Responsibilities:
- Prioritize all action ('improvement') items.
- Status track all action items.
- Implement all action items.
- Disseminate feedback (via several media).
- Database administration (defects and actions, see above).
- Generic analysis (periodically review trends to catch defects which individual causal analysis teams may not have noticed).
- Visibility of success stories and recognition.

Benefits:
- 54% reduction in defects through causal analysis (Mays, 1990).

Figure 7.11   A description of Action Teams as practiced at IBM development labs (Source: Jones (1985), page 155).

---

† The 1990 report (Mays, 1990) reported about one person per 200 professionals, or 0.5% of total cost. The five per 150 number is from Jones (1985).

7.4.4   Summary of Differences from IBM's Method

The method recommended here differs from IBM's practice mainly in taking a smaller scale and more immediate approach. But the reader must develop a style appropriate to their own culture.

Process improvements can be suggested within the logging meeting, which in the IBM method is only used as a defect-logging meeting.

The analysis of root causes (called 'causal analysis' by IBM and 'process brainstorming' here) is done immediately after the logging meeting. The reason for this is so that the understanding is still fresh in the Inspectors' minds from the logging meeting. If the causal analysis meeting is held days or weeks afterwards, time will have to be spent first in reviewing the defects and refreshing the background which may have been forgotten by then. Both methods capitalize on the fact that the Inspectors and developers will have a much truer picture of the real causes of defects and therefore should be involved in the analysis of root causes.

The process brainstorming meeting is limited to 30 minutes to improve the overall efficiency of the defect prevention process, and also to help gain acceptability. Managers will be more likely to approve an additional half hour to an existing meeting than a separate two-hour meeting, which may also involve people having to travel to get there.

Another reason for analyzing defects immediately is that over time we tend to forget the pain caused by things which have already been fixed now, and this has a significant negative impact on our will and resolution to put the causes right.

The size of an organization also has an effect on the best way to organize the process improvement activities. Organizations the size of IBM may be quite happy with the method which obviously works well for them. However, the process improvement part of Inspection is certainly not limited to large organizations, so the way of organizing it should be tailored to fit. The method described in this book can be tailored for any size of organization, but is based very firmly in the IBM experience.

There are also aspects of small organizations which should be preserved when the method spreads within a larger organization. Most participants in Inspection experience a closeness to the Inspection metrics, the involvement with small teams in analysis of the data, and the discussion about what to do to improve things.

7.5   Process Change Management Team Organization

7.5.1   Process Change Management Teams

In early Inspection practice (1972–1984) someone leading the Inspection leaders, typically a quality assurance manager, analyzed the Inspection metrics periodically and made suggestions to management about potential improvements to the software engineering process.

In 1983 IBM began the practice of encouraging grass root groups to analyze data which they themselves or their peers had generated. The Process Change Management Teams (PCMT) concept is a development of this idea (see Figure 7.12).

PCMT members may have received special additional training, be managed by a manager outside a deadline-driven project, and might be temporarily on full-time assignment. They may also be permanent PCMT employees.

A PCMT might choose to delegate the detailed work of analyzing the causes and cures of frequent serious defects based on their analysis of the metrics. Delegation avoids the PCMT being a bottleneck. Delegation could for example be to consultants, quality

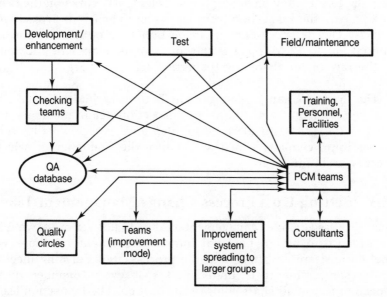

Figure 7.12   Process Change Management Teams relationship diagram.

improvement teams, people between projects or PCMT staff if there are enough.

PCM Teams are driven by the QA defect database of defects and costs. They can access other groups to do the improvement prototypes, and can influence change anywhere. Successful improvement knowledge is spread by them to others in the organization.

7.5.2   Informal Process Improvement Groups

The PCMT members can also be organized more informally and on-the-spot to find process improvements based on their own process brainstorming suggestions. This works when it is not in sharp competition with project deadline pressure.

This amounts to a 'democratization' or 'empowerment' of the management process. Professionals are encouraged to analyze their own Inspection data, to recommend and to carry out improvements, and then to use their metrics (not only from Inspection, but also testing and field costs for defects) to determine just how well their ideas have worked.

The Process Change Management Team analyzes current defects and initiates experiments to reduce the probability that similar types of errors will be committed in the future.

The Process Change Management Team is ultimately funded and staffed to do real organizational change work. The Inspection team, by way of contrast, may well be disbanded long before action can be taken on defects they have identified. The PCMT works on the future work *process*, the Inspection team works on the current project work *products*. The defects found in Inspection of products are the raw material for the PCMT, just as the software development documents are the raw material for the Inspection team (see Figures 7.13 and 7.14).

The Process Change Management Team can choose to make use of anybody, from consultants to Inspection team members who initiated the ideas, to attempt to find and experimentally verify process improvements which will reduce the frequency of selected defect types in the future.

7.5.3   Setting Up a Process Change Management Team

When Process Change Management Teams do not yet exist, we make it a practice to assign personal improvement items to those who show enthusiasm and insight at the process brainstorming meeting. At the same time it is understood that every member of the Inspection team will share some of the burden. The Inspection leader will lead the process of assigning process improvement experiments,

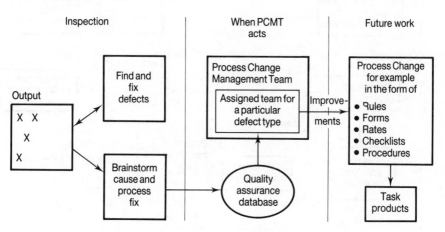

Figure 7.13   Where the Process Change Management Team fits.

and effectively acts as a one-person Process Change Management Team.

It is important that the people assigned can somehow really find time – even if it is just a few hours a week, to analyze the defect and experiment with cures. It may well be necessary to have a special budget to which you can charge this activity. It may also be necessary to protect your new enthusiastic 'consultants' (checkers) from their immediate supervisor – who may not be interested in long-term improvement, just this week's deadline.

Participating in process improvement activities is a wonderful learning process. People are frequently thrilled at the opportunities it provides to show their hidden talents. They will rapidly turn up improvements of real value. These improvements will often be used as pilot experiments to get support from upper management, who hopefully (we can't guarantee it) are interested in real organizational improvements in practice.

7.5.4   Advantages of Process Change Management Teams

The advantages of the Process Change Management Team form of organization are:

- Individual defect analysis is done by grass roots participants, frequently on single defects rather than anonymous statistical data.

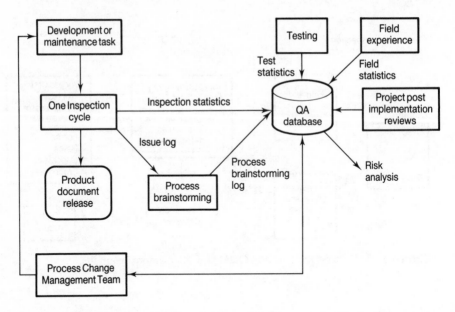

Figure 7.14   Inspection in the context of the larger quality improvement process.

This leads to more accurate interpretation of the real causes of the data.

- The final selection of economically worthwhile defect types to work on is made by the PCMT, based on analysis of the QA database. The database indicates frequency of defects and their repair costs at different stages.

- You are empowering younger people who are as intelligent and as well-educated as anybody else to play what is traditionally a managerial/consultant role. They can control their own work processes. It is interesting and they love it.

- The reaction time is shorter from defect identification to cure than if the data is handled at a higher organizational level. Days or weeks of reaction time, rather than months to years, is the result.

- You can avoid the 'big brother is watching you' feeling, which people often get when metrics of defects are sent to others in the organization. (We fix our own processes.)

- Experience at IBM (Mays & Jones, 1990 and Mays, 1992) shows that the total error reduction even with initial project use is about 50% in all phases (development, testing, field use) at a cost of 0.5% development cost. In 1993 Mays reported 70% error reduction after 2–3 years (see Chapter 17 in this book).

7.5.5   The Right to Improve

It sometimes seems that an organization actively works to prevent improvement to its own processes, through bureaucracy, apathy or simply 'we've always done things this way'. When the possibility of real improvement is perceived by software development professionals, their enthusiasm and idealism can only benefit the organization if the changes can be implemented. It is a great shame if real grass-roots positive initiatives are squashed inadvertently by organizational mass. See Tom Peters, *Liberation Management* (Peters, 1992) for a lot of practical inspiration on this subject.

One attempt by us to protect the rights of inspectors to improve their organization is shown below. This represents political dynamite in many companies. It changes personal empowerment. But it is the kind of dynamite that top management will hopefully support.

Inspector's Bill of Rights
  (1) The author has the right to participate as a checker in the Inspection of their product.
  (2) Anyone has the right to turn down an invitation to participate in a particular Inspection team.
  (3) Every professional has the right to become an inspector.
  (4) All Inspectors have the right to perform checking roles which they are interested in, able to do well, and learn from.
  (5) Inspectors have the right to suggest any issue or improvement, not already logged, without justification, question, discussion, approval, or consensus from others, any time.
  (6) Inspectors have the right to search for and identify issues and improvements outside of their assigned specialist roles.
  (7) Inspectors have the right to log and suggest any improvement suggestion to rules, procedures, master plans, and checklists.
  (8) Inspectors have the right to log a question of intent to authors and to get an oral answer at the end of the logging meeting.
  (9) Inspectors have a right to confidential treatment of any action, suggestion or discussion they make during the team meetings.

(continued)

Continues

(10) Inspectors have the right to initiate any written or oral dialogue with team members or other company professionals or management, which is stimulated by their experiences on the team, and which has the objective of improving the product or the process.

(11) Inspectors can take any reasonable initiative to improve their professional knowledge, when they recognize that this would be valuable as a result of experiences working on the team.

(12) Inspectors have the right to participate in process brainstorming in order to suggest improvements in their work process which would remove causes of defect occurrence.

(13) Inspectors have the right to access and use any source materials which arguably might help them discover major defects.

8
The Inspection Leader

This chapter is primarily intended for the Inspection leader, and may be skipped by those who are not leaders. It is assumed that Chapters 4-7 have been read thoroughly before reading this chapter.

8.1 Who is the Leader?

8.1.1 More than a Moderator

Fagan's original term for the leader role was 'moderator'. This is the person who manages the Inspectors on a day to day basis, and should not be confused with the Inspection champion. 'Moderator' was chosen to emphasize that the Inspection meeting was led by someone other than the product author, which previous review techniques, such as structured walkthroughs, had advocated.

'Moderator' no longer describes the more complex total role of the Inspection leader (see Figure 8.1). When the leader (or anyone else) leads an Inspection meeting, the term 'moderator' may be used for the meeting control role. But the overall job of professional trained Inspection leader needs a broader term, to include tasks such as planning, entry check, exit check, and follow-up which are important parts of the leader's work, but outside the role of the person who chairs the logging meeting.

The leader is a coach, a teacher, an administrator, a manager, a friend, a supporter to the inspectors. The leader should do everything needed to make Inspection work well. The leader has considerable power to make things happen, and to prevent bad things from happening. The leader is no mere policeman of the rules, but can exercise considerable creative energy, just like the coach of a ball-team, to make the team perform at a superior level.

The following material is intended to give detailed guidance to the leader throughout the many parts of the Inspection process. It does not replace leader training, because a major function of training

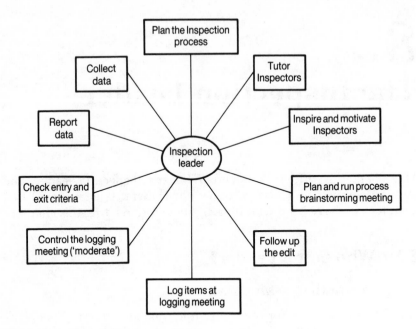

Figure 8.1   Inspection Leader tasks.

is to gain initial experience (that is, make the inevitable mistakes) in a 'safe' environment, where no real harm is done by a wrong approach. The training environment enables real hands-on learning to take place quickly and effectively.

8.1.2   Why the Leader's Role is Critical

The Inspection leader is responsible for making the entire Inspection process function. Inspection leader is a part-time job done on a voluntary basis. Time used should, naturally, be credited and billed to the appropriate project. Inspection leaders are especially trained for their job, they have been approved by their trainers, and continue to be approved by whoever 'manages' them in their Inspection leader role.

Inspection is essentially a 'reactive' discipline. It tries to ensure that all work is directed to the goals and designs intended. It does not set the standards, it only enforces them.

Truly great software products come about through the high aspirations of the whole software development organization, those who want to be the 'best of the best', and through the efforts of their software engineers who turn these ambitions into practical realities by finding the appropriate designs and products.

The world's best designs can be spoiled by poor implementation. Inspection can help in the effective communication of the aspirations, the designs, and the final product. Software development is becoming an engineering discipline, where many people must communicate effectively with each other. Because we are only human, we need a human-based method to improve our human attempts to communicate complex ideas to one another. Inspection helps us improve that communication, and the Inspection leader helps to improve the Inspection process.

8.1.3 Self-assessment Test for Inspection Leaders

If you, as an Inspection leader, believe that you are currently running Inspections correctly, answer a few simple questions to assess your own performance:

- What are the demonstrated optimum rates for checking and for the logging meeting?
- What is the numeric level of probable remaining defects which you accept as an exit condition?
- What is the percentage effectiveness of your process in finding defects?
- How do you officially certify Inspection leaders?
- What sort of numeric objectives do you set at the kickoff meeting?
- How much time do you use on average per item during a process brainstorming meeting?
- How many specialist defect-searching roles do you assign per checker?
- How often does a checklist or rule set get changed or improved as a result of the process?

If you have difficulties in answering these questions, then this is a sign that the way Inspections are carried out in your organization does not conform with the best current practice described in this book.

8.2 The Master Plan

The first task of the Inspection leader, when a product is available for Inspection, is to plan. The master plan is the Inspection leader's document which guides the execution of the Inspection process. A master plan is produced for every candidate document put forward.

The first step upon receiving a candidate document is to register it by beginning to record details about it in the master plan. This is a formal written document which contains any data the Inspection leader wants to communicate before the checkers start the individual checking work.

Sample master plans, both blank and filled in, are shown in Appendix C. The structure of the master plan is outlined in this section, and the information which is recorded in the plan is discussed more fully in the following sections.

The basic structure of the master plan is:

(1) Header
(2) Documents
(3) Participants and roles
(4) Standard rates
(5) Data from individual checking (blank for recording).

The details of each of these sections is shown below.

8.2.1   Header

The header of the master plan is structured as shown in Figure 8.2.

The 'header' can include any necessary things not covered in the rest of the document. For example:

• Inspection leader: name, telephone number.
• Author(s) name.

Header	Leader	Name, phone
	Author	Name
Documents	Product(s)	Title, pages, status
	Date	Inspection request
Participants and roles	Entry	Entry criteria
		Entry status
Standard rates	Kickoff	Date, time, location
	Logging	Date, time, location
Data collection (individual checkers)	Brainstorm	Date, time, location
	Exit	Exit criteria

Figure 8.2   The 'header' of the master plan.

- Description of the author's candidate product: title, number of pages, status (for example, failed exit). This references the full product document, but only part of it might be checked at a time, as described in the following section of the master plan.
- Date Inspection requested/initiated.
- Entry criteria which apply: document tags generic and specific, version or date.
- Current entry status: failed criteria, compromises, passed criteria, any remarks.
- Kickoff meeting: date, start time, probable or latest end time, location.
- Logging meeting: date, start time, probable or latest end time, location.
- Process brainstorming meeting: date, start time, probable or latest end time, location.
- Exit criteria to be applied: document tags generic and specific, version or date.

8.2.2   Documents

Figure 8.3 illustrates the structure of the 'documents' section of the plan.

The documents section contains information about all of the documents which the Inspectors need to know in order to perform this Inspection, as follows:

- Sources: references and page numbers of relevant source documents.

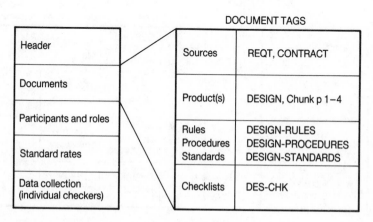

Figure 8.3   Documents section of the master plan.

- Product(s): references and page numbers of relevant product documents.
- Rules: the rules, procedures and standards which should have been used by the author in producing the candidate document from the sources.
- Checklists: the lists of questions which each individual checker will use in order to guide their checking to find the greatest number of unique Issues. All Inspectors will receive the same source, product, and rule documents, and may also receive the same checklists for general checking, as shown here (design checklist). Each Inspector will also receive the appropriate checklists relating to the role which they have been assigned (see next section on participants and roles).

8.2.3   Participants and Roles

The 'participants and roles section' is structured as shown in Figure 8.4.

The name of each Inspector is given, with their role assignments and the procedures they are to use. The document role assignments are made by using the document tag.

A checklist-defined role assignment is made using the tag of a role checklist.

The procedures are the Inspection procedures which apply to the specific Inspector with regard to their place on the team (leader, author, checker, scribe). This is a way to make sure everyone has access to a brief and updated set of procedures, especially when they

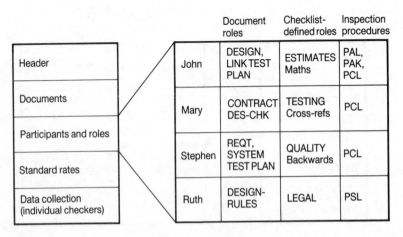

Figure 8.4   Participants and roles in the master plan.

are new Inspectors. A 'starter kit' of procedures is given in Appendix B of this book.

8.2.4 Standard rates

This section is concerned with the volume and speed of the Inspection process. It can be used to give instruction regarding the recommended rates, for all checkers or for individuals, as shown in Figure 8.5:

- checking rates (for example, 'pages studied per hour');
- item logging rates (for example, 'three items logged every two minutes');
- brainstorming rates (for example, 'three minutes per issue for 30 minutes' and 'two product pages reported per hour');
- edit rates (for example, 'expected edit rate eight minutes/major defect').

8.2.5 Data Collection

The data collection section is organized as shown in Figure 8.6.

Each individual checker must record the information shown for their own individual checking part of the Inspection process. The first thing which happens in the logging meeting is that the Inspection leader will ask for this information so that it can all be collected and stored (anonymously) in the QA database.

The pages 'studied intensively' (at the optimum rate) would be likely to include the candidate product document and perhaps the

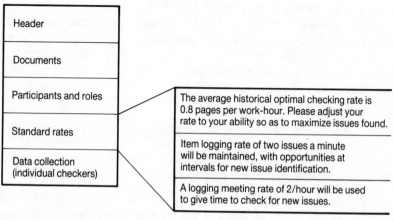

Figure 8.5 Standard rates.

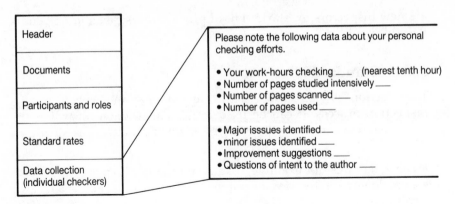

Figure 8.6 Data collection.

documents for which the checker was assigned a document role. The other 'scanned' pages (at any rate the checker chose) would include parts of the product document outside of this chunk. The total number of pages used includes all source pages, product pages, rules, procedures, and checklists. Any page looked at is counted.

Note that issues can be identified in *any* document looked at.

8.3 Entry Criteria

The Inspection leader's first task is to check all the formal entry criteria for the type of document to be Inspected. This is done in parallel with drawing up the master plan. In fact, the master plan would not be issued to any Inspectors if the candidate product failed its entry criteria, although there would be some information recorded for the document in a master plan.

Entry criteria are any set of conditions which your organization insists should be met before proceeding with other phases of Inspection. They can be determined and revised by experience. The main purpose of having entry criteria is to:

- avoid continuing an Inspection process if it would probably be wasted;
- motivate document authors to do things properly, so that the rest of the Inspection cycle will be productive.

The following are the basic entry criteria which should be met before an Inspection is allowed to proceed. In some cases, particularly when Inspections are first begun, these criteria may not all be met.

8.3.1   Source Documents

All relevant source documents:

- must exist and be available in writing (paper or screen);
- must be explicitly identified in the master plan;
- must themselves have successfully exited from another Inspection, or at the very least be explicitly identified in the master plan, by the leader, as 'not exited' (see also Section 8.4.2 below).

8.3.2   Rates

The optimum checking and logging-meeting rates are known (or estimated). The task product material (candidate document) is chunked by the leader (see Section 8.4.1 below) so that no one issue-logging meeting session will need to exceed two continuous hours of issue-logging time.

8.3.3   Leader Qualification

The Inspection leader is trained and still certified (on the official list) as a leader.

8.3.4   Voluntary

The authors have volunteered that their product is ready for Inspection. The Inspection leader should not force authors to put the candidate document forward for Inspection before they are reasonably confident that it is ready for Inspection, and comfortable with the idea of it being Inspected. However, the leader can strongly encourage that scheduled dates for the candidate product being prepared for Inspection be adhered to. This is a question of balance, and the individual authors concerned. Some authors will want to continue 'polishing' far too long, when Inspection would be more effective at finding defects in the document than they can be on their own. These authors should be encouraged to release their document for Inspection. However, other authors will 'meet their deadlines' by releasing a product far too early, when it would be more effective for them to find their own errors rather than leave them to the Inspection team. This situation should be detected in the checking of entry criteria.

8.3.5   Candidate Product Document Quality

The candidate product documents must, in the leader's opinion, be of a reasonable standard. They must contain no obvious major defects upon cursory (1 minute) examination by the leader.

8.3.6 Author/Editor

The author, or the editor, accepts the invitation to be a member of the Inspection team. The reasons for this are:

- to motivate the author(s) to do a better job, through knowing they will confront their peers at the Inspection meeting;
- to help the author(s) save face, by personally being an effective issue finder, along with the other Inspectors;
- to ensure that the issue logging is of a satisfactory quality for the editor, by having it monitored during the meeting.

8.4 Selecting Materials

The objective of the Inspection materials selection process is to ensure that the team gets a correct, complete and updated set of all materials which they will need to do their job effectively.

8.4.1 Selecting Product Documentation (Candidate)

The Inspection leader is responsible for unambiguously specifying the extent of the candidate material to be covered during one Inspection cycle of individual checking and a logging meeting.

This will be done in the master plan, as a chunk of the candidate product. There is no restriction on planning for multiple chunks at one time and doing so in one single master plan.

The leader must also consider such things as actual meeting room booking times, necessary start-up overhead time, and process brainstorming meeting time, as well as the logging meeting. So for example, if a meeting room is available for two hours, and administration (say five minutes) and process brainstorming (say 30 minutes) are to be included, then there is only one hour and 25 minutes available for the issue logging meeting. The material must be chunked to fit this space, taking the optimum rate into consideration.

The candidate is the product or part of a product (a chunk) which is to be Inspected in a single Inspection cycle of individual checking and a logging meeting. The candidate may be more than one product document if they are very small and related (for example, maintenance changes).

It is more likely that only a portion of the candidate document will be Inspected at a time, if the candidate is large. In this case, the product will be the relevant pages or sections to be checked. The master plan may contain information for more than one chunk. Copies of the documents to be checked will either be readily available, or distributed at the kickoff meeting or independently.

The Inspection leader is free to use any appropriate chunking strategy. The normal chunking limits are set by using 'lines', 'test cases' or 'pages'. But the leader may elect to divide the material in terms of other types of chunk. For example, a program source listing could be chunked by 'logic', 'data', and 'documentation notes'. The ultimate test of all chunking methods is their relative ability to produce major defects per hour of human time used.

The way in which the length of a chunk is determined is that it is not to exceed known, or presumed, optimum rates of checking and logging (see Section 8.5), given the actual time available to Inspectors. There is in any case an absolute maximum of two hours for the logging meeting which must not be exceeded.

Another chunking strategy may be for the entire team to study the product chunk pages intensively, but each member of the team to scan different sets of pages (for example, 4–6). Another strategy is sampling, where the chunk to be studied intensively includes, say, the first page of each section, or every tenth page.

Although electronic copies of material are permissible, it is often preferable to supply paper copies to all checkers so that they can mark the material with hi-liters (color background marking pens) and notes, in any way they see fit. It is the leader's responsibility to ensure that each checker has the material in the form needed.

The leader is personally responsible for ensuring that confidential material is kept confidential. Mark it as such before copying, and on the master plan.

8.4.2   Selecting Source Materials

All Inspectors must have either a copy of, or access to, all necessary source documents.

Source documents are defined here as all those documents (except standards, manuals or other generic instruction) which were used (or should have been used) to generate the product document(s) currently being Inspected.

For example, for a maintenance change, the source documents would include the change request, the previous version of the document, and any other related documents which may have been affected by the change. The task product document would be the changed version of the document and any other related changed documents.

There should be no dependency on human memory or verbal instructions. If necessary, the leader will ensure that any information which affects judgement of the inspected work process is written down for all to see.

Source Document Status: Exited from Inspection

One of the basic principles of Inspection is that any source documents used have ideally already been checked themselves and have successfully 'exited' from Inspection earlier (see Figure 8.7).

If they have *not* exited, we must proceed with great caution and explicit recognition of the untrustworthiness of our sources (marked on copied sources given to checkers) 'NOT EXITED'.

Checking against an un-exited source can lead to a situation where defects in the source document are 'successfully' preserved in the product.

What About Sources at the Very First Inspection?

At initial start-up of Inspection, no source documents have previously been Inspected and exited successfully. We must be fully aware that such uncontrolled, un-exited documents could and often do contain between seven and seventy defects per page .

A sound practice, indeed a generic entry requirement ('all sources must have exited'), is to Inspect and exit the source documents, or at least a sample of them, before continuing work creating and checking the task outputs. If you do not even take a partial page sample, then you do not know how defect-ridden the source is. This effectively makes the Inspection of your product dubious, since large numbers of defects in the source hide equally large numbers of defects in the product.

The source document is subject to renewed checking during the Inspection, even assuming it has exited from its own Inspection earlier. But you do not, at that second Inspection, normally have the benefit of the correct rules, checklists or your sources' *own* source documents (see Figure 8.8). These all ideally *should* be used in checking your source document. You cannot really check your product document properly by simply looking at it for intelligibility. It can be perfectly clear – but perfectly wrong. Clarity is not the same as correctness in relation to rules and source documents.

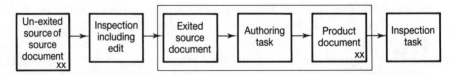

Figure 8.7 The concept of an 'exited' source. Anything less leads to a Garbage In – Garbage Out result.

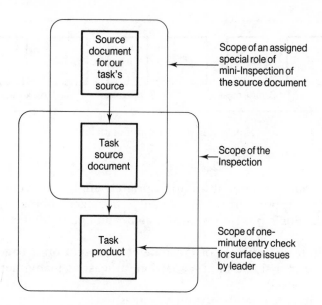

Figure 8.8   Source documents and their sources.

This could lead you to conclude that Inspection can never get properly started, which is not in fact the case. The practical compromise (and we have to realize that it *is* a compromise) is for the Inspection leader to perform a 'mini-Inspection' (see Figure 8.9), or a few-page sample Inspection on the source document to make sure that it is 'reasonably suitable' to be used as a source document.

What if the Sample Shows that the Source is in Very Poor Shape?

Here are some tactics for dealing with this situation:

- Send the sample details to the source owner. Ask if they can clean up the entire document. Ask for a deadline when this will be done. A sample of a few pages can be enough to convince management and source owners that it would be wrong to proceed without cleaning it up.
- Send the details via your manager to the manager of the owner of the source document. Ask if they want to be responsible for the defects this document creates for you and others. Ask if they would like some help to Inspect the document and clean it up.
- Clean up the document yourselves, and send a copy to the official owners. (You are taking over their job and should get their budget.)

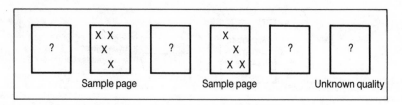

Figure 8.9   Issues (X) found in mini-Inspection of source.

- Raise your concerns at an appropriately high management level, getting support from the quality manager, about what the organization's position is on source documents as defect-ridden as these:
  - include an estimate of those defects present on a page but *not* found in a single mini-inspection (at least as many more as you have found);
  - extrapolate total defects on all pages;
  - estimate additional cost to clean up using Inspection (try one work hour per major, defect-finding cost);
  - estimate cost *not* to clean up (try nine hours per major, later);
  - translate 'failure to clean up the source document' into 'project delay weeks', assuming constant staffing. Ask management if they will be fully responsible for the delay. (Yes, it is only a rhetorical question!)
- Write down the details of your efforts and conclusions for your files. Consider sending a copy to your project management.
- Get your management to sign a statement to confirm that they have told you to go ahead with current (low) quality levels of the source document, and that they accept all responsibility for downstream problems. (Hopefully they won't be dumb enough to sign it. Maybe they will act to correct the situation.)

However, it is also important to be practical and to realize that Inspection has to start somewhere. If we simply throw up our hands in horror, we will not improve the quality of the existing product even if the source is not perfect. It is a matter of degree and judgement; a truly horrendously poor source should be rejected, but we do need to make a start with what we have if we are to make any progress at all.

And What if Your Source Documents Have Not Exited Inspection?

Whenever the source documentation itself has not properly exited from its own Inspections, the leader must determine and supply those source-production rules and the source's own source documents, which would have applied to them during the missing Inspection.

The leader could delegate the task of finding appropriate sources and rules to the relevant role players. It might sound time-consuming to find and check sources/rules, but consider the following before you dismiss it as impractical:

- You can make do with a sample (as little as a quarter page can be useful) which will give you hard evidence of the type and quantity of defects in the source document.
- What would you say if you found five or more major defects in the quarter page? (we usually do!) Would it be meaningful to continue checking your product using the defective source? (hint: never!)
- This is better than mounting a full Inspection on the sources, as at least it can be used to put pressure on your source document suppliers via appropriate management levels.
- If you do not identify the source defects, then you will fairly get blamed for letting them enter into your product document. The only truly unrealistic thing is to expect somebody else to send you a zero defect source document which has not even tried to exit a proper Inspection.

What to Do When No Source Apparently Exists

It is very unlikely that a product document has really been created without the benefit of any form of source information. Our experience is that people are unaware of the applicable source documents, and that the organization has done a poor job of helping them to become aware. If no source can be identified, or created from oral sources, then you should ask why the product document was written in the first place, since it is apparently unconnected with any documented organizational plans or needs!

If a product document has apparently been created without the benefit of a source document, you should not simply give up and check without a source. You should consider the following:

Search for Missing Sources

Search high and low, using other experts in your organization, to identify and get for your team the source documents which should logically have been used by the author. The fact that the author did not know about, find or use, what was logically necessary for correct production of the product document, according to the rules, is no valid reason for avoiding the use of the valid source documents in

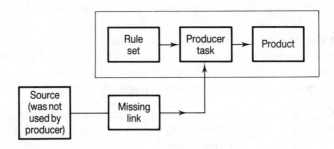

Figure 8.10   The missing link.

Inspection. On the contrary, such source documents will be a valuable source of information about potential defects (see Figure 8.10)!

Authors cannot logically, and should not in practice, generate products from thin air. Neither should they be checked, in the same way, without these missing source documents. Use Inspection to improve the process which should have been carried out.

Should you Proceed?

If you do find source documents of which the author was unaware, you must (during the planning stage, the leader evaluates this) evaluate with the author whether the author should first make use of the new source document to upgrade the product document, before the checkers use it.

Inspection Leader to Construct Source Information

If you find that the source information has not been written down previously, or you cannot find it, then the leader, during planning, must attempt to set down in writing the source information that can be captured from oral sources, as well as possible. The leader must attempt to validate the 'new' source data, for example by getting someone to sign it off as being correct, complete, and intended. This source may then be distributed to the Inspection team, or perhaps first be used by the author for an upgrade of the product document. Do whatever saves effort in total for the project.

8.4.3   Selecting Software Engineering Standards, Rules and Procedures

The leader shall determine all applicable standards and guidelines for the process whose task product document is being Inspected.

These include rules, procedures, outside 'standards' (perhaps imposed by policy or contract), checklists, entry and exit criteria or other mandatory guidelines. They include all rules, procedures and standards which should have been used, whether they were used or not.

Indicate in writing on the master plan exactly which manuals and standards, including the revision level, are applicable to this particular Inspection, and which parts are invalid, inappropriate or low priority.

Ensure that the applicable portions of the standards are really the latest updated versions. The author may have applied an outdated version, or may have depended on memory and experience. This point is a way for the leader to ensure that the task product material conforms to the latest and most up-to-date standards. When they haven't been given a standards document to work with, the checkers should always get the latest updates, unless an older version is needed for contractual reasons.

Whenever large bodies of standards are applicable (for example, defense standards, or large corporate manuals), the leader should attempt to highlight a few selected, shorter passages or pages, which are particularly applicable to this Inspection. If not, there is every danger that nothing will be read, and the standards will be totally ineffective. In addition the leader should consider giving one Inspector the role within the Inspection of being the 'watchdog' of the standards, so that they are taken seriously by at least one participant.

Whenever too few copies of a standard are available, the leader will either get enough copies for the team, indicate where they can be found or borrowed, or give instructions for finding them on computer databases.

Make selected copies, or give a selected page of instructions, to any Inspector who has a special role and can benefit from such specialized instruction.

Create, if necessary, and supply specialized local standards, whenever adequate standards are not available from ordinary sources. For example, if no applicable rule set can be found, it is the Inspection leader who must draft the first one, however crudely. Missing or inadequate standards will in any case be logged as issues or improvements at the logging meeting.

Consider assigning special checking roles for these or doing a mini-Inspection on the documents or at least sampling the quality of the standards documents. Sampling even a page or less can be well worth the effort. You don't want your team wasting its valuable time checking against poor quality standards, and if they haven't been through exit yet, you probably have a problem there right now.

Standards which cannot exit should be equipped by you with adequate 'health warnings' such as:

* 'not exited from any Inspection: beware and report any issues in this document'.

8.5 Rates of Checking and Logging

8.5.1 Individual checking rates

Individual checking rates should be lower than you may have expected. A typical rate for effective individual checking of a software development task product lies between 0.5 and 1.5 pages per hour, that is, a rough rule of thumb of one 'page' (non-commentary, 600 words) per hour.

One page per hour shocks most people initially. But it is a very much better default planning rate than the three to 30 pages per hour which people seem to use intuitively. If you have not collected data from even a few relevant Inspections, then you do not have any evidence to contradict this rate, which is based on extensive real experience, so you would be wise to heed this advice.

If in doubt, try the rate on a very small check like a quarter of a page. Or get different checkers to use different rates in the same Inspection. In both cases you will quickly convince yourselves of the necessity and virtue of the slower rate.

For some documents even slower rates are profitable. Going down to 0.1 (non-commentary, 600-word) page per checking hour can easily make sense for corporate policies, million-dollar contracts, and critical project requirements. It is a lot cheaper then paying your lawyers for controlling the damage later!

Remember the slow checking rate is not just for checking the page, but for cross-checking against a typical assortment of rule sets, checklists, role checklists, and source documents. You may also make several passes through the product document, checking for different things each time.

You should normally get specific rates for each different type of task product material (for example, source code, test plans, contracts, user manuals) computed from your own metrics.

Experience data:

In a published oil company information technology corporate-wide policy statement, we found (February 1991) that a checking task rate of 0.33 page per hour (page-sized printed document) gave 44 major defects per page, and

---

Continues
three other groups operating at about 2.8 to 3.2 pages per hour of checking effort could only find about 20–23 major defects per page.

Suppose the document in this oil company policy case above contained six pages or that we decided to sample six pages of it (it had about 37 as I recall). Checking at one third (0.3 page/hour) of a page per hour would take 18 hours per checker. If there were three checkers, that amounts to 3 x 18 hours (54 work-hours), or seven days' work for checking. The faster rate (3.2 pages/hour) would only take six work-hours. On the surface it looks as though Inspection is much more expensive. Using the same example, the 22 defects *not* found by the faster rate (3.2 pages/hour) will cost at least 88 work-hours (using four hours saved per major found) if not 660 work-hours (using 30 hours saved). So by 'saving' 36 (54-18) work-hours in the Inspection process, it will *cost* us at least 88 work-hours later. In the worst case it will cost us 660-18=642 work-hours! This is a 660/18=36.7 to one ratio of savings. The extra work of slowing down to find the extra defects was a small price to pay considering that the document was a major computer services purchasing policy for world wide distribution.

Source: personal experience of Gilb client in Europe

Keep in mind that for every major defect you identify, most companies reckon they save at least four hours of time later. Some like Shell (Doolan, 1992) and Applicon Inc (see Barbara Spencer's case study, Chapter 12) save 30 or more hours. The question is not how much it will cost to go at this rate during the checking process, but how much *more* it will cost later if we do not.

One client found that each downstream software error cost on average five hours. Others have found nine hours (Thorn EMI, Reeve), 20 to 82 hours (IBM, Remus), and 30 hours (Shell) to fix downstream. This is compared to a cost of only one hour to find and fix using Inspection.

The chief Inspection leader or facilitator, who coordinates all Inspection leaders, will be expected to supply updated rates to leaders. Another alternative is to let the leaders look up the current optimum checking rate in a database. Optimum rates are computed using data on 'pages studied', 'hours used', and 'major defects found' for a number of Inspections. The point where 'defects-found-per-hour' peaks is the optimum rate. This rate will vary as ability and quality of documentation improve.

The Inspection leader will publish the expected individual time-use in the master plan.

8.5.2   Checking Duration Discretion

The Inspection leader needs to allow the individual Inspectors to exercise discretion in their time during the individual checking work as well. Individuals have substantially different rates of working ability. Even for people of a peer group, differences of ten to one have been measured in several software studies. For this reason the optimum individual checking and logging rates can only serve as a guide for the group average.

The rates allow us to encourage people to spend more time than they would otherwise do under pressure. We can defend the rates in terms of the 'value created', by finding more defects when using the lowest rates, compared to the much greater cost of finding those same defects later.

Here are some examples of things which the Inspection leader can say to Inspectors who are worried about performing their individual checking at the proper rate:

- Keep on using checking time, as long as you find that you are noting new issues every few minutes.
- If you find no issues whatsoever for a quarter of an hour, and you have been through the document once, then perhaps you should quit. Maybe you are faster than the average.
- Don't let the recommended rate get in your way of finding unique potential major defects. They are worth several hours of saved time to us, so err on the side of too much time, rather than too few major issues found. It's in the company's interest.

8.5.3   Optimum Logging Rate

The purpose of Inspection is to detect potential defects as cost-effectively as possible. When a group of people are in the logging meeting, every minute is actually four or five or more work-minutes, taking all the people into consideration. To be most cost-effective, we want to log as many issues as quickly as we can.

There are several aspects which limit the top speed at which we can log issues. One is the physical means of recording the issues. Handwriting is fairly slow, but typing is also limited. It is essential that every issue logged is comprehensible afterwards to the editor, otherwise the time 'saved' by logging so quickly is actually wasted because the editor can't make sense of what was logged. These factors make a logging rate of two issues per minute a realistic fastest rate.

However, another important aspect is to allow enough time for synergy at the meeting, so that the Inspectors are able to find new issues. If the logging rate is too fast, this will not happen.

8.6   Selecting Inspectors

8.6.1   General Considerations

Participants cannot be expected to attend more than a maximum of two meetings per day, and normally no more than one per week. All participants have other tasks because no-one is a full-time Inspector. Remember that adequate individual checking time is essential before each logging meeting.

Participation in Inspections should be spread as evenly as possible among all relevant employees. This is:

• to spread the workload;
• to share the competence;
• to ensure that all have a learning experience;
• to ensure that all participate in process brainstorming and resulting software engineering process improvement.

The Inspection leader must ensure that meetings are realistically scheduled so that all participants can arrive at the meeting on time. Further the Inspection leader must ensure that participants can stay for the entire meeting period (issue logging and process brainstorming). They must be made aware (in the master plan or the kickoff meeting) of the planned timings and uncertainties, and accept them.

Meetings, once scheduled and accepted, should be regarded by all parties as the highest priority task for all participants, and the immediate supervisors of participants must accept this. This obligation includes not only the meeting, but also to ensuring that adequate time *before* the logging meeting is spent on approximately optimum-rate checking, by each individual.

8.6.2   Whom to Select

• The Inspection leader is responsible for selecting a team of Inspectors to perform the checking tasks.
• The leader will determine and inform participants (in the master plan) about appropriate time-charge account numbers.

- The leader will invite someone to Inspect, but they are not obliged to accept a particular invitation to be a checker.

  There should, however, be some form of motivation, so that all potential Inspectors are happy to accept some invitations sometimes – perhaps with leaders or other Inspectors they prefer to work with. There should be some element of 'popularity contest' for both parties, which motivates them to be acceptable to each other.
- The leader should try to select the strongest possible team, from the following points of view:
  - their ability to spot major issues
  - their ability to spot 'downstream' issues,that is, potential defects for recipients of the Inspected product
  - innocence. A trainee or someone inexperienced and non-expert in the products which are being Inspected should be invited to every Inspection. Generally one novice is invited to each Inspection, since an Inspection team consisting of all novices is not ideal.

Including a novice is particularly appropriate when they are likely to have to consume, or be dependent on, the task product document. The novice will give the most sensitive warning about intelligibility. Seeing both good and bad practices helps in on-the-job training, and should also help to avoid pitfalls. This is one time when short-term maximization of issues found is not the primary consideration for the leader. A major objective is to develop the younger, less experienced, staff in a responsible and controlled way, in order to avoid future problems, that is, to prevent future potential defects.

- The Inspection leader selects someone from the author team, preferably the one who will perform the editing. Note that this is an entry criterion.

An example of an Inspection team selection table is shown in Table 8.1. This can be extended to show many more types of documents and participants. It can be used to guide Inspection leaders into inviting those types of participants found most desirable and effective at any one meeting type.[†]

The left-hand entry contains the type of employee, that is, their current main job function. The top line is the type of document to be Inspected: contract, requirements specification, architectural or logical design, detailed or physical design, test plans, test case designs, code, technical documentation, or user manual. For any

† From an idea by AT&T in their *Technical Journal*, March/April 1986.

document type, the relevant type of employee to invite to Inspect that document can be seen at a glance.

Table 8.1   Team selection table.

Employee Type	Contract	Reqts.	Archit. Design	Detail Design	Test Plan	Test Design	Source Code	Tech. Doc.	User Manual
Task author	x	x	x	x	x	x	x	x	x
Req. analyst	x	x	x	x	x	x			x
Architectural designer	x	x	x	x	x	x		x	
Detailed designer			x	x	x	x	x	x	
Programmer				x	x	x	x	x	
Tester	x	x	x	x	x	x	x	x	x
Maintainer		x	x	x	x	x	x	x	x
User	x	x	x		x	x			x
Manager	x	x	x		x				x
Marketing	x	x	x						x
Legal department	x	x						x	x

8.6.3   How Many People on a Team?

Your own data on team size and results will help you determine how many Inspectors to invite. A general rule is to have two to three people in total including the leader for maximum efficiency (major issues per work-hour), and four to five people including the leader for maximum effectiveness (percentage of total majors found in Inspection). This is based on research done in the Danish electronics business on software Inspections by Søren Nielsen, and confirmed in principle by research done by John Kelly of Jet Propulsion Labs (JPL). It is not particularly difficult for you to analyze your own data with various team sizes, to find out what is best for your purposes.

8.6.4   How to Invite Inspectors to Participate

- Use personal contact, telephone, electronic mail, common friends to encourage people to participate in Inspection.
- Use the master plan to give them the official planned invitation.
- Inspection should normally be voluntary – not ordered by a manager.
- Make use of a list of potential Inspectors.

The potential Inspector list should contain practically every professional in your area. At one client of ours the spreadsheet file contained data on last Inspection date, next committed Inspection date, number of Inspections done in total since a date, and whether qualified as team leader.

8.6.5   How to Motivate Inspectors to Participate

People are motivated to participate by:

- the chance to learn new things;
- the opportunity to contribute to other work areas than those which they usually can influence;
- the opportunity to socialize and get to know other people better;
- the opportunity to show their special abilities to a broader audience;
- the opportunity to represent their special-interest professional group;
- peer pressure (being recognized as a team member, helping move the team forward).

Here are some constructive reactions an Inspection leader might try if a particular Inspector seems reluctant to accept the invitation to join your team:

- Appeal to them directly for help: 'We really need your help!'
- Ask if you can possibly do anything to help clear the way for their participation.
- Ask if this is an exceptional case, and whether they would normally be prepared to say yes.
- Make sure they know that your project is willing to fund their time (if that is the case).
- Point out that you and your team will be pleased to reciprocate, and to be Inspectors on their teams on an equivalent exchange basis.
- Consider an initiative in contacting their boss in order to change their priorities. Work out the advantages for that boss and be prepared to sell the case.
- Point out that they will broaden their knowledge and job skills.
- Point to company management statements, about the need for this kind of activity: 'quality' initiatives (if there are any).
- Promise them 'coffee and doughnuts'. And deliver.
- Tell them who else will be on the team; they might be motivated if certain people they respect are on the team.

8.6.6   Should the Inspection Leader also be a Checker?

Inspection leaders need to 'manage' the checking of the Inspectors. If they choose to do so, they may also undertake a 'checker' role in addition to their Inspection leader role. They should do so if they are technically capable and if doing so improves their team's net ability to find major defects per hour of time used. The Inspection leader should *avoid* becoming a checker:

- when they are not technically qualified;
- when doing so would detract from the time which they would have for managing the checking of others, so as to ensure that other Inspectors get the most from their own checking;
- when the contribution of their own issues at the meeting would reduce their ability to 'milk' issues from their Inspectors.

8.6.7 Advice from Leaders to Checkers during the Individual Checking Phase

Here are some points of advice that leaders should give to Inspectors before individual checking. These points could be put on a written handout procedure (see PCC in Appendix B, procedures for checker during checking), or they could also form the basis for advice from the Inspection leader to the checkers during the kickoff meeting.

Maximum Unique Potential Defects

Your objective, during checking, is to find the maximum *unique* major potential defects (issues). Unique issues are those which no other Inspector offers at the logging meeting. Major defects are those which we can save effort by capturing now rather than at test or in field use. Of course you won't know until the meeting whether or not the issues you found were unique, but one point of the roles and checklists is to help you to find issues which other checkers are less likely to find.

Familiarization

You are to familiarize yourself with the material (checklists, rules, procedures, candidate product, and source documentation). This is to enable you to take advantage of additional time you have during the logging meeting to find more issues. It will also allow you to make use of new insights you gain during the meeting as a result of issues found by other Inspectors.

Checklist

Make use of every question on the checklist to search for that kind of potential defect indicated by the question.

Checklist Improvement

If you can think of additional questions for the checklist, or better ways of writing existing questions on the checklist, make a note of them. These are valid 'improvement suggestions' in the checklist and can be logged at the meeting.

In particular, if you have found a unique potential major defect for which there is no question on the checklist, then there *is* a need to improve the checklist so that it asks questions designed to find those issues. It is your personal responsibility to suggest that new checklist question.

Rules Improvement

Make full use of the rules provided. Either the documents must agree fully with the rules, or the rules themselves may contain a potential defect or issue you can report (as a rules improvement suggestion during logging).

There may be applicable rules which are not provided. This is particularly true for source documents, for which the Inspection leader will not always supply you with the applicable rules. But these source rules still apply, and you should be looking for potential defects in them too, if you know about them. Ask colleagues for such source rules if that is the easiest way to find out.

If rules or procedures which you are using are ambiguous, unclear, less than useful or incomplete then you have found an area to suggest improvement! Note it and report it. Don't get mad, get even!

If rules are in apparent conflict with other source or product documents, report it as an issue. You don't have to worry about whether the rules or the documents are 'wrong'. That is for the editor's judgement. Just report apparent problems. If the 'real problem' is with the rules, the editor will determine this and report it to the appropriate rule owner.

Source to Product Correlation: How Far Should You Trust the Sources?

You are expected to check systematically that all source information has been faithfully translated to the product document. You may question the completeness and updatedness of the source documentation as handed out to you by the Inspection leader, particularly if you have any knowledge of more appropriate documents.

The source documents should ideally be marked as exited or not, and in both cases an estimate of remaining defects per page should be made. If there are no markings and you conclude that inspection has not even been attempted, this is an 'entry' violation. Someone is asking you to work with poor tools! You can safely assume that such sources contain dozens of major issues per page. These will prevent you from checking the product correctly. Get angry, if you must, but 'get even' again by finding many of those issues in the source and reporting them.

Part of your job as an Inspector is to provoke other people in your organization to take quality of what they write as seriously as you do. Make your information suppliers give you good quality documents.

Missing or wrong source documents are of major importance. Suspicions of this should be immediately reported to your Inspection leader. This is so that other Inspectors can benefit, the same day, from your insight, or so that you can receive immediate feedback from the Inspection leader if you have misunderstood something. With correct source documentation, you can complete your checking under the correct assumptions.

Using Your Time

On the Inspection master plan, the Inspection leader will have estimated the average amount of time (or the checking rate in pages or lines per hour) to be used by Inspectors in individual checking.

This will be based on the average optimum rate experience of the time needed by your colleagues previously, on this class of documentation, to maximize their defect-finding ability. (But if no experience is available, an estimate, of about a page per hour, based on similar documents and people will be used.)

You may well benefit from more time, or need less time than the average. In addition, the particular document at hand may be more or less complex than the average. The time indicated in the plan is a guide, and it represents official company 'permission' to use that time. Do not allow yourself to be pressured to do a bad job, which merely increases the time needed by your company to get the correct job done for your customers on time.

However, you alone are in a unique position personally to correct that time estimate with regard to your ability and to the documentation at hand. In addition you may have been assigned one or more 'roles' for checking which need more or less time than any 'average'.

The important thing is to err on the side of caution. The value of 'major defects found' can save from four to one hundred or more hours of project time later for someone in the company. It may save us a customer, our reputation in the market, and our own jobs.

So, if you are hot on the trail of major issues, keep checking!

Practical tip
As a guide, if you can find a major issue at least every hour,
you should continue, particularly if you think the issue would
probably not be found by your colleagues.

Remember, the fact that the defect *might* be caught by testing or
early customer trials is irrelevant. By catching the defect now, we
save time and money – this is the whole point of Inspection. We are
not here even to consider leaving some defects to others to clean up
later. We want them all! We want all defects even though we
realistically know we cannot expect literally to find them all during
one Inspection. If in doubt about the checking time you are using,
consult with your Inspection leader.

Issue Search Methods

You may have been assigned one or more special roles, but these do
not in any way limit you from identifying any potential defect
elsewhere. Your team-mates *with* the appropriate role for a particular
defect type will probably only find 50% to 80% of the actual existing
ones – and *you* can (must!) back them up and find the others.

Go Wild! Get Creative about Finding Defects

You may use any method of looking for potential defects that you
want to. Use your imagination and all the automated tools available.
The most productive thing you could do would be to use such a
unique method that you turn up issues that no other teammate
would even dream of! Even 'cheating' is allowed. For example, you
may decide to check the source document against its own source
documents, or against updated decisions on the project, which may
not have been considered by the Inspection leader or author. No
holds are barred in winning the war against defects!

In principle, you do your checking separately from your
Inspector colleagues. Nevertheless, feel free to ask them questions.
Feel free to contact anyone inside or outside the organization who
might help you turn up a potential defect.

**Summary of Inspection Leader advice to Inspectors for
individual checking**
(1) Maximize unique major potential defects (issues) you find.
(2) Familiarize yourself with all documentation for further
issue-finding during the logging meeting.

Continues

(3) Exploit the checklists for ideas on potential defects.

(4) Improve the checklists if you can.

(5) Exploit all given and implied rules. Improve them if needed.

(6) Exploit all source documents fully, but look for potential defects in them too.

(7) Use the allotted time, but use more or less time with respect to your individual ability and particular role and documentation difficulty. Err on the side of more issues.

(8) Use any defect-search devices you want to, especially unusual creative ones.

8.7   Reserving Meeting Rooms

In addition to the people issues in Inspection, like motivating and encouraging individual members of the Inspection team to participate and be productive, the Inspection leader is also responsible for the administration details of the Inspection process, such as reserving rooms for the kickoff and logging meetings.

• Reserve sufficient time for both an issue logging meeting at the optimum rate, a process brainstorming meeting following that, and a few minutes for administrative overheads and 'unforeseen' incidents.

• If necessary, be prepared to make use of any available space. An enclosed meeting room is the preferred environment, but other spaces have been found to function. At some sites the need for meeting rooms will very likely exceed their capacity, and you will have to be inventive. An unused executive office, the canteen or cafeteria outside of eating hours, or simply sitting around somebody's desk are all alternative possibilities. Outdoor cafeteria benches or lawns are great in good weather.

Don't ever let the lack of ideal meeting space be an excuse for inaction. As the need grows and the Inspection method is clearly paying for itself, management can be persuaded to fund more meeting space. One client has gone as far as to dedicate certain rooms as 'Inspection rooms'.

• Give precise written instruction (usually in the master plan) as to the location. More than one Inspection meeting has been delayed by people having difficulty locating it. Include a simple foolproof map whenever you invite people who have never been to that meeting room before.

- Work out local parking, traffic, and transportation conditions and advise participants coming from outside your site.
- Advise any outside guest Inspectors of security requirements and arrange to have them met in the lobby. Such outsiders can be a valuable component in Inspections.
- Give visitors a local telephone message number or fax so that they can be reached, but without unnecessary interruptions during the meetings.

Generally only one logging meeting should be scheduled per day for a team or participating individuals, although in exceptional circumstances one in the morning and one in the afternoon may be permissible.

8.8 Assigning Specialist Roles to the Inspectors

8.8.1 What is the Purpose of Roles?

A 'role' is any viewpoint, any potential defect search method, any specialization which helps checkers focus more narrowly and effectively (see Figure 8.11). It should increase the probability that they will find 'unique' defects (those found by no other team member).

One key activity of the Inspection leader, which can greatly influence the productivity of Inspection, is allocation of effective specialist roles. Every professional needs to be used to full effect. This will not happen if everyone is searching for everything.

The team has to specialize in order to get time to be effective. Individuals need to be able to focus on things in which they are especially interested and competent, confident that their team-mates are covering the other areas at the same time.

Note that more than one person can have the same role, and that one Inspector can have several roles. Any Inspector can feel quite free to 'wander' into other people's roles. The test of 'wandering' validity is whether they performed their assigned roles as well as others, and whether, in wandering, they have additionally managed to dig up major issues which others failed to find. It could be said that allowing wandering is a way of keeping the people who *do* get a particular role 'on their toes'.

> **The primary role assignment rule:**
> Maximize total major issues found by the team.
>
> **The secondary role assignment rule:**
> Assign roles with regard to the talents and interests of the individuals involved – and with their agreement.

8.8.2   Types of Roles

There are three types of roles: document roles and checklist-defined roles and procedure-defined roles.

Document Roles

An individual checker is given a special responsibility to pay particular attention to one or more of the documents used in the checking process. This assignment is in addition to the candidate product, which every checker looks at very carefully. A document role contains two responsibilities:

- check the document itself for issues;
- exploit the document to discover issues in all other documents.

A document role is assigned in the master plan to individual checkers. It is assigned using the document tag. It can be assigned for all checked document types (sources, products, checklists, rules, Inspection procedures).

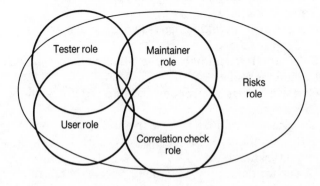

Figure 8.11   Some example 'roles'; there are many other possibilities.

This means that although all checkers have the same documents to use, different individuals will be looking more thoroughly at each particular document. Thus a detailed examination (the magnifying glass) is done by at least one checker on every document. This is what is meant by document role.

Checklist-defined and Procedure-defined Roles

The best method we have found for defining how to 'play a role' is to write up to about four special checklist questions which define what to do. This is the best advice from an experienced senior expert to anybody who has got the role. It in no way limits the role player. But we have found such role checklists to be very much better than assigning a name to the role such as 'tester', 'legal beagle', 'risk analyst', and assuming the checker would know what was intended.

For example, the checklist for estimates may contain questions about feasibility of performance estimates for the design, or could be related to project delivery estimates. The role checklist for quality may contain questions about measuring maintainability, usability or performance. The procedure roles contain a checking procedure, such as reading the document from back to front (backwards).

Checklist and procedure roles should be assigned during planning. They can be stored and retrieved from Inspection libraries, or made up on the spot.

Some examples of roles are shown in the list below.

---

(1) Read from the last page forward (a procedural role).
(2) Concentrate on finding issues in source documents. Document role.
(3) Concentrate on finding issues in checklists or rules. Document role.
(4) Concentrate on finding issues which violate rules. Document role.
(5) Concentrate on finding issues which violate checklists . Document role.
(6) Check all cross-references and implied correlations. Procedure role.
(7) Check all calculations, measurements, data, estimates, and predictions. Procedure role (but could be a question in a checklist role!).
(8) Check for ambiguity, unintelligibility. Procedure or checklist role.

(9) Check for internal consistency. Procedure or checklist
      role.
(10) Check against any external (to software development)
      applicable company standards (documentation, ethics,
      policy, general procedures). Procedure role.
(11) Check all graphics and symbols. Procedure role.
(12) Check that there is a test planned for each requirement
      stated (procedure or viewpoint role).
(13) Check that the procedures for using the system
      correspond to user workflow (user viewpoint role).

8.8.3   General Tips for Assigning Roles

- Use your own imagination. Get to know your Inspectors' talents
  and interests. Analyze where you are weak in finding major
  defects; then dream up a role which will find those issues.
- Make it fun and challenging. Give roles which will allow
  individuals to make a unique contribution to the team.
- Confer with the more adventurous Inspectors to find fun, unusual,
  and interesting roles. 'What could you do to find major issues,
  using a searching strategy or specialist viewpoint which we have
  not exploited yet?'
- Rotate roles so people learn different things. Do keep in mind that
  roles never keep any Inspector from looking for any and all issues
  any way they like! But roles do give license to spend more time
  and focused energy.
- Take a look at the major defects which pop up in practice and
  consider how to find more of them, more easily.

8.8.4   Summary of the Planning Procedure for the Inspection Leader

(1) Write all decisions about the Inspection at hand in the master
      plan (one-page form).
(2) Make sure the product document(s) is as clean as the author can
      and should deliver (entry criteria).
(3) Determine all source documents which the author *should* have
      used, that is, all source documents which are logically necessary
      for correct and updated product document writing. If necessary,
      write down unwritten 'sources' (a telephone request for a
      change, for example).
(4) Determine all necessary rule sets for transforming the sources to

the product document correctly. If necessary write down unwritten rules yourself.

(5) Select all useful checklists to help your team find defects. If necessary generate initial lists. Delegate to role players to build initial lists or to find them. Remember that checklists must illuminate existing rules and cite them.

(6) Check your Inspection library for useful artifacts (such as rules, forms, checklists).

(7) Create up to four special roles for each checker which should, in your opinion, increase the team's probability of finding more major defects. Roles should be defined by up to four questions on special role checklists.

(8) Select or write any useful Inspection procedures. These should be selected from the Inspection library or written by you. They shall be used especially to make sure that participants are absolutely clear about the expected and best known practices.

(9) Determine optimum rates for checking, for the logging meeting and for special roles.

(10) Select a balanced team of experts, trainees and special interest outsiders.

(11) Agree as to the best meeting (kickoff, logging, process brainstorm) times and places with team.

(12) Plan possible kickoff objectives, strategies, things to teach.

(13) Mark all participant documents with a reference tag in upper right corner. Make sure lines are numbered (or equivalent). Make copies available, as required by checkers, with respect to roles they have.

8.9   The Kickoff Meeting

8.9.1   Purpose of the Kickoff Meeting

In 1985, Carole Jones at IBM reported that IBM had adopted an improved version of the 'overview meeting' (from Fagan's version of Inspection) as a major way of getting far more oriented towards 'defect prevention'. This version of the kickoff meeting is shown below.

Kickoff Meeting: The Entry Sub-stage as seen by IBM
Meeting objectives:
• Review available input.
  – do all members understand what is available?
  – is everything from the previous stage complete?

Continues
- Review the process and methodology guidelines.
  - discuss output requirements (examples, guidelines, Inspection leader expectations).
  - make use of incrementally improved kickoff procedures.
- Review error lists.
  - most common error causes.
  - increase awareness for prevention before doing task.
  - update checklists constantly.
- Set team goals.
  - expected error detection rates.
  - documented in a quality plan.
  - establish own team goals (these are for internal motivation and never published).
  - group discussion about project errors (emphasizes quality rather than schedule).

Source: Jones (1985)

Notice that IBM classifies kickoff as a part of the 'ENTRY sub-stage' of a development process, a wider view than an Inspection kickoff as in this book.

The Inspection leader can use the kickoff meeting for any purpose which helps to promote a more effective Inspection team. Inspection metrics are fed back into the Inspection process at the kickoff meeting, and new targets are set by the team for continuous improvement. Over time, certain Inspection practices will be measured by Inspection metrics to be more effective than others.

8.9.2 Format of the Kickoff Meeting

The kickoff meeting varies in the time it consumes. The time needed depends on the objectives of a particular kickoff. It can be one or more hours if detailed initial training for some or all Inspectors is required. This is where Inspectors are to be given any necessary training to do their job.

If there are a number of new Inspectors who will be involved in their first Inspection, or who have not been involved in many, then the kickoff meeting can be used to reinforce the general principles of Inspection, such as how to look for potential defects by comparing documents, not by criticizing people according to personal preferences.

The documents to be used in individual checking and logging may be handed out at the kickoff meeting. This also gives the

Inspection leader the opportunity to explain anything about any of the documents which may need clarifying. For example, the scope of the checking to be done, exactly what the current chunk consists of, may be more clear from an explanation than simply from receiving the documents in the internal mail.

Roles, which were probably assigned during planning, may be explained and accepted in the kickoff meeting. Adjustments or improvements to role assignments can be negotiated at the kickoff.

The team improvement targets for the Inspection process are also set at the kickoff meeting. This may include review of their metrics from recent Inspections, with areas of possible improvement highlighted.

For example, 'the individual checking rates have been creeping up to 1.8 pages per hour which is greater than the optimum of 1.4 for our group. We suggest that the team should try to slow down and see if our defect-finding ability improves as a result.'

8.9.3   The Purpose and Rules of Checklists

Checklists are needed for the checking process alone, and are not normally used in production of the product document. The 'rule set', by contrast, dictates the relevant software engineering process which generates the product document itself, using one or more source documents.

As checklists are an analytical tool for the Inspection checking and logging meeting, they need to be available in time for the Inspectors to do individual checking, because this is primarily when they are used (see Figure 8.12).

Note that 'rule sets' function exclusively as if they were checklists during any form of checking. Checkers are continuously asking, 'was this rule followed, or broken?' We learned in 1988 at Douglas Aircraft that it was silly to rewrite a rule into a checklist question. Let the rule be used directly to check that it has been applied. Checklists should be used to extend our understanding of rules. All checklist questions should refer to specific rules, which they interpret (using a source arrow '<-'). Here is an example.

Rule set (fragment)
RUL19:   All statements should be unambiguous.

Checklist (fragment example)

CK21: Are all statements unambiguous to test planners for purposes of constructing all tests needed to verify that requirements are met?<-RUL19.

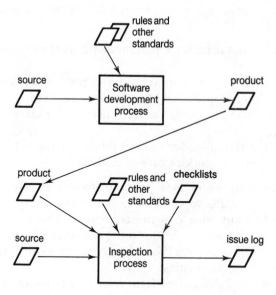

Figure 8.12   Checklists are used only during Inspections.

A checklist may deal with one entire specific software engineering process (for example, system test planning), and all its
documents and their relationships. A checklist may cover only one
type of software engineering document (for example, software test
cases or scripts). A checklist may cover more than one engineering
process from a particular point of view (for example, maintenance
changes from a configuration management point of view). There are
checklists for particular roles, as described above.

From the point of view of the Inspection leader, the checklist is a
tool for:

- instructing the checkers as to what to search for;
- describing clever defect search techniques;
- describing special roles in detail (all these save Inspection leader
time);
- increasing the defect-finding ability of the team (majors/work-
hour);
- defining and pre-classifying defect/issue types (major, minor);
- encouraging continuous improvement by storing good checklist
questions for future use.

The leader should be responsible for both the library storage of the
checklists, their reuse and their improvement as practice indicates.

8.9.4   Generating Checklists

The Inspection leader has the responsibility for generating checklists:

- when they do not exist for a particular product or source document type;
- when those that do exist are considered poor or useless for finding issues, or when people have begun to ignore them;
- when there are problems in the checklists that need fixing or improving;
- when the Inspection leader needs to define a special role by means of a special set of questions on a checklist.

The Inspection leader may provide Inspectors with one or more checklists appropriate to each document type being Inspected. In particular, when any source document, rule or checklist itself has not itself exited, the Inspection leader must consider planning to provide appropriate additional checklists for these un-exited documents to support special checking roles.

A hand-drafted document with four to 20 checklist questions is much better than nothing. A checklist is a dynamically modified document, largely under Inspection leader control anyway. Faults in it will soon be improved upon as a natural part of the Inspection process.

The checklist is normally kept simple and brief by insisting on a maximum of one page – no matter how many questions you can think of. For this reason virtually all questions should lead to the identification of major defects rather than minor ones. At most a single question can be used to 'define' minor problems. For example: 'Are there any spelling, punctuation or grammar errors which ought to be cleaned up? (minor)'.

All checklist questions should be based on written rules and should therefore directly refer to the rules they support. For example: 'CK-13. Are all quality concepts measurably defined? <- Rule Q-16'.

There is a checklist-writing rule set in Appendix D of this book, which defines how to write a checklist. This can be used to Inspect a new checklist, if necessary.

Checklist Inspection, and successful exit from it, might be chosen by you as an entry criterion for Inspections using that checklist. However, it is up to you as an Inspection leader whether or not you Inspect checklists. It does provide a good short exercise for the team, and sloppy checklists can waste time. Certainly, checklists which are going to be used frequently or by many people deserve a proper Inspection.

Experience shows that hastily-compiled checklists written by amateurs cause more lost time and lost results.

It is the special responsibility of the leader to sense during a problem logging meeting that a suggested improvement in a checklist should be made, and to take time to get this logged.

8.10   Preparing for the Logging Meeting

8.10.1   How can the Inspection Leader help Inspectors?

The Inspection leader's primary obligation is to do everything which helps make Inspection succeed. There are no formal limits to the imaginative, intuitive and psychological initiatives the Inspection leader can take.

Here is one example of such an initiative, a checker's procedure, which is a handout from the Inspection leader to inspectors to make sure that their task is well-defined in all details:

Checker's procedure

(1) [ ] Receive master plan.

(2) [ ] Notify Inspection leader of possible conflicts, non-attendance, or inability to do checking.

(3) [ ] Check over the material. Tell Inspection leader if there are any problems with the assignment.

(4) [ ] Checking

    (a) [ ] record your start of checking time.

    (b) [ ] review your assigned roles (in invitation). Re-negotiate roles with Inspection leader if you can do better with one or more other roles.

    (c) [ ] arrange the material, all items visible on your desktop.

    (d) [ ] scan* and/or read* source document(s).

    (e) [ ] scan* or read* the rule sets.

    (f) [ ] scan* the checklist.

    (g) [ ] scan* the entire product document (if it is all supplied).

    (h) [ ] read* the product document chunks to be Inspected during the next meeting.

    (i) [ ] check by comparing source to corresponding product.

        (i) by using the checklist questions,

        (ii) by using the generic and specific rules.

Continues

      (j) [ ] count the potential defects you suspect exist (that is, issues) in terms of major, minor.

      (k) [ ] record the stop time, and write issues found and minutes used on the places provided on the master plan, so you will have them ready, as the logging meeting starts, to tell the Inspection leader.

      (l) during checking

         (i) mark the problems directly in the document(s),

         (ii) write down the appropriate checklist item identification code when possible,

         (iii) write down the appropriate rule identification code when appropriate.

(5) [ ] Show up promptly for the meeting. Allow time for unexpected problems like parking, so you are not the cause of a delay.

(6) [ ] Tell the Inspection leader your time and issue counts (approximate is good enough), at the beginning of the meeting, when requested.

(7) [ ] Issue reporting, during the meeting.

      (a) at the appropriate time and place, as indicated by the Inspection leader, suggest the issues you have found, if nobody else has already suggested them

      (b) use the shortest possible 'telegraph style' sentence and speak clearly and slowly enough for the scribe to record properly. 'Seven words or less' is the report ideal.

      (c) indicate the type of issue (major or minor) if you can.

(8) Process brainstorming after the problem logging meeting:

      (a) [ ] Follow the instructions and lead of the Inspection leader.

      (b) [ ] Try to suggest root causes for major issues found by the group.

      (c) [ ] Try to suggest some simple immediate correction which would help remedy the cause of the defect.

      (d) [ ] Volunteer to follow up with more detailed cause analysis or corrective action. Play your part to root out the defect causes early.

Source: from A.W. Brown, Douglas Aircraft Co, Jan. 88, modified (terminology) by TG March 1988, 1992.

This example is not intended as a full and best possible procedure list, but it is a real one for a real user, to fit a particular situation and a particular stage of development. See Appendix B on procedures with reference to the procedures for checkers for more advice.

8.10.2   Teaching by Wandering Around

Often new Inspectors will have a number of questions, but they may be reticent about actively approaching the Inspection leader about them. The Inspection leader should ensure that all Inspectors, experienced as well as novices, are free to ask any question at any time, and they must not be made to feel foolish for asking it. Effective learners always ask questions. The asking of questions should be taken as positive evidence that Inspectors are actively using the technique and developing in their knowledge.

Wandering around is the best way to solicit these questions in an atmosphere which is generally non-threatening (on the Inspector's home territory), and is a good way to increase Inspection learning and effectiveness. The Inspection leader should be available during the time when the team is doing their individual checking.

8.11   Conducting the Logging Meeting

8.11.1   Purpose of the Logging Meeting

The major task of the logging meeting is to get oral assertions about potential defects, which are at this point called 'issues', from the Inspectors and to write them down in the issue log. This includes both issues identified in individual checking and also new issues which come to light in the meeting. In addition, questions to the author as well as improvement suggestions, either for rules, procedures, standards or checklists, or improvements to the software development or Inspection process itself are logged. The generic word for these three types of things logged (issues, questions, improvements) is 'item'.

The person who writes the items down is called the 'scribe'; the Inspection leader is the scribe by default.

8.11.2   The Logging Meeting Rules

The fundamental rules of the logging meeting are:

- No explanations (or presentations) are allowed by the author or anyone else, unless requested specifically in the form of a logged question of intent to the author. Then only brief answers are permitted at the end of the meeting without discussion.

- No suggestions for fixing potential defects in the product document and source documents are permitted at this meeting; this is the job of the editor/owner alone later.
- No other comment or discussion is allowed about whether an issue to be logged is really a potential defect or not. The answer is always to log it anyway and the editor will sort it out later. Only assertions of issues, questions or improvement suggestions are permitted to be reported.
- No repeating of items already announced by others (which are already logged).
- No comment (negative or positive) on an issue assertion by anyone. Brainstorming rules of criticism suspension apply here.
- Maximize issues noted per minute (about one or two per minute), but also allow time to find new issues in the meeting.
- Give issue reports as briefly as possible, avoiding wordiness.

8.11.3   Additional Suggestions for the Logging Meeting

Here are some other suggestions for running the logging meeting. These are not fixed requirements or rules for the meeting, but the use of some of them may prove to be very helpful.

- Allow the 'weakest' (youngest, newest) members first priority at reporting an issue when several raise their hands to indicate issues to report. This allows them to contribute and be recognized as contributors.
- Let a secretary (or other non-participant) actually log the items (be the scribe). This is the Inspection leader's responsibility, but the logging process is often the bottleneck in productivity, and the Inspection leader should be more concerned with paying attention to the Inspection team, rather than being worried about noting down the issues.
- Use a lap-top computer or personal computer to capture items. This avoids handwriting problems, allows later analysis by text ('give me a list of all issues which mention 'cross-referencing'), and makes a real-time display of items found for the team members.
- An alternative simpler way to get a real-time display of items logged is to write the issue list directly on overhead projector foils during the meeting.
- Make it into a game with rewards: 'Company-sponsored lunch if we exceed normal major-issues-per-page finding-rate by a factor of two', or 'an extra hour of lunch today if we find more than three major issues per page.'

- Chart the team's progress on a public wall-chart, for example team results ('issues found per page' for example) against company averages.
- Give the Inspection team a name: 'The Desert Rats', 'The Vikings', The Space Hackers', or whatever turns them on.

8.11.4   Inspection Leader Duties at the Logging Meeting

Here is a list of the Inspection leader's duties at the logging meeting, which you can use and update as you get more ideas. See also Appendix B (Procedures).

Inspection Leader Procedure (example)
(1) Get started promptly. On the minute.
(2) Try to get someone else to be the scribe for you (not a checker).
(3) Gather orally, and note 'Inspection summary' data from checkers (time used for checking, major and minor issues found).
(4) If any Inspector arrives having used inadequate checking time or with less than 10% of the number of Issues that other Inspectors have claimed they found, either excuse them from the meeting, or ask them to be the scribe. This is not a punishment, but is the best way they can contribute under the circumstances. They are allowed to report items even if they are the scribe.
(5) Make clock notes of start and stop time for each phase of the meeting process (administration, logging, problem brainstorming, non-Inspection matters).
(6) Note the approximate time of any major digressions and interruptions, or the sum of them. They should not be included as Inspection time. You could use a chess clock for this.
(7) If too few fully prepared Inspectors arrive on time, cancel the meeting. Suggest they do their individual checking instead.
(8) Make sure that the editor (author, usually) who is present at your meeting, is aware that they are expected to monitor the issue logging and to react if the issue as logged would be unintelligible to them during edit. Seat them so they can directly see the log as written.
(9) If you have done checking, or if you otherwise spot potential defects, then be the last to offer them. Give all others a chance first.

What to tell your Inspectors about the Logging Meeting

Here is a Procedure for Inspectors for the meeting, which the Inspection leader could hand out to them. You might like to improve it and tailor it as a tool in your job as an Inspection leader.

Inspector Procedure (example)

(1) Be a team player. Do everything you can to improve your team's total score at the end of play.

(2) Contribute items rapidly, briefly, clearly (to the scribe). Make sure others can hear you too.

(3) Encourage, assist and 'applaud' contributions from your teammates.

(4) Do not criticize, explain, defend, show scorn, haughtiness or otherwise 'turn team-mates off '.

(5) If you want to 'show off ', then find major issues which no one else has found.

(6) Arrive on time and be prepared to go into action on the dot. In fact to do this, plan to arrive a few minutes early. Allow a safety margin for traffic, parking, weather, and other contingencies. Don't use them as an excuse.

(7) Use your valuable time during the meeting to find more issues than you found in checking. Keep looking for new issues all the time.

8.11.5   The Scribe

The 'scribe' is the person who writes down the items reported in the issue log. In some review methods, this role is called 'recorder'. The Inspection leader is usually the scribe, and has the responsibility for getting the items written down in the log. But if there is anyone else who can undertake that function – someone not otherwise engaged as a checker, like a guest of the meeting – then this frees up the Inspection leader to concentrate all attention on the checkers reporting issues, which is usually an advantage for getting more recorded.

It is not unheard of to pass the pen after one scribe is worn out.

Guidelines in how to fill out the issue log are given below.

Scribing Procedure (example)

How to Fill Out the Issue Log

(1) The Inspection leader (try to avoid using a checker who has issues to contribute) is responsible for filling out the log.

(2) For maximum productivity, the Inspection leader can try to find someone else to record the items (a trainee, a student, a secretary, a meeting guest, or someone who failed to put in checking time as needed).That way the Inspection leader can concentrate on getting the maximum flow of issues from the Inspection team. Aim for between one and two issues per minute recorded.

(3) Record issue severity (M, m) and other item classifications (?, Imp., New) by circling the code on the form (Major, minor, question, Improvement, New issue at meeting). But do not stop to discuss them at all! Remember, it is far cheaper and probably more accurate for the Inspection leader or the editor to do that classification later alone, rather than in the meeting.

(4) Identify the location of the issue. Give reference to the exact source item, the exact rule number, the exact 'checklist' question number.

(5) The Inspection leader should paraphrase the issue report telegraph-style, when necessary, thus teaching and encouraging Inspectors to do likewise themselves initially. This saves the scribe some time, which is often the bottleneck.

(6) Make it into a game to deliver the issue report with the fewest possible words. Set a ten-word maximum. Tell people that the entire process of making the assertion and noting it down should not take more than 30 seconds. 'Seven words or less!' is a good guideline.

(7) If the author or editor is present (and they should normally be) then ask them to monitor the issue log. One suggestion is to seat the author next to the scribe for this purpose. The editor should be charged with reacting to the material logged if they are not sure they can understand it when editing. Remember that there is no question of defending or proving the issue report, only of clarifying what the assertion actually is.

(8) A multiple-location issue can be recorded once, but the count of issues can be recorded approximately, at the extreme right side. It should be equal to the number of distinct places that have to be corrected.

Continues

(9) Normally a meeting-log form will be used, either paper forms or computerized forms. In some instances, for example with large graphic diagrams, it has been quicker and more accurate to make issue notes directly on the diagram. The central requirement is that the logging captures all the information needed by the Inspection leader (to compute the issue metrics) and needed by the editor (who needs to be sure of what the potential defect is).

In addition to the fundamental process of logging items (issues, improvements, questions) at the logging meeting, there are a number of other considerations for the Inspection leader, in order to maximize the flow of issues and side-benefits from the meeting.

8.11.6   Brainstorming of Issues

The logging meeting is a cousin of the 'brainstorming' process. We want to maximize the flow of potential defect assertions, no matter how seemingly trivial or 'silly' these may seem to be at the moment.

Make no mistake. We are 'really' after major defects. Minor defects (like spelling errors) are 'nice' to clean up. Issues that are not truly defects of any sort are not really 'welcome' (but we log them anyway because it is quicker). Also the penalty for being too critical initially about what we log, may well be that we end up missing the really big ones.

There are several reasons for this.

- If we get too critical initially then we may discourage any member of the Inspection team from suggesting a certain issue (which may turn out to be a very major one) they have in mind. They may misjudge the importance of it themselves, and not have the stomach for the implied criticism from their team if it judges their issue not worthy of logging.
- The time taken to discuss and pass judgement on a suggested issue could be better spent finding other issues and logging them. It is particularly unproductive to have five people discussing for five minutes whether a purported potential defect is really worthy of logging, when that same team could be logging five or ten more issues in the same time period. It is a far better use of time to let the editor alone decide what to do with the potential defect assertion, than to try to solve the problem in committee.

- If one of your Inspectors, however young and inexperienced (and remember we want some inexperience on the team!), suspects there is an issue, when there 'objectively' is not, then you definitely have a problem somewhere. It could be with training, documentation, recruitment, supervision, or tools. But the 'misinterpretation' is a sample of what could happen when the same individual is using this documentation for maintenance. They could misinterpret it and cause a real error to occur.
- Even a 'silly' problem assertion can stimulate someone on the team to suddenly 'see' a real issue. Even a silly brainstorming idea can stimulate someone to think of a much better one. We have seen this happen in practice. Someone asserts a 'silly' issue and another team member counters with 'no, the real issue is . . . '. Of course, we are not allowed to reject the first ('silly') issue either. It is normally logged (unless the proponent retracts it before it is logged).

8.11.7   Issue Logging Flow Rate

During your early Inspections, you can expect to keep the process moving at between one and two (or slightly more) issues per minute. If it is substantially lower, then you are mismanaging the meeting. You are probably allowing too much comment and discussion.

This rate is only possible if the available issue density is relatively high – say ten or more issues per page. Density is usually this high and even much worse initially.

After software engineering authors have been involved in a few Inspections, their work will improve automatically and remarkably (50% fewer defects committed each new document written!). This will lead to a lower issue rate per page; more like one issue or less per page and about one major issue or less every four pages, which is what characterizes a mature pre-checking document which would meet normal entry criteria.

Practical hint:
We usually use issue logging forms which allow exactly ten issues per page. We get the scribe to note the page number as the logging proceeds. After a while you can make a quick estimate of the rate. Say half an hour has passed and you are just beginning on the fourth page. You have logged about thirty issues, one per minute. Not bad. But not as good as it might be. It is time for the Inspection leader to try to speed up the process. This can be done by announcing that the rate is fairly low and we should try to focus on getting the issues

Continues

more quickly noted down during the rest of the meeting.
Even better, the Inspection leader can inject a little friendly
competition by reminding the team that some other team has
just done an Inspection at twice the rate – or by simply
challenging them to improve their own rate.

Remember that the optimum logging rate also allows time
for the discovery of new issues in the meeting which may be
10–20% of the total final number. This means one or two
newly discovered issues on every logging sheet. If you feel
this is not happening, encourage the team to be more active
in looking for new issues.

Be Diplomatic

There is a natural human tendency towards discussing the issue
reports. The Inspection leader's job is continuously to suppress this
discussion, in favor of more real issue identification.

The Inspection leader must always be a diplomat when doing
this so as to avoid turning people off. It is very easy to hurt someone's feeling by cutting them off in public, and we don't want team
members dropping out because of that.

You have to keep in mind that the tendency to want to discuss
some issues is very strong and very healthy. Your job is to deflect
this energy until later – not to suppress it forever.

Practical hint:
Other than the logging meeting, there are several other
possible times for discussing the issues.
- Remind people that the editor will do the evaluation. We
  get judged on the quantity of issues logged.
- Ask people to make a written note of their concern, so as to
  be sure to bring it up later. Or, to hand it over to someone
  like the editor or the Inspection leader.
- If you have new Inspectors who are not used to this culture
  of 'issue identification only', then remind people at the
  beginning of the meeting that you will diplomatically have
  to resist all attempts to discuss the issue assertions. If it is
  publicly announced in advance, it will not seem like a
  personal attack, but more of a friendly reminder of the
  rules of the game.

Continues

- Don't say 'no'. Say 'later'. The process brainstorming meeting, immediately following the logging meeting, is the place to raise some of these points.
- Thank people for every attempt at a contribution. They mean well! 'Thanks. We don't want to lose your ideas, so would you please make a note of them for the process brainstorming meeting. Remember the game here is to log issues and to avoid all activity except item logging at this session'.
- Even though the formal rules prohibit discussion, the Inspection leader can and should exercise reasonable discretion in allowing it. A ten or twenty second exchange of remarks every few minutes might be worthwhile and not too damaging. You might allow it 'for free' while the scribe is busy noting the current issue, and other activity is temporarily stopped. It might be the spark that stimulates the finding of further issues. It might have an educational value for many participants. It might be useful to let the steam off at that moment, and be done with it. It might be fun. A good laugh every few minutes at a high-paced issue logging meeting is highly recommended! The trick is to know when and how to cut it off if it threatens to get out of hand. Therein lies one art of being an Inspection leader.
- Sometimes a person will get out of hand. Their rank or seniority may inhibit the Inspection leader from doing too much about it during the meeting. This should not stop the Inspection leader from diplomatically hinting privately afterwards, that it would be appreciated, if most of those comments could have been reduced in length and channeled elsewhere – because 'our meeting was only finding issues at half the expected rate (as a result)'. The final resort is to avoid inviting the talkers to the next meeting. If they wonder why, tell them.

Set Targets for the Meeting

'Let's see if we can beat our previous meeting record of 90 issues logged per hour'. Or 'Let's see if we can find more than three major issues per page, within the time allotted.' This target-setting is expected in the kickoff meeting, but can be reinforced at the logging meeting.

The point is to make it a game and to give people a reason to be a team player. If you can connect these targets with even symbolic rewards, like enlarging the following lunch break by 10 to 30 minutes, going home early, public bragging about the result of the team effort, so much the better.

Pacing the Meeting

You need to make full use of your allotted time. That means starting on time, ruthlessly (even if some people have not arrived yet). It also means continuing at an even pace. Too high or too low a rate of pacing can mean that potential defects are missed, or time is wasted.

Pacing is usually done by the Inspection leader citing pages, lines, or sections in sequence on the product document. The exact pacing mechanism may have to be adjusted dynamically by the Inspection leader depending on the flow of issues. If there is a high flow, you need to focus better by taking smaller sections of the material at a time. If there are only a very few issues per page, then a page at a time is fine.

Some types of Inspection use a role called a 'reader', who 'paraphrases' the material aloud as a pacing device. This has the advantage of providing a visibly different perspective on the product document, and can reveal potential defects, particularly of misunderstanding. The theory is that by forcing someone to interpret the material, we have provided a test of intelligibility. This is true, but this is really a holdover from reviews which did not have the other mechanisms which Inspection has for deciding intelligibility (rules, optimum rates, checklists, source documents, and defined roles).

Therefore the role of reader is not recommended in this book, mainly because it takes too much time for the benefits which it provides.

If you as Inspection leader want to hold an experiment where you use a reader, this is a good experiment to perform. Just be careful not to start experimenting until the basic Inspection process is well established. Also look at the results produced both with and without the reader. If you can demonstrate experimentally that the use of a reader leads to more issues per hour being logged, then by all means use them.

8.11.8   Searching for Additional Issues during the Logging Meeting

It is a common failure for checkers to report only issues they identified during their initial individual checking. Yet the logging meeting itself provides additional time and stimulation for searching for and finding additional issues. Indeed, that is a major justification for the

logging meeting (other justifications are education, peer pressure
and collation of overlapping results into one set of issues).

One of the ways to measure whether the pace of the logging
meeting was correct is the number of new issues found during the
meeting. If it is less than 10–20%, you are probably going too quickly.
Note that the logging form must have a way of recording 'new' issues,
and that they also need to be reported as such by the checkers.

The things to watch out for are Inspectors who are staring into
space, while they wait for the section of the material, where *their* next
checking issue is noted, to come up. Most Inspectors should be
avidly scanning rules, checklists and documents trying to find
additional issues.

We sometimes dramatize this by asking them: 'what would you
be doing now if I said that the company will pay you $1000 for each
additional major issue you find during the meeting?'

8.11.9 Nurturing the Inexperienced

The Inspection leader must be prepared to act as Big Brother or Sister
to inexperienced Inspectors. Here are some suggestions.

- Make a note of those who may need additional help. They may
  have the least experience in Inspection, or in the company, or in
  dealing with this particular class of documentation. Sometimes it is
  just people who are shy and reticent by nature.
- Visit them during their checking, to make sure they get a good
  start.
- Encourage them; especially during the meetings – even when they
  do 'inexperienced things'. Do not *ever* criticize them in any way in
  public.
- Thank them for trying – even if their report is not always a major
  issue.
- Get to one or more other team members privately and ask if they
  will, both during checking and at the logging meeting, help,
  encourage, and protect the newcomer.
- During the meeting, when several people indicate that they have
  an issue to report, intentionally choose the newcomer first to make
  the report.
- Don't hesitate to praise them even for 'obvious' major issues.
- Remember, the most vulnerable member of the team is the author.
  The newcomers need to be especially reminded not to criticize the
  author or their work (directly). For example, 'Analyze the discrepancies, don't criticize the quality or intent'.
- The author needs to be considered as a person in special need of
  attention by the Inspection leader. Failure to be sensitive to this

has resulted in authors walking out of Inspection meetings in uproar. The author needs to feel that they are privately being helped by their 'family', and that they are a contributor to the critical analysis of their work product.

What to Do in the Case of Revolt or Protest

On more than one occasion Inspection leaders have allowed things to go 'too far'. On two occasions we know of (below) the Inspection leader was relatively inexperienced, was without more senior guidance in the room, and did not know how to control the situation. Their Inspectors walked out in anger.

The Case of the Team Walkout

The immediate cause of the first situation was that the leader-distributed source documentation was not the correct one. It was not really the correct input to writing of the product document. This frustrated the Inspectors in their checking attempts. But the Inspection leader did not understand why and persisted in continuing the meeting. One of the participants, a manager, wrote a 21-item criticism the next day. The Inspection leader had not been properly trained as an Inspection leader, and was without experienced guidance.

Looking at the situation afterwards, here was our advice to the Inspection leader on what he should have done ideally, or next time:

(1) Apologize to them.
(2) Explain frankly that you are a trainee Inspection leader and need more instruction on this point.
(3) Take the blame entirely on your own shoulders. Do not blame the Inspectors for anything, no matter what!
(4) Stop the meeting. You can resume or restart later when the problem is cleared away. Don't waste the team's time by continuing.
(5) Note the protests or remarks of the Inspectors. Don't be shy of asking for their help in analyzing what went wrong!
(6) Analyze the situation together with your chief Inspection leader or champion.
(7) Check out your correction of the situation privately with the main protesters before you resume the meeting.

The Case of the Angry Author

In the second situation, one of our new Inspection leaders was doing her second Inspection. She had done a really great job in the face of her immediate management opposition in getting even her first

Inspection done. Her problem came when conducting the logging meeting. The author, a senior engineer, stormed out in anger.

It seems the author had no training in Inspection or motivation to find defects in his own work. He was known as the superstar type who believes that his work is basically perfect and did not ever need to be checked. The issue-reporting process must have been a severe blow to his ego (rather than the aid to making him look even better that it is intended to be). But the crushing blows came during the logging as his major issues were reported by his 'inferiors'. They were called 'defects' as they were reported, and the term irritated the senior engineer after a few dozen were reported.

This is one reason why we now use another word (issues) and make sure that everyone understands that we are only logging 'potential purported problems', not a fault or defect in the author himself.

The fundamental mistake seemed to be in allowing the Inspectors during the logging meeting, or perhaps also afterwards at the process brainstorming meeting, to speculate on all the possible 'better' ways in which the superstar 'could' have done the work. There were, we agreed, very many correct ways of doing the work, and each individual has an opinion. A distinction had not been carefully made between this myriad of possibilities and the objective requirement for proper work quality.

In a sense, this was an improper use of both the logging and brainstorming meetings. The objective is never to suggest corrections to the author's work uninvited. Corrections to a work product of the author is always the province of the editor during editing, who is usually the author and the owner of that document.

Brainstorming may focus on the ultimate organizational reasons that the issue cropped up (like improper training or standards, never individual author faults).

The author felt that he was being unjustly picked on. His way was, he felt, at least as good as any of the suggestions. He was under severe time pressure to get his work out as is. His management did not really even care about the defects (this of course was a major known problem in the company and the reason we were starting to use Inspection to remedy the problem).

In addition to this, we found that the division's management environment was still hostile to Inspections. They had grudgingly agreed to cooperate only under clear pressure from higher management, but they were not really supportive. Just determined not to be seen as obstructionist!

This was not unexpected, since top management was pressing for increased quality on the one hand, but still only measuring supervisors' performance on whether they got the work out the door on schedule – irrespective of the quality.

This is a common situation. Top management had been warned that they needed to change the old patterns, otherwise Inspection was not going to help anybody, but merely be viewed as a fly in the ointment. But it was a start-up situation in its third month, and many of the necessary motivations were simply not in place.

Conclusions and advice:

(1) We have all learned a valuable early lesson. Authors are very sensitive and need particular attention from the Inspection leader.

(2) Authors probably should not join their first Inspection without either brief training (two to six hours of lectures), reading this book, or being a checker of someone else's work first.

(3) The Inspection leader has to make a more careful distinction between 'could be' reports and 'should be'. 'Could be alternatives' should not be permitted in Inspection, and only result in ill will, if offered unsolicited. 'Should be' is what we are after in the edit, and that is the sole choice of the editor to make. Issue reports should concentrate on objectively and analytically pointing out a potential defect which the author as editor would perhaps like to look at, based on the objective rules, standards, checklists, and source documents.

Small Tricks Developed by Inspection Leaders

Sometimes the most useful part of a hands-on training course with an experienced Inspection instructor, or the interaction with fellow Inspection leaders is to pick up 'helpful hints' or 'small tricks'. They are often very easy to do but can make quite a lot of difference to making the Inspection process more effective.

Some 'tricks' are as subtle as being hidden in a suggested paper form as one single field of information. See Appendix C of this book on Forms. Each 'trick' seems to solve a real problem with the Inspection process, at least in a particular environment, at a particular stage in implementation.

Many of these 'finer points' of Inspection will not necessarily be appreciated by novices, but they are at least recorded here for you to pick up sometime in your use of the method. No doubt other practitioners have their own local variations, which are often largely undocumented.

Inspection leaders should be aware of 'small tricks' and notice which are useful, and at least make sure that they get spread to others in the same organization, and to a wider audience.

Some examples of 'small tricks' are listed below, although they may also be mentioned elsewhere in this book. Credit to specific people and approximate date of first use is indicated when possible.

- The editor/author sits next to the scribe and monitors logging in real time, interrupting if necessary to ensure intelligibility for editing (Mary Apt, Douglas Aircraft, 1988).
- The use of logged questions of intent; to the planner (the '?') to avoid reporting 'issues' (or potential defect) when you may suspect that you do not understand the author (Douglas, 1988).
- The use of the inoffensive term 'item' to cover the total set of issues, improvements and questions logged (Douglas, 1988, Winsor Brown and Bob Wiebe).
- The concept of a super-major defect as one which 'blows the project out of the water' (Citibank, London, 1986).
- The concept of measuring additional issues, first discovered and logged during the problem logging session (as opposed to checking phase) and promoting continuous improvement in it (Cindy Arksey, Boeing, 1989).
- Collecting information from checkers about their checking metrics, as use for entry criteria to the logging meeting.
- When the data about checking is collected at the beginning of the logging meeting, distinguishing between the individual's pages intensively studied at optimum rates, and other individual pages scanned in which issues were reported (including sources, rules, checklists, product commentary).
- During logging, first report issues and improvement suggestions in non-product documents (source, rules, checklists) before reporting the ones in product documents, as a way of prioritizing and emphasizing that we are after those issues too, and that they are important.
- The notion of one-page-everything to keep things simple: one page maximum rule sets, checklists, entry, exit, data summary forms, master plans.
- The distinction between generic and specific rules, checklists, entry and exit criteria, reflecting the very large number of applications of the Inspection method and the need to avoid redundancy or repetition of the same rules.
- Define a 'page' as 600 words and use a word processor word count feature to count pages accurately. This was integrated with the notion developed that the 600 words must be significant 'non-commentary' text (Los Alamos National Labs, New Mexico, 1992).
- The leader should find out during the checking time whether in fact all checkers have had adequate time to do the job at the optimum rate. If not, the logging meeting should be rescheduled to give them time, rather than discovering this problem at the beginning of the logging meeting (Magne Ribe, Ericsson, Hisøy, Norway, 1991).

8.12   Conducting the Process Brainstorming Meeting

8.12.1   Timing

You should plan for the process brainstorming meeting to continue straight after the logging meeting, although a short (three-minute) break would probably be a good idea.

This means that when you schedule the room (and the people) for the logging meeting, you need to make sure that they are also booked for the extra half hour of the brainstorming meeting. Note the start and stop times of the meeting.

The Inspection leader's job in the process brainstorming meeting is to guide the discussion in a very focused way so that the results that we want are produced in the minimum time.

Allow a maximum of 30 minutes for the process brainstorming meeting.

If ten issues are to be discussed in 30 minutes, then each issue can only have three minutes, which is very short. Since there are three things to discuss for each issue, this gives only one minute for identifying and understanding the defect, one minute to brainstorm causes and root causes, and one minute to brainstorm action ideas and process improvement suggestions. Although it may be very difficult to keep to this timetable, it will be highly cost-effective to do so.

People

The same people who were at the logging meeting also continue into the brainstorming meeting.

If there are one or two additional people who you feel should attend the process brainstorming meeting, they may be invited to join at this point. This can create difficulties if the logging meeting does not take the full two hours, so you may want to ask the additional people to be ready to come at a minute's notice at any time within the last part of the logging meeting, or else at the scheduled time. You would of course have to call them into the meeting if it starts earlier than scheduled. People from the Process Change Management Team, for example, may want to attend to gain a fuller understanding of the defects, root causes, and suggested improvements.

Identifying What to Discuss

When the logging meeting finishes, you must identify the issues, that is, potential defects, which will be discussed at the process brainstorming meeting, and this must be done very quickly.

Uncritical Atmosphere

It is important that the uncritical atmosphere of the Inspection logging meeting is preserved in the process brainstorming meeting, but it is more difficult now because we are discussing the defects or issues, not just identifying them.

Particularly when the causes of the defects are considered, it is easy for people to begin to find fault with the author instead of identifying the faults in the process which the author was performing, which led to the defect arising. If the process is faulty, no one can do a good job. For example, if you are told to stick the leg of a table back on with sticky tape instead of wood glue and screws, even the best carpenter cannot do a good job. The fault is in the process description, not the individual.

It is the Inspection leader's responsibility to ensure that the root causes, those which lie in the process, are brainstormed, even though they may be related to the individual author. You could ask whether anyone else had ever made a similar error, for example, to illustrate that the root causes are in the process.

The issues to discuss will normally be the ones raised in the logging meeting, but sometimes there will be other issues or identified defects which should also be discussed at this brainstorming meeting. For example, if one of the issues raised at this Inspection team's previous meeting turned out to be far more serious than was realized at the time, you might want to schedule time to discuss that defect.

More details on the brainstorming meeting are given in Chapter 7.

Small Scale Improvements (Individual 'Candle' Ideas)

It is important that the process improvement suggestions always include small improvements which can be accomplished by a single individual on their own. If every defect resulted in one of these small scale improvements, even if nothing else were ever done, things would begin to improve. Stress the importance and role of each person in 'lighting a candle rather than cursing the darkness'. Avoid megolomanic ideas (like 'fire the Chairman'). Get participants to be practical.

The actions which a single individual can do ('candle' ideas) should be carried out by at least the person who suggested it, and anyone else who feels that they could also take this action. These 'promises' to improve quality in a small way should be recorded and also passed on to the PCMT via the QA database. They should be monitored from time to time to see whether they had any effect, whether they could be improved, whether other organizational processes have stopped them being effective, or whether they could be spread elsewhere in the organization.

Large Scale Improvements

The larger improvement suggestions should also be transferred to the PCMT via the QA database. It is important that every improvement suggestion is recorded, so that Inspectors know their good ideas are not simply disappearing down a 'black hole'. It is also important that they get feedback on their suggestions, for the same reason, whether any organizational changes have been planned or taken place yet or not.

8.13   Collecting, Delivering, and Using Metrics

8.13.1   Collecting Metrics

The Inspection leader is responsible for collecting Inspection data about time used and Issues and defects found. The metrics themselves are the lifeblood of Inspection. They are key to its survival and productivity and must be totally integrated in the Inspection process on a daily basis.

It is the Inspection metrics which give the basic foundation for controlling the process of software development. The essence of statistical process control is that the process is continuously measured, and the results of that measurement are plotted so that we can see what the process is doing over time. The plot of the metrics will show whether the process is in or out of control. Figure 8.13 and Figure 8.14 show an example of each.

Before you can even begin to know whether your software development process is improving, you need to know where it is now. As Watts Humphrey puts it: 'If you don't know where you are, a map won't help' (Humphrey, 1989).

The first thing which the Inspection leader must do is to establish a baseline of measurements about the software development process. This is what Inspection of products provides, by measuring defects.

Once you have accumulated sufficient metrics and you have established that your software development process is in control, then you can begin to experiment by making changes to that process, and observing the results. This is what the Process Change Management Team does. But without the Inspection metrics as a measuring instrument, the results of any experiment are not based on fact, but only at best on 'gut feel' – which can be quite wrong.

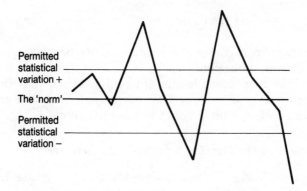

Figure 8.13 A process outside of statistical control (see Deming, *Out of the Crisis*, 1986).

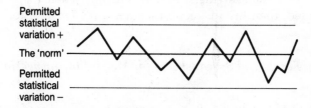

Figure 8.14 A process within statistical control.

Where are the Metrics Collected From?

The Inspection leader has some assistance from others in collecting and judging metrics:

- Inspectors collect data about their individual checking time and the major and minor issues which they have found then;
- the editor will make the final judgement on the classification of the issue and will suggest the final defect metrics.

Although various people may help with classification, the Inspection leader is finally responsible for getting it done properly and turning it over to the Inspection database. There are usually various forms (see Appendix C on Forms) to guide the Inspection leader in the data collection task.

There are basically four sources of metrics:

- what the checkers report about their individual checking (major and minor issues found and time spent);
- the logging meeting itself (major and minor issues logged and time spent);
- final metrics, from the editor (final counts of major and minor defects, editing time spent);
- your time as Inspection leader (planning, overseeing Inspectors, follow-up) – this is outside any additional time you may have spent as a checker, which would be counted above.

What Happens to the Metrics After they are Delivered?

The Inspection leader is responsible for delivering the Inspection metrics about each product Inspected and each cycle for a product which is chunked, to what we have called the 'QA database'. However, it is not necessarily the province of a QA department, and it is not necessarily a database! It is simply some way of keeping track of all the Inspection data in one place, so that analysis of the results can be performed. It needn't even be on a computer, but would very likely be stored in at least a spreadsheet.

If no QA database exists, and it will not when Inspections are first installed, then the Inspection leader is responsible for setting it up.

The Use of Forms and Spreadsheets for Metrics for Inspection Metrics

Appendix C of this book gives a number of examples of forms used for the collection of metrics. Some organizations have also used spreadsheets.

An example is given in the Racal Redac case study in Chapter 15 using an Excel spreadsheet to capture basic Inspection data. The basic spreadsheet looked like an ordinary form, but this form then automatically transmitted its data to another spreadsheet which logged all the basic data and computed totals.

8.13.2 Analyzing Your Own Metrics

The basic metrics of your own Inspections as a leader should be analyzed and compared to other results. Each Inspection leader should regularly be supplied with a suitable updated report to allow this to be done. They should be encouraged to make use of the data in order to improve their methods and their team's performance. They should be given access to both Inspection and test and field metrics which are necessary for full understanding of the economics of Inspection.

In many organizations, an appraisal is held (perhaps annually) of an individual's performance at their job. With the Inspection metrics, you as an Inspection leader can appraise your own performance and your team's, by regularly checking the Inspection metrics against test and field metrics for the products which have exited Inspection. It is the responsibility of Inspection leaders to keep track of their own success.

In a small organization, there many be only a few Inspection leaders, and the teams may vary, so the metrics may only be valid for the whole Inspection process and group of Inspectors.

In a large organization, there may be a sizable team of Inspection leaders, under the direction of a facilitator or senior leader. In this case, the performance of particular Inspection leaders within the Inspection process can be monitored – not for apportioning blame, but to identify where the process (the Inspection process this time) needs to be improved.

One example is the use of the computer as a 'watch-dog' for about a dozen deviations from the norm. This has proved useful and even irreplaceable (due to the large volume of Inspections) for spotting leaders who need help, additional advice or redeployment.

Examples of Using Inspection Metrics

Inspection metrics can be used as a tool to predict how many items should be logged in the logging meeting, as described below.

Experience data:
Predicting the Next Step
Based on past experience, I expect the total number of items logged at the logging meeting to be 30–90% more than the most items found by any one checker during individual checking.

What's the value of predicting how much we will find in the logging meeting? After all, we will find what we find. There's little we can do to control what we find at this point (assuming, of course, that we are careful to observe the optimum rate, specialized roles, and so on).

The Deviation Principle:
If you have a clear idea of what you expect – beforehand – any deviation will attract your notice and indicate a possible problem.

Continues

If you had no prior expectation, you're far more likely to accept whatever happens without question. In this case, deviation from the expected 30–90% increase should trigger the immediate awareness that something might be going wrong; this particular logging meeting might not be nearly as effective as assumed.

In this example (predicting the number of items to be logged at the logging meeting), another reason for prediction exists. When you have a fair idea of how many issues will be logged, and how long it takes to log each issue, you can tell whether or not you allowed enough time for the logging meeting.

Source: Ed Barnard, 1992, Cray Research, Inc., Minnesota, USA

See Ed Barnard's case study (Chapter 13) in this book which gives more detail on this point.

Inspection metrics can be used to predict the amount of time which the editor will need to investigate the issues raised at the logging meeting, as described below.

Experience data:
Estimating Editing Time

Based on the number of items logged in the logging meeting, I predict how long it will take the editor to complete editing. (I base the prediction on the total number of items, not just issues in the candidate document.)

This sets an expectation for the editor, which is especially important for people new to Inspection. The editor might have figured on half an hour's work to clean everything up and get very frustrated after four hours and no end in sight. However, if I tell the editor immediately after the logging meeting that, based on past experience for documents of this type, it should take eight hours, the editor has a much more reasonable expectation.

If the estimated edit time is 36 hours (for example), but the editor absolutely does not have 36 hours to spend on the project, at least we know there's a scheduling problem before beginning the edit. We will have to make tough choices, but at least we can make informed choices.

Continues

This statement of edit time, said out loud at the end of the logging meeting (I quickly calculate the figure while the other participants relax and discuss all those issues they couldn't mention during the logging meeting), gives other participants an idea of what we mean by statistical process control – we can set numeric expectations based on past experience, and feed current experience into the process of setting future expectations.

If I predicted eight hours of edit time and the editor comes back claiming completion in half an hour, I know to carefully investigate this questionable situation.

Source: Ed Barnard, 1992, Cray Research, Inc., Minnesota, USA

8.14   Editing

8.14.1   Controlling Editing Time

It is the Inspection leader's responsibility to ensure that editing is assigned to one or more people, and carried out properly. The Inspection leader's responsibilities include those listed below.

The Inspection leader will compute the estimated editing time by multiplying the total issues (minor and major) by the average experience factor for editing in the Inspection database.

For example, one client found the editing time averaged two minutes per issue. They found 42 issues in a seven page Inspection and computed that the editing time was likely to be approximately 42 (issues) x two (minutes), or 84 minutes. The author (editor) was asked if she had time to tackle this the same day. She said yes, and got the work done. She also asked what would happen if she used more time than the estimate. We said that this would be noted and merely result in an update to our ability to predict editing time better next time.

If more than one person will be needed to complete the edit process before a deadline, the Inspection leader will, as far as possible, ensure that the extra people are made available by the responsible manager.

If the Inspection leader does not have sufficient authority and cannot get enough people to do the job on time, then the Inspection leader must inform the project manager who is responsible for meeting the deadline. The manager will then know of the problem and the options available, and can take appropriate action.

8.14.2 Help the Editor(s)

The Inspection leader is responsible for instructing the editor/ author through to successful exit, including coordinating any editing done by more than one editor.

In particular this means informing them that exit is conditional upon visible reasonable action taken on all logged issues. It also implies that they create formal written change requests for documents outside their immediate control. The change requests must be recorded (for example, in a configuration management system) so that issues raised in the documents outside the scope of this Inspection cycle can be followed up.

There are several advantages to letting the author do the editing, which the Inspection leader should bear in mind:

- they are familiar with the material;
- they will learn from fixing defects;
- they will feel better if they, rather than a stranger, have to decide on the exact action to take on an issue/defect.

It is not taken for granted that the original author will do the editing, because:

- the original author (of the product document or change) may not be available;
- the author may not be available in time to meet a deadline;
- the author may need one or more assistants to get the editing done by a deadline;
- it may be desirable to have another person do the editing in order to familiarize them with it, and thus to guarantee understandability of the work.

8.15 Verifying that Work is Completed: Follow-up by the Inspection Leader

The Inspection leader is responsible for verifying that the editor(s) have attempted, reasonably, to take action on all issues. This is an 'edit checking' process, which is called follow-up.

The Inspection leader is not responsible for ensuring that the actions taken are perfectly correct. The work of the editor is taken on trust (the best basis for constructive work relationships), but in any case the quality of the editing will be further checked in later Inspections, when it is a source and in testing.

However, the Inspection leader is free to check out the quality of an edit attempt to any extent, particularly to ensure that the editor has done a reasonable job as defined by the applicable written rules for the product.

This is particularly important when the editor is new to the material or the company. In general, full checking on the details would both be uneconomic and probably inaccurate.

The editor shall have indicated in writing how each issue was handled, and signal, for example, by a tick on the issue log, that it is completed. It must be possible for the Inspection leader to see immediately, explicitly, and exactly all the changes carried out by the editor, even if the editor has to create a written cross-reference or list of the changes.

The editor shall have completed the final severity classification of all defects.

The Inspection leader needs particularly to check that the editor has inserted suitable cross-reference notes in the product documentation when change requests have been raised. This is so that all who are dependent on it are aware of the potential changes.

The following are *not* required for completion of the follow-up process of Inspection, since they may take some time to come to fruition:

- action taken on a source or other document as a result of a change request;
- response or acknowledgement to a change request;
- action as a result of an improvement suggestion to rules, procedures, standards or checklists.

All of these cases are outside the control of the Inspection team and Inspection leader, and must not be allowed to prevent the Inspection cycle for this particular product being completed. The Inspection leader checks that change requests have been raised, not resolved. They are resolved outside the Inspection process.

If the Inspection leader can see that the edit has not been completed properly, then they must note that a vital exit condition has not been met. The first step is to encourage the editor very seriously to put more effort into completing the edit properly.

If the editor has failed to classify a few items, then the Inspection leader could undertake it personally, rather than delaying exit.

8.16   Exit

The final stage of the Inspection process for products is the exit, which mirrors the entry stage. Just as we did not allow products into the Inspection process if they were not of adequate quality, so we don't allow them out of the Inspection process unless they are of adequate quality. The exit process is the sole responsibility of the Inspection leader.

8.16.1   Exit Criteria

Basic (generic) exit criteria are listed below. However, you should also look for a more specific exit condition list when using this general one.

The main principle of the exit stage is that you as Inspection leader have checked that all exit criteria have been met before signing for approved exit.

Basic generic exit criteria are:

(1) All editing has been completed (that is, you have successfully validated the edit in your follow-up).
(2) All necessary change request cross-references are inserted in the product document.
(3) Data summary is completed and sent to the database.
(4) There are no more than 0.25 (or two to three for beginners!) major defects per page remaining, calculated based on removal effectiveness (between 30% and 88%) and defect insertion rate (one of six attempts fails, according to IBM).
(5) Check that the rate (pages or lines per hour) of individual checking and of the logging meeting did not exceed the known optimum rate by more than 20% on average. (Otherwise you may have missed too many defects which will then be sent on to others, even after correcting the defects you did find.)
(6) Either the author/owner or the Inspection leader can veto the exit based on their subjective belief that release would be a danger to their document customers.

Completing Statistical Reports

The Inspection leader can now complete the Inspection data summary based on the final data from follow-up, and this must be done before exit from Inspection is permitted.

The reason why the handover of statistical data is a generic exit criterion is to ensure that the entire system is really kept up-to-date. Inspection needs up-to-date metrics about what is going on to keep it supported by management.

The exit condition of delivering statistical data is the rough equivalent of not paying people their travel expenses until they have delivered the expense report.

The data summary needs to be entered into the Inspection or QA database in some way. Some companies let the Inspection leader do this personally (key it in). In some cases it may be done automatically. In some cases it might be sufficient to hand in copies of these sheets to someone responsible for the metrics.

The issue logs also need to be filed for future reference. File them either as a binder of Inspection issue logs by Inspection number or in a computerized QA database. They need to be kept in case anyone wants to analyze them, such as the Process Change Management Team.

8.16.2   Successful Exit Constitutes a Milestone Deliverable

When the Inspection leader signs off on successful exit, the work is officially complete. Authors can now claim to have met their deadlines. The work is deemed safe for processing by other people in the 'downstream' work processes. Note that successful exit for the author's product is usually an entry condition for the next work process, their 'customer', and for the next Inspection where this product document is a source document.

The status of the product document is no longer a 'candidate', but is now of 'exited' status. If Inspections are carried out properly, this gives some kind of guarantee of quality for that document, although even the best Inspections only find up to 88% of the errors. So even exited status certainly does not guarantee perfection!

If the product has been chunked into several sections which were checked separately with several different logging meetings, then all Inspection chunks must be completed before the document itself can exit from the Inspection process.

An Inspection which has not completed its exit is not a true Inspection. The power of the Inspection method is that it demands that the job is finished and completed, and not skimped at the end for lack of time. If quality products are to be produced, this is where it is critical that the job is done right.

There is no point in knowing that you have lots of defects if you have not fixed them correctly and thoroughly. This doesn't give you good quality, it gives you known levels of poor quality.

It is absolutely essential, therefore, that you as Inspection leader resist all pressures to cut corners at this stage of Inspection. Insist that all exit criteria are fully met.

8.17 Managing Change

8.17.1   Process Change Management Teams (PCMT)

In the description of process brainstorming, we recommended an initial informal process which effectively makes a Inspection team itself into a change agent. At some point you may wish to strengthen the institution of change and might consider using the concept of Process Change Management Teams.

The task of the Process Change Management Teams (PCMT) is, with the support of a manager, to ensure that improvement suggestions logged during process brainstorming are really followed up, and that they do result in real improvement in the organization.

If you are a leader, and you sense the need for more effective follow-up of the logged improvement suggestions, then you can argue for a budget and appropriate powers and go about seeing how you and your fellow leaders can make the change happen.

Managers of the leaders should note that this is an excellent training ground for future managers. The achievements reflect on the whole group as the improvements roll in – not just for the improvements themselves, but for the way in which they were arrived at.

8.17.2   Becoming a Local Champion

You may be reading this book and there is no Inspection in your organization. You have an excellent opportunity to become the local champion of Inspections. Some champions have had such good results that they got Corporate recognition (awards from the Chairman), unfortunately not all as generous as the $50,000 Outstanding Contribution award Michael Fagan received in 1979.

Alan F. Brown of ICL England has also received awards. (See his case study chapter on Inspections in Gilb, 1988). Some have not, like one individual at Douglas Aircraft, who has not yet received formal award recognition of his champion role (that is not his company's style) – but many top managers are well aware of who he is.

It seems that the Inspection method itself is so powerful that people assume the person promoting it must be some kind of an exceptional genius. In fact, few are, but the world needs heroes and we shouldn't disillusion them.

The 3M Company is reported to have a rule.

A 'good' idea without a champion – 'not approved'.
An idea with a self-appointed enthusiastic champion – 'give it a try'.

There are plenty of 'good' ideas. It takes the hard work of a champion to turn them into useful change. For further reading on the role of a change agent, see Bouldin (1989) or Pressman (1988).

8.18   Managing Leaders

8.18.1   Who Manages Inspection Leaders?

The Inspection leader is a 'freelance' job. It comes as a supplement to some other main job. Just as the normal manager of the Inspector/ checker may not be trained or able to lead an Inspection, the manager of the Inspection leader manages the leader in their 'normal' life, but is probably not aware of the special needs and requirements of managing the Inspection-leading aspects of their subordinate's role within the company. So the problem arises of how to manage the leaders in the Inspection task.

It is important that that the Inspection-leading part of the leader's work is adequately managed. The right balance between Inspection-leading and other work must be struck. The time spent on leading Inspections is all part of the cost of the Inspection process and therefore needs to be controlled. The Inspection leader also needs to have someone to turn to when they encounter problems in leading the Inspections, someone who knows and understands those problems and can help to solve them.

Initial management of leaders may well come from the champions, those people who were most keen to get Inspections started within the organization, but that may be only during the start-up phases.

There may be some people who were instrumental in getting Inspections started, or who were early supporters of the technique, who received some of the earliest training, and who after a while have more experience than the other newer Inspection leaders. They can be called senior leaders, and they may be given a relatively formal role in managing the leaders.

Another possibility is to assign management of the Inspection leaders to the quality function (for example, quality assurance). This has worked well in many organizations, since Inspections are obviously a quality improvement technique.

Each organization must find their own solution. The solution may change over time, and it may vary from one part of the organization to another. It is important to realize that there are alternatives, and if one method is not working, try another.

8.18.2 The Chief Inspection Leader Role

In a larger organization, there is a need for more formal professional guidance for Inspection leaders which neither their classroom trainer nor their boss can give. The 'chief leader' is usually a practicing leader who is formally assigned the task, and can use time to deal with problems which leaders struggle with. The chief leader might undertake some of the following tasks:

- Certify new leaders by taking responsibility for monitoring their first two Inspections after their initial training.
- Assist other leaders on request with any difficulties they may have. Provide a shoulder to cry on when an Inspection turns sour, to analyze and correct the situation.
- Analyze metrics with a view to seeing opportunity and need for improvements in the Inspection process. Look for both exceptionally good and exceptionally bad results.
- Attend logging meetings with a view to bringing ideas to their leaders and picking up new good ideas.
- Communicate to their group of Inspection leaders any improvements in the Inspection process.
- Solicit any ideas for improvement of the Inspection process from other leaders.
- Experiment with improvements to the Inspection process.
- Provide feedback to Inspection trainers about weaknesses and suggested improvements in the training courses for leaders, managers, and new Inspectors.
- Participate as a leader trainer.
- Keep practicing as an Inspection leader.
- Be a model for others of really good Inspection leadership.
- Help improve tools: procedures, checklists, rules, forms.
- Take advanced education, attend conferences, join the Inspection user group (SIRO in USA, QA Forum in UK, Ariadne in Norway for example[†]), visit other organizations to get relevant new ideas.
- Sit on company councils or task forces for improving software engineering.

8.18.3 Certification and Re-certification of Leaders

Inspection leaders need to be certified for roughly the same reasons that aircraft pilots require certification. They are in charge of something which is very important and the way they do their job can

[†] SIRO (Software Inspection and Review Organisation), PO Box 61015, Sunnyvale, CA 94088-1015, USA; Quality Assurance Forum, 17 St Catherines Road, Ruislip, Middlesex HA4 7RX, UK; Ariadne Consulting, Storgt. 18, 1440 Drøbak, Norway.

make a large difference to the organization they work for. Although not doing Inspections properly is not generally considered a life or death situation, in fact software defects have been instrumental in resulting in death in a number of different types of software, from medical systems, aircraft control systems to robot control systems. Even the use of 'ordinary' software such as a spreadsheet or word processor, if used for a critical application, could have serious or fatal consequences.

Leaders do not merely become leaders by appointment or accident. They should have had a two or three day course on the theory of Inspection, two days for experienced checkers and three days for complete beginners without Inspection experience. The training for Inspection leaders should consist of a fairly large percentage of practical work in running an Inspection in a classroom situation, where they can make their inevitable learning mistakes in a 'safe' environment, and can ask the many questions which will occur when they actually do it for the first time themselves. It also allows the trainers to observe and correct any initial misconceptions before the leader starts for real.

Next, the new Inspection leader should carry out two real Inspections under the eye of the chief leader, a senior leader or their Inspection trainer. This, if successful, leads to initial certification of the leader, which means they appear on the official list of certified leaders. It is an entry criterion that a certified leader must lead an Inspection.

During their tenure, which probably should include a minimum number of hours 'flown' each year, their metrics will be compared to norms and any negative deviation corrected.

Metrics are used to help the leader do a reasonable job. However, if after a reasonable amount of experience, a new leader is unable or unwilling to do a job comparable to acceptable leaders, then that person needs to be removed from the leader certification list. Since this is a part-time job, most people do not feel too threatened by this. They may well have already concluded themselves that the job of Inspection leader was not for them. It is important that the certification qualification is not diluted by allowing leaders to remain on the list when it is common knowledge that they are not pulling their weight. It will not help those who are trying to maintain the high standards of Inspection leadership within the organization if those standards are not adequately enforced.

8.19   Advanced Leader Pointers

This section contains some practical pointers and tips on becoming a better Inspection leader.

8.19.1 The Leader as a Diplomat

Inspection is a 'people-intensive process'. People are very sensitive to criticism. They are also sensitive to encouragement, appreciation, and praise. The leader needs people-management skills, as opposed to technical skills. These skills can be improved with adequate awareness and training.

The necessary people skills for being a leader will be necessary and useful for the remainder of your engineering and management career. Don't be afraid to develop them.

Positive and Negative Strokes for Authors

The person who is most sensitive in the Inspection process is the author. No matter how well prepared the author is, no matter how well they understand the motivation for the Inspection process, no matter how well they understand that everyone is helping to improve the quality of their work, a logging meeting still feels like a personal attack, particularly the first time the author is in the 'hot seat'.

It is a very important part of the Inspection leader's job to protect the author from what may feel like total devastation. Here are some tactics which may help.

Avoiding Negative Strokes

- No criticism of the author is ever permitted in the logging meeting.
- No unsolicited advice. No saying 'you should', 'you ought to', unless the author specifically asks for help, in which case keep it brief, or better still postpone it until after the logging meeting.
- Allow questions of intent ('Give me your wisdom, author, I don't know if I understand').
- The author is also a checker, often the best one. Give praise where due when this happens.
- The author is always present when their work is Inspected.
- Privacy – don't talk outside of the team about issues raised.
- Separate the product from person, and focus on product.
- The author was working inside a software development process which may be defective, virtually guaranteeing that the product cannot be perfect.
- The issue/defect count includes all document problems, including sources so the count does not only refer to the author's work.
- The author (as editor) has power to decide what to fix. The editor can reclassify issues and decide what are really defects and need to be fixed, and what needs to be sent to others.
- The team is jointly co-responsible for the quality of the product.
- The leader must protect the author's ego. Warn the author that a large number of items may be reported, tell the author that issue or

defect data will not be used against them (and make sure it never is!).

- Do not report detailed information to supervisors, use aggregated data to retain anonymity.

Giving Positive Strokes to Authors

Here are some tactics which will help to give positive strokes to the author:

- Remember that everyone takes their turn in the 'hot seat', and you will be doing the same thing to them another time. It won't be personal on your part then, so it is not personal on their part now.
- The author has an audience that can appreciate a job done well in spite of issues raised.
- By giving time voluntarily and working on finding potential defects, checkers are showing that they care. They are also showing that they accept co-responsibility.
- Recognize that causes of some issues come from input documents (source, rule set and checklist).
- Trust the author (as editor) to fix and classify problems.
- Later rewards will come as a result of delivery of superior product in the end ('making the author a hero').
- Intersperse compliments to the author for clever, concise or clear work during the meeting. Start and end the meeting by having everyone find something good to say about the product.

8.19.2   General Improvements to the Process

Dealing with Bureaucracy

If you are part of a large company, then a frustrating bureaucracy probably exists. It is not evil in intent. But few bureaucracies (except perhaps Inspection!) are intentionally designed to encourage and permit change. Inspection requires change. So you have to expect to deal with your bureaucracy to get Inspection installed and working well.

Any rule, order, or management attitude which hurts successful use of the Inspection process needs to be challenged, in the name of the results you are trying to get with Inspection. This includes challenging not only things related to the Inspection process (like eliminating older ways of reviewing). It includes challenging surrounding disciplines such as development rule sets, forms, codes, tools.

The beauty of Inspection is that you can prove the need for change using Inspection statistical data, and you can prove that your changes are working in practice – before suggesting that others might like to get the benefits you have proven are possible.

Improving Teamwork

Your job as team leader is constantly to emphasize the shared responsibility for the quality of work performed and delivered. Your team, which normally includes the author, is jointly responsible for:

- a correct Inspection procedure;
- finding about 60–88% (maximum possible normally) of the remaining defects in all documents run through the Inspection process;
- helping each other to learn Inspection;
- helping each other to understand the documents' content;
- helping colleagues and 'customers' of the documents to get quality input to their work (you are not done until a proper exit is achieved);
- giving honest assessments of defect root causes – to ensure cause removal;
- assisting team-mates in any way they can during Inspection;
- visibly respecting each other and all involved authors.

You need to emphasize team results – 'improvement suggestions logged' or 'major issues logged per minute'. You need to ask strong team members to give novices the first option for logging issues and improvements. Strong team members should show their strength by doing for the team what others cannot.

Improving the Inspection Process

The Inspection process itself undergoes continual improvement in the following ways:

- individuals get more skilled;
- existing written rules get applied gradually, which were not yet in force or heeded;
- new rules are tried out;
- procedures are improved;
- checklists are improved;
- authors improve their software development skills and learn to avoid defects.

The leader should be aware of the need and ability for Inspection to improve forever. Your job is to use every opportunity to promote improvement and change. You can exercise great power in this respect.

There should be a feeling of friendly rivalry amongst Inspection teams and leaders. The Inspection metrics should be used to compare results so that all can emulate the better performers.

There should be some means of communication amongst leaders so that experiences can be shared. You could use an informal newsletter, or have meetings and joint presentations amongst leaders. (See the case study in Chapter 15 for a sample newsletter.)

Sometimes leaders participate as checkers or authors on some other leader's team. Improvement then can happen as a result of observing a better practice. Or, an improvement can be the result of a diplomatically-given suggestion to the host leader.

Leader responsibility ends with successful exit of the material. The team may dissolve, and the leader may get a different team the next time.

8.19.3   How to Run Inspections under Deadline Pressure

What to Do

- Follow the Inspection process standards (rules, procedures, entry, exit). Leaving defects in the documents will never save real time on the project, unless you can deliver garbage, in which case you certainly don't need Inspection to help you.
- Respect the optimum rates of individual checking and rate of checking at logging meeting. Even small deviations can result in leaving behind defects which will cost far more to remove during testing and field trials.
- Keep doing Inspections! It saves project time.
- Inspect on a sampling basis, and keep careful track of what has been Inspected and what has not (to prove how much time was wasted later by not Inspecting everything).
- If your manager claims that Inspections are too expensive, ask 'compared to what?'
- Inform management of the risks they are taking, and the estimated extra costs downstream if the defects remain where they are. Get the management to sign their acceptance of these risks.

What Not to Do

- Don't extend logging meetings over two straight hours without chunking the material.
- Don't cheat on Inspections by going faster than the optimum rates and thus push defects over to colleagues or customers.
- Don't use fewer people. The number of people on an Inspection team should be the economic optimum. Reducing it means losing productivity and time. Sometimes, this is an indirect loss like sales

lost due to defective product, which doesn't become evident until a long time later. So there is a real problem of how to convince people to care about the whole, rather than their narrow part.[†]

8.19.4   The Inspection Leader's Bill of Rights

Here is a 'Bill of Rights' for leaders which we originally gave to the first graduation class at Douglas Aircraft in January 1988. It seemed to inspire the young engineers to immediate constructive action.

Bill of Rights for Inspection Leaders

(1) You have the right of access to all documents that are relevant to your work (anything which will help your team to identify potential defects).

(2) You have the right to take any action that should optimize the team's work time. You also have the obligation to validate the actual value of the action.

(3) You have the right to use at least three work-hours per week in pursuing any idea or experiment which can, in your view, improve your team's effectiveness (issues found per work-hour).

(4) You have the right to at least half an hour for a process brainstorming meeting after the logging meeting.

(5) You have the right to contact anyone in the company to ask for information, documents, advice or experience that will help in your defect finding or process improvement.

(6) You have the right to resist deadline pressure in order to do the quality work that is necessary to save downstream costs and time in delivering products to customers.

(7) You have the right to supplement or modify your tools (like the checklists or rules) if you can thereby increase your team's productivity.

(8) You have the right to request and use all metrics.

(9) You have the right to take any initiative and to encourage others in taking initiatives that will improve the consistency of delivered quality.

---

† The problem of motivating people to care is treated stimulatingly in Tom Peters *Thriving on Chaos: A handbook for management revolution*, also Tom Peters *Liberation Management* (1992) and Jan Carlzon *Moments of Truth*.

8.19.5 Summary

There is no official rule book for Inspections. Indeed, Inspection has to be flexible in order to continue to give better results. There are many different environments in which Inspection can be helpful. What works in one may not work so well in another, because of differing objectives in using Inspection. Some want document quality improvement, some want to improve the learning environment for employees, some want to break down communication barriers separating their employees, some want a continuous process improvement programme. Whatever the objectives, they will also change as circumstances change, and the role of Inspection must reflect this.

The only basic rule is statistical process control. If you do not collect metrics on defects and time usage and make intelligent use of it, you can have no factual data to support your opinions. You are not doing Inspection.

The Inspection leader has responsibility for the Inspection process, and is more than a meeting moderator. The leader's role is critical to the success of Inspection. The following summarizes the main leader tasks:

Select Inspection Material

- Identify and if necessary chunk the task product document(s) submitted as a candidate for Inspection.
- Check all formal entry criteria for the candidate product.
- Check that all relevant source documents are of acceptable quality (ideally exited from Inspection).
- Identify relevant parts and versions of rules, procedures and standards.

Select Inspection Team/Book Venue

- Identify potential checkers, and confirm acceptability of selected checkers with author.
- Verify checkers' availability for individual checking, kickoff meeting and logging meeting (ensure enough checkers are available).
- Reserve meeting rooms for kickoff, logging, and brainstorming meetings.
- Select, evaluate, and update checklists to be used by Inspectors in checking, including role checklists.
- Assign roles (in master plan).
- Send out Inspection master plans.
- Distribute Inspection materials: candidate product or chunk,

source document(s), relevant rules, procedures and standards, and checklists (alternatively, this may be done in the kickoff meeting).

Conduct Kickoff Meeting (if held)

- Hand out materials (if not already distributed).
- Give background information about materials if required.
- Confirm roles or re-assign.
- Suggest and negotiate acceptance for numeric objectives and corresponding strategies for the current cycle of the Inspection process and emphasize finding unique major issues.
- Confirm optimum checking rates.
- Confirm logging and brainstorming meeting venue.

Logging-meeting Leader Preparation

- Obtain blank copies of issue logging forms, or electronic recording machine.
- Complete the Inspection summary header with pre-logging meeting data.
- Remind Inspectors (if necessary) to be there on time and check if they have carried out their checking or have plans in place to do so.
- Arrive early.

Conducting the Logging Meeting

- Record start time of meeting.
- Note Inspectors' checking time and other data requested in the master plan on the Inspection summary.
- Remind Inspectors of the rules and aims of the meeting.
- Control logging of issues in all documents (product, source, rules, checklist).
- Control logging of questions to the author and improvement suggestions.
- Ensure all issues are recorded (by scribe or self). Ensure that the editor monitors recorded issues so that he or she will be able to understand them later.
- Ensure that adequate time is allowed for identification of new issues in the meeting (synergy) and ensure the newly-found issues are noted as such in the log.
- Record stop time of meeting (maximum two hours).

Conduct Process Brainstorming Meeting

- Record start time of meeting.
- Select issues/potential defects to analyze.
- Control discussion of defect causes and improvements.

- Encourage brainstorming of improvement keywords.
- Record stop time of meeting.

Generate Metrics

- Verify or increase legibility of recorded issues, if necessary.
- Classify issues' severity (major and minor) if not recorded (editor can correct this judgement).
- Tally the number of issues logged and time spent on checking to Inspection summary.
- Record the number of new issues raised in the logging meeting on the Inspection summary.
- Fill out any other data required by the Inspection data summary page.
- Estimate editing effort.
- Assign editing and agree schedule/deadline.

Follow-up

- Verify that all recorded issues have had some reasonable action taken.
- Verify that required change requests have been raised.
- Record final metrics in data summary as given by the editor.

Exit Check

- Check all exit criteria.
- Act to remove exit problems if necessary.
- Give exit sign-off when all exit criteria have been met, and record in QA Database.

9

The Inspection Experience from Specialist Viewpoints

The purpose of this section of the book is to look at the Inspection process from the point of view of particular participants. Some description of the method will be repeated. The objective is to help individuals to understand what to expect, and it makes useful reading for beginners joining an Inspection team.

9.1 Inspection from a Checker's Point of View

9.1.1 Initial Approach

You will first hear about Inspection from someone in your organization whose document has been Inspected, who has been on an Inspection team, or from an Inspection leader, or from someone else who is trying to get Inspection up and working or spread throughout your organization.

You will register your interest with the team leader, chief team leader, quality assurance department, or whoever will be organizing the Inspection, so that your name will be put on the list of potential checkers who will be invited to take part in an Inspection.

9.1.2 Training: Formal and On-the-Job

Your might then be sent on a one-day or half-day training course so that you understand the purpose of Inspection, the need for the rigorous discipline required, and will have some idea of what is expected of you in your checking time, and what takes place during the meeting.

More likely, if there is an Inspection culture already in your organization that you can join, you will simply appear at your first kickoff meeting, and learn on the job. You will be taught whatever you need to know in a number of ways. The main source of learning is the Inspection leader, who is trained to be your teacher. In addition, there are strong silent teachers such as written procedures for each sub-task, rules, checklists, and master plans that you will be given, as well as your own observation of your team-mates.

9.1.3   Getting Started

You will be asked if you can join a team by the Inspection leader. Your acceptance will depend partly on your ability to find the necessary time and to be in the right places with enough time for individual checking and meetings with the team.

You will get a set of materials starting with a one-page master plan. This will tell you where and when meetings will be held, your special roles, and list all documents you will need to work with. These documents will include:

* *procedures*: informing you of expected best practice for your participation in each sub-task of Inspection.
* *rules*: these will tell you how documents should have been written in relation to their source documents, and will define the notion of an 'issue'.
* *checklists*: these will give you specific questions to ask of the documents so as to identify issues, in addition to those the rules will help you find.

You might be given copies of some documents, you might have to find other documents on your own (especially for a special role), and access others electronically (based on retrieval codes in the master plan).

9.1.4   Kickoff Meeting

Any documents not already distributed to checkers should appear by the kickoff meeting. Most documents should be marked with a reference tag in their upper right corner, for ease of reference in the master plan and in the entire Inspection process. Sometimes, line numbers will have been added to each page to be used (see Figure 9.1). Some documents may not be used in their entirety, so the relevant sections to use will also be pointed out (for example, 'use checklist questions CDES16 -> CDES35').

Your special issue-searching roles will be assigned in the master plan. If you are unhappy with your role, the Inspection leader may be prepared to change it. Remember that you are free to find issues which are outside the scope of any role you have been given at any time. You will probably be given a checklist which defines your particular role.

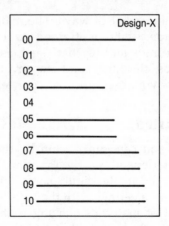

Figure 9.1 Example of reference tag and line numbers for ease of reference.

The leader will provide group or individual instruction on the next work process, 'checking'. This will include general methods, special roles, interpretation and use of procedures, rules, checklists, source documents, and co-operation among team members. The objective is to get all team members ready to play their part effectively and find as many major issues as possible as a team.

The team, led by suggestions from the leader, will attempt to improve their past performance as a team. They will adopt self-chosen quantified improvement objectives. 'We will try to find more than five major issues per 100 lines of code'. They will then adopt self-chosen improvement strategies designed to help them attain those goals. 'And we will slow down our checking rate to 0.8 pages per check-hour'.

This procedure is designed to inject continuous experimentation, creativity, and 'sport' into the Inspection process itself. The process brainstorming and Process Change Management Teams, by contrast, are more likely to attack and improve the software engineering processes surrounding Inspection.

9.1.5 Individual Checking

The time you spend in individual checking is probably the most important in the Inspection process. You must spend enough time so that you will be effective at finding issues. This involves studying the documents, comparing them against each other, going through rules and checklists, all with a 'fine tooth comb'.

Your aim is to find as many major unique (nobody else on the team finds them) issues as you can. Concentrate on major issues.

Think about the consequences of a potential defect. Think of the financial or legal effects, for example. Think of how a problem here might affect other documents or code 'downstream'. .

Try to find not only the obvious issues, which probably everyone will see (but note them anyway in case they don't), but the really difficult and obscure ones, particularly if they will have major effects or repair costs later on. Try to find something which no one else could have thought of, but you noticed because of your expertise and experience, and which, had you not noticed it, would cause serious problems later on.

Recommended Checking Time

The checking time agreed is a guideline, not an absolute law. There is considerable individual variation from the average upon which optimum rates of checking are calculated. If you have used all your recommended checking time but are still finding issues, carry on. On the other hand, if you have not yet used all of your time, but have spent a reasonable amount of time at it and haven't found anything new for ten minutes or so, then stop. Consult with the Inspection Leader about what you have done.

Record or note the issues you have found in any way you like provided you will be able to make sense of it during the meeting. Record the time you actually spent in the checking activity. Also note the number of pages (or lines) studied, scanned, and used, and major and minor issues, which are requested at the bottom of the master plan.

You should look for issues not only in the candidate document being inspected, but also in the source document, the rules, procedures and checklists. Since Inspection only finds 80% of existing issues at best, the use of a previously exited source document should reveal some of the issues missed last time.

What if You Find a Lot of Issues?

If, when you first start your checking, you find that the product document or an exited source document are obviously very full of issues on each page, notify the Inspection leader immediately. It will waste everyone's time to spend a lot of effort on rubbish. The Inspection leader should have already checked the document as part of the entry process so that it couldn't get as far as this in such a bad condition. But Inspection leaders aren't perfect either, and if they are not expert in dealing with this particular type of document, they should get it entry-checked by someone who is.

9.1.6   Logging Meeting

Report your checking metrics (noted at the bottom of your copy of the master plan) to the Inspection leader when requested to do so in the meeting. How much time have you spent, and how many issues have you found (classified at least by your initial major/minor judgement)?

As the Inspection leader takes the group through the documents, report the issues which you have found in as concise and objective a manner as possible. Give document, page, and line number references first (if that's the way the Inspection leader requests them). Give the tag reference for the rule violation or checklist question. If needed, describe the issue in the minimum number of words to get the idea across – a maximum of seven words is a practical guideline.

Pay attention to the other issues being reported. Use the report of issues which you did *not* find to stimulate your thoughts about other issues which might be there but which you didn't see during checking. Much of the value of the logging meeting is to stimulate you to find additional major issues.

The Inspection leader's word is final in the running of the meeting. If you are cut off in something which you want to say, there will be a reason for it. If you don't stick to reporting issues objectively, according to the rules and checklists, this will be cut off immediately. If you get into involved discussions or arguments – the leader will stop you. If your idea is a 'valuable technical insight', there is no space for it here. Make a note to yourself about it. Later you can pass the idea on to the author or editor in private. We don't want to inhibit your creativity – just direct it to where it will be most productively used.

The main activity at the logging meeting is reporting and finding more issues for rapid-fire logging at a rate of one or more per minute. Any other conversation leads quickly to side-tracks and can lead away from the Inspection process.

Process Brainstorming Meeting

If a process brainstorming meeting is held immediately after the logging meeting, this is the time to think of ways to improve your work process so that the type of issues found will be less likely to occur again.

The leader will pick a sample of about ten serious issues for three-minutes of discussion each.

The first minute gives you a chance to find the issue in your documentation. At the same time your team will suggest a cause category (communication, oversight, transcription, education) for the purpose of focusing your ideas in the particular area.

The second minute you will brainstorm keywords (no criticism or analysis) as to the reason why you think errors leading to issues like this are committed.

The third minute you can brainstorm keywords about what types of changes in your work process might be implemented to prevent such issues from occurring in the future. This is a chance to be creative, and to start change in your local work environment.

There are no right or wrong answers here. Your ideas will form part of the inputs to a deeper analysis to be done by a 'Process Change Management Team'.

9.2   Inspection from the Author/Editor's Point of View

9.2.1   Submitting your Work for Checking and Approval

If you would like your own work to be Inspected, start thinking about any improvements which you may be able to make *before* your document is ready to be checked. Have you yourself checked it against the complete set of generic and specific rules for producing it? You should make sure that your document is as good as you can reasonably make it *before* it is submitted.

When your product document is ready for checking, inform your supervisor or the Inspection leader, and submit a copy of it.

You will be included on the team. Your presence as author is an entry requirement to the Inspection process. You will be included in the master plan with especially assigned issue-searching roles.

9.2.2   Kickoff Meeting for the Author

Attend the kickoff meeting with the other checkers. The Inspection leader may have been able to find additional documentation which you were not aware of when you produced your document which might help to improve it. You will be given this at the kickoff meeting.

There are two main things going on at the kickoff meeting: training and Inspection improvement.

9.2.3   Checking by the Author

It is vitally important for you to do the checking as well as the other checkers. Don't assume that you will not be able to see anything new in it just because you wrote it in the first place.

The role which you were assigned, and the checklists you were given, should enable you to bring a fresh outlook and to find things which escaped you before. It may be that the Inspection leader has discovered a source document or rules which you had overlooked and which should have been taken into account, and you may be able to put your finger on the relevant areas very quickly.

If you feel, when you begin your checking, that there are a lot of issues that you would prefer to put right before the logging meeting, notify the Inspection leader immediately so that the decision can be made whether or not to cancel the checking process. Remember you are not aiming at absolute perfection before checking, although you don't want to put up a document which does not show your best level of professionalism. It needs to be, within reason, about as good as you can make it before you volunteer it in the first place.

The Inspection leader will have made an entry check already. The leader will have tried to determine whether your candidate document was ready for checking, or if it has too many issues after a simple surface check of a few minutes. Remember that finding lots of issues in your own document when checking doesn't make you a poorer author, it makes you a better issue-finder. Then, when corrected, it makes you a better author.

9.2.4   Logging Meeting for the Author

Don't be threatened by a large number of issues being logged. If you are the unlucky 'guinea pig' whose work is being checked this rigorously for the first time, it can be a rather daunting experience! Once you have been through it a few times, however, you soon realize that everyone has their turn in the 'hot seat' and issues are found in everyone's work.

A major purpose of the meeting is to help you – to improve the quality of your product document. Every issue found is a distinct quality improvement. What your friends and team-mates find now is confidential and private to the Inspection team – both as to quantity and to detail. This is your last chance to improve things before your document is exposed to a less friendly public. Make the most of it.

A practical tip is to say 'thank you' to every issue reported (even if you can't bring yourself to say it out loud – at least not every time – do try to think it to yourself). This can be a great help in establishing your own positive attitude, and will also help to put the other Inspectors at their ease. They may feel uncomfortable criticizing a friend, especially if they don't know you appreciate it.

The way time is spent in Inspection bears no direct relationship to the total quality of the document. All of the time is spent on issues. Furthermore, the document itself does not actually deteriorate throughout the meeting (which is what it feels like), but it actually improves (which you will appreciate afterward when editing).

Questions of Intent

The checkers will log questions of intent for you to answer at the very end of the logging meeting. Additional issues may be logged as a result of your answers. You (as editor) are not obliged to make any written changes as a result of such a question. It is in the log to give you the opportunity, if you want to upgrade your document, to 'explain' in writing to readers who might not have been present at your reply to the question or who might not remember or have understood your explanation. Think of this as protecting yourself from continuing to be misunderstood.

9.2.5   Process Brainstorming Meeting for the Author

The process brainstorming meeting will highlight some of the handicaps under which you were working when you produced the document. The focus is no longer on your document or you. The entire team will focus on the present working environment; the training, the time to do the job, and the tools to do it correctly.

Here is your chance to contribute directly what the other team members can only guess at. What was the real underlying reason for an issue? Do you need better training and information from your company? Do you need better tools? Were you given far too little time to do the job by your boss?

The author is the star of this scene. The prime purpose of the whole exercise is to find out from you where the company is creating its own difficulties, and what it could do better in the future. Don't just gripe in the cafeteria! Tell management how they must improve your working environment, or themselves take responsibility for their contribution to the problems.

This is Deming's basic teaching. Management is to blame for systematic lack of quality. Process brainstorming is how we tell company management what we think is the real problem with the software development process.

9.2.6   The Author in the Role of Editor

You are normally responsible for editing your document. You will systematically analyze and edit each item on the issue log.

Not all of the things logged as issues will actually be defects in your document; there will also be issues found in the source documents, the rules, and checklists.

Sometimes what is logged as an issue is a 'misunderstanding' on the part of an individual checker. However, if it is possible that something can be misunderstood in this way, then really that is a problem, at least in the explanatory materials (like comments). It may indicate deficiencies of training. For example, your analysis says: 'this wording is company shorthand for the concept, but the new graduate hadn't been told.' As a result, you could choose to add an explanation in your text, to avoid any future misunderstanding. You might choose to add a glossary of terms in your document. You might choose to send a change request to the owner of the generic rules regarding the use of 'company shorthand'. You might choose to send an improvement suggestion to include company shorthand in the induction course for new employees.

Nobody can Dictate Exactly What you Change

No checker can determine exactly how you handle the issue. You are responsible. The checkers are just giving you signals as to how things are actually read. We never blame the individuals involved; neither the 'novice' checker for not knowing company culture yet, nor you, the author, for not realizing how little some other people know.

You must focus first on correcting the situation so that your document cannot be misinterpreted by anyone who might have to work with it. Secondly, you will consider correcting the situation at a higher level, by suggesting that the process be improved.

Your decision on what to do for the edit is final, but every issue logged must have some action taken; a change, further explanation, a change request, and so on. The one thing you are not allowed to do is to ignore any logged issue. A logged issue is not necessarily an 'error' on your part. It is, however, proof that the real organization out there did have, and thus will probably continue to have, some sort of problem in the future unless you act to prevent it now.

Notify the Inspection leader when your edit is completed. The Inspection leader will check your edit, and will tell you if they regard it as complete. Passing the edit check is only one hurdle your document must pass in order to achieve exit status.

10
Installation and Training

How can something so good ever fail?

> 'We tried Inspections here once, but they were a disaster. We're never doing that again.'

> 'Inspection is a dirty word here now. We can do reviews but we don't dare call them Inspections.'

Inspection can be the most cost-effective quality improvement method ever used in your organization. But the way in which Inspection is introduced into the organization is critical to achieving those benefits.

Change introduced in the wrong way may well engender suspicion, resistance, resentment or even sabotage (we'll make sure it doesn't work here). Once an attitude of 'never again' is established about a certain technique, no matter how good the technique is in itself, it is doubly hard if not impossible to make it work in practice.

The case studies in this book (Chapters 12 to 17) are written by people who played an active part in getting Inspection installed in their respective organizations – with varying degrees of success. The aim is to provide 'real world' illustrations of what can happen within the process and within an organization, and in particular what difficulties they encountered and the solutions they found to them. The case study from Trevor Reeve of Thorn EMI (Chapter 14) gives an example of a good implementation plan for managing the change process in installing Inspection.

10.1 Installation

10.1.1 Implementing Change within an Organization

Just as software development follows a life cycle, and the Inspection process has a series of steps, so the process of introducing change to an organization also follows a cycle, which is briefly outlined in the change steps described below.

A number of books, seminars, and consultants describe 'change management', and give much useful advice for managing any type of change to working practices. Introducing Inspection will change the way people work, sometimes very dramatically. With foresight, the change can be properly managed, and the technique can be successfully integrated into the company culture. If the change process is not regarded seriously enough, the whole technique may be lost.

Absorbing Change

Change must be both 'pushed' and 'pulled' in order to move. A management sponsor gives visible support to the changes proposed, as well as ensuring that the change process is adequately resourced. The 'change agent' or 'champion' is given the responsibility of managing the change process itself.

The people in an organization go through a number of phases when they change the way they work:

- initial contact, hearing of Inspection for the first time;
- awareness of Inspection itself and the fact that it may affect me;
- understanding of what Inspection really is;
- trial: experiencing for myself how Inspection works (on someone else's document);
- buy-in: wanting to have my own documents Inspected;
- experience: volunteering one of my own documents to be Inspected;
- practice: gaining skill in doing Inspections;
- proficiency: improving the practice of Inspection;
- institutionalization: Inspection is part of my organization's process;
- internalization: Inspection is 'second-nature' for everyone.

People should not be pushed too quickly from one stage to the next. The best implementation plans take people gently but surely through one stage at a time.

The Change Equation

There is a psychological equation[†] which expresses the dynamics of why people change, and also explains why some people find it very easy to change and others find it difficult. This can help the change agent to find ways to help people change when they do find it difficult or threatening.

† from Ian Beech, ICI, Macclesfield, UK, and Mike Migdoll, Bank of America, attributed to Gleicher and Beckhard.

Change happens only if a function of three things (a, b, and c) is greater than something else (z).

$$f(a, b, c) > z$$

where a = dissatisfaction with the current state

b = a shared vision of the future

c = knowledge of the first practical step to take

and z = the psychological cost of changing to the individual.

The psychological cost of change is the emotional and mental effort required by the individual in terms of the disturbance to their normal ways of working and the extra time and effort they would need to invest in order to do things differently.

Some individuals are happy to change very readily; their threshold of change is very low. They may well change if only one of the change factors has been met, although this type of almost 'change for change's sake' is often ineffective. If they do not know the practical steps which they should take, for example, they may change to a worse way of doing things just because they are dissatisfied with the status quo. Other individuals find it very difficult to adjust to change. They like their normal routine and are very unhappy when it is disturbed for any reason.

In order to convince someone who is strongly resisting change, it is not effective to try and lower their change threshold; this is a basic part of their personality. However, it is generally effective to raise the other 'objective' elements. This type of person would need additional and more detailed knowledge of the steps to be taken to get from current working practices to full Inspections. They may need a fuller vision of the future, and may need to be more convinced that a continuation of the current situation would be intolerable.

Crossing the change threshold cannot be rushed. Above all, give the reluctant changers enough time to convince themselves. Although they will not be the first to volunteer their work to be Inspected or to become Inspectors, once they do change, they often become the staunchest defenders of the new technique (because they don't now want to change to anything else).

Principles of Software Process Change

A wide-ranging discussion of the changes in a software development organization is found in Watts Humphrey's book (Humphrey, 1989). Humphrey's principles of software process change are:

• major changes to the software process must start at the top;
• ultimately, everyone must be involved;

- effective change requires a goal and knowledge of the current process;
- change is continuous;
- software process changes will not be retained without conscious effort and periodic reinforcement;
- software process improvement requires investment.

Suzanne Garcia points out that installing Inspections can be a way of moving an organization from a lower level of software process maturity to a higher one (Garcia, 1991).

10.1.2   The Role of the Champion or Change Agent

The Champion

There is no doubt that when starting with Inspection it is essential to have a strong enthusiastic leader of the change process. All really successful efforts to install the Inspection process have had a person you could name as the real champion of the effort. If you cannot find a champion for the cause, you should hesitate to install the process.

Champions who have made a good job of the implementation of Inspection have been well rewarded with corporate glory and cash prizes. For the method is so strong in results that everybody assumes that the champion is personally responsible, which in a sense they are.

However, a champion who does not heed good change management guidelines can also be held responsible for the failure of the implementation of Inspection. When people are looking for a scapegoat, for example, when a deadline has been missed, the person who was most visible in pushing for change is an easy target. The missed deadline is immediately visible, while the benefits of increased quality deliverables are not evident until later.

This chapter is aimed primarily at the champion of Inspection within an organization, and at the change agent. The champion can be a highly supportive manager, a member of the quality assurance department, or a day-to-day trainer and implementor of the method. 'Championing' can even be a team effort. The champion may or may not be the same person as the change agent. For example, the champion may be the quality director, who is determined that Inspections will be installed but does not have the time to directly manage all the day-to-day details of the implementation. In this case, a change agent is appointed, perhaps from the quality department, or (often preferably) one of the development staff.

The change agent is given the responsibility for the implementation of Inspections within the whole organization. Often this person is someone who had an initial contact with Inspection through a seminar or course, recognizes the benefits to their own organization, and would ideally have the following skills and experience:

- recent and extensive experience in software development;
- progressive rather than reactionary personality;
- practical and business orientation, as well as technical background;
- highly developed analytical skills.[†]

Another list of characteristics is given by Humphrey (Humphrey, 1989):

- enthusiastic about carrying out the change;
- technically and politically capable;
- respected by the people they will be dealing with;
- has management's confidence and support.

The steps which the change agent must take in implementing Inspections are given below.

10.1.3   Assess Organizational Readiness for Inspection

There is a right and a wrong time to try to implement change to an organization. If everything is currently going well, and you are meeting your deadlines and having no quality problems with your software in the field, then you do not need Inspection (yet). Even if this is not true but most people believe that it is true, it is still not the right time to start Inspection. If people are not dissatisfied with their current situation, then change is unlikely to succeed.

If the organization has recently been reorganized, is newly formed, or has recently undergone a major change, such as acquiring a software development or testing tool, then introducing yet another change is not likely to succeed. Wait until the other changes have settled in or bedded down, and problems are arising.

If there are significant quality problems and people are ready to try something other than what they are doing now, then Inspections have a good chance of succeeding in improving software quality, provided the implementation is carried out correctly.

10.1.4   The Business Case

Benefits

The first task to be done is to build a business case for Inspections. The whole point of Inspection is to save money. If you cannot find a

---

† adapted from Bouldin (1989). *Agents of Change*, Yourdon Press, Prentice-Hall.

way to justify Inspections, then do not implement them. The costs and benefits outlined in Chapter 2 should give you some idea of the benefits which can and have been achieved in other organizations. However, you should put together a business case for your own organization, with the quantified objectives which Inspections should achieve. If you do not put together your own business case, you will have nothing against which to evaluate the success of your Inspections.

Inspection is worth implementing if it will meet business objectives such as improved quality, improved time to market, reduced cost of testing, improved productivity, and reduced cost of maintenance. The money saved by using Inspection should outweigh the overall cost of implementing and running Inspections in order to justify the training and continuing support costs. The following checklist gives suggestions for ways to quantify the benefits of Inspection:

- quantify the present penalties associated with poor quality software, including time and effort to fix bugs and possible or worst-case consequential loss;
- identify current areas of greatest risk to the business where the consequences of poor quality will be most serious;
- estimate time/effort/money spent now on other types of reviews.

In constructing the business case, be conservative but not too cautious. The business case will be more credible if it is based on real figures and clearly not exaggerated, but do not hesitate to claim the real benefits which will be there for the taking.

A simple business case can be constructed in the following way:

- find out how much time has been spent on fixing a representative sample of faults in the field;
- take a median salary cost for the fault fixer;
- calculate the salary cost to fix a fault;
- multiply by the salary loading figure (overheads and so on, usually two to three times);
- multiply by the number of faults discovered in the field.

This will give a quantified estimate of rework costs to the software maintenance or development organization.

If possible, put a quantified cost on consequential loss which may be caused by faults in software. These costs are often many times greater than the software rework cost. For a bank, for example, if the on-line banking service were to fail for a day, the costs would include not only the fault fix and retest effort, but the re-entering of all lost transactions which would have had to be recorded manually. Consequential loss would also include lost business as some customers decided to move their accounts to other banks, and a damaged market image which would deter other potential customers. Even if you cannot quantify consequential costs, be sure to include an estimate of them in your business case anyway.

Costs

The costs of getting Inspections started include training costs, which are covered in the next section, but also the effort needed to organize early Inspections, including the design of standard forms and checklists. In addition, many organizations find that they may want at least to 'tidy up' their standards before they begin to use them in Inspections.

The initial reaction of many managers is that the cost of Inspection is too high. If a figure such as 15% of development effort is quoted, they immediately translate this into a 15% delay on their already tight timescales and are horrified. Investing this time upfront often means that they feel they will be using up their project contingency right at the beginning. This is not actually the case, as Figure 10.1 shows.

Experience data:
Jacqueline Holdsworth at Lloyds Bank found that the way to overcome this fear of delay was to put the managers through a simulation, in order to develop confidence that Inspections would actually save them time. The 'Applied Process Improvement Simulation' gave teams a product to make, with a deadline and budget. After the first cycle, they would typically have achieved 10–20% of their targets, and were complaining about the unrealistic schedules and impossible deadlines. After half an hour of training in process improvement, they achieved 100% of their targets in the next cycle, including planning time. In fact they often had done no planning in the first cycle.
Source: Jacqueline Holdsworth, independent consultant

Return on Investment

The return on the investment in Inspection will not happen instantaneously. There is an initial cost before benefits begin to be visible, as shown in Figure 10.2.

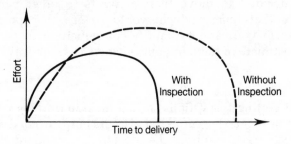

Figure 10.1   Distribution of effort on using/not using Inspection.

Hypothetical Example: Calculation of Inspection Costs and Savings

Suppose that 100 defects are produced per week, which would cost 30 minutes each to find and fix at Inspection time. If we assume that Inspection is 80% effective (this is probably rather high for an immature Inspection process, 50% may be more conservative), then Inspection can find 80 of them, for a total cost of 40 hours.

There will be 20 defects which will slip through the Inspection net and be looked for in test execution. We will assume that accumulative testing is also 80% effective at finding errors. The cost of finding and fixing an error in testing is at least ten times more than finding it before it has been built, so the cost to find and fix one of the errors is 300 minutes, that is, five hours, and 16 defects will be found. This gives a cost of 80 hours for defect finding in testing.

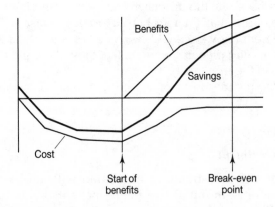

Figure 10.2   Return on investment using Inspection.

The remaining four defects will cost 100 times more to find and fix in the field than if they were found in Inspection, so these will cost 50 hours each, for a total field cost of 200 hours.

The total cost of these errors is therefore 40 + 80 + 200 = 320 hours.

What would be the cost if we did not do Inspections, but test execution was the first defect-finding opportunity? Assuming 80% efficiency again gives 80 defects which cost five hours each to find and fix, for a total of 400 hours.

But 20 defects now slip into the field, where they cost 50 hours each, for a total of 1000 hours. This gives a total cost of 1400 hours without Inspection, compared to 320 hours with Inspection.

Net saving with Inspection 1400 − 320 hours = 1080 hours, 154 days or 30 work-weeks. So, in this hypothetical example, you would need 30 extra people each week to cope with the fact that you are not using Inspection.

The 1 − 10 − 100 ratio of cost in Inspection − test − field is a widely-accepted industry norm, but is actually quite conservative. IBM found that their numbers were actually 1 − 20 − 82,[†] so the savings with Inspection would be even more dramatic. Do you know what these figures are for your organization? Does anyone know?

Another way to calculate costs is to estimate the cost of fixing a major defect. One client found that it cost $4000 on average to fix a major defect if it was not found and corrected by Inspection at an early stage.

One of the problems of achieving organization-wide quality improvement is that the test and field service people may not be on the software development manager's budget, so why should they pay (even a little) to save (a lot) for someone else? This is why Inspections must be supported from the highest management level, to ensure what is best for the organization as a whole.

10.1.5 Management Commitment

When it is evident that a good business case exists for implementing Inspections, the next step in the change process is to gain top-level management commitment. Without top-level support, the change agent will not have the power or resources to implement Inspection properly.

The business case is the main 'selling' tool to convince management that Inspection is needed. However, if top-level management is not aware of how much they are losing through poor quality, it will not see any gains through improving quality.

---

† IBM Santa Teresa Labs, Horst Remus, late 1970s.

If after presenting the business case to top-level management the Inspection implementation does not have their full support, then do not continue trying to implement Inspections without it. It can be effective to do a small-scale experiment, keeping careful track of Inspection costs and benefits, to help convince them in six months' time, but it is difficult to 'grow' Inspections from the bottom up without support from the top.

Remember that Inspection may be turned down at this time for reasons which you are not aware of, such as political maneuvering or imminent organizational changes. If it is turned down now, continue to keep records of what not doing Inspections is costing the organization.

10.1.6   Getting Bottom-up Demand

Although management commitment is essential, it is not ideal to impose Inspections as a management dictum. Once you have commitment, the actual take-up of Inspection is best from the bottom up. It is hard enough to change the way you work, and to have your work criticized in great detail. At least if you have volunteered your work to be Inspected, you have taken the responsibility yourself for getting into that situation.

The role of the change agent at this point is to begin the process of 'selling' the concepts and practice of Inspection within the organization, and this is a far more significant effort than simply buying in the training, which is simply the tip of the iceberg. This is where the change agent publicizes Inspection, puts on informal seminars to raise awareness, starts a newsletter, gets regular mention in the company magazine, takes out an 'advert' on the system start-up message or e-mail, and anything else which will raise the profile of Inspection.

In order to succeed, Inspection must be demanded by those who will use it. They will not demand it unless they have been 'sold' on the benefits, realize that they could do better than they are doing now, and know the steps needed to start Inspection (the change equation again). People must be convinced about Inspection. Inspection is hard enough to do even when you want to, and people can easily find ways to sabotage Inspection if they don't want it.

It is also important that Inspection will actually benefit those who will be using it. They have a right to know the metrics of their own team, and to be rewarded for raising quality levels.

10.1.7   Pilot Project

A small-scale project should be chosen as the first step in implementing Inspection. Everyone involved should be given thorough training and adequate management support. A local business case should be made for the pilot project, and the results achieved should be carefully recorded.

It is very important that the first pilot attempts to use the method are done as well as possible. Avoid compromise on central things like optimal rates, having rules and written source documents. Plan well, and get a first-class team together.

Some compromise with 'perfect' use of the method is inevitable. You should be pleased if you are able to make use of 20 out of 40 basic ideas. For example, you should expect that you may have to violate the generic entry condition that the source documents have exited their Inspection process. You should point this out, as well as other violations, and their consequences, when any evaluation is made of the pilot attempts.

Use the pilot project to develop workable forms, checklists and standards. Experiment with individual checking and logging rates. The most important thing is to record the metrics and use them to refine the process throughout the pilot project.

The purpose of the pilot project is to get an in-depth assessment of the suitability of Inspections within the organization, and to evaluate internal procedures and practices with respect to Inspection. It is only through the actual use of Inspection on a real project that the way forward can clearly be identified, and it is important to make a formal evaluation at the end of the pilot project so that the lessons learned can be applied. The following list gives some idea of the topics to be covered in the formal report on the pilot project for the review by management (who need to support and fund the next stage):

- overview of the pilot project experience;
- quantified benefits achieved;
- comparison of benefits achieved to the local business objectives and success criteria for the pilot project;
- comparison of local business case objectives with the organization-wide business case – will the benefits scale up?
- problems encountered and how they were solved;
- was the pilot a fair trial for Inspection? (Were the objectives realistic? Was sufficient time allowed for the learning curve? Was adequate training and support provided?)
- summary of lessons learned for future use of Inspection in the organization;
- any special conditions making this project exceptional, so that benefits or problems may not be typical;
- investigate the use/requirement of Inspection in other business

areas, for example, marketing, product release, production/ operation, subsidiaries, suppliers.

If the benefits achieved from the pilot project were not as expected, then do not proceed immediately in implementing Inspection throughout the rest of the organization. Analyze why the benefits have not been achieved. It may be helpful to call in outside expertise at this point (experienced Inspection users from another organization or consultants). If Inspection was not correctly carried out on the pilot project, select another pilot project to try. Do not implement a faulty Inspection process!

If the benefits are achieved, then a substantial publicity blitz is needed. Managers need to know that the technique actually works and saves money for them. Other potential Inspection leaders and Inspectors need to know that the benefits can be achieved. Sharing experience of those on the sharp edge ('My work was Inspected and I lived to tell the tale') is probably the most effective way to gain buy-in from the next wave of Inspectors.

10.1.8 Wider Implementation

Whatever implementation step is taken after the pilot project, it needs to be planned and managed. The level of training for experienced users should now be deepened, while providing the initial level of training for new users.

Wider organizational aspects can also be considered at this point, such as addressing the current working practices now affected by the use of Inspection (for example, configuration management, metrics collection, testing practices).

As part of the planning for this phase, ensure that the change agent is given adequate resources to implement Inspection in the rest of the organization, including publicizing, scheduling training, integrating with internal and external user groups, producing internal manuals and guidelines, and integration with other software engineering methods and tools.

The most important part of implementing Inspection is to assess the business benefits. Your experience is of most value to your own organization if the benefits gained (and problems experienced) are carefully and accurately chronicled. It is only by comparing actual benefits achieved, so far, to those predicted in the initial business case estimate that you will be able to see if Inspections were worth implementing. Your experience is also of immense value to others about to embark on the same path, so publicizing your results is very valuable.

Publicize experience data, especially any dramatic or striking ones. Set up an infrastructure to measure defects found in testing and after release, counted or weighted by severity. Analyze trends in Inspection efficiency and effectiveness. Compare current metrics to original business case figures.

Expect to encounter resistance. People in general do not like change, but they like unexpected change even less. Technical people are often very resistant to changing their technical ways of working.

Learn from experience, but do not attempt to spread Inspection too quickly. A common mistake is to try to do too much too soon.

Depending on the size of the organization, the change agent may want to adopt a phased approach to the wider implementation of Inspection. This is usually a good idea, so that the newcomers to Inspection can have adequate support from the change agent, champion, and existing Inspectors.

Forming an inter-disciplinary team can be a wise move, as recommended by Bouldin (1989) This team brings together the mutual concerns of many software developers so that Inspection can be tailored to the organization as a whole. Then the Inspection implementation team members also serve as 'mini change agents' in their own work areas. This worked well at Boeing, 1989.

The process of 'selling' Inspection internally is never finished. Any technique needs a constant push in order to keep it moving. There is a built-in inertia with all methods which take effort to do well, and they tend to fall off in their effectiveness if a careful watch is not kept. There will also always be new people to train, or new managers to inform.

Experience data:
Implementation planning for Inspection used at Bell Labs
- The key: rather than giving individuals a set of skills, the software Inspection program was installing a process in an organization.
- Training for individuals made sense only after managers could be counted on to support the new process.

(1) Four steps for installing Inspection at Bell Labs
    (a) The overview seminar.
    (b) Needs assessment and planning meeting.
    (c) Discuss present development methods.
    (d) Select people for further Inspection planning and co-ordination.

Continues
      (e) Determine exit/entry criteria, checklists, forms.
      (f) Determine qualitative and quantitative goals for
          Inspection.
      (g) Determine Inspection implementation and training
          schedule.
      (h) Determine trial groups (if any).
      (i) Modify the Inspection workshop's first teaching
          module to fit languages used by actual groups.
      (j) Select Inspection workshop case study. Run a practice
          meeting.
(2) The Inspection workshop
      (a) One day course to train leaders and participants.
      (b) Includes practice meeting (case study).
      (c) Distributes the project's Inspection manual.
(3) Half-day management seminar (after 10 Inspections are
    completed).
(4) Review and evaluation activities (after 10 Inspections are
    completed).

10.2   Checklists for Installing Inspection

10.2.1   Issues in Installing the Method

Here are some issues which you will need to address when implementing the method in your organization.[†]

Getting and Retaining Management Support

- Who will be responsible for major decisions regarding the installation of the process? Who will this be when the process is installed in new places?
- Who is going to be the initial senior Inspection leader and to champion the installation of the process? Overall, or in various independent centers?

---

† This list is adapted from the list of issues generated by Mr I. Pal and his team at Texas Instruments in Bangalore, India, October 1990, and from work generated by a team at Hewlett Packard Printer Division, Boise, Idaho shortly before that.

- Do we need a short course for managers in successful installation of the process, as opposed to understanding and supporting the process in general?
- How are we going to sell this to management?
  - Shall we get them to do it once?
  - Which data shall we give them?
- Can we persuade management to make the initial 15% of project budget investment early in our process (in the attempt to save even more downstream)?
- How shall we conduct the longer-term communication with management about this process? How can we make sure that management is kept informed about how much Inspections are saving downstream? Who is responsible for keeping the flow of information about Inspection success to managers at a steady rate?
- How can we ensure that middle management fully supports Inspection?

Management of the Inspection Process

- Who is responsible for measuring the success of the process?
- How will we settle disputes (for example on leader certification)?
- How are we going to keep track of leader performance?
- How shall we represent Inspection leaders at a higher level?
- How does the overall organization of the process look in terms of types of people and authority?
- How are we going to deal with the metrics from this process?

Training and Certification

- How will senior leaders be appointed or emerge?
- What training should be given to management? Inspector checkers, Inspection leaders, senior Inspection leaders, the chief Inspection leader?
- How shall we train future Inspection leaders of the process? Three to five days of practical-based trial Inspections?

Products to be Inspected; the Checking/Logging Process

- Which documents shall we check?
- What will the generic entry and generic exit criteria be? How will they be improved? Who will 'own' them?
- What rules should there be about people's supervisors being present at team meetings?
- What kind of quality improvement measures and objectives are we going to have for the Inspection process itself?
- Who is responsible for bringing documents up to entry level acceptability?

Rule Sets, Procedures and Checklists

- Should we have generic rule sets for all documents?
- Should there be rule sets for checklists?
- Who is going to make initial specific rule sets for the documents we choose to check?
- How will we resolve disputes over rule set content?
- What about the forms we need? Their initial design and improvements to them?
- Who will own the rule sets? How will we capture improvements in them and change them?

The QA Database

- How are we going to measure the success of this process? Of the sub-processes? What should be in the QA database?
- Should the data from this process be kept as part of an existing quality or process database?
- Should the database contain provision for integration with other future databases (field errors for example)?
- How will the database be set up? How will it be maintained? Who will have responsibility for it?
- What level of confidentiality and accessibility is needed for the database?
- How will Inspection leaders be tracked in the database?
- Should the data summary from a particular Inspection be made available for anybody (supervisor, originator)?

Process Improvement

- Who will have the authority to make decisions about the process?
- How and when do we form Process Change Management Teams?
- How shall we go about assisting the Process Change Management Teams in actually implementing changes to the software development processes?
- Do we need to teach statistical process control (Deming, Juran) to change processes effectively?

10.2.2   Basic Recommendations for Beginners

- Do not try to follow *all* rules at the beginning.
- Do recognize that you cannot get the full benefits until you do follow the recommended process correctly, and that it takes time for this to become established.
- Start with something very important. It will be an upstream document, perhaps a feasibility study, contract, high-level

requirement specification, acceptance test criteria, or a high-level system design.

- Start small. A sample of one or a few pages of a larger document, done properly, will show how powerful the method is. Expect to find five to 20 or more major issues per page in such cases.
- Start with documents which your management, and their management, can deal with (not too technical for them).
- Use a checking rate of about one 'non-commentary' page (that is, pages with real information on them, not contents or heading pages) per individual checker work-hour, until you have data indicating another rate as optimal. This may seem slow, but if you only do one or a few sample pages, you will see the result.
- Make a list of the recommended things which you are *not* practicing properly at this time. This is a reminder to both you and your management that the process cannot be fully judged just yet; that there is more potential in it.
- Try to get some Inspection team leader training for the leaders. A public course might do. There is a wide variation in quality and content of leader courses on the public market. Choose carefully. If this is impossible, someone who will undertake to study this book thoroughly and take the contents seriously could achieve a great deal.
- Capture a full set of metrics about each Inspection. About ten numbers and parameters at least (see Figure 10.3). More details about metrics are given in Appendix C (Metrics and Forms).

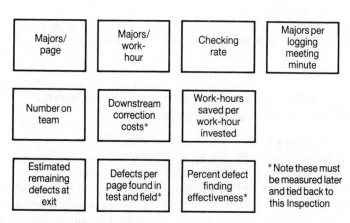

Figure 10.3   Ten basic statistical parameters.

- Analyze and compare the data immediately (same day):
  - What rate are we using? (checking, logging and more checking) How does this compare to what we know about optimum rates?
  - How many defects are we likely *not* to have found (for example, if we only found 30% to 50% of them)?
  - What is the cost (hours or money) to find and fix a major defect?
  - What (approximately) would such defects cost to fix later? (Usually 10 to 100 times more, but try to look at real current costs, and sample a few 'fixes' in practice.)
  - What then is the (approximate ratio) of saving to cost, even at this early stage?
- Start wherever people seem to want help, but do challenge the skeptics to join in and make up their own mind based on experience.
- Don't force anyone to have their work Inspected. Give lots of support to the brave volunteers who go first.

10.2.3 Recommendations for People Doing Older Versions of the Inspection Process

- Take the self-assessment test in the Preface at the beginning of the book. Make a list of things which your older process does differently from the recommendations in this book. This will help you recognize the differences.
- Note particularly (for example): optimum rates, tuning and learning from the data, process improvement, training leaders, specialized roles, continuous improvement of checklists, improvement suggestions in the rule sets themselves, issue logging at high rates (one or more items per minute), not discussing solutions to the issues during logging.
- Once you feel you have learned the new process pretty well (at least ten trials would be necessary) you can challenge the old system to a comparative test.

10.2.4 Questions and Concerns on Introducing Inspection into a Small Organization

It may appear that Inspection is more suitable to large organizations, since it has been successfully used by many of them. However, it is equally applicable to small organizations, but it does need to be adapted for this kind of environment. Some penetrating questions asked by Tony Bird of Serco Services Limited, Gloucestershire, UK are typical of the concerns which need to be addressed by small teams adopting Inspections.

Question 1. Cost seems Frighteningly High

The cost of Inspections is quoted at 15% of project cost. This seems frightening, even allowing for the savings in later activities, testing and so on (assuming we are good at it). Are there ways to mitigate the perceived cost/reduce the risk?

Answer 1

There is no way to tell whether the cost is too high without knowing what the current cost of errors in the field is. The whole purpose of Inspection is to save money – if you are not losing any through defects, then don't bother. However, you are likely to find that defects are already costing you well over 15% of development time. If you are typical, it may be 100% or more.

Try to get a 'feel' for current error costs. Analyze one or two serious errors, and estimate how much they cost to put right. Use loaded salary costs for people's time, if time is recorded in time sheet data. (Loaded salary is salary and overheads, usually two or three times basic salary.)

Also don't expect savings to appear instantly (see Implementation section of this chapter). Also see general business case type benefits in Chapter 2 of this book.

Question 2. Small Team

Will it work with a very small team, say six people? There will not be a separate QA team. All team members are responsible for quality matters.

Answer 2

It will work using a small team, providing that the team members are united in wanting to make Inspections work, and there are no serious personality clashes within the team.

With few people in the 'pool' of Inspectors, every Inspection is likely to be with the same people. This has the advantage of sharing knowledge about improvements gained immediately. The disadvantage comes if there is an individual who does not or cannot adapt to the ego-less Inspection culture. See also experience data below.

Question 3. Infrastructure

The necessary infrastructure (documentation, standards, quality goals and so on) are not yet (or partially) in place. Does this mean we cannot proceed yet?

Answer 3

You can always start with Inspection no matter where you are now. If your infrastructure is in place, it would make the early Inspections easier, but either way, the Inspection process will find problems in your existing standards. If you have no standards, you would need to write some up informally to get started. If you have partial standards, use them and supplement them where needed. You can always start to improve, and everyone has to start improving from where they are now.

Question 4. Partially Complete Project

How does one apply Inspections to an existing project that is perhaps 40% complete?

Answer 4

Inspections can be applied to a 40%-complete project; the question is what should be Inspected first, the documents completed early in the project or those just nearing completion now? It is still important to Inspect the highest level documents, even though they have been 'signed off'. Any major defects found will still have a major effect on the rest of the project if they are allowed to continue past the 40% complete point. It is better to fix them now.

Question 5. Limited Sample

Given limited resources, is it acceptable to apply Inspections to a (key) sample of a project and apply less formal controls to other parts?

Answer 5

Yes, do apply Inspections to the key sample of most important documents. You cannot Inspect everything at once. Inspections should be phased in gradually, but continue your existing less formal controls at the same time for other areas.

Question 6. Inspection Overload

I fear that Inspection overload will occur.

Answer 6

Inspection overload may well occur, if you try to do too much at once. Aim to make progress in installing Inspections gradually. Remember to keep track of progress and make sure that everyone else sees that progress as well – publicize the benefits gained in small areas.

Question 7. Statistical Overhead

The overhead of collecting and analyzing metrics – administration might be disproportionately large in a small team.

Answer 7

Collecting and analyzing metrics should be kept to the minimum to give you the information you need. A small team may collect fewer metrics than a large organization, but no one should collect metrics they don't use. So collect what you need, and use what you collect.

A simple spreadsheet can easily be set up to both collect and analyze metrics. However, don't forget to allow time to interpret and do further statistical analysis and act on the knowledge gained from the information.

Experience data:

At one organization with a small software development team, the manager was very keen for the programmers and analysts to use Inspection, so we had a couple of trial one-hour Inspections, one with two analysts and the team leader, and one with three programmers. The analysts experiment worked very well; a number of serious defects were found which could be put right before they were designed into the system.

However, when we came to try Inspection with the programmers, we found a serious problem. The programmers were a mixture of in-house and contract staff, but that had nothing to do with the problem. One of the individuals was a rather arrogant youngster (whom we will call 'Fred') who had spent the last few months in 'polishing' his program, even though he was supposed to have written at least three other programs in that time. The other two programmers had been far more productive in writing the software which was needed in their fairly tight timescale, although there were some suspected quality problems.

Fred's code was Inspected first. The other two programmers had not found any issues in Fred's program, which normally indicates insufficient individual checking. A few minutes were spent looking for issues, but then it was decided to move on to the other programmers' code. There were many issues to be found here, since the code had been

---

Continues

produced much more quickly, but many of those noted by Fred were minor, for example, standards had not been followed in comments, and so on.

Although Fred was good at identifying issues, he was completely unable to follow the issue-reporting standards in terms of objectivity. Instead of phrasing a defect as 'Comment standard not followed at line 55,' he would say 'Any idiot should be able to write comments in the standard form – can't you read?'

Because of Fred's antagonistic personal approach, which he seemed unable to change in spite of repeated warnings, he was quickly thrown out of the Inspection meeting. Because there were so few people involved in the whole project, Inspection was abandoned at the programmer level for this organization. It became evident, by the sigh of relief when he walked out of the door, that the personality friction was a contributing factor to why the other two programmers had not (dared) to find errors in Fred's program.

10.2.5   Organizational Issues

- Make sure you have a way to train new Inspection leaders (public course, in-house training by an experienced leader) and ways to certify them after the training.
- Make sure you have someone to undertake analysis of metrics who understands Deming's methods. (See Deming's *Out of the Crisis.* (Deming, 1986). Key ideas: don't change the process until it is in control. Improve the basic process continuously. Don't change the process for special problem causes which might be due to a particular person or incident.)
- Make sure that all costs of the method are clearly justified in terms of the benefits.
- Make sure you present this clearly, imaginatively, and continuously to management.
- Make sure the ongoing support of the process is attached to someone like a quality director who really cares and understands.
- When you know what you are doing – expose the process to top managers on documents they are concerned with (policy, strategy, budget, contracts, sales proposals, re-organization plans). This will be useful and get their support, if it is done in the right way. An outside trainer or consultant may be useful in presenting your case to top management in a non-threatening way.

10.2.6   Budget and Time Planning

- At least one person needs to be allocated as a chief Inspection leader to support the process for a substantial part of their time initially.
- You will probably be using about 15% of a project budget on Inspection when you are mature. This cost will probably replace costs of other forms of quality improvement, and will save you the costs of allowing the defects to escape downstream.
- Allocate more time for getting the Inspection effort started – less towards the end.
- Allocate some budget to break in the new process.
- When the process is used and the savings are made downstream, you can expect to save 30% to 50% of the total cost or time you would otherwise have spent in performing the same software development activities. In other words, Inspections will help you be more productive as well as increase your quality levels.
- The maintenance costs for a system may go down by one order of magnitude, half due to fewer defects, half due to easier changes.[†]

Initial planning by the leader can take 10 to 16 hours for the first Inspection cycle, due to the creation of new forms and checklists, and due to the greater amount of teaching needed for new participants. When Inspections are well established, the planning time will be more like one hour for each Inspection cycle.

The usual initial state of written material is that it is filled with a surprising number of defects. Five to twenty major issues found per page is normal, so do not be disheartened by it. The authors of the material have to learn better habits. They do – quickly. In five or so cycles they can halve their errors each time. When you are finding less than one major issue per page from experienced authors, then they have learned what the expected rules are.

10.2.7   Priorities

- Do the most profitable documents first (generally 'upstream' such as contracts, requirements).
- Sample parts of large documents to establish how infected they are (expect 20 or more major defects per page).
- Get your management involved by checking their documents, with them on the team.

---

† This has been validated in software engineering (ICI (1981), The Standard Bank (Johannesburg) (1979).)

10.3 Formal Training

10.3.1 The Balance of Theory and Practice

There are a number of alternative approaches to the provision of formal training in Inspection. The important thing is to balance the theory of Inspections with practical hands-on experience.

This book may be seen as an alternative to training. It does give you a firm grounding in part of what is covered in training in the theory of Inspection. In fact, it gives you far more than you would normally cover in a short course.

However it is important to supplement the book by formal training to communicate the essential ideas by an experienced trainer who can answer questions as they arise. Another advantage of formal training is that early mistakes can be made in a 'safe' (classroom) environment.

On the other hand, Inspection is a technique which is not fully understood without practical experience; theory alone is not enough. Formal training generally includes the first taste of the Inspection experience, and allows the many questions which inevitably come to light as a result of that first experience to be resolved immediately as part of the training course. Further involvement of trainers can also be helpful as Inspections get started, in the form of consultancy support or occasional workshop clinics to discuss problems or questions which have arisen in early Inspection experience.

Training for Inspection leaders is essential, and background briefings for managers are very helpful. Training for Inspectors may be a full day including practical work, a half day, or even no formal training at all, allowing them to learn through the experience of the early Inspections they attend. A special 'training' Inspection for new Inspectors is another alternative, provided Inspections are already well established.

The different forms of formal training for these groups are discussed below.

10.3.2 Inspection Leader Training

Inspection leaders should be formally trained, and ideally formally approved (certified) as Leaders of the Inspection process.

Inspection leaders are formally approved or 'certified', after their courses, by instructors who work with small groups (about six pupils per instructor). Their approval is based on their ability to lead Inspections in practice, rather than their ability to memorize Inspection rules.

IBM has used three-day courses internally; many courses offered by independent Inspection training companies also use a three-day course for Inspection leaders. The three-day courses are intended to allow the leaders to begin to lead Inspections, and include one day of theory, observation of real Inspections (live or video), and practical experience.

There is no doubt that much of their real training comes on-the-job, by means of feedback from metrics, and guidance from a chief Inspection leader or Inspection coordinator. Inspection leaders are still considered 'a little wet behind the ears' until they have managed at least five or six Inspections.

At SEMA Group in the UK (see also case study in Chapter 16), no additional classroom theory is given to new Inspection leaders, since they will already have had a day of theory when they became Inspectors. The trainee leaders generate checklists, perform Inspections which are video-taped, and analyze the tapes. Each trainee leads an Inspection at least once.

Once trained, Inspection leaders should be monitored to ensure that they are improving their techniques all the time, and are not slipping back into poor habits.

At Douglas Aircraft from 1988, there was extensive use of a computerized Inspection metrics system. They maintain that the volume of Inspection (hundreds) made it impossible to monitor Inspection leaders except by looking for deviant patterns in their reported metrics. About a dozen ranges of reasonable numbers (such as '0.5 to 2.5 issues logged per logging meeting minute') are examined both to find simple incorrect data being reported, and to find problems with the leader's application of the process they have been taught. Some problems can be corrected by further personal instruction being given to the Inspection leader.

10.3.3   Orientation Courses or Awareness Briefings

If managers are expected to 'buy-in' to the Inspection process, particularly when they need to allow what seems to them to be an extra 15% of software development effort early on, they need to know what they are buying in order to give their support. Overview courses or presentations at a management level are very helpful especially after a pilot project, when Inspections are to be spread more widely within the organization. At Lockheed, a two-hour briefing was found to be very valuable in gaining managers' commitment.

IBM Santa Teresa Labs report that they found in the beginning (1977) that they had to give a one-day Inspection appreciation course for managers. This was to help managers appreciate that they would actually save total time using Inspection, in spite of the early overhead costs incurred in the project. These early costs had begun to tempt inexperienced managers to stop Inspection.

At the ICL OASIS Group, where Inspection was led by Alan F. Brown and his quality team, nearly all of the 180 software engineers were (at least in the early days) given a one-day orientation course. This was on the assumption that the day would be saved by more rapid practical work being done. From this pool of people with the theory, Inspection leaders were chosen and trained on the job.

IBM (C. L. Jones, *op. cit.*) reports that additional training is needed to prepare people to work on Process Change Management Teams.

10.3.4 Inspection Training

New Inspectors are trained in a number of ways. The most formal classroom training they will usually get is a one-day overview. Bell Labs, for example, reports using a one-day workshop to train Inspection participants.[†] Even that is not practiced by some, such as IBM. The difference is probably that one-day courses for new Inspectors are useful when Inspections are first started up, but are less necessary if there is already a 'culture' in place for new Inspectors to learn from. Inspectors can then learn on the job with the help of trained Inspection leaders and peers, and the use of rules and checklists.

Suzanne Garcia from Lockheed reports an experiment where trained Inspection leaders ran a series of groups through a 'training Inspection', where a real document was Inspected but in a learning environment. When some of these people later attended the formal training course (one day, half theory and half case study), they felt that it only marginally added to their knowledge, although most of them did get something useful out of the class.

Inspectors are trained on the job through their exposure to a number of Inspection components, detailed below:

- Software task rules, together with corresponding source documents, form the basic definition of what an Inspector uses to find issues during individual checking and the logging meeting.
- Inspection checklists define a set of advanced questions additional to rules which the Inspector is expected to ask about the particular types of document being Inspected. Checklists should not define new rules, but should help to interpret existing rules better.
- Rules, procedures, the master plan, product documents and sources read by the Inspectors give examples both of clear and complete writing, coding and planning practices, and also of poor practices. Inspectors can learn from both.
- The activity of their peers at Inspection meetings teaches Inspectors rules of conduct and what they can be expected to react to, and how.

† P. Fowler. *AT&T Technical Journal*, March/April 1976, 107–8.

- The Inspection leader is the official guide for Inspectors and will teach them whatever they need to know to succeed.
- Process brainstorming meetings provide a regular opportunity for learning and creative thinking on the job.
- Process Change Management Teams provide an opportunity to learn more deeply about the Inspection process by allowing participants to consider process improvement mechanisms.
- Inspection metrics, when presented to team members at kickoff meetings, provide an opportunity to teach something about Inspection. The lessons are enhanced when Inspection metrics are compared to the dramatically higher costs of coping with the same defects at test and maintenance phases.

Summary of Ways to Teach New Inspectors

- classroom lecture;
- classroom practical work (training material, not real documents);
- classroom practical work on real documents;
- videos of Inspection situations;
- observation of real Inspections;
- study of Inspection documents (source, product, rules, checklists, master plan);
- Inspection leader to take 'under their wing';
- peer activity and behavior at logging meeting;
- process brainstorming meeting;
- metrics (Inspection, test, and field).

10.3.5 Training the Chief Inspection Leader

The 'chief Inspection leader' is the one who manages the Inspection leaders while they are functioning in the Inspection leader role. The chief Inspection leader is not usually the line manager of the Inspection leaders.

The chief Inspection leader must see to it that the Inspection leaders have all the information and support they need to perform effectively.

In really large operations there may be a hierarchy of levels of management of Inspection leaders, which may have a formal support function for the chief Inspection leaders. This may provide advanced training, discussion of common problems, statistical support, sharing of experience, and mutual support and advice.

Who is Qualified to Teach Those Who Lead the Inspection Leaders?

As with most subjects, the teacher will be better for having participated in Inspection as a checker, having planned and led logging meetings as an Inspection leader, and later having been a chief Inspection leader or a quality assurance specialist. Many a teacher has had to learn 'one jump ahead' of the students, and this has functioned well enough.

In actual practice, those in this top position with regard to Inspections tend to be to a large extent self-taught as they progress the technique in their own organizations. They would typically learn from interaction with their peers at conferences or in Inspection user groups such as SIRO (in the US) or the BCS SQMSG or QA Forum (in the UK). See Bibliography for contact details.

10.4 Summary and Conclusions

10.4.1 Summary

Organizations follow a natural process of change. The person responsible for managing the implementation of Inspection into an organization, the champion or change agent, must follow a recognized change cycle in order to be successful.

The business case for Inspection must 'sell' the benefits within the organization, and must be used to prove that Inspection really works. Management commitment is essential, but Inspections must grow from the ground up in implementation. A pilot project should be used to introduce Inspection on a small scale before more widespread use is attempted.

There are a number of concerns which have been listed in this chapter which must be addressed by the change agent, and recommendations have been given for special circumstances such as those already using an older review process, those without any review process, and small organizations.

11
Overcoming the Difficulties

Inspection isn't easy. There are now a large number of organizations all over the world who have attempted to install Inspection, and not surprisingly, their success has been mixed. You can see some real life examples in the case studies in Chapters 12 to 17 of this book. This chapter provides an opportunity to build on their experience and avoid some of their frustrations and failures – and to look at some of the ways to improve the Inspection process itself.

11.1   How to be Sure Inspections Fail

There are no guaranteed ways to make absolutely sure that Inspection will succeed in your work environment. However, there are a number of ways to ensure that Inspections will fail. The more of the things listed below which you do the less likely it is that Inspections will succeed.

11.1.1   Technical Issues

- concentrate on trivia;
- get personal in criticism;
- omit edit and follow-up;
- don't keep metrics, don't look at metrics, or never tell anyone what they are;
- don't keep track of rates of checking or logging, or ignore them;
- don't experiment, for example, with slower rates, to find your optimum rates;
- don't let lack of checking hinder the logging meeting;
- Inspect anything regardless of initial quality;
- don't ever upgrade your entry or exit criteria or checklists, rules, and procedures;

- don't allow any changes in source documents or standards;
- don't use checklists or roles; have everyone cover the same ground;
- allow any amount of discussion in the meeting.

11.1.2 Organizational Issues

- make costs visible, keep benefits hidden;
- decide when to Inspect without author's agreement;
- don't keep people informed about Inspection progress and goals;
- let the manager moderate;
- use defect metrics for individual personnel appraisal;
- don't provide training, especially for Inspection leaders;
- don't certify leaders;
- don't provide ongoing support to improve the Inspection process;
- don't allow what is learned in Inspection to have any effect on software development processes;
- if things begin to go wrong, ignore them;
- never allow any change to the Inspection process.

11.1.3 Implementation Issues

- don't plan the implementation of the technique;
- expect miracles, instant benefits immediately;
- don't bother with management commitment, start bottom-up;
- implement organization-wide from the start, impose top-down;
- expect people to be immediately convinced of the value of Inspection;
- don't allow extra time for the initial learning curve;
- don't take notice of existing practices or previous review experience;
- don't design forms or spreadsheets;
- expect 'teething' problems to disappear without effort;
- expect people to remain convinced over time without further input;
- don't check whether anticipated benefits have happened;
- don't keep track of any savings due to Inspection.

11.2 Why the Inspection Process Fails

11.2.1 Particular Examples of Failure to Practice Inspection Properly

Here are some examples of the ways in which people fail to practice Inspection which are still common even amongst those claiming to do Inspection properly. This is not a complete list. It contains only the most deadly sins. Use it to evaluate your status.

(1) Failure to train leaders for at least three to five days.
(2) Failure to certify leaders initially and regularly as sound practitioners.
(3) Failure to establish, and update, optimal rates of checking activity and logging meetings.
(4) Failure to establish and upgrade appropriate 'entry' criteria to Inspection.
(5) Failure to clean up the upstream documents, over-emphasis on code as an object of Inspection.
(6) Failure to establish and maintain strict 'exit' criteria.
(7) Failure to continually upgrade issue identification checklists with powerful questions, based on experience. Initially brainstormed checklists are notoriously useless.
(8) Failure to upgrade document and code production rule sets so that Inspection using them becomes a much easier task.
(9) Failure to control the process centrally, using a database.
(10) Failure to take the next step of 'defect prevention' (Jones, 1985; Mays, 1990).
(11) Failure to conservatively calculate the profitability of Inspection and thereby gain control of the process and management support.
(12) Failure to collect experiences and share them in a company library (things like checklists, rule sets, metrics, process improvements, forms, encoding methods).
(13) Failure to continue to search for and report defects in all documents – irrespective of which organization they come from, or whether they have exited Inspection earlier – particularly source documents and rule sets.

11.2.2 The Background Reasons for Failure

Most software professionals have heard of Inspection by now. Some well-known industrial companies have many years' experience in using it. However, poor practice of Inspection is widespread, a fact of which the practitioners themselves are not always aware. The reasons do not only lie only within their own internal poor practice, but because they are working against a background that does not provide them with the support they need. This includes:

- inadequately detailed literature on correct practices;
- inadequate availability of public courses or private offerings;
- inadequate internal training of leaders (Inspection leaders) – often zero to a few hours when current indications are that a week is necessary to become a beginner;
- inadequate public models of what to expect from Inspection, so that we could recognize poor practice through our poor results.

11.3 Early Attempts at Process Improvement Failed

The process known widely as Fagan's Inspection clearly intended that someone should analyze the statistical data, find causes of defects and 'fix the process'. Michael Fagan (the founder of software inspections) held that improving the process was primarily a management responsibility. In the years 1976 to 1980 at the top level of the large IBM development labs a typical result seemed to be that it took a year to analyze a process error and get approval to develop a cure. It took a year and $1 million to build the cure. The cure didn't work, or was not profitable, and was dropped.[†]

In short the process improvement process took years, was very risky, and looked at few alternative improvements. Inspection itself was still very successful at finding defects and resolving them, but did not score documented success at fixing the process, removing common root causes.

Later, IBM found a more effective prevention approach, as described in Chapters 7 and 17.

11.3.1 Some Measures to Improve the PCMTs

Local Process Change Teams

It can be fruitful to encourage the Inspection team to be their own Process Change Team, at the stage when it is not yet organizationally practical to form outside PCMTs. In this case, the Inspection team allocates its own process improvement suggestions to specific individuals during the process brainstorming meeting. These individuals could do the process fix alone, or form an informal team of two or three colleagues, probably from the Inspection team members. They would attempt to make local improvements. If successful, these improvements could be spread company-wide in a relatively short time.

Experience data:
At Douglas Aircraft Co in early 1988 in the MD-80 Group, an Inspection Team we had trained, decided to tackle the problem of errors in all the Engineering Orders ('E.O.s', the basic change mechanism).

---

† Our sources are Mike Fagan (Kingston Labs) and Ken Christensen (STL) in personal notes.

> A great many defects resulted from the incorrect filling out
> of an E.O. A new E.O. cycle had been costed at about $2,965
> each on average, three years earlier. There were about 3000
> new young inexperienced engineers out of a total of about
> 8000 design engineers.
>
> There were about ten different major variations of the same
> E.O. form. One young engineer explained that the company
> school trained you on three of these variations. In practice,
> these were not the frequently used variations. The information
> on how to fill out the form correctly was in a standards manual
> several inches thick. The individual engineer did not have a
> copy of the manual. They only learned about errors when an
> external checking function discovered them.
>
> I remember some of the initial brainstorming included the
> idea of a computerization project, so that everybody got
> computer guidance as they were filling out the form.
>
> About a week later, the team of three young engineers
> showed me their basic solution. It was to have ten different
> templates, one for each major form variant. The templates
> were cut out in each part of the form that you could validly fill
> out. This physically encouraged correct data and prevented
> incorrect parts of the form being filled out.
>
> In addition they included notes in relevant places about
> valid codes and their meanings, as well as warnings so that
> engineers were further guided in correct filling out.
>
> It worked wonderfully. In addition, they made an enlarged
> version with more detail which engineers could pin up in
> front of their desk.
>
> Within a few months, the company had spread the
> innovation to all engineers. It became a plastic template in
> color. It got top management attention.
>
> One engineering director told me. 'We could have used
> that idea forty years ago!' He then asked me 'How did you get
> those kids to think of that idea?' I replied that nobody had
> ever given young engineers the time or direction to think of
> improvements. They were told to do their work according to
> company standards. Improvement was left to management.
> *Source*: Tom Gilb Personal Experience of Douglas Aircraft
> Local Process Improvement Teams

11.3.2   Making the Distinction between Practical and Unrealistic Change Ideas

One procedure which was formally introduced at a banking
organization in London was with regard to the immediate

practicality of brainstorming suggestions. We found that it is all too easy to suggest very costly or impractical ideas. Some of these may be 'correct'. But if nothing is likely to come of them, people will quickly feel that the process brainstorming is a waste of time.

We introduced the rule that you *may* suggest a global improvement idea, but you were *obliged* also to put in some effort to identify a local improvement idea. Global ideas were typically things we could not possibly do alone because of cost, time or political implications. For example, 'Get rid of the management,' 'Build a huge new computerized system.' Local ideas were things which we could conceivably find time to do and could implement at least in our own environment to see if they worked. For example, change our rules, entry criteria, exit criteria, checklists, give information, teaching, additional time.

11.4 Typical Installation Problems and Solutions

11.4.1 Cultural Resistance

Resistance to change is natural, even healthy. The new must prove it is better than the old. Inspection is easily misunderstood. It makes seemingly outrageous claims to be ten times better than anything people have done before in finding defects. It demands much more time to check documents than people feel they have available: 'one page per hour?!' Some organizations are quite successful without ever using it. People are naturally skeptical until they experience it and then also see the numbers for costs and benefits.

There will always be some people who want to try new things and who want to try this new thing in particular. Concentrate on these 'leaders'. Help them succeed in what they want. This will provide the basis for others having the desire and confidence to try. It is remarkable how fast the cultural resistance breaks down and the method spreads when you get a good start.

11.4.2 Lack of Management Support

You do need support from management – active 'official' support for time, budget, and a recognition of the necessity of first-class quality improvement methods. You can aim to get support in stages:

Stage 1. Point out how the results expected from Inspection are the ones they have on their agenda. (Find out what their official objectives are and tie into them.) They are bound to have some quality and productivity objectives and you can always use Inspection to improve upon them.

Stage 2. Demonstrate the method on existing documents, preferably those that have been approved by conventional reviews, inspections or management approvals. The contrast is always effective. You will always find 5–20 major defects per page, even when reviews have been used on the same document previously.

Stage 3. Involve key managers on at least one process of checking documents they can relate to amongst their management peers – their own strategic plans or a key contract or a bid. It is usually necessary for them to experience Inspection themselves to appreciate and understand the mechanisms. No amount of convincing presentations does so much good in the same time. In effect, they are being asked to spend half a day of their busy lives (do it in the evening if you have to) in order to learn how to get control over all the paperwork they will be responsible for during the rest of their working lives.

Do not exaggerate. Do not promise to much. Do not let people get involved in minor defects. In fact during trials you might make it a point to not look for them, not log them, and not report them! Be conservative. The realities are in any case convincing.

11.4.3   No Rules

You can expect the following situation regarding rules:

(1)   There are existing software engineering standards. Nobody uses them. They are not in useful shape. Too voluminous, too much trivia.

(2)   There are several areas needing rules for which there are no standards whatsoever.

Experience data:

A contract modification just about to be sent by fax to the customer by the marketing director, for a $20 million contract which was at least 80% software work, had no written rules. We made some up on the spot, just before a top executive checking and logging session one afternoon as shown below:

CON-1:   All individual promises to the customer which involve cost or human effort must have a *specific estimate* of how much effort or cost is involved, in this or some other available document.

CON-2:   All statements which could possibly be ambiguous or willfully misinterpreted by our customer must be written so that no dangerous wrong interpretation is possible.

Continues

These were powerful rules, because the marketing director had made promises committing the software engineering staff to specific accomplishments and a deadline. As usual, he had not calculated the consequences. He had not evaluated the true resources available. In fact, that was the very reason we had to send the fax explaining what we were going to accomplish that year. The customer was angry about delays already. The managers all agreed that violation of any of these rules constituted a genuine issue they would want to deal with.

About seven major defects per page were found in a four page fax, by the executives themselves.

Source: author's client

Do not hesitate to 'make up' reasonable rules, which the producer has not yet seen. Try to get the author to agree that if these rules were followed, it would result in a dramatic quality upgrade to the document. Get the author to agree that, given time to do the job, they believe that the document should be upgraded to this quality level.

Make it clear to all parties that defects found against a new set of rules do not constitute errors on the part of the author. They constitute new agreements about the quality levels of documents. The author is a pioneer in the upgrading of quality in work done! To be fair, you should give the author the opportunity of editing the document with respect to the new rules, before checking, so that the worst excesses are cleaned up.

11.4.4   No Access to Source Documents

Some of the necessary source documents are not normally made available to certain types of professionals. Programmers do not normally read the contract or the marketing plan, yet these documents could well contain vital information for checking their work. In theory the required information has found its way to requirements and design documents. In practice, especially without a rigid entry/exit and checking process, many vital things are not where they should be.

There are two ways to overcome this difficulty:

(1) The leader, during planning, manages to dig out required source documents.

> One leader, just trained by us, showed us that he had found a total of seven additional source documents for code checking, in addition to the three the coder knew about and had used. The coder immediately admitted lacking three of the documents, and disputed the other four, which were resolved later.

(2) The organization improves its process, so it is more obvious which documents must come into play. The most powerful tool we can recommend is to impose on authors a direct detailed cross-reference to the source documents they have used.

It is not unknown for leaders to have to 'fight their way into a vault' or change security procedures to give them access to what they must have in order to do their job properly.

11.4.5 No Quality Assurance Database

Normally, there is no statistical database for this process in your company, so you have to make one yourself (see Figure 11.1). Until you do, there are some small but solvable problems:

(1) You cannot know the optimal rates of checking (but you can guess, and keep it slow).
(2) You cannot be sure of the checking costs, and thus the profitability of the process. Profitability is high if Inspection is done properly, and the results of finding major defects speak for themselves to all participants.
(3) You probably cannot determine the downstream costs (finding and fixing defects in test and field), and this data is the most powerful single argument for doing this process. You can argue by referencing those who have, for example Reeve in his case study in Chapter 14 in this book.

11.4.6 No Checklists

There are usually no checklists, at least no really useful and significant ones available to begin with. Do not get somebody to draft checklists all at once. This is invariably wasted effort, because:

- too much trivia gets on the lists;
- the lists are too voluminous;
- such lists have no credibility;
- there tends to be no way to get rid of them, except to ignore them.

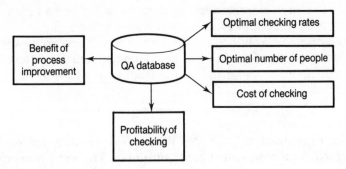

Figure 11.1   Some useful results from having a QA database and its data available.

Building a Checklist from Experience

You have plenty of 'checklist' questions in your rules (which perform as checklists when in the hands of a checker). The purpose of checklists is to add value which is not already present in the existing rules, and this is best done by a gradual process of building and modifying checklists when significant learning has been done (see Figure 11.2). It is better to start with no checklists, with rules only, than to produce misleading checklist questions.

Remind the leaders that they are the key to building good checklists. During logging, when it is apparent that some people are finding major/super-major defects, while others who could have found them have not, then it is time to take a break and get them to share their knowledge in the form of an improvement suggestion logging with a recommendation for revisions to the checklist.

If the leader (or any other Inspector) knows of a recent case of a defect which caused significant problems because it wasn't found earlier (perhaps the reason why Inspection is wanted now), this can become a critical checklist question.

11.4.7   No Clear Leadership for the Process

When there is no clear and strong leadership, the quality improvement process will not survive because it will not be done properly. It will therefore not have significant results, and will not be perceived as a solution to current needs.

Conventional wisdom says that 'quality' initiatives must come from the top to succeed. Certainly, they must have serious support high up. But they need very active and capable 'champions'.

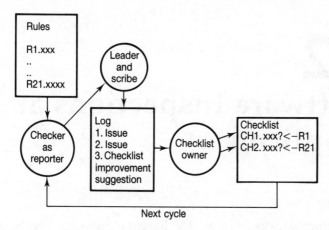

Figure 11.2 Checklists need to be developed 'one question at a time' and 'through hard experience'.

Probably the type of person who has read the book this far. Yes, *you*. Champions typically have no particular formal power. They get their power by proving that the new method really works and by parenting it until it can safely stand on its own.

Certainly it is natural for a quality assurance function to assume some leadership in this matter, and certainly they must be converts. But some individual is always really responsible for the persistent month-after-month activity, which gradually drives the method into the culture of the organization.

Such champions are not easily 'appointed' to the job. Our experience is that they seem to appoint themselves. They think it is necessary for the organization. They realize that it will succeed. They know it probably will not hurt their career, in or out of this company. They make it work.

12
Software Inspections at Applicon

This chapter was written by Barbara Spencer, Senior Software Engineer at Applicon, Inc., MI. It describes how software Inspections started at Applicon, and offers some observations and tips on the methodology. The case study was written two years after its Inspection program was initiated. Applicon is a leading supplier of mechanical design automation software specializing in integrated solutions which shorten product cycles and improve productivity from engineering through manufacturing. 'Issues' and 'defects' are referred to as 'problems' in this chapter.

Implementation

Formalized software Inspections at Applicon had their beginnings in 1990 when our engineering organization was assessed using the Software Engineering Institute's (SEI) software maturity scale. Based on the findings of the SEI assessment, an action plan for process improvements was drawn up which called for, among other things, implementation of some type of peer reviews.

Later that year, a dedicated software process group was formed. As a member of the software process group, I attended Tom Gilb's Software Inspection leadership course. I had no previous interest in Inspections; in fact, the process sounded to me like a pillory for software engineers. However, the course sparked my enthusiasm and interest in Inspections.

The engineering organization had no previous training or program in Inspections or other peer review methodology. In general, people were not fond of change. Given the initial environment and the size of the engineering organization (about 200 people), the implementation of Inspections seemed a daunting project not likely to succeed. However, the support of management and the potential benefits of Inspections motivated me to assume the challenge of bringing Inspections into use and to make a commitment to ensure the success of the project.

First Year's Activities

Initial plan

Send one person to external training
Provide two-day Inspection leader training to interested individuals
Identify pilot groups for Inspections
Report and evaluate results
If positive results, proceed with implementation.

The initial plan was carried out. About 10% of the engineering staff volunteered to attend the initial Inspection leader training. Tom Gilb's course materials were used, along with a locally-created toolkit including a data summary form, log sheets, severity definitions, and document-specific checklists. The attendees included software developers, project managers, and the members of the software process group.

The students' responses were enthusiastic. Four additional project managers were briefed on Inspections, and agreed to do some Inspections in their groups. The process of leader certification began with self-certification of a chief Inspection leader (myself) and certification of four additional leaders, using material in process where there was management support. The initial Inspections were done on requirements, specifications, and code which were under active development.

The results of the initial two Inspections of 52 pages of requirements and specifications yielded 66 major problems at a fast checking rate of 15 pages per hour, a surprising number of problems (although in looking back, we could have found more problems had we Inspected at a slower rate). Feedback was solicited at the end of the meetings from two long-time skeptics. They liked the Inspections and wanted to do more!

A decision was made to proceed, and the plan for the first year's implementation consisted of these activities:

First year plan (1991)

Create toolkit of forms, checklists, and handouts
Teach two-day Inspection leader course semi-annually to interested individuals
Encourage Inspection of software project documents and code
Create Inspection database in Excel
Collect and report data monthly to engineering staff.

The first year's activities generated interest mostly at the grass-roots level. The toolkit underwent several improvements based on feedback collected at the Inspection leader courses and from practicing Inspection leaders. By inviting them to observe or participate, managers were persuaded to allow Inspections in their groups.

Introduction of a Formal Software Process

In the first year (1991) a parallel activity of the software process group was defining and implementing a formal software development process. A software process model was drafted based on IEEE standards. Management approved the model and mandated its use for all projects under active development about the same time as the Inspection program was begun.

The parallel introduction of a software process model and software Inspections proved beneficial since the two activities complement and support each other. The use of a software process requires producing several types of documents. These documents need formal review, which provides an incentive for doing Inspections. Inspections are especially useful to engineers who are writing requirements and specifications for the first time since they are prone to making a lot of mistakes.

The Inspections and software process model are complementary in other ways. Supporting standards for process documents such as requirements and specifications are needed by the development staff and software Inspections call for the use of standards. Also, a coherent software process demands consistency of all related project documentation, and software Inspections support consistency checking of the target documentation against its sources.

The software process group produced several standards the first year and Inspected most of them. Managers and developers outside the process group were invited to participate. Three or four managers were persuaded by these initial experiences to do Inspections in their groups.

The process group also Inspected a software engineering course in ten pieces or 'chunks'. These Inspections provided the software process group with valuable first-hand experience in the roles of producer and Inspector as well as Inspection leader. The value of these experiences helped solidify the group's commitment to implementing the process.

First Year's Results

Inspections were starting to be part of the organization's culture. Most who tried Inspections responded with enthusiasm, but only four groups were continuing to do Inspections – not surprisingly, those groups in which the manager required them. Most groups tried a few Inspections and then interest waned as deadlines approached. A few managers ignored Inspections altogether, citing schedule pressure as the reason.

However, the positive overall response by those who did participate and the first year's results were deemed good enough to continue with the program.

First year's results (1991)	
Number of document Inspections	39
Number of code Inspections	9
Average efficiency	0.8 hour to find and fix a major problem
Average effectiveness (documents)	2.3 major problems per page
Average effectiveness (code)	28.7 major problems per KLOC
Average checking rates	9.9 pages/hr. (docs); 300 lines/hr. (code)
Completed Inspection leader training	48
Certified leaders	8

One surprising statistic was that the document Inspections produced on average more than twice the number of major problems than did the code Inspections (45 opposed to 18). There appeared to be several reasons for this, the overriding one being that the number of problems in the code was lower. This was partly because most of the Inspected code had already been unit or field tested, or both.

At the end of the first year (1991) a second SEI software process maturity assessment was done. The organization was rated at SEI Level II, showing improvement. The resulting action plan called for more use of Inspections. This recommendation, coming from an outside authoritative source, was a major boost for Inspections. Plans for holding Inspections started showing up in managers' quality objectives for 1992.

Second Year's Activities

Four additional action items were proposed to senior management and accepted for implementation:

Second year plan (1992)
One hour Inspection overview presentation for senior management
Two hour Inspection overview presentation for project managers
Mandatory Inspection of requirements and specifications for all major projects
Requirement that at least 20% of the people in each group have Inspection leader training.

Management Support Needed

By the end of the first year it was clear that increased management support for Inspections was necessary for a successful implementation.

The senior Engineering managers were given an Inspection overview presentation. Product managers from Marketing attended. Inspection overviews were also given individually to the Vice Presidents of Engineering and Marketing; both endorsed the program and agreed to make Inspections of upstream documents mandatory. The Inspection leader's signature indicating a completed Inspection was added to the list of required approvals for the requirements and specifications.

The Vice President of Marketing notified his department that Inspections were required for approval of all mandatory documents produced. Thus interdepartmental Inspections between Marketing and Engineering began. These high-visibility Inspections and their support by Marketing helped establish Inspections in Engineering's culture. Most of the participants in the interdepartmental Inspections were managers, and many became convinced of the value of Inspections for catching problems early and for exchanging information.

Second Year's Results

The results shown for 1992 are cumulative. An interesting thing to note is that in 1992, 54 code Inspections were done. These were strictly voluntary and were done by several groups who needed to carry out careful examination of changes to code which could not be tested. For these Inspections, checking rates slowed down a great deal, reducing the average rate in 1991 of 300 lines of code (LOC) per hour to 200 LOC per hour. The expected results were observed: the rate slowed down, and the number of major problems found increased from an average of 28.7 per thousand lines of code (KLOC) to 53.3 per KLOC.

Second year's results (1992)	
Number of document Inspections	100
Number of code Inspections	63
Average efficiency	0.9 hour to find and fix a major problem
Average effectiveness (documents)	2.5 major problems per page
Average effectiveness (code)	53.3 major problems per KLOC
Average checking rates	9.1 pages/hr. (docs); 200 lines/hr. (code)
Completed leader training	70
Certified leaders	28

By late 1992, at the time of writing, over 170 Inspections have been completed with reasonable results. Inspections seem to have a life of their own; constant nurturing is not needed to keep the process going. Many managers are now requiring Inspections of more than the two mandatory documents. The regular use of Inspections (two or more per month) in well-managed projects is motivating non-participating managers to reconsider their position on Inspections.

Inspections are a regular activity in over half the groups and many people including skeptics have come to believe in their value. The only person in the software process group who did not attend Inspection leader training made the following remark two years later, and one year after moving back into technical development: 'If we were to throw out all the process improvements and keep only the most worthwhile one, we should keep the Inspections.' He had just participated in an Inspection of a critical document in which over 180 major problems were uncovered.

A Combination of Activities Brings Acceptance

Other activities of the software process group contributed to the acceptance of Inspections. Metrics and names of certified leaders were reported monthly. Several articles were published in a quality awareness newsletter. A tutorial on Inspections was created and presented at a corporate software conference. Inspections were observed by members of the process group. Improvements were made to the process based on feedback received. All engineers attended a one-week software engineering course during 1992 which included an overview of Inspections. All these activities gave increased visibility and credibility to Inspections.

One unexpected indication of acceptance is the emerging popularity of the Inspection leader role and the apparent status of certified leaders. Casual conversations in which people discuss who is a leader, who is certified, and brag about their certification are not uncommon. At first the role of leader was important only among new hires. However, apparently not to be outdone by the new hires, several senior people have made a point of becoming certified.

By now it was becoming clear that a combination of activities was contributing to the acceptance of Inspections – leader training, certification, use of a software process model, SEI action plans, presentations to management, mandatory Inspections of key documents, involvement of other departments, involvement of management, training of Inspectors, using feedback to improve the process, and reporting data.

Long-term Strategy

The long-term strategy for implementing Inspections is now as follows. Each year, development groups are required to Inspect more of their pre-code documents. In 1993, project plans and designs will be added to the list of documents for which Inspections will be required. Code Inspections remain optional at least until 100% of the pre-code documents are Inspected. The strategy is designed for maximum benefit by targeting early software process documents where software problems have been shown to be created in larger numbers (TRW, 1978) and at a greater cost (Boehm, 1981).

Results will be improved by slowing the checking rates. The plan is to slow the rates by at least 50% in the next two years.

The strategy is also designed for gradual acceptance. Groups cycling through the software process model at first are required to Inspect only two key documents per year, based on the projected release schedules. This gives them a chance to gain experience with Inspections and for results to improve before doing large numbers of Inspections.

Costs

Since Applicon did not hire an outside consultant to give training, most of the cost of the implementation consisted of in-house training – development of supporting materials and training courses, planning and executing training, and obtaining feedback. Tom Gilb's estimate for installation is one person full-time for one year. At Applicon, this proved fairly accurate, except that the installation was spread over two years, with about 50% of the job devoted to Inspections.

The cost of implementing Inspections is not restricted to the cost of its core staff. The cost of training must be taken into account. So far, 70 individuals have attended a two-day Inspection leader training course and about 50 people have attended a two-hour overview presentation for Inspectors and managers.

The ongoing cost of maintaining Inspections is approximately 25% of one full-time job in the software process group. The cost covers minor improvements, maintaining a statistical database, and training of Inspectors and leaders. Major changes or improvements to the process cost an additional 25% of one full-time job.

The actual Inspections more than pay for themselves. The average cost of one Inspection is not considered part of the overhead of Inspections but rather part of the overhead of maintaining an effective software development environment.

Benefits

The benefits of Inspections have yet to be measured at Applicon in terms of reduced numbers of software problems reported after release. Customers and field personnel have reported clear improvements in software quality since process improvement efforts began, but since a formal software process was introduced at the same time as Inspections, it is unclear how much of the benefits can be attributed to Inspections. The expectation is, however, that software quality will continue to improve as the usage of Inspections increases.

Baseline measurements of productivity in terms of number of work-months and number of lines of code produced are currently under way as the organization launches its first comprehensive software metrics program. Though the numbers are not yet available, some conclusions may nevertheless be drawn.

The initial reaction of management and developers was that developing software using a formal software process and Inspections would take longer. Early results show that this was not the case. On the contrary, productivity appears to have remained about the same or increased. It is expected that productivity will improve as the usage of Inspections increases.

Applicon's average efficiency of one work-hour to find and fix a major problem compared with its estimated average of 30 work-hours to fix a software problem after release suggests a possible savings ratio of 30 to one with Inspections. However, this may be misleading. First, there is no one-to-one correlation between customer-reported bugs and major problems reported in Inspections. Also, it is notable that the estimate does not include any of the time spent for either the customer or field personnel to report a problem or possible losses due to customer dissatisfaction, nor does it include overhead for maintenance.

Inspections must be profitable in any organization to justify their use, and improvements in quality and productivity form the basis for their profitability, which eventually must be measured. However, Inspections offer other benefits in addition to enhancing profitability.

In the area of human interactions, Inspections are having a transforming effect on Applicon's development environment. This transformation can be observed in groups that have a well-established Inspection process. In these groups, there are increased instances of people openly discussing problems, better sharing of information, more cooperation and teamwork, and generally less ego involvement and one-upmanship. These effects have occurred in several groups including the software process group. Inspections tend to create an atmosphere in which people are comfortable discussing problems, and can help break down barriers between developers, as well as between developers and managers who participate in Inspections as peers.

Problems and Solutions

Several problems were encountered in implementing Inspections at Applicon. An early problem was lack of metrics. The organization first had to invest in training, gain experience, and do enough Inspections to generate metrics. Only then could it prove to itself that the Inspections were useful.

Resistance was a problem. Often it was difficult getting Inspections started in groups, especially those in which deadlines were approaching. Managers did not want to make the initial investment to try the process. Individuals who were experienced with other types of peer reviews, such as reading-style inspections, technical reviews, and walkthroughs, preferred what was familiar to them and tended to resist the adoption of the new procedures. The solution has been to ignore the resistance and focus on those people who are interested in championing the Inspections. Peer pressure generated by the champions tends to take care of the problem.

Another problem was establishing and maintaining an effective Inspection process by enforcing sufficiently slow checking rates. The results should, after all, be more than worthwhile; they should be as good as possible. Yet the recommended checking rate of 1–2 pages per hour has not yet been accomplished. People in their initial enthusiasm tend to Inspect too much and do not understand the importance of the slow checking rates. A typical perception is that simply too much project documentation exists with too little time to do slow Inspection of it all, even of the upstream software process documents. It has continually been a challenge for the process group to insist on a minimum level of rigor and to keep the process afloat.

A related problem is what to count as pages or lines in code and document Inspections. For example, should comments be counted in code Inspections? Revision pages in documents? After quite a bit of experimentation the current solution is to count whatever is going to be Inspected. What will be Inspected should be based on what is important for the longevity of the company.

An easy problem to fix is to not 'train the trainers'. Initially, non-certified trained leaders were relied on to give hands-on training to new Inspectors. This has not worked well. New Inspection leaders do not have sufficient experience to train new Inspectors and many are not experienced in conducting training. At Applicon we've learned it is better to give formal Inspector training of at least one day and to include practice Inspections with the help of certified leaders.

A related problem has been scheduling of training. Inspections are not well suited for late phases of software development such as alpha or beta testing, but are ideal for early phases such as requirements definition. The best way to time training may be to offer initial or refresher courses to project groups prior to beginning projects so the information is fresh and people can practice what they have learned.

Problem Reporting Meeting

Finding effective scribes was an early problem. Generally, no one was interested in the task. Leaders did not want to record; they found it interfered with running a meeting. Many had poor handwriting when under pressure to write quickly. Those leaders who recorded (leaders assumed the task by default) found they could not keep up with the pace of the meetings, and Inspectors were getting bored waiting for them to finish writing down the problems. The eventual solution was to eliminate the role of scribe and have Inspectors log their problems during the checking stage. The focal meeting of the Inspection process was renamed a Problem Reporting Meeting. The elimination of the scribe has been an improvement to the process; this change is described in detail.

The scribe was first dropped when two groups rejected the scribe role. Log sheets were handed out with the Inspection packets and Inspectors were asked to log their problems during the checking stage. The Inspectors adopted the new procedure without complaints. Inspectors crossed out duplicates during the problem reporting meeting.

The software process group then tried the pre-logging procedure. The process group found that logging problems during checking required more effort, but was worthwhile since writing down the problems helped in reporting them. The main difference noticed, however, was the improved flow of the meetings. The meetings moved along at a comfortable pace when there was no waiting for logging.

The advantages observed as a result of pre-logging problems and eliminating the role of scribe in the meetings are summarized as follows:

Advantages of pre-logging problems

Inspectors take the proper time to prepare and prepare more carefully
Problems are recorded with greater accuracy
Inspectors classify their problems (many didn't previously)
Inspectors show up prepared to report their data (number of problems, severities, time)

Advantages of pre-logging problems (continued)

Meetings move at a comfortable rate
Meetings are more interesting
Saves an estimated meeting time of 20%.

For the sake of efficiency, a second variation on the process was invented. Deadline pressure was on for one set of materials, so the process group tried a new technique: to report only the major problems and skip over the minor problems. To retain the educational value of the meeting, the group agreed that minor problems would be restricted to typographical, punctuation, spelling, grammatical, and other such cosmetic problems that do not affect the understanding of the technical content of the material.

The meetings became shorter. The group's time was spent reporting only major problems. Minor problems were passed along to the author for correction with no loss of ability to correct them.

Since then, these procedures have been implemented throughout Engineering. Many Inspection meetings have been conducted without incident or complaints. Problem Reporting Meetings are interesting, little time is wasted, and the pace is comfortable.

Advantages of reporting only major problems

Encourages people to find major problems
Meetings do not digress into a discussion of minor problems
Inspection meetings are more interesting
Saves an estimated meeting time of 10%.

The overall effect of these two changes has been improved meeting efficiency of at least 30% and increased credibility for Inspections.

Keys to Success

The following keys to success are lessons learned at Applicon which might be helpful to others who are interested in implementing Inspections. Other factors also helped make the program a success as well but were not as critical.

Management Support

Management support for Inspections, especially at the highest levels, has been crucial. Funding a dedicated software process group gave support in a concrete way, allowing for appropriate training at all levels and an in-depth understanding of the process by at least one individual. Management commitment to attaining SEI Software Maturity goals helped convince people at all levels that the Inspection activities were part of a long-term program rather than a passing fad. Participation in training, and support of the mandatory document Inspections, also helped make Inspections a reality at Applicon.

Inspection Process Definition

Another key to the successful implementation of Inspections at Applicon has been a process definition based on the kind of metrics that distinguish Inspections from other types of reviews. The parameters employed at Applicon are:

Inspection process definition

Size of target document: 10 pages of documentation or 250 lines of code (maximums accepted are double these amounts)
Checking time: two or more hours
Checking rate: 5–10 pages or 125–250 lines of code per hour
Size of Inspection team: 3–7 people
Problem reporting meeting: two hours maximum.

In this way, the organization solved the chicken-and-egg problem of doing Inspections based on its own optimized statistical values before metrics were available by using average industry values. These parameters provided reasonable results for the initial start-up.

In addition, the following were insisted on:

Inspections led by trained leaders
A leader certification program
Entry criterion: document readiness
Inspection packet: product document, rule set, checklist, and at least one source document
Exit criteria: edit, metrics, edited document made available to Inspectors.

Target Inspection Material

Another key to the success of Applicon's Inspection program has been the choice of Inspection material. The approach of Inspecting material that offers the greatest benefit – upstream software process documents – is a good choice. The Inspection of these documents has helped sell the process. Many people, including managers, who participated in these Inspections became strong supporters of

Inspections in their groups and went on to do more Inspections than were required.

Champion

Especially in the beginning stages, having at least one person in the organization who is committed to implementing Inspections is essential to keeping the organization on track. Many subtle issues can be misunderstood in the early stages, but more importantly, any new program is, like a young plant, in need of constant care. Many small tasks that appear trivial or mundane help a young process to grow into a new activity for an organization. By having a person assigned to champion the process, sufficient time can be given to carry out whatever tasks are needed for a successful implementation. Enthusiasm is contagious and can be quite beneficial.

Problem Definition

The topic of defect or problem definition (which is an interesting and important sub-project) was given a great deal of thought when applied to Applicon's Inspection program. Problem definition at Applicon is given a broad meaning, since all types of problems have something in common – they cost money.

Each organization must define for itself what a 'defect' is in Inspections. The problems and challenges in an organization typically go beyond software bugs reported by customers and field personnel. An example of this is ease of use, which is clearly a growing software requirement in today's world. Ease of use is being redefined almost continually with no end in sight for what will increase customer satisfaction.

Defining 'major problems' for the organization is another interesting challenge. Given all the kinds of losses that companies suffer and the opportunity to use Inspections as a tool to help correct and prevent some of those problems, I believe it is a serious mistake to limit a major problem to just a malfunction of software. To begin to get an idea of the kinds of problems which are causing loss, problem reports can be examined. However the biggest losses, such as loss of market share due to lack of innovation, may become the future basis for problem definitions.

Also, quite often, there are problems that need to be solved within the organization which cause various amounts of loss or lost opportunities for the company. Problems take many forms such as portability and maintainability of the software and may not always be apparent to customers.

By applying a sufficiently broad, customized definition of 'problem', Inspections can be used not only to prevent software bugs, but to prevent other sources of loss as well. In addition to helping make an Inspection program as profitable as possible, an effective problem definition is a subtle but powerful tool for communicating new standards of excellence.

Metrics

Metrics are extremely important in Inspections, although this is not at all obvious at first. It is easy to skip or skimp on this part of the job. However, setting up an Inspection spreadsheet is simple and is something every organization that is serious about their Inspections should do.

There are several reasons why Inspection metrics must be kept. Inspections must be profitable to justify their existence, and metrics are the tool for measuring Inspections' profitability. Metrics are essential – without them, the parameters of the process cannot be optimized. It is in part the use of metrics in Inspections that differentiates the process from technical reviews and walkthroughs. Without measurement, there is no way for the organization to know how it is doing with its Inspections, so how can it improve them?

Tips for Implementation

The following tips are offered for implementing and improving inspection programs.

Make a strong, objective case for Inspections. No amount of enthusiasm can achieve what even one convincing set of metrics will do to persuade an organization to adopt Inspections. Engineers are persuaded by facts. Build a logical, objective, bulletproof case for Inspections, and you will have the support of your most extreme skeptics. Take sufficient time to adequately educate the trainers with a thorough knowledge of the process so they can properly answer the questions they will be confronted with.

Adopt as much rigor as possible. People tend to form habits early on, so make sure the habits they form are desirable. When implementing Inspections, teach and demand as much rigor as the organization will bear. This will yield the best possible results. Carefully solicit and monitor feedback to be sure that you are not expecting too much. Be aware that if too much or too little rigor is applied, the program could fail. Often, finding the right amount is like walking a tightrope. It is better to err on the side of rigor since that is what will make Inspections a success.

Do whatever it takes to maintain longevity of the process. The goal should always be to keep the process alive, no matter what. Get to the bottom of the challenges that are presented and find solutions to them. Incorporate the problems and their solutions in the training materials and educate people about the possible pitfalls – utilize the problems to advance the process.

Solicit feedback and continuously improve the process. Stay in touch with the people who are doing the Inspections. Participate in each role of the process – Inspection leader, Inspector, producer – to understand it in depth. Observe Inspections regularly to find out what is working and what isn't, and make improvements that could benefit the organization. A lot of small improvements can have a significant impact on the overall program.

Customize the process to your organization's needs. Be responsive to the people who are doing the Inspections and adapt the process to their needs. Listen carefully. Make it their process! Good Inspection leaders are the best champions and role models. Educate people in the importance of process. Only make changes that do not violate the process. Update the training materials. Find ways for people to modify the process, so they can share the ownership of it.

Organizations usually change slowly. Although people often prefer otherwise, it is helpful not to expect too much too soon when implementing Inspections or implementing a change in the program. Don't expect the organization to change all at once. Allow people to complain, and welcome their feedback. Educate people at all levels as much as the organization will allow. Inspections are a form of behavior and because of this, change is usually more likely to succeed when implemented slowly. This is not a problem unless expectations are otherwise.

Take into account subjective issues such as cultural behavior. Cultural behavior is something which, although subjective, can nevertheless bring about loss in a company. Consider the effect, for example, of fear in the workplace. In an organization in which people are afraid of reprisal or confrontation, or find Inspections intimidating, an entire Inspection program can easily fail. People simply will not find or disclose enough problems to make the process pay for itself. Identify and acknowledge the subjective issues and find strategies to address them.

Teach Inspections with care and sensitivity. The way the Inspection process is presented will have an effect on the way people perceive Inspections. Since our society tends to teach us that mistakes and errors are at best a source of embarrassment and are potentially damaging to a person's reputation, a good Inspection program will counteract these beliefs. People often need to be reminded that not only does everyone make mistakes, everyone gains much of their most valuable experience when given an opportunity to learn from their mistakes. Understanding and utilizing this point is key to a successful implementation.

13
One Person Getting Started

This case study was written by Ed Barnard, Senior Programmer Analyst at Cray Research, Inc., Eagan, MN. The terms in this chapter (logger, issue, and so on) differ from those in use at Cray Research. To ensure that I am correctly understood, I have written this case study using terminology consistent with the rest of this book.

This case study is an example of what you can expect as you begin using Software Inspections. I will lead you through a one-person software development project, concentrating on my thought processes, showing you the lessons I learned along the way.

I will show you why 'upstream' (planning phase) Inspections worked out much better than 'downstream' (coding phase) Inspections. Software Inspections provided little additional benefit to the coding phase of this project – but the planning phase Inspections cleared the way to discover that the project, as originally planned, could well end in disaster.

Part One of this case study focuses on the project.

- 'Setting the Scene' introduces the company, the author, and the project.
- 'Upstream Inspection' leads you through the creation of a high-level document, from the perspectives of both the author and Inspection leader. I will illustrate the details of writing a document for Inspection and dealing with Inspection-raised issues.
- 'Customer Visit' demonstrates the success or failure of the project document, and of the Inspection process which created it.
- 'Project Success' balances the successful 'upstream' Inspections against the limited value of 'downstream' Inspections in a single-expert environment.

Part Two focuses on leading the Software Inspection process.

- 'Do It Yourself Metrics' demonstrates ways to use Inspection metrics as an individual Inspection leader. While merely applied common sense, this area is rarely touched on in Inspection training or literature.

- 'Inspection Roadblocks' provides an honest confession of why certain Inspections have not worked out for me.
- 'Conclusion' distils what I learned into a final commentary.

Software Inspection is an extremely formal process. If you are not careful, formality can become an end in itself, replacing common sense. In order to demonstrate that such nonsense is not inevitable, I have written this case study as an occasionally humorous treatment of a serious project. I trust this approach will in itself demonstrate a valuable technique of keeping formality in its place; I hope you enjoy this story as you learn from my experiences.

> At Cray Research, we take what we do very seriously, but we
> don't take ourselves too seriously.
>
> From *The Cray Style* corporate statement

PART ONE: THE PROJECT

1   Setting the Scene

1.1   About the Organization and Author

Cray Research creates 'the most powerful and highest quality computational tools for solving the world's most challenging scientific and industrial problems.' A unique environment and culture hides behind this Mission Statement; this case study will give you a glimpse inside.

> Economy comes from high value, not from low cost. Aesthetics
> are part of quality.
>
> From *The Cray Style*

This study takes place as Software Inspections were being introduced at Cray Research. I was a 'bug fixer' in the operating system group of the Software Division. I was responsible for the older low-level tape subsystem software, assigned to fix all reported defects in this subsystem. With lots of advice, I did so. I was relatively new to both software development and Software Inspection, but not new to the industry. I have spent 13 years with Cray Research supporting, documenting, teaching, and now developing operating system software.

While I call this a one-person project, it really was not, of course. I had help from numerous areas, but most especially I had a mentor, far more experienced than me with software development in general and this tape subsystem in particular.

1.2   Problem

I hate to admit that our Cray X-MP™ computer system (Figure 13.1) software had problems. However, at the time of this study, we had a customer who pushed the limits of our tape subsystem harder than anyone else. When this customer purchased higher-speed tape channels (4.5 million bytes per second transfer rate, or 4.5 Mb/sec), the heavier load uncovered reliability problems. This situation was unexpected, since things were fine at the normal channel speed (3.0 Mb/sec).

How can a mere tape drive overwhelm a CRAY X-MP supercomputer?

It's not easy – in fact, only one customer in the world has been able to do so. Tape data flow is from the magnetic tape through the tape control unit, into the Cray I/O Subsystem, and on into the CRAY X-MP mainframe. Data flow is identical for the reverse direction. In the customer's case, the I/O Subsystem is the bottleneck, running at its maximum capacity. With enough modern tape drives at one end, and an ever-faster Cray mainframe on the other end, the customer was able to overwhelm the I/O Subsystem. The newer Cray I/O Subsystems no longer contain the architectural bottleneck I alluded to above.

1.3   Solution

We decided upon the following alternatives.

- Give the customer more hardware. The customer would no longer be 'pushing the limits' so hard and, presumably, not be encountering these problems. The book value of this hardware giveaway would be upwards of a million dollars.
- Give the customer the newest hardware, which would include our newest software. With our newest offering, the problem disappears. The architectural bottleneck allowing a mere collection of tape drives to overwhelm the system has been removed, in addition to the new software being incomparably more reliable. We normally charge several million dollars for this newest hardware.
- Fix the existing customer environment. The projected 3–6 developer months are a trivial cost in comparison to a possible hardware giveaway.

The changes would be in my subsystem, so the solution became *my* problem. I had the chance to save the situation ('all in a day's work'), or fail and cause the megadollar hardware giveaway ('you useless imbecile'). I became highly motivated, as they say, to achieve a favorable result.

> We look first to our customers to define Cray quality – and we do our best every day to deliver it.
>
> From *The Cray Style*

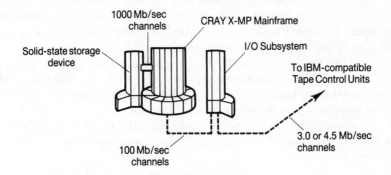

Figure 13.1   A CRAY X-MP computer system.

1.4   Get Started

Upon accepting the situation, I had:

- An objective: make the customer happy.
- A strategy: make the suggested software changes.

We knew when to get started (yesterday at the latest), but did not know when to quit – when is it good enough? I thus started heading two directions in parallel:

- The 'real work', writing, Inspecting, and testing the software changes.
- The 'overhead', in the form of a formal requirements document and a plan for its achievement.

> The Cray approach is informal and non-bureaucratic but thorough. People are accessible at all levels.
>
> From *The Cray Style*

This case study looks at the 'overhead' phase first, including a visit to the customer. I will then discuss the 'real work' briefly, concentrating on what has *not* worked for me. Finally, I will examine some lessons I have learned as an Inspection leader.

2   Upstream Inspection

2.1   'To Somebody with a Hammer, Everything Looks Like a Nail'

I decided to try a new approach with the requirements document. I had recently attended Tom Gilb's training on Result Delivery Planning. The planning course had little to do with Software Inspections, but (like Inspections) focused on achieving a top-quality result. None of us course graduates had yet any experience in using these planning techniques. This project seemed an ideal place to apply what I had learned; I was excited at the prospect of doing a better-quality job than I ever had before.

Several of us quietly declared this project the 'guinea pig'. I would create a 'proper' requirements document and project plan and two of the other graduates agreed to help Inspect the result with an eye to using this as an example or template for their own work later on. I did not burden my manager with details about 'guinea pigs' and formal documents. I hoped that, in the fullness of time, the result would speak for itself.

> With informality, however, there is also a sense of confidence.
> Cray people feel like they are on the winning side. They feel
> successful, and they are. It is this sense of confidence that
> generates the attitude of 'go ahead and try it, we'll make it work.'
> From *The Cray Style*

2.2 Writing the Document

The informal objective was quite clear (see Figure 13.2).

What I wanted to do was quantify 'at least as reliable,' so that we could conclusively demonstrate success to the customer when the time came. I separated what I planned to accomplish into the components shown in Figure 13.3, and tried to show that hierarchy in the requirements document. (This breakdown applied what I had learned in the Gilb planning course.)

I followed the Rule Sets, creating a page and a half of complex text. It was the best I could create, so I declared it ready for Inspection.

2.3 The Software Inspection

I gathered a volunteer Inspection team. Three of the four of us had attended Gilb's planning course; the fourth was included as a sanity check. All of us, you will recall, were interested in putting Gilb's planning principles into practice.

> People like taking responsibility for what they do and thinking
> for themselves. At the same time, we work together and are
> proud to share a single mission – to create the most powerful and

---

The system must be at least as reliable using 4.5 Mb/sec tape channels as it currently is using 3.0 Mb/sec tape channels.

Figure 13.2 The informal project objective.

highest quality computational tools for solving the world's most challenging scientific and industrial problems.

From *The Cray Style*

I thought I did pretty well, but everyone else found my requirements document incomprehensible – even those who had attended the same course I had. I suffered from a typical author's blindness. I found almost no issues during Inspection while the others found dozens and dozens of major (or worse) issues. During the logging session, we ran out of time after logging a mass of super-major issues. (A super-major issue is one which, by itself, could potentially invalidate the entire project.) Figure 13.4 illustrates the Inspection data.

2.4 Document Upgrade

After correcting a tremendous list of serious defects, I had expanded the document from a reasonable page and a half to an intimidating five pages. The Inspection leader (me) and the author (me) got our heads together and figured out that something was seriously wrong – a mere edit of the existing document was not getting us where we wanted to be.

So now what? The informal requirements statement was quite clear to all involved, but the formal statement was incomprehensible gibberish. Furthermore, the requirements document was (I thought) produced according to the teaching of Tom Gilb himself, and according to the Rule Sets he provided in his course materials.

I decided the problems fell into these general categories:

- The Rule Sets turned out to be either incomprehensible or easily misunderstood in practice.

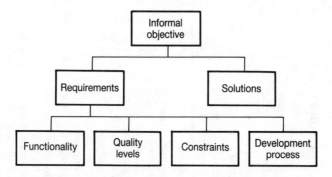

Figure 13.3 Organization of project plan.

Insp.Ref	ewb0010		Doc. Type:	plan		Submitted:	6/11/92
Chunk:			Pages:	1.50		Pages Insp:	1.50
Leader:	ewb		Plan Time:	3.00 hours			
Kick off Meeting			# people:	4			
			Duration:	68 minutes			
			Total meeting effort	4.53 work-hours			

Checking Activity   # Checkers: 4

Role	Super Major	Major	Minor	Question	Improv.	Totals	Problem Pages	Pages Studied	Check Hours
Leader									
Author		3	1			4	2.00	1.50	1.50
Chckr 1	5	35				77	2.00	1.50	1.50
Chckr 2	9	4	2	10	2	27	3.00	1.50	2.00
Chckr 3	9	13	3	3	3	31	2.00	1.50	1.50
Summary	23	55	43	13	5	139	9.00	6.00	6.50

Logging Session   Date: 6/15/92

Scheduled start	14:00
Actual start	14:07
Logging start	14:42
Questions start	15:49
Logging end	16:10
Brainstorm start	16:10
Meeting end	16:10
Total meeting effort	8:12 work-hours

		# people:	4
SM/Major	80		
Minor	1		
Other	1		
Total	96		

Net pp. studied	1.50
Logging time	1:28 hours:mins
Logging rate	1.09 items/min
SM+Maj/page	53.33

Adjusted Defects
Fixed SM/Majors	132
Fixed Minors	17
Change requests	45

Completion date:	7/7/92
Follow-up cycle:	22 days

Follow-up

Leader time:	0.50	hours
Experience factor:	8.00	avg. editing mins/item
Est. Editing time:	12.80	hours
Actual Editing time:	13.00	hours

Total Inspection Effort
27.88 work-hours,   26 days elapsed

Figure 13.4 Data for the first Inspection.

- The requirements document used jargon and special formatting that had meaning only to myself.
- In the desire to define measurable objectives, I contrived measurements that had little practical meaning and thus appeared as nonsense.

I found it much more satisfactory to blame my inadequate document on the faulty Rule Sets rather than deal with my own authorship. I switched roles from requirements document editor to de facto Rule Sets editor and upgraded the Rule Sets, based on the issues raised in the Inspection.

2.5 Rule Set Upgrade

Rule Sets should require as little specialized knowledge as possible. However, the Inspection showed that these Rule Sets assumed everyone had attended the planning course, and were therefore useless (Figure 13.5). My planning document likewise tended toward incomprehensibility.

> The purpose of a Rule Set, for a checker, is to help find major (or worse) defects. If the rule only identifies trivia, throw it out. If the rule is useless to a checker, either throw it out or transform it into a useful item. Useless rules are parasites, sucking life from your organization. Kill them.

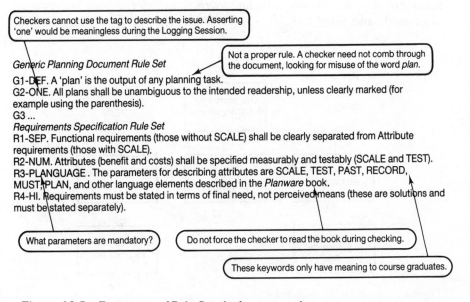

Checkers cannot use the tag to describe the issue. Asserting 'one' would be meaningless during the Logging Session.

Not a proper rule. A checker need not comb through the document, looking for misuse of the word *plan*.

Generic Planning Document Rule Set
G1-DEF. A 'plan' is the output of any planning task.
G2-ONE. All plans shall be unambiguous to the intended readership, unless clearly marked (for example using the parenthesis).
G3 ...
Requirements Specification Rule Set
R1-SEP. Functional requirements (those without SCALE) shall be clearly separated from Attribute requirements (those with SCALE).
R2-NUM. Attributes (benefit and costs) shall be specified measurably and testably (SCALE and TEST).
R3-PLANGUAGE. The parameters for describing attributes are SCALE, TEST, PAST, RECORD, MUST, PLAN, and other language elements described in the *Planware* book.
R4-HI. Requirements must be stated in terms of final need, not perceived means (these are solutions and must be stated separately).

What parameters are mandatory?

Do not force the checker to read the book during checking.

These keywords only have meaning to course graduates.

Figure 13.5   Fragments of Rule Sets before upgrade.

I reorganized the Rule Sets, separating generic rules from planning-specific rules, so that we could create a hierarchy of one-page Rule Sets (Figure 13.6). Figure 13.7 shows how I made a specific Rule Set more useful.

2.6 Another Round of Requirements

The stated project objective had now evolved from the simple one-liner in Figure 13.2, to the page-and-a-half attempt that we Inspected, to a five-page rewrite. This rewrite had very little content change; I was simply trying to create a more palatable format, defining my terms and explaining what I was trying to accomplish.

2.7 Another Software Inspection

I finally had a document that I hoped was readable. I was assuming all along that it was technically correct, but I should have known better!

I gathered a second Inspection team. Half of the team was different from the first team, and provided as close a perspective to the customer's point of view as we could manage.

The document was clearly an improvement – we were able to see past the formatting issues and move on to the technical faults. After the first few minutes we closed the log to all but super-major issues and questions that might lead to identifying such issues. With so many issues identified of such magnitude a mere major issue is so much noise – not worth writing down. I asked for peoples' notes afterwards and filled out the log to 173 issues.

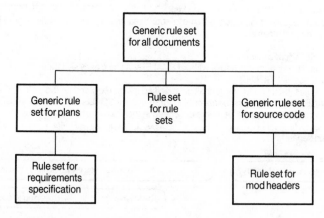

Figure 13.6 Rule Set hierarchy.

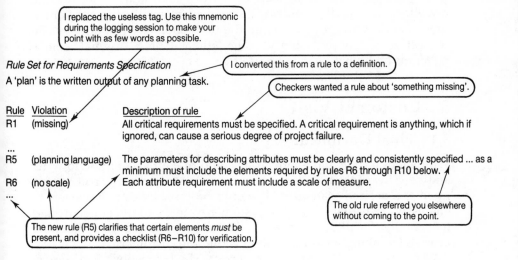

Figure 13.7 An upgraded Rule Set fragment.

2.8 Reality Check

Why, you should ask, am I presenting a document with dozens of reported issues as a case study? I chose this document because I wrote it myself, so that I need not be shy about advertising its inadequacies. I am showing you a 'worst case', rather than a complete 'success story'. When you first start out, even if you find things less smooth than expected, you will know that is normal.

When first beginning effective Software Inspections, people are often shocked with the sheer volume of issues raised. Even though the author had the best of intentions, you may well find documents with upwards of a hundred serious defects per page. Be aware of this possibility. In fact, if you are just getting started with Inspections and you are not finding documents with dozens of major defects per page, you should find out why. (Consider the possibility that your Inspections are far less effective than they should be.)

You will have noted that thus far I have acted as author, Inspection leader, editor, statistician, Rule Sets editor, logger, checker, and now project historian. Is this really a one-person project? Would it not be better, and more in keeping with the principle of peer review, to have someone else deal with the Inspection details and let me stick with authorship? Yes!

This multiple-role approach created several problems. I had no sanity check; as leader I could not tell the author he was on the wrong track. Discussions between the leader and editor (again, myself) were equally fruitless. I struggled to justify the substantial time necessary to properly set up the Inspection. We did not have an Inspections resource library, other than Gilb's original course materials and what I created myself.

3 Customer Visit

3.1 Final Document

With enough time and energy, one could of course continue to write and rewrite such a requirements document, hopefully converging upon the desired statement. It would be terribly silly, however, to endlessly try to state what the customer wants, and never get around to actually fulfilling that want. We short-circuited this planning process by taking what I had and visiting the customer.

This document was far from perfect. The Inspections had proven that beyond a shadow of a doubt. However, it did still serve its intended purpose – to provide a point of discussion with the customer. We would have concrete issues before us to discuss, validate, or modify. I intended that by the time the visit was over, everyone would have the same understanding and expectations.

3.2 Planning the Visit

You might recall that I had not burdened my manager with my hidden agenda for the requirements document. It was time to show what we had produced. I had boiled the requirements back down to a single page, followed by a short list of issues to discuss with the customer.

My manager took it well. This Gilb-inspired thing was not nearly so daunting as she had feared. We discussed how to handle the actual visit. Out we flew.

The next hurdle was the local Cray staff – the salesman and software representatives. We gave them a dry run of the presentation and asked if there were any surprises we should know about.

The Cray staff were quite pleased with what we had to say. We were obviously taking this project seriously and had put some good thought into understanding what the customer *really* wanted. This meeting was quite short – nothing more needed to be done except meet the customer.

3.3 The Visit: Feedback to the Process

The meeting went well, and the customer was favorably impressed with our preparation and the sincerity of our effort. We obviously had more in mind than a 'quick fix' of dubious value.

Here are some things we had 'done right.'

- We came well prepared, bringing the right information and the right participants to the meeting.
- We visited the customer, keeping them informed.
- We visited the customer, taking the trouble to ensure we really understood the customer's needs.
- We visited the customer, finding out our misunderstandings while there was still time to correct the situation.
- We demonstrated an awareness of exactly what quality was of interest to this customer, and also demonstrated precisely how we intended to deliver that quality.
- We kept discussing matters until all present were certain we all had the correct understandings.
- All issues discussed arose from the presented document. As author, I would never have anticipated all issues without benefit of the two Inspections. Likewise, with merely the informal objective written down, I think it unlikely that all critical issues would have been discussed in this meeting. I discovered that there were several major misunderstandings on my part.
- The customer is a data center which in turn provides service to their own customers. Every past problem has reflected on their own ability to provide service. Even though they have all been resolved, the series of past problems has placed their own credibility at stake. If they enable these higher-speed tape channels one more time and anything goes wrong, they will take them out of production and never use them again. In other words, we have exactly one more chance. No mistakes, innocent or otherwise, will be tolerated.
- If something breaks, it does not matter to the customer what it is that broke. It does not matter if it's new code I wrote, or something else. In other words, if there are any problems to be found anywhere, I'd better find them!
- After all that work of trying to figure out what we should measure to prove success, I discovered I had the wrong tape subsystem performance measure. We agreed upon the correct measure during the meeting.
- Reliability is the overriding concern. Increased performance is a very distant second. As noted above, if there is any degradation in service quality, it's all over.
- Finally, since no other site in the world has this customer's tape subsystem capacity (that's the whole 'problem'), I had hoped to do the stress testing at the customer site. This suggestion was greeted with a resounding 'No.'

3.4 Oops!

The customer's own credibility was wound up in this project. They were interested, out of self defense, in exactly what we planned to do with this project, and offered their advice and expertise. The discussion turned to our software development process. I obviously had not given enough thought to stress testing by this point (I had figured the customer could do it for me), but was proud of the fact that I was subjecting the coding changes to Software Inspections. (Inspections were nothing new to this customer, but the customer was well aware that these were just being introduced within Cray Research.)

I briefly described our Software Inspection process, including entry and exit checks and criteria. I explained how to predict the number of defects remaining in a document based on the number found and corrected and presumed effectiveness of the Inspection team. I blithely went on to explain that I allow no more than three major defects to remain per 50 lines of (assembler) code. I hastened to add that I intended the exit criterion to eventually be one-tenth that (three major defects per 500 lines of code), but 'we're not there yet.'

Oh my, did I cause a stir! The customer staff couldn't believe I was serious. The Cray salesman could not believe it. Software Development was declaring to the customer that we ship code knowing it has three bugs per page (we don't!). My manager could not believe I would say such a thing. Other expressions of disbelief were lost in the uproar.

Fortunately, all present quite literally did not believe I meant what I said. They asked me to define exactly what I did mean. I explained that I meant certifiable bugs or the equivalent. For example, suppose there is a spot where the commentary does not match the code. The code is correct, but it is quite likely that later on someone will incorrectly modify the code (based on the misleading commentary), thus introducing a bug. I would call the code/commentary mismatch a major defect.

It was clarified by consensus (without my saying anything) that major, minor, and so on are terms that apply to Inspection data but have no meaning in the real world. The important concept is what the customer can observe in the existing system. So long as the code is working, the customer does not care that the accompanying comments might mislead someone sometime in the future. There is no defect observable by the customer *now*.

Once I understood what a defect was (namely, something that will cause a customer job to quit), it was explained to me (politely, but firmly, and from several directions) that the acceptable number of defects is zero. Period. Not three in fifty lines, or one in ten thousand lines. Zero.

Zero defects was, of course, my goal anyway. I wouldn't introduce defects on purpose. At the same time, I was trying to reconcile zero defects as expressed above with the idea of predicting the remaining number of defects based on Inspection data. If the Inspection result indicated more than zero major defects likely remained, some of which could be real bugs, what do I do?

We wound up the discussion with this understanding: If I had probable cause to believe there is a single customer-observable bug in the new or changed code, 'don't ship it.' This conclusion seemed obvious when stated like that, but we sure took the long way around to arrive there.

This discussion was continued, with the Cray salesman and my manager, all the way back to the airport. By time we arrived, I was quite clear on the subject. My manager later complimented me on how well I took the verbal walloping. (I had kept firmly in mind The First Solo Flight Principle: 'Any landing you can walk away from is a good one.')

3.5   Inspection Data Useful?

Given the preceding discussion contrasting defects as defined by this customer with defects as defined by Software Inspection, must I conclude that Software Inspection results are useless except to the people that run the Inspections?

Certainly not – but I clearly need to modify my version of the process and, perhaps, the terminology I use. 'Defect' in the sense of customer-observable bug is relevant for code shipped to a customer but seems less relevant in a requirements document. (A missing requirement could not be a defect until the resulting defective code is shipped to the customer.)

I should be collecting a separate piece of information – those defects which are also customer-observable bugs. This idea is hardly a new one, and it would serve two specific purposes in my environment:

- In addition to the exit check being based on the predicted remaining major defect density, another criterion could ensure we have reasonable cause to believe the document contains zero customer-observable defects.
- With Software Inspections still in the introductory stage, many managers understand the concept of customer-observable defect (bug) better than the more esoteric major defect as defined by the Inspection process. Bug count has more concrete meaning than, say, understandability by a novice.

Let me hasten to point out that the Inspection-defined major defect remains a key piece of information. If you focus entirely on 'bug count' and ignore, for example, understandability by a novice, you have little hope of improving your software quality (especially if you ever hire a novice).

4 Project Success

4.1 Upstream and Downstream Inspections

Thanks to the 'upstream' planning (Inspection input and customer visit), I discovered that merely correctly writing the code I had planned was no guarantee of project success. The critical factor was that the customer observe *no* problems, regardless of the source.

Correct code was critical, but so was stress testing. If I had merely concentrated on writing and Inspecting code, I may well have entirely missed that critical factor. In other words, the 'upstream' planning and Inspection effort paid off. However, only about half of this code was ever Inspected – the remainder passed informal but rigorous review.

4.2 The Single-expert Environment

I discovered that it is quite difficult to justify code Inspections in a single-expert environment – when the objective is removal of customer-observable bugs. (Numerous important people, you will recall, had clarified this as my single most important objective.)

In my case, only two people were likely to find serious defects in the code Inspected. These were my mentor and myself, and only I was actively working with this subsystem. The area is so specialized that it was even difficult to find 'novices' to help Inspect. The novice perspective was valuable, and did lead to better code documentation. The novice perspective, however, had no impact on the project's critical objective.

We tried several Inspections, but discerned no difference in customer-observable bug detection between the Inspections and our normal review process. Since the total number of customer-reported problems escaping the two of us is very small, we have very little data to contrast rigorous reviews with Inspections in this single-expert environment.

4.3 Incomplete Success

What is the final result of this project? It has not yet been delivered to the customer (the customer is not yet ready, as of this writing). However:

- Stress testing is complete and the customer is happy with the result. Numerous 'fine tuning' improvements were made along the way, based on the experience gained.

- The tape subsystem is now even more robust than originally planned – it now correctly handles obscure hardware failures I had never even heard of before the stress testing commenced.
- Unrelated potential problems have arisen with other customers during the time period of this case study. Our tape subsystem was suddenly showing problems that it never had before. I suspect this is related to more and more sites stressing the latest tape technology harder and harder.

Fortunately, in every case I was able to send out the software I had just stress tested – and it solved the problem. In fact, the software completing the stress testing has solved every reported customer problem.

> The creativity, then, that emerges from the company comes from the many ideas of the individuals who are here and from the teams of Cray Research people who make these ideas into quality products for our customers. And that is the real strength of Cray Research.
>
> From *The Cray Style*

PART TWO: LEADING INSPECTIONS

1 'Do It Yourself' Metrics

1.1 Change in Focus

I took the Inspection process as far as I could with this specific project. Now it is time to step back as leader and see what I can learn.

I believe it is important to set the best example I can for my peer leaders (Figure 13.8). Since Software Inspections derives much of its power from statistical control of the overall (development) process, it is important to exemplify that concept at the personal level. In other words, if I am to support the use of process metrics, I should set the example by using them myself in some way. This is quite simple, as I will show you – merely applied common sense.

Not many of you should presume to be teachers, my brothers, because you know that we who teach will be judged more strictly.

James 3:1, New International Version

Figure 13.8

1.2 Your Numeric Experience

Fortunately, your metrics have great value for you as Inspection leader. They represent a large portion of your experience – if you trouble to make use of this experience. Don't leave their use to someone else!

If you analyze your own metrics with the view of optimizing your own job as Leader, you will probably continue to improve rapidly. You will begin to understand Software Inspections 'in the bones', subconsciously supporting rather than sabotaging the process control aspect. Without realizing any direct benefit from gathering metrics, for example, I might well tend to get sloppier and sloppier in this respect, losing effectiveness as a leader.

Each of the following subsections provides an example of statistical analysis leading to performance improvement.

1.3 Estimated Editing Time

Based on the number of issues logged in the logging session, I predict how long it will take the editor to complete the editing. (I base the prediction on the total number of issues, not just problems in the author's document, because the editor must deal with *all* logged issues in some fashion.)

1.4 Anticipating the Outcome

Let me bring out another important principle, using the previous example where I predicted eight hours of editing time but the editor came back in half an hour, claiming completion. What if I had not troubled to make the prediction, thus setting no expectation for myself or the editor? I must have a clear idea of what to expect *beforehand*, so that any deviation will attract my notice and indicate a possible problem.

This principle applies to all aspects of the Inspection process. For example, a high-level document barely past the 'brainstorm' stage can be expected to have a high defect density. If the individual checkers find only a few issues to raise, you must question whether individual checking is as effective as you would otherwise assume. If individual checking raises many issues but very few more appear during the logging session, you should again examine the process's effectiveness. You should be able to examine your own Inspection data and come up with numeric ranges to match this intuitive hypothesis.

For a document late in the development cycle, such as the final segments of program code, you could reasonably expect to see very few issues raised. If something violates this expectation, you ought to immediately investigate the cause. Suppose that very little was found during individual checking but the floodgates are opened during the logging session. Again, investigate before matters go any further.

With experience, you will 'anticipate the outcome' intuitively and automatically. If you base your habit on numeric data (as in the eight-minutes-per-item editing example), you will be much more credible. Your habits will refine themselves based on your ever-greater background of (numeric) experience.

1.5 Logging Strategy

One problem to address immediately was that I sometimes ran out of time in the logging session. There were likewise other times where we ran out of things to say and, in keeping with the formality of the occasion, were afraid to say anything extraneous.

I realized we needed two different logging session strategies. If I expect to log very few issues (for example, 20 or less over the course of an hour), I call this 'low density' logging. 'High density' logging is where we're likely to have our hands full getting it all down in time.

- With 'low density' logging, we can afford to relax a bit. So long as the intent is clearly to pull out additional issues, we can stray farther afield. In one code Inspection, for example, we closed up the printed code listing entirely and discussed what we would do next. In the ensuing discussion, we opened the listing back up to check on this and that – and found a live bug.
- With 'high density' logging, the leader must keep more careful control. We will have to stay strictly to the task at hand and not get sidetracked by relatively minor stuff. We have to move right along with a terseness and directness that would be impolite in a more relaxed setting.

1.6 The Limiting Factor

Realizing that I needed two styles of logging strategies was a useful conclusion. However, there was still a problem to address: I was sometimes running out of time at the logging session, even though I used the 'high density' strategy. There was obviously a limiting factor out of control.

I examined the logging session's issue logging rate (see Figure 13.9). With one notable exception, I was unable to exceed 1.0 or 1.1 issues per minute – 60 or 65 issues per hour. (I first focused on the exception. This was the Inspection where I had collected notes and added to the log afterwards. In reality we logged 75 Issues in 75

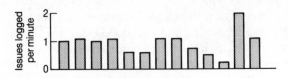

Figure 13.9 Issue logging rates.

minutes.) Examining the data, and thinking back over the sessions, I realized the limiting factor was how fast the scribe could write.

Once I understood that we never exceed 60-65 issues per hour, I suddenly understood why I was often running out of time. If we have 120 issues, for example, and only 60 minutes for the logging session, we are *guaranteed* to run out of time.

I thought it would be useful to know, at the start of the logging session, whether or not we were likely to run out of time – so that I could do a better job of directing the session. It seemed to me that the tool I needed was to be able to predict the number of items likely to be logged, and compare that to the number of minutes set aside for the session. This would also provide me with numbers to back up my intuition about logging strategies. It turns out that a better answer would have been to make the logging session more efficient, but this concept of personal data analysis remains relevant, using actual numbers to back up your intuition.

This case study describes how I examined my logging session performance, assuming the limiting factor is how fast the logger can write issues in the log. Barbara Spencer describes elsewhere in this book how she has eliminated this limiting factor, so this aspect of the problem disappears.

1.7 Metrics to Back Intuition: Personal Data Analysis

How could I predict the number of issues to be raised in the logging session? To do this, I examined the individual checking activity results. I looked at the total number of issues found (not worrying about duplicates), and also at the checker finding the most issues. In the first Inspection (see Figure 13.4), for example, 'checker 1' found the most issues during individual checking (77 issues), with a total of 139 found (see Inspection Reference 10 in Figure 13.10).

Figure 13.10 consolidates the data from several Inspections. Figures 13.11 and 13.12 look at this data in a couple of different ways. I arbitrarily decided that 'the most number of issues found by a single checker' was a better predictor than 'total number of issues found by all checkers.' I therefore expect the total number of issues

Inspection reference	Most found by single checker	Total found in checking	Actual issues logged	Actual increase over total	Actual increase over most
1	45	57	45	−21%	0%
2	42	64	74	16%	76%
5	68	103	159	54%	134%
6	39	53	55	4%	41%
7	41	50	55	10%	34%
8	48	65	96	48%	100%
10	77	139	96	−30%	25%
11	27	33	64	94%	137%
12	21	31	52	68%	148%
14	5	10	14	40%	180%
16	71	136	173	27%	144%
18	89	166	55	−67%	−38%
Average				*20%*	*82%*

Figure 13.10   Predicting the number of issues logged.

logged at the logging session to be 30–90% more than the most issues found by any one checker during individual checking.

This complicated conclusion may well seem vague and therefore not too useful. Remember, though, that the whole point of the exercise was to better understand a limiting factor – which was that I was running out of time at the logging sessions and thereby failing to get all issues logged. I believe that understanding a limiting factor, and being able to deal with it numerically, is always useful. In fact, it was this very analysis which allowed me to understand the need for Barbara Spencer's improvement to the logging process.

Again, this conclusion expresses numerically your intuition that, if a lot of issues were raised during checking, to expect a lot of issues during logging. Likewise, if only five issues were raised during checking, you should expect only another 2–5 issues during logging. Remember that if checking turns up five issues but logging turns up 50, you have immediate cause to question the effectiveness of that particular Inspection.

1.8   Problem Density

By coincidence, the log for the second requirements document Inspection totaled 132 major and super-major issues – the same as the number of defects I had corrected on the first round. (Remember that when it's logged, it's an issue; when the editor does something about it, it's a defect.) This tells me that neither Inspection was especially effective.

Let me explain my reasoning. Suppose we are 50% effective at finding issues, and find 132 issues the first time. The editor removes

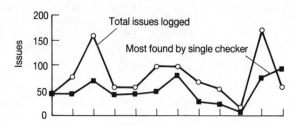

Figure 13.11 Checking (by single checker) and logging activity.

these 132, leaving the other (presumed) 132 issues undiscovered and uncorrected. Assuming a second Inspection to be equally (50%) effective, one would expect the second Inspection to uncover another 66 issues, which is 50% of the remainder. Instead, we uncover another 132 – implying 100% effectiveness. Since 100% effectiveness is quite unlikely, we must conclude that the document has such a high defect density that finding a mere 132 is a small dent. Keeping in mind that both logging sessions were cut off for lack of time, it's more likely that the document contained several hundred major and super-major issues, and that both Inspection teams were equally effective at finding issues in the time allowed.

1.9 Stay Within Established Norms

The above data analyses were aimed at process improvement – that is, helping me to lead more effective software Inspections. They bore no relationship to anyone else's experience. However, you must also compare your experience to common practice. What is common practice? That should normally be established by the senior Inspection leader(s). If you are just starting, you must use other companies' experience as the basis for common practice.

Examine the Inspection data in Figure 13.4. You will see that I did the following things correctly – that is, my data matches the default values listed elsewhere in this book.

- I followed the correct procedure of kickoff meeting, checking activity, logging session, editing, and follow-up. I conducted entry and exit checks and collected suitable Inspection data.
- The Inspection teams consisted of 4–5 people, chosen to provide varying perspectives. I established specialized roles for each checker.
- The assigned checking rate was one page per hour, the presumed optimum. Also worth noting is that the checkers actually followed

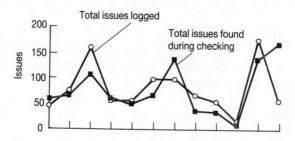

Figure 13.12   Checking (total) and logging activity.

this rate. The default logging session time is the same as the checking time; we followed this guideline.
- The issue logging rate (see Figure 13.9) is pretty consistently one item per minute, which falls at the low end of the desired range of 1–4 items per minute.

It is important to realize what you are doing correctly. You obviously want to keep on with the good habits, but there is another reason for knowing this information. Inspections cost a lot of time and trouble up front, and certain aspects will seem unreasonable and counterproductive at times. You may then be called upon to justify your existence, and it will benefit all concerned if you can immediately put the situation in its proper perspective.

> Always be prepared to give an answer to everyone who asks you to give the reason for the hope that you have. But do this with gentleness and respect...
>
> *1 Peter 3:15, New International Version*

1.10   What Happened to the Entry Check?

As an astute reader, you are probably asking yourself why I bothered to Inspect a document known to have dozens of serious defects. The document should have been subjected to the entry check (it was!) – that is, the Inspection leader should have made a cursory examination of the document, and other Inspection materials, to ensure that the whole package was good enough. Otherwise, we should not be wasting the Inspection team's time.

How did this document get past the entry check, since it obviously should not have? Here are the reasons. I am explaining what happened in the hope that you will not fall into the same trap.

- The author submitting the document and the leader accepting it for Inspection were the same person (me). As previously noted, I was suffering from a typical author's blindness; I was equally blind as leader.

- You'd think I would have figured this out for the second Inspection. However, I had just completed thirteen hours of editing for that single page and a half, so it just *had* to be perfect!
- None of the source documents had themselves been Inspected, let alone exited an Inspection. This situation is typical when just getting started – we do the best we can, but realize this may be a source of extensive confusion and error.
- As author, I was 'breaking new ground' in an area where I had little experience. We were just beginning to attempt to use Gilb's planning techniques, and had no examples or common usage to work from.

2   Inspection Roadblocks

2.1   Leader Overhead

This early in Cray's Inspection history, I had no other Inspection leaders to call upon for my project. I myself was just getting started, and unfortunately had to spend a lot of 'overhead' time for each Inspection (Figure 13.13). I averaged five hours of planning and follow-up time per Inspection, in addition to my duties as author, checker, and editor.

This time added up too quickly, getting in the way of the 'real' project work. I felt the time was better spent on actual project work. Eventually, of course, Inspections would be better established and various Inspection leaders could share the load.

2.2   Chasing After Typos

I had a mistaken idea of what a 'major issue' was. I reported lots of picky stuff as major issues, and sent the other checkers off to do the same. Based on my own misunderstanding, I declared that all Rule Set violations were major issues. At the same time, I created a source code Rule Set which declared 'all text should be free of spelling and grammatical errors...' (I have always been very picky about grammar and spelling, even when I don't know what I'm talking about.)

I made no distinction between a 'live bug' and a fumbled comment in the code. The code checkers were well aware of the difference in customer satisfaction between tripping over a bug and the never-to-be-seen fumbled comment. To the average intelligent checker, then, the code Inspection appeared to be primarily an exercise in 'chasing after typos'.

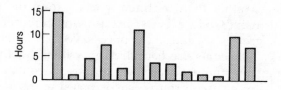

Figure 13.13   Leader time per Inspection.

2.3   Unnecessary Formality

I had incomplete success attempting to introduce explicitly formal Inspections in the explicitly informal Cray Research environment. The logging sessions were a lot smoother, for example, once I understood the need for 'high density' and 'low density' strategies. We would use formality where absolutely necessary, and nowhere else.

I made matters more difficult by creating unnecessary rules. In addition to encouragement to 'chase after typos', for example, I included the rule 'the code should use symbolic constants...' Symbolic constant use was an important programming practice, but so universally understood that the rule just got in the way during checking.

2.4   Process Support

I felt bad about not leading other Inspections, and I was stress-testing myself as much as I was my tape subsystem. I most especially felt bad about leading Inspections entirely on my own; we had no senior leader or the equivalent to share resources or experience. Even though various management reports stated that we were 'doing Inspections' here and there, I saw few indications that this made a difference. Inspections were not yet part of our culture.

3   Conclusion

3.1   Project Focus: Communication

With sufficient communication, Software Inspections would be unnecessary. In a single-expert environment, I discovered that we communicate as well by other methods – the Inspection adds little value to the program code being Inspected.

However, Software Inspection has proven a powerful communication forum for higher-level 'upstream' documents. It is much easier to gather a diverse group of interested persons at the 'upstream' stage, rather than continually draw from the same tiny pool of 'downstream' code experts. By drawing representatives of different work groups together, we once saved an author several weeks of work – someone else had already written exactly what he was designing. In another case, a proposed common set of requirements between two groups was exposed as trying to cover two very different sets of needs. In both cases, the Inspection provided an 'eye-opening' understanding of the other group's work. Faulty assumptions were exposed, and participants went away pleased with the accomplishment.

Software Inspections have their place. You should be able to demonstrate their value (or lack thereof). Inspections are only one of the many forms of communication necessary in the software development process. Equally important are the feedback from peer discussions, internal and field tests, and customer visits. Use the communication tool which best fits the situation.

3.2   Leader Focus: Keeping on the Right Track

An Inspection leader should be able to continuously improve his or her performance. I have shown several examples of examining my own performance. I should be able to 'audit' myself, demonstrating that I am keeping on the 'right track'. I should be able to keep myself headed in the right direction, even if nobody else is available as an outside observer.

I attempted to demonstrate the value my Inspections are adding to the development process. Where I saw little added value, I examined the situation and changed accordingly. I discovered I was collecting insufficient information to demonstrate Inspection value (that is, 'bug count'). I now collect and report Inspection value in terms of customer-observable defects prevented (while retaining other major and minor counts).

You only get one chance to make a good first impression. Please ensure, for example, that your checkers feel their time was well spent, rather than just 'chasing after typos'.

14
Implementing Document Inspection on an Unusually Wide Basis at an Electronics Manufacturer

This case study was written by Trevor Reeve, Engineering Quality Manager and British Standard 5750 Program Manager at Thorn EMI, Crawley (previously MEL), Institute for Quality Assurance Lecturer and Member of the American Society for Quality Control.

Introduction

This chapter describes one practitioner's experience of introducing and applying document Inspection in a major UK company over the past four years. It also describes how we see the technique as differing from the established practices of peer review, design review, and walkthrough, as well as how it may be used as an integral part of the product appraisal process from initial proposal to customer acceptance on any type of product.

The only justifiable reason for the existence and use of any management, development, production or quality control technique is that of economic viability, that is, one that gives a return on investment greater than 1:1. The development and application of the document Inspection technique has and is being shown to meet these criteria.

The primary objective of this chapter is to show how the techniques described in the rest of this book were integrated into the overall product review process and successfully introduced to one particular rapidly changing organization.

The secondary objective of this chapter is to add further weight to the argument that the principles of quality (process) control are equally applicable to any product developed whether it takes the form of a hardware engineering, software engineering, sales, marketing or management planning document.

Why Inspect Documents?

Documentation is used as a vehicle for written information about ideas, requirements or achievements in order that other people may use this information for various purposes. However, these documents are written by error-prone humans, and therefore contain defects and ambiguities. It is evident from studies of the relative cost of fault correction that it makes sense to stop these documentation defects occurring as early and as efficiently as possible in order to minimize product costs to ourselves as developers, producers, maintainers (see Figure 14.1) and users.

It makes sense for any organization to reduce costs by reducing the incidence of defects being propagated from proposal through to end product/service use as early as possible in the product development life cycle.

How is Inspection Different from other Techniques?

Before you can introduce a new technique into an organization you have to prove to yourself and others that this will be beneficial. One measure is to compare it to alternative practices to which documentation has (at best) been traditionally subjected:

	Found at stage 1						
Occurred at stage	1	2	3	4	5	6	7
1. Proposal/contract	1.0	1.3	2.4	3.3	6.8	26	96
2. System requirements	–	1.0	1.8	2.4	5.1	19	72
3. Preliminary design	–	–	1.0	1.3	2.8	11	39
4. Detailed design	–	–	–	1.0	2.1	8.0	30
5. Unit test	–	–	–	–	1.0	3.8	14
6. System integration/test	–	–	–	–	–	1.0	3.7
7. Operation/usage	–	–	–	–	–	–	1.0

Figure 14.1   Relative cost of fault correction.

(1) Design review: a formal documented and systematic critical study of a design proposal by specialists, as required, and not necessarily engaged in the design (British Standard BS4778).

(2) Walkthrough: a review of the concept, examining the validity of proposed solutions and the viability of alternatives.

(3) Peer review: an informal review carried out by colleagues or associates.

Unfortunately the application of the above techniques to ideas and products defined and supported by documentation by managers and engineers of all disciplines is in most cases poorly controlled and inefficient. For example;

(a) Most people at design reviews have not seen and do not use the defining and supporting documentation. They consequently do not have time to truly study and review all aspects of the proposed or achieved design before or during the invariably short design review meetings.

(b) Design reviews and walkthroughs appear to be held with the object of completing a checklist in as short a time as possible in order to satisfy a requirement from the Quality Assurance department. Thus the object of the activity is often not fully understood by either the designers or the attendees at the meeting.

(c) The time spent by most reviewers when checking a document is invariably too short. Thirty minutes is not untypical for most documents of any size from 10 to 200 pages in length.

(d) Document defects, if they are recorded at all, are rarely analyzed for systematic causes, and consequently preventative actions and process improvement are rarely implemented.

The alternatives to Inspection can be summarized as follows:

Reviews	– much less effective in finding defects
Walkthroughs	– far fewer defects found but same cost
Testing	– too late for avoiding higher downstream correction costs for 60% of the defects
User complaint	– bad for your reputation and higher costs to fix than at test
Auto inspection	– requires machine interpretable specification language
Peer checking	– far less effective

Peer checking is the least effective, but most used, of all defect removal techniques within the electronics industry.

	Inspection	Walkthrough	Design Review	Peer Review
Proven cost-effectiveness on all types of document	Yes	No	No	No
Metrics feedback into process	Yes	No	No	No
Trained leader	Yes	No	Yes	No
Uses sources	Yes	No	Yes	No
Uses standards	Yes	Yes	Yes	No
Meeting control	Yes	No	Yes	No
Entry & exit control?	Yes	No	Exit (Yes)	No
Authorship standards improvement due to learning	Yes	No	No	No
Use of experts and peers	No	Yes	Yes	Yes

Figure 14.2 Comparison of review technique features.

Document Inspection is part of an Integrated Product Review Process

In order to obtain maximum benefit from the document Inspection technique, it should be used as part of an integrated product review process. Figure 14.3 illustrates how this may be (and has been) done.

Figure 14.3 shows a typical product life cycle based on the waterfall model, indicating the normal points at which walk-throughs, design reviews, and document Inspections are performed during the product life cycle.

The product review process normally begins some time after project start at a point just prior to completion of the design process, that is, when the major part of the design decomposition and definition activity has been completed. Subsequent design reviews are then performed regularly until release to customer is satisfactorily achieved.

Design review and test activities at best confirm defects in the design or at worst do not detect the majority of the in-built defects at all, that is, the customer finds them in the first few units – evidence based on the assumption that some 62% of defects in any product arise from deficiencies in the product requirements and management control documents.

In-house analysis of defects at Thorn EMI has shown that document Inspection removes at least a further 50% of these documentation errors very early in the product life cycle.

It can be seen that document Inspection is applied to all documentation produced on a project from proposal to final drawings (including changes), or code and test paperwork;

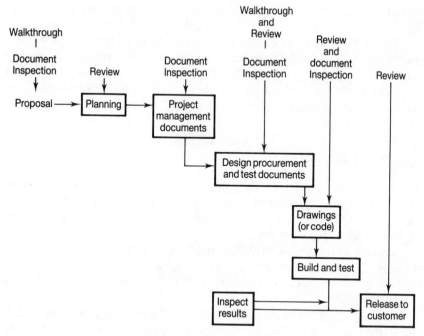

Figure 14.3   The Product Review Process.

walkthroughs are applied to establish the validity of the concepts and reviews are used to establish proposed or actual conformity with all product requirements including documentation, performance, safety, availability, quality, and cost.

Establishing Inspection within the Organization

Organization Profile

The following notes outline the author's strategy, experience, and results obtained in establishing Inspection in MEL, a former division of Philips, now taken over by Thorn EMI, over a period of four years. The organization totals approximately 1500 staff working in the world defense electronics systems markets.

Since the takeover by Thorn EMI, the technique has been spread to other parts of the company working in the civilian equipment market. The spread of the technique into the new larger division resulting from the merger and acquisition process has had to overcome significant culture differences. Furthermore, the use of the technique has been adopted by other divisions of Thorn EMI involved in the civilian equipment markets.

The only champion of the technique has been myself. Tom Gilb then gave a one-week Inspection leader course – though of the 25 staff trained that week, only about five of them today regularly lead Inspections. All other leaders have been trained in-house on one-day courses, coupled with advice and 'nursing' through their first two or three Inspections.

Application Profile

The technique was originally intended for software documentation, but initial trials on project planning documentation and an ever-expanding appreciation of the possible benefits quickly resulted in its use on all types of company documentation from major proposals for aircraft systems, to study reports including hardware, systems, software, quality, and production specifications and plans, irrespective of whether the document in question had a direct effect on product quality.

To date, over six hundred Inspections have been performed with the expectation that the one-thousand barrier will be broken some time in early 1993.

Implementation

To date two hundred staff from all disciplines and grades have been on one-day Inspection leader training courses run by myself. In addition, all original MEL managers including the managing director have been on one-hour Inspection overview courses or been given individual presentations or tutorials. The task of monitoring Inspection activity has recently been devolved from myself to the product assurance managers within the company.

The Target Material

Types of documents Inspected started with quality plans, and were then extended to cover software source code (now dropped, due to lack of cost effectiveness – not enough defects found per man-hour), software design and test specifications (all levels), study reports, hardware designs and test specifications, system design and test specifications, proposals, program management documents (for example, configuration and program plans), contracts and, most recently, purchase specifications and printed circuit board design and test specifications, procedures, and standards. Further application of the technique to cover all contractual documents, drawings, and internal specifications (for example, information technology and financial requirements) is expected to occur during 1993 with all contracts using it to a lesser or greater degree by the end of 1992.

Support for and Opposition to Inspection

Inspection was first adopted by the product support division, because of their responsibility for rectifying faults caused at least in part by imperfect design or inadequate drawings. Support also came from the more enlightened managers who realized that failure costs were too high. The MEL managing director publicly proclaimed his unqualified support and commitment, as did the MEL technical director.

Resistance to Inspections (in the form of resistance to change, 'not another QA rule', what do they know? Big Brother watching) was certainly there, and has been gradually overcome by personal credibility, education, publication of results, lots of talking and helping practitioners, examination of underlying principles, as well as getting and publicizing top management support. A key factor is the dogged total commitment, determination, and stamina of the champion.

The Sequence of Events in Implementation of Inspection at Thorn EMI

(1) Knowledge of the Inspection technique was obtained at course(s) and from other operators such as Tom Gilb and his clients and colleagues.

(2) The organization requirements were established as being acceptable, that is, the organization would listen to and was ready to accept new ideas for improvement (Total Quality Management and Quality Improvement).

(3) A plan of campaign was formulated.

(4) In-house support was obtained from likely potential Inspection leaders in the software group.

(5) An in-house course (less costly than public courses) was run by an external consultant (Tom Gilb) for these potential Inspection team leaders.

(6) Positive course opinions were distributed to everyone who would listen – including management.

(7) The campaign plan was improved.

(8) Two or three 'off the cuff' Inspections were performed on various documents very shortly after the internal course.

(9) Results from these first Inspections were published.

(10) A draft Inspection procedure was produced based on data obtained from courses and first Inspections.

(11) More Inspections were performed with help from the champion in various groups.

(12) Inspection overview talks were given to groups of engineers (all disciplines) and managers (lower and middle) in all departments, each time reporting on the most recent successes of the technique on various types of software documents and proposing benefits to be obtained if it were employed on other types of document.

(13) Explanations of the modus operandi and cost effectiveness of the techniques were given to senior managers including the managing director.

(14) More Inspections were performed on a wider range of engineering and project management documentation.

(15) The Inspection procedure was further improved to fully reflect the lessons learned from Inspections held to date.

(16) The product appraisal process was revised to incorporate the technique into the normal activities performed by the organization on all types of document from contract to lowest level design and test documentation including drawings.

(17) One-day training courses were given to likely participants – to date (December 91) over 200 people have been trained in document Inspection.

(18) Inspection workshops have been held with experienced Inspection leaders to improve the understanding of the process.

(19) Inspection paper work and results have been analyzed to find ways of improving the performance of the leaders.

(20) The process has been introduced into Thorn EMI Electronics following the acquisition of MEL from Philips.

Note that throughout the campaign, and for the foreseeable future, publicity and advice about the benefits and application including teaching of the technique was and is being given to management and everybody likely to be involved in its application.

Benefits

The document Inspection results (Figure 14.4) were reported over a four-year period since the introduction of the technique. These show the results of a typical analysis of problem types across all documents Inspected over a six-month period.

Types of document covered ranged from system, hardware, and software design documents to software code and change notes.

It is interesting to note that the above results do not vary a great deal over time. Although the authorship standards improve, Inspection teams become more effective in their activities even though the actual number of defects found decreases, particularly in the downstream documents. An example of this phenomenon is shown in Figure 14.5, where the curve has been derived from the results of two hundred Inspections performed by the same Inspection/document producer team during a twelve-month period on different projects.

The majority of the defects found were detected using the following general checklist:

> Identification – what is it?
> Legibility – can you understand it?
> Understandable – does it make sense?
> Grammatically correct – is it?
> Correctly spelled – is it?
> Logical layout – yes?
> Clear in meaning – not ambiguous
> Complete – no significant omissions
> Self-consistent – is it?
> Consistent with source documents – is it?

The unusual wave shape in Figure 14.5 is explained by the fact that the authorship standards are improving and defects of a particular sub-type are decreasing in the document. Then the Inspection team improve their checklists and ask themselves (and the document) more searching questions. Thus the number of defects detected in the documents tends to rise and fall – but quality standards are improving overall. Later analysis of defects in downstream documents and tests show marked reductions in defect

Missing data	30%
Ambiguous data	30%
Incorrect data	3%
Additional data	5%
Inconsistent data	11%
Other (standards, etc.)	10%

Figure 14.4   Document Inspection problem analysis.

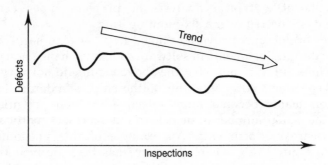

Figure 14.5   Defects found by team versus Inspections performed in a 12-month period.

levels and defect correction times. It is likely that the above pattern is not unique as it is tending to occur in other organizations where Inspection has been introduced.

Savings are of the order of at least £500,000 per year. Quality increased and development time has been reduced significantly.

Costs

Start-up costs were of the order of £50,000 in the first two years (champion's time plus consultants' Inspection leader courses plus internal training). Running costs indicate that savings are of the order of ten times the costs of Inspections.

Lessons Learned at Thorn EMI

With hindsight, the following are some of the major lessons learned and problems seen during the introduction of the technique in the past four years:

(1) Inspection needs a committed and dedicated champion with a conviction of the benefits of Inspection and an absolute commitment on their part to the process.
(2) As much knowledge as possible of its application in other organizations needs to be gathered to convince the skeptics.
(3) A thorough understanding of the underlying principles needs to be obtained to ensure a meaningful cost-effective implementation. There must be some knowledge by at least one person (not necessarily a quality professional or manager) on the deeper principles of the Inspection technique.

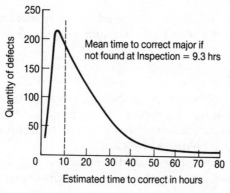

Figure 14.6   The 'cost of quality'. The average saving for finding a major was found to be 9.3 work-hours, versus a cost of about one work-hour to find and fix a major. Thus majors save about eight work hours net each.

(4) Publicity and education are needed to gain acceptance in all parts of an organization.

(5) Proper initial and follow-up training is imperative to ensure correct application of the technique and realization of its full benefit.

(6) Full support and guidance need to be constantly given to new team leaders during their initial Inspections with regular debriefs being held during the years to keep up the momentum and keep staff aware of the latest problems and practices.

(7) Constant vigilance and encouragement to ensure the technique is being correctly implemented are needed to ensure its full effectiveness.

(8) No amount of publicity regarding its benefits is enough.

(9) The pressures of delivery or time need to be withstood at all costs, to maintain quality.

(10) The amount of time spent on the initial introduction was vastly underestimated because the technique requires culture change.

(11) The introduction of the technique needs to be done in stages to avoid frightening people off unfamiliar concepts like basic process, role usage, causal analysis, and process brainstorming.

(12) An awareness is necessary that Inspection can appear to threaten people's self-esteem, and can lead to important culture changes within the organization. In this respect, care and foresight are necessary before introducing it.

(13) The optimum checking rate for most documents appears to be 600 words per hour.
(14) Code and drawings do not need to be Inspected if the source documents have been Inspected and exited satisfactorily.

In Conclusion

Inspection does not solve poor design, organizational, cultural or production problems. However, if applied at the right time, correctly, and in conjunction with other techniques it helps to significantly reduce business costs.

However there must be a readiness in the organization to listen to new ideas and an acceptance that improvements in ways of working are needed.

Then – take it slowly. Publicize results all the time. Don't stop after one or two years, but keep doing it. Introduce the various elements of the process over a period of time. Change, consolidate, publicize results, and then introduce the next stage. The keys to successful introduction of the technique are communication, publicity, dedication, commitment, and understanding.

Footnote (January 1993)

The application of the technique has provided a solid foundation for meeting the document and design control requirements and the company's quality system recently achieved certification ISO9001 (International Standards Organization Requirements for Quality Management Systems).

15

Inspection at Racal Redac

This case study was written by Grahame Terry, Software Engineer at Racal Redac (UK).

Organization

The company is a world-class software house, producing tools for the electronics design industry. Some three years ago, we were becoming aware of the variety of developing quality improvement techniques and were keen to apply some of them. The organization comprised some 100 or so development staff, plus marketing and management people. The development was organized into teams of various sizes, averaging about ten people.

Application

The application is a large suite of programs; mature software from diverse sources, written to diverse standards. The majority of software development at this time was in maintenance and enhancement rather than writing new programs.

Implementation

Inspection was first introduced to the company in the summer of 1988, and in that September we had an Inspector's training course for some 25 people. The next stage was to set up a pilot scheme to evaluate the method, which was driven by a steering committee. In the first months we identified document types and roles for those documents, developed first-cut checklists and a handbook, and held our first Inspection in late November. As we gained confidence, we held seminars to inform other people about the method. Towards the

Inspection						Times	(effort-hours)					Elapsed days	
insp Ref.	Doc. Ref.	type	Pages	mod'r	no. of insp.	mod'r	prep	mtgs	TOTAL	rework	mins. logging	Insp.	follow up
21	MPC3	spec	8	JS	4	1.0	9.0	7.9	19.4	0.0	55	11	7
22	ICS0015	spec	7	GT	4	1.8	5.2	4.3	12.6	0.0	14	4	5
TOTAL			15						32.0				
AVERAGE			7.5						16.0			8	6

	Defect counts				Post-rework			Rates				
insp Ref.	major	minor	MAJOR /PAGE	% defs. in mtg.	major	minor	DCRs	prep'n pgs/hr	logging def/min	productivity def/hr	maj/hr	mins/ def. fix
21	48	55	6.0	8%	48.0	55.0	0	3.6	1.9	5.3	2.5	0
22	23	8	3.1	0%	22.0	8.0	0	5.4	2.2	2.5	1.7	0
TOTAL	71	63			70.0	63.0						
AVERAGE	35.5	31.5	4.6	4%	35.0	31.5	0	4.5	2.0	3.9	2.1	0

Figure 15.1   Racal Redac Metrics on Microsoft Excel™ Spreadsheet.

end of this phase, we improved our working practices document and had our first attempt at reworking documentation standards.

The results of these early trials had showed clearly that our documentation standards were unusable and largely unused. We redesigned our standards definitions until we had something which was useful and could be Inspected against.

The second phase started in November 1989 when a small group of Inspectors were sent on an Inspection leader course, and learnt about Inspection as part of a process improvement system. This produced quite a change in direction when we could see what we were doing wrong. Previously, we had been given the idea that checklists and roles

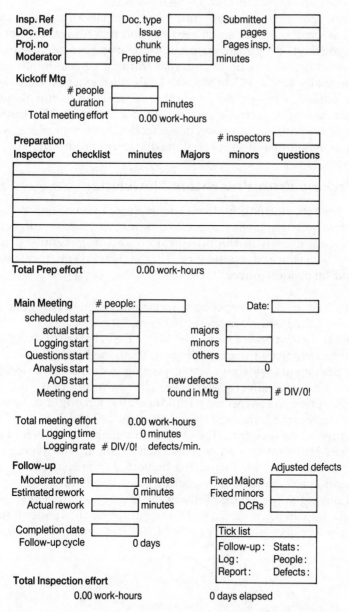

Figure 15.2   Racal Redac data summary sheet on Excel spreadsheet.

were central to the Inspection process and indeed that by using the
checklists, Inspection could be carried out by checkers who were not
skilled in the roles they were given. In reality, checklists and roles are

minor tools in the Inspection tool box; the most effective tool is to use skilled staff to do what they know best!

Our Inspection techniques improved dramatically. We wrote an Inspection handbook, laying out the rules and procedures, and set up an effective method of capturing Inspection data using spreadsheet tools.

Meanwhile, we set up an internal training course for Inspectors and eventually sent another batch of leaders for external training.

The second phase produced another 20 or so Inspectors. However, we were having to scratch around for documents to be Inspected. Although we now had a reasonably effective system in place, we had lost the momentum and support of the document producers.

The Process Error Prevention Newsletter

In July 1990 we started *PEP* (for Process Error Prevention) *News* in an attempt to get the latest Inspection news, and above all benefits, more widely known in the organization and to generally drum up more enthusiasm and volunteers. This is an excerpt from our first efforts at Inspection journalism;

> ...we have done 12 Inspections so far under the new regime and some of the results are presented here.
>
> First the important news, the Major Defect rate is falling! As you can see from the graph (Figure 15.3), the level of defects in the documents which we are Inspecting is dropping noticeably. Nice to see this effect so early, well done the authors!
>
> Excepting the Inspector's Handbook (which ought to have a low defect rate!), the best document was CAD0088, a requirements spec from the CAD area which had a Defect Level of 0.67 Majors/page, an excellent achievement. The average Defect Level for the documents Inspected so far is 1.62 Majors/page, so we are inspecting some good stuff.
>
> Looking at the productivity of the Inspection Process (Figure 15.4), we can see a nicely stabilizing graph as the moderators and Inspectors become more practiced. The best Inspection team so

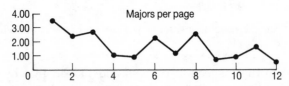

Figure 15.3   Majors per page.

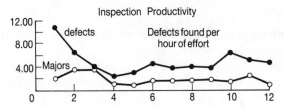

Figure 15.4   Inspection productivity.

far is the one which did Inspection Number Three, achieving a defect finding rate of 3.5 Majors per hour of effort. Well done that team!

The average rate of finding defects over an Inspection is just short of two Majors/man-hour which shows an excellent return since a Major defect represents anything from two hours wasted work to an Immediate bug!

The significance of the defects being found can be seen from the average defect-fix times seen below. This graph (Figure 15.5) is showing a slight rise, indicating that we are finding more important defects and not so much trivia.

...the steering team has made many improvements to the Inspection process, documents can now be turned around within a week, and we are setting up the mechanisms for code Inspections. A Glossary of Terms is being produced to ensure a consistent use of terms and abbreviations. The documentation structure is being rejigged to make it easier for people to produce and maintain documents. These are all results of recording and analyzing defects and seeing what sort of things are going wrong.

Nineteen new Inspectors have been trained since the beginning of the year, bringing the total up to 28. We have a short (two-hour) training course on the Inspection process and this can be used to train both Inspectors and authors. We have another 20 odd volunteers for Inspector training and these will be brought

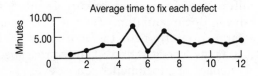

Figure 15.5   Average time to fix each defect.

into the scheme during the coming months. Are there any more volunteers?

So, if you are writing specs, how do they measure up?
Can you beat the best?
Volunteer your documents for Inspection and find out.
Source: Racal Redac *Process Error Prevention News* (July 1990)

The third phase began as part of a general quality improvement drive in September 1990, when Tom Gilb was called in. We now fully understood the method, we reworked our checklists and task standards, and lots of good things were said (and promised). But we still could not find much to Inspect. As a final throw, we simplified the documentation standards radically to entice people into writing Inspectable document sets.

The system was just becoming effective when a company reorganization hit us and we lost the core of the Inspection drivers. It has not been used since.

Target Material

Initially, two approaches to quality improvement through Inspection were considered: top down, Inspection of a documentation suite from the earliest specifications onward, and bottom up, Inspection of source code.

There was a far greater volume of code than there was documentation and our Inspector team consisted largely of software writers. We had a history of code reviewing which had proven beneficial, so code Inspections looked attractive. We were not then aware of the importance of having Inspected source documents to Inspect against! We felt it would be useful to Inspect mostly against the standards.

We rapidly confirmed that it is impossible to apply new standards to old software and impractical to Inspect the myriad changes generated by maintaining and enhancing old code. So we shelved code Inspections, at least until we knew how to run effective Inspections.

Ours was not a document-oriented culture. We had an established software architecture, code look-up tools, and adequate commenting culture which together greatly reduced the need for low- and mid-level documentation. Teams were small and well focused and a large proportion of the work was in maintenance, using bug reports as the 'specification'. Thus source specs were fairly rare and a sequence of documents only ever occurred when Inspection demanded it.

Politics

Our Inspection training was aimed at the document users. These were the people most likely to benefit from high-quality input and we had heard that Inspection was a 'grassroots' improvement scheme where a better culture grew upwards from the lowest level. Our primary document producers were not part of the development staff and were all too busy to find out what Inspection was all about! So documents were not being volunteered for Inspection and those we hijacked had not been written using the recommended style and guidelines.

For the same 'grassroots' reason as above, our middle management had not been involved in the initiation of the scheme. Although we held specially targeted seminars to spread the word on Inspection, management did not take up the idea of 'Inspection exit' as marking the completion of the various development stages. Thus Inspection was not incorporated into the product management guide or into individual project plans.

Consequently, over the first eighteen months we carried out something like twenty Inspections and a similar number in the nine months after our conversion to better practices.

Costs and Benefits

Inspection showed the deficiencies in our standards, both definition of and use of. It resulted in a major rewrite of the standards definitions making them considerably more effective within the documentation structure. This was followed by a revamp of the structure so that it was a better model of the way people worked. The end result was a documentation standard which was flexible, helpful, and Inspectable.

Several spin-off ideas, collected on the way towards Inspection, have proven useful and have crept into the development cycle. I believe that the efforts we made to install Inspection did a lot to raise people's awareness of quality issues, accountability, and effectiveness. We now have a considerably higher level of commitment to improving both the quality of our products and the effectiveness of our working environment, but oriented towards configuration management, process automation, and automatic test rather than Inspection.

Compared to many other quality improvement techniques, Inspection is cheap. Our costs were in training for the Inspectors (one session in-house plus small groups for internal training) and Inspection leaders (eventually about a dozen people) and in time for the steering committee and Inspection management. With the semi-automatic Inspection logging system we set up, administration of

Inspection was a simple task. Much of the time spent by the steering committee was on setting up the environment for Inspection and implementing the process improvements discovered by Inspection.

Downside

We found many trivial defects because our original method and emphasis were wrong. This gave the method a bad name and dampened morale among the Inspectors.

We found it very difficult to estimate the severity of a defect and also difficult to measure the effect of removing defects. This was partly because other quality improvement initiatives were being implemented simultaneously, but also because of the relatively long time scale between Inspecting a document and getting feedback from users of the resulting software.

Critique

We were too slow! We took far too long getting the method right and lost momentum and support by finding the wrong sort of defects. Our standards were not in a form where Inspection could be usefully applied and the improvements instigated as a result of Inspection were not implemented forcefully enough or quickly enough.

We were too ambitious! We tried to turn our specification mechanism from something which was pragmatic and largely verbal (between highly experienced, tightly focused individuals) into a formal document-oriented system. This imposition of standards was not perceived as useful and I agree with the concept that where a system appears to be working, don't mess it about!

Were I attempting to install Inspection again (and in an appropriate environment I would have no hesitation), I would consider the following stages and be very careful not to mix the objectives. For stages 1 and 2, I would have a full-time administrator, although this should not be necessary once the system is running.

> Stage 0: be sure that your working practices (actual, not theoretic) are of a form likely to benefit from Inspection.

> Stage 1: get your Inspection mechanisms installed and working but be flexible and expect change!

> Stage 2: get your standards working, use Inspection of real documents to evaluate the standards.

> Stage 3: start to evaluate documents and integrate Inspection into the development cycle. Fine tune the system.

16

Inspection in the Sema Group (UK)

This is a case study by Denise Leigh, Production Manager and (latterly) Technology Manager in the Communications Division of (UK) Sema Group.

Introduction

When I started work at Sema, a review procedure had been in operation for a number of years. The procedure included preparation, some role allocation, note-taking, and advice on minimizing time spent solving problems. It had guideline status only, and not many people applied it in its entirety.

The first project into which I introduced Inspections in the Communications Division of the Sema Group had available to it five Inspectors and one Inspection leader, all externally trained and with no practical experience.

Some measure of the acceptance of the value of the technique today can be gained from the division's investment in directly related training. At the end of April 1992, out of 207 technical, sales and managerial staff, 156 had been trained as Inspectors (and a further 16 booked on internal training courses). Seventy-four had been trained as [Inspection] team leaders (and a further 19 booked on internal training courses).

The First Project

In late 1986 a prospective customer requested figures on the number of residual defects in software delivered by the Sema Group's Communications Division.

We were confident of the quality of the systems we produced, but had no such figures. Rather than confess to the lack of availability of such figures, I used the opportunity to ask the customer, who had been using Inspections for a number of years, for help in introducing the technique.

An initial two-hour Inspection course and two places on a team leader's course were kindly made available by our initial contact.

The project in question was an eight man-year project carried out over ten months. In the event this turned out to be just the first phase of a three-phase project. The specifications provided were incomplete and had not, at the start of the project, undergone Inspection. The timescale was tight. The chain to the end customer went back and forth across the Atlantic through a number of intermediaries. The software was to be a mixture of new and reused code.

The project had available to it five trained Inspectors and one team leader, all inexperienced. The team leader chaired all the Inspections. Most Inspections included some Inspectors trained solely on the job.

It was decided to Inspect the upstream documents down to and including detailed logic design specifications. Code and unit tests were reviewed by the three team leaders. No customer representatives were present at Inspections. Metrics were collected but not used. I took to heart the injunction 'management must keep out of the way' and did not even glance at the metrics, relying on the project manager and the team leader to do so. They didn't.

Five months into the project, the team leader produced a memo of which the following is a summary:

Subject: Inspections

Noted below are the problems highlighted with Inspections and some suggestions to resolve the problems:

(1) Lack of checklists and guidelines for Inspectors.
   Team leader to consider.
(2) Are the right documents issued for Inspections? (e.g. should the source documents be issued with the documents under Inspection?)
   Guideline needed.
(3) Too much time spent on trivial problems (e.g. spelling, grammar).
   Guideline needed.
(4) Method is not applied correctly?
   Simplified approach learnt on training course applied. Should Inspection technique as described by Fagan be applied? Should our own approach be defined?

(5) Insufficient attention paid to comparisons with source documents.
    Checking time needs to be increased.
(6) Insufficient time to check.
    Inspections to be scheduled in downstream bar chart.
(7) Difficult to find the right reading level.
    Trial and error appears to be the only solution.
(8) Can be difficult to identify potential Inspectors with the right skills
    May need staff management assistance.
(9) Entry and exit criteria not clear.
    Definition needed.
(10) Work on next phase starting before Inspection performed.
    Guideline needed.
(11) No mechanism for processing defects which get discovered in source documents.
    Guideline needed.
(12) Downstream Inspections (e.g. detailed design) need Inspection leaders and readers who are familiar with the development.
    Guideline needed. When should an Inspection leader/reader be external to the project? When should they be internal to the project?

In spite of these concerns, as a result of using Inspections, two out of the three areas completed system tests in the time allotted.

In the third area, the system test team encountered a defect density three times higher than in the first two, and spent most of the Christmas break working overtime. It turned out that the detailed logic design document for that area had exhibited a very low number of defects. Closer examination showed the document to have been written at a level too close to its parent document. The next level down (coding) was therefore a large step away from its parent, and was reviewed by the area's supervisor rather than Inspected. Its review and unit testing were superficial. The project manager, despite having been warned of the potential weakness of the area's supervisor, chose not to exercise additional caution.

Lessons Learned from the First Project

The section on lessons learned relating to Inspections in the debrief document produced at the end of the project reads as follows:

The main lessons learned by the project were:

• Despite what other people say, do not try to miss out any of the steps.

- Use Inspectors from outside the project team, to inspect design documents thoroughly.
- Give the Inspectors defined targets.
- Do not replace technical reviews with Inspections; a technical review will find problems an Inspection will miss; include the technical review in the Inspection framework.
- There should be no attempt to economize on the Inspection time, especially at the detailed design, code and unit test stage.
- The separation of defects into 'majors' and 'minors' should take place after the item has been updated and the changes reviewed, not at the time of the meeting.
- More metrics should be collected from the Inspections; this should be done continuously throughout the project; more use should be made of these metrics to check that the Inspections are sufficiently thorough.

In addition it had become apparent that:

- Any newly written test harness was as much in need of Inspection as the software being tested.
- Relying on 'peer' review entailed a potentially high risk factor.
- Rules for producing various documents needed to be tightened and had to be an input into the Inspection process, that is, items needed to be Inspected for conformance not just to their parents and peers but also to any rules they were supposed to be adhering to.

The factors which project members thought had made the most contribution to the impact of Inspections were:

- mandatory preparation;
- formal follow-up of defect removal;
- earlier detection of defects;
- use of entry and exit criteria.

Overall the project turned out to be very successful. The project manager, who was reporting to me at the time, attributed its success largely to the use of Inspections. At the end of the project we produced an Inspection process standard, inclusive of metrics to be collected.

Spreading the Word

Over the next three years attempts to use Inspection on other projects appeared initially somewhat less successful. In hindsight, the main factor for failure was lack of training. One project manager at the time recorded his difficulties as follows;

- Inspections attempted too early in the review cycle as first (or only) instead of last review step;
- documents not in a fit state for Inspection;
- readers' lack of preparation resulting in inefficient meetings;
- attempt to resolve disagreements (not fix defects) in the meeting;
- team leader scribing and classifying defects during the meeting.

In 1989 two large projects provided the opportunity for looking again at the best way to use Inspections. By then my talks at a previous technical conference and internal metrics users group were beginning to have an impact and there was some interest in Inspections in other divisions.

Training which had been received externally had not been perceived to be good value for money. Eventually, I was able to persuade the operation and the internal training department that it would be worthwhile to invest in the development of an Inspectors' and team leaders' course. This proved to be a turning point in the use of the technique, with converts becoming in turn preachers.

The standard was updated to reflect the lessons learned, thus allowing projects to proceed on a solid base. The results were very soon apparent in the increased efficiency of Inspections and the improved quality of items produced.

Current Status at SEMA

Usage

The use of the technique has evolved from a local enterprise, to a default in the Communications Division, to a technique currently spreading across the group. The technique, which was originally applied solely to design documents, is now used at all stages of the development life cycle.

Customer Involvement

Inspections are routinely mentioned in proposals and the customers' proposed involvement in upstream Inspections specified. A four-page glossy leaflet has been produced for staff and customers. Customers are invited to attend Sema Group's Inspectors training course or are given briefings as appropriate.

Standards and Forms

A Sema Group standard has been produced and Inspected. It contains a set of forms designed to be used before, during, and after the process.

Training

The cavalier 'on the job' training has been replaced by:

- formal training, given by Sema's training department, consisting of one-day Inspector training and a two-day team leaders' course, both of which include live Inspections;
- informal training, consisting of people sitting in on Inspection meetings as observers (usually just before or after courses), support to team leaders from the chief team leader or project Inspection coordinator, and team leaders' bi-monthly meetings.

Using Metrics

The collection and analysis of data and the production of associated metrics have become the norm rather than the exception. Projects use a spreadsheet to collect data which is then collated on a divisional basis for analysis as described in the following sections.

Controlling the Inspection process

We collected process-related metrics on the planning and on the efficiency of Inspections. Data related to out-of-meeting activities includes:

- checking time total;
- logging meeting duration;
- administration time total;
- edit time.

   Data collected during the meetings includes:

- size of team;
- material coverage rate (pages per hour);
- defect detection rate (number of defects per minute detected during the Inspection meetings).

These metrics are used to plan and organize Inspections in terms of:

- size of team;
- duration and number of Inspection meetings required;
- recommended length of checking time.

During the logging meeting, metrics are used for checking the efficiency of the meeting in terms of:

- defect detection rate;
- material coverage rate.

Given the immediate use of the data, process-related metrics have proved easy to implement.

Monitoring Document Quality

Document-related metrics are used for assessing the quality of a document relative to its peers. Data includes:

- defect density (for example, number of defects per page);
- defect distribution by category (type and severity);
- document quality number (a formula which takes into account the number and severity of defects as well as the size of the item).

Document-related metrics are used to:

- contribute towards a preliminary, then a final, decision regarding the need for re-Inspection;
- spot anomalies – upon close examination these may prove to reflect exceptional circumstances, in which case further action is required – they may indicate a process problem or they may identify the item in question as a potential trouble spot;
- identify weaknesses in the project (for example, lack of expertise or training);
- identify areas in the development process in need of investment and quality potential benefits (for example, further training, standards, tools).

Examples

The following examples illustrate the use of metrics on three different projects code-named Napoleon, Wellington, and Nelson.

On Napoleon an analysis of defects by type indicated that over 50% were documentation-related. A two-page documentation guideline was produced. As a result documentation-related defects fell drastically. A proposal for the production of a divisional standard, complete with expected pay-back, was put forward.

On Wellington a league table of potential trouble spots was used to identify the need for additional testing and/or more senior resources. This was an evolutionary development. Half a day a week was allocated to supporting the first live version of the system, which ran on a 24 hours a day seven days a week basis. In the event, half a day was used for defect identification and correction over a period of three months.

On Nelson, metrics and the level of defects discovered during tests helped convince the skeptics of the value of code Inspections. The use of Inspections at every level resulted in the eventual abandonment of unit tests. The team had become very confident of the quality of the software and when hardware problems caused the postponement of the system tests, no rescheduling or overtime working were considered necessary. In the event, system tests finished ahead of schedule.

Nelson was run as an evolutionary eight work-years' project, which produced 22,000 lines of non-comment code as its final delivery. There were five sets of system tests, which uncovered a total of 90 defects. In the year following the first evolutionary step delivery a total of 35 defects were uncovered by the customer in integration and live running. No defects have been reported in the six months following the final delivery.

Graphs and Residual Defects

Data from 230 Inspections for which the document size is measured in pages has been analyzed and is captured in the illustrations which follow (Figures 16.1 to 16.5). Some interesting points are worth highlighting:

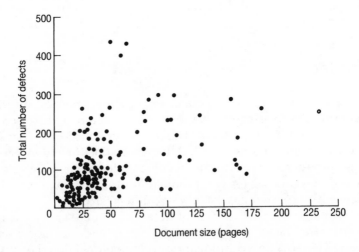

Figure 16.1 Total defects against document size.

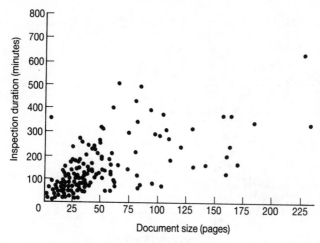

Figure 16.2   Inspection duration against document size.

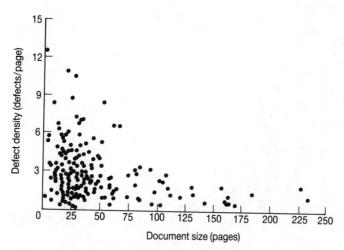

Figure 16.3   Defect density against document size.

- Large documents appear to have been Inspected at a high number of pages per hour. The defect density (defects per page) for such documents appears to be low. While a number of explanations could be put forward, my favored one is that people find it hard to check and Inspect large documents, which leads to a 'let's get on with it' attitude.

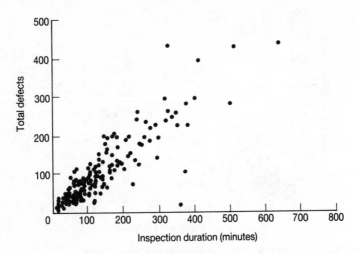

Figure 16.4 Total defects against Inspection duration.

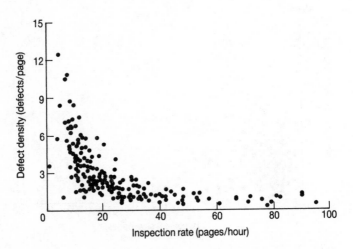

Figure 16.5 Defect density against Inspection rate.

- The number of defects per minute against total Inspection duration is linear for Inspection durations up to four hours. Thereafter the detection rate starts to slow down, potentially indicating difficulties with handling large documents.
- The defect density drops sharply with the increase in material coverage, reinforcing the message 'go slow'.

Conclusions

Inspections have proved successful in all the areas they have been introduced. This is due in large measure to their formal structure.

The use of Inspections has had a major impact on how people relate to quality and also on team spirit.

For the process to continue to be successful, scope for experimentation and for the introduction of new ideas is needed. Any changes to the process must be introduced in a controlled, measurable way.

Recommendations

From my experience of introducing Inspections, I would make the following recommendations:

- Have a champion.
- Use a pilot project.
- Enroll management. The bottom-up approach is too slow.
- Buy in training and support for at least the first project. Then decide whether you want to set up your own.
- Set in place a simple metrics collection with clear goals (a spreadsheet will do for a start). Have data available for more complex analysis later.

17

Practical Aspects of the Defect Prevention Process

This case study is by Robert G. Mays, a senior programmer in the Software Process, Assessments and Technology Department of the IBM RTP Networking Laboratory.

Introduction

This chapter describes the Defect Prevention Process used in the IBM Corporation. The Defect Prevention Process is a set of practices that are integrated with the development process to reduce the number of errors developers actually make. It has proven effective in improving product quality and improving the development process, at a reasonable cost for implementation. Our discussion here focuses on some of the practical aspects of the Defect Prevention Process, such as how to conduct causal analysis meetings.

Overview of the Defect Prevention Process

The Defect Prevention Process (references 1–4) was developed in 1983 in IBM's RTP Networking Laboratory in Research Triangle Park, North Carolina. Since then it has come to be used in every major development lab within IBM. It is an accepted method for improving processes and reducing defects not only in software development but also in such diverse areas as hardware design, manufacturing, and secretarial and administrative processes.

In the 1980s, other forms of defect prevention were also practiced within IBM, notably the On Board Shuttle development organization in the Federal Systems Company (references 5–6) and in application development projects in the UK (reference 7). These other processes were similar to the Defect Prevention Process in that they used

336

causal analysis to develop preventive actions. However, the Defect Prevention Process provided a more comprehensive process which could be readily taught and implemented by other development organizations.

The process uses a simple concept – do causal analysis on your defects and implement changes that will prevent those defects from recurring. However, it is far from simple to implement methods and procedures that can be successfully deployed within a development organization and bring results. In this respect, the Defect Prevention Process is similar to Inspection, which also has a simple concept – have people look at the development work products to find defects – but is likewise far from simple in actual implementation.

There are four key elements of the process which are integrated into the development process. Software development is usually divided into process steps (also called 'stages' within IBM), such as design steps, code, unit test, functional test, and so on. The Defect Prevention Process is applied at each process step, including the test steps. The following description summarizes a typical application of the process in a software development organization (see also Figure 17.1).

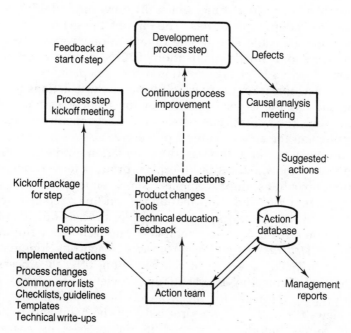

Figure 17.1 The Defect Prevention Process.

(1) *Causal analysis meetings* Developers perform regular causal analysis of defects and problems occurring in the process and suggest preventive actions. Causal analysis meetings are attended by the people who created the defects. These meetings can be held during the development step as defects are discovered and fixed, or may be held at the end of the step.

Each meeting usually lasts two hours and is attended by the members of a single development team. (Development teams in IBM generally number four to seven people.) During the meeting, the following areas are covered for each defect:

(a) What is the defect or error?
(b) What is the cause of the defect? How was the error introduced?
(c) What actions would prevent this sort of error from recurring?

In the last half hour of the meeting, the team also addresses broader questions concerning trends and commonalities in the defects, and problem areas that the team has encountered that can be improved. These broader questions result in additional suggested actions.

(2) *Action team* A team of people from the development area implements the suggested preventive actions. The action team members work part-time, generally devoting 10–15% of their time to action team duties. The size of the action team varies depending on the size of the organization, from three to four members for a small organization of 20–50 people, to eight to ten members for a large organization of 200–250 people.

Each action team member implements those actions for which he/she has the expertise. If the action team does not have the expertise, the appropriate person in the organization is sought to implement the action. Typical preventive actions include process improvements and process documentation updates, new and enhanced tools, education offerings, product improvements and communications improvements. Many actions require saving documentation and information in on-line 'repositories' for access by the developers, for example, process documentation, common error lists, design templates and technical write-ups.

(3) *Process step Kickoffs or Process reviews* Each development team holds a Kickoff meeting at the beginning of each process step. The Kickoff meeting is essentially a review of that process step to prepare the team for the work of that step. The team leader reviews the details of the process with the team and points out the things that have changed in the process as a result of implemented actions.

The process step Kickoff meeting (in earlier papers we called this the 'Stage Kickoff meeting') usually lasts 1–2 hours. The information presented in the Kickoff is tailored to the specific step the developers are about to begin. In the cases where the developers do not follow a 'staged' process (for example, developers who diagnose and fix defects in production software), the team conducts a 'periodic process review', reviewing some aspect of their specific processes every two or three months.

(4) *Action database*   Because the number of suggested actions tends to be large, a database is needed to track them and to provide data about the Defect Prevention Process itself for management control. The action team uses the database to record each action and its status. The action's status is updated in the database as it is assigned to an action team member, investigated, implemented and finally closed.

It is critical that these key elements be integrated into the development process to insure successful implementation of the Defect Prevention Process. The Defect Prevention activities need to become part of everyone's job, just as Inspection activities become part of what developers do.

Relationship to the Inspection Process

The Defect Prevention Process complements the Inspection process. Developers conduct their Inspections and fix the work product. As a natural extension, the developers then conduct causal analysis on a portion of those defects in order to improve that process step so those defects do not recur.

However, the Defect Prevention Process can also be applied to development steps where there are no Inspections conducted (for example, test stages), to processes where Inspections are not usually done (for example, administrative processes), and on defects that are discovered in other ways than through Inspections (for example, software defects found in production). The Defect Prevention Process thus has a broader applicability than just to the Inspection process.

Clearly, causal analysis should be conducted after Inspections but should causal analysis be done *immediately* after an Inspection? Several IBM experts in Inspections and Defect Prevention strongly recommend *not* to conduct a causal analysis meeting as part of an Inspection meeting or immediately following it, for the following reasons:

(1) Energy level: the Inspection participants have already gone through a long meeting. Some rules of thumb recommend that

the Inspection should not proceed for more than four hours per day because the Inspectors' effectiveness declines after that much intense mental effort. To add an additional 2-hour meeting to the end of a long meeting will result in a very ineffective meeting. To do causal analysis properly the participants need energy and enthusiasm to come up with good ideas. The causal analysis meeting itself is limited to two hours for this reason.

(2) Wrong participants: the people who attend the Inspection are not the same set of people who need to attend the causal analysis. The causal analysis participants should include the entire development team, so there can be a real synergism of ideas and a balanced view of the process that was being followed. And the causal analysis meeting should not include 'disinterested' parties, that is, those who were not directly involved in that part of the development process, for example, planners, testers or information developers. These people will not be able to address the specific process issues that need addressing nor propose the types of preventive actions that are needed.

(3) Defects are not verified: right after the Inspection, we don't yet know if many of the issues raised are defects or not. Such items must first be investigated to determine if they are in fact errors. It is quite unproductive to attempt to do causal analysis on such an item because it will always be open to the objection that it isn't a defect, it doesn't have a cause and there's nothing to prevent! On the other hand, once an item has been identified as a defect, it may well be one of those that we should analyze because of what actually went wrong. You need to do the investigation after the Inspection to decide conclusively if the item is in fact a defect.

(4) Focus is on only one person's defects: it is desirable to have defects from *several* people discussed at the same causal analysis meeting, to deflect the sensitivity from any single developer. If several developers' defects are discussed, no one developer is put on the spot to explain the causes of his/her errors. In contrast, right after an Inspection, the developer would be the sole focus of the causal analysis. Moreover, the Inspection itself is a cause for sensitivity from which the developer deserves at least several days to recover before participating in a causal analysis meeting.

A second reason to mix defects among several developers is that there develops a much broader perspective on the causes for the defects, how to prevent them, what trends there are in the errors being made, what the underlying process failures are, and so on. You will miss this broadness of perspective if you concentrate on just one person's errors. The developer himself/herself can also get the misimpression that he/she is a poor performer for having made these errors, when in fact, all developers make errors. The focus of causal analysis is not on an individual developer, the developer's defects or even the causes of these defects; the real focus is on suggestions for process improvements.

(5) Difficult to screen/select defects prior to the causal analysis: we generally can't afford to do causal analysis on 100% of our defects. This means that we need to be selective about which defects to analyze. We can't rationally make selections without viewing a large set of the defects. We do not have such a large set after a single Inspection.

Within IBM, the causal analysis meeting is conducted after Inspection defects have been investigated and fixed, when the defects from several developers can be pooled and selected. That way the development team gets a broader view of the defects that have occurred in that step and can propose more effective preventive actions.

Practical Aspects of Defect Prevention

The balance of this chapter discusses some of the practical aspects of the Defect Prevention Process:

• What is a defect?
• Selecting defects for causal analysis;
• Conducting a causal analysis meeting;
• An example of an actual causal analysis meeting;
• The action database;
• Action team operation;
• Repositories;
• Process step Kickoff (process review) meetings;
• How much does this cost and what's it worth?

We are describing the Defect Prevention Process from the perspective of software developers, although almost all of these practical aspects apply as well to Defect Prevention activities done by others such as testers, planners, information developers, hardware engineers, and so on.

What is a Defect?

For students of the Inspection process, what a defect is should be clear. Generally, a defect is identified as something that is incorrect in a work product. There are Major and minor defects, a Major defect being one which if left uncorrected would be identified by a customer as needing correction. In other words, a Major defect is a failure to meet customer expectations.

For the Defect Prevention Process, we generally use a broader definition of a defect. We need to improve everything we do, so we should not feel limited just to software product defects. Our software development Lab at Myers Corners Road in Poughkeepsie, NY (see reference 2) developed the following definition of a defect:

> Anything which impacts or interferes with maintaining or improving quality and productivity.

Thus we can look for defects to bring to causal analysis beyond the traditional sources of software Inspections and testing. Good indications that we have had a defect are the fact that we had to repeat something (rework), that there was a slip in a committed delivery date or that an internal or external customer was not satisfied. We need only take the time to record the fact that a defect has occurred and what the particulars were, in order to bring it to a causal analysis meeting.

Selecting Defects

The defect rates during software development are generally such that most development organizations cannot analyze every defect, nor is it usually worthwhile analyzing them all. Some subset of the defects should be selected for analysis. There are a number of guidelines by which an organization can make such a selection. The overall goal is to select a subset that is representative of the whole and which will place emphasis for prevention where the organization wishes. Some typical selection strategies are:

- Select every fifth Major defect such that there is a balanced set from each developer participating in the causal analysis meeting. Eliminate any obvious duplicates but make a note that that particular type of defect occurred several times. Do not analyze minor defects.
- Group similar or related defects together into subsets. Pick a typical defect from each set to do detailed causal analysis on but describe the whole set of defects to the team during causal analysis.
- Analyze every severity 1 (most severe) defect and a balanced subset of the other defects. Do not analyze severity 4 (low impact) defects.

• Analyze every defective fix that we ship to a customer. Analyze a subset of the defects we encounter in developing fixes, in Inspection, test and certification of the fix.

Conducting a Causal Analysis Meeting

The causal analysis meeting is a structured meeting. Its objective is to examine defects and generate suggestions that will prevent those defects in the future. The structure of the meeting is crucial in order not to waste the participants' time. The structure is needed to guide the participants through the thought process of 'defect' to 'cause' to 'suggested actions'. Less structured forms of meeting, such as brainstorming, are just not able to focus on all of the details that must be covered.

The participants of the causal analysis meeting are a causal analysis leader and the development team members. The leader may or may not be a member of the team. The team is the group of people who are working together. If the project has no formal teams, the participants are those people whose work is related (for example, they follow the same general process). Sometimes the best set of people to do causal analysis is composed of members of the same department.

Managers do not attend their employees' causal analysis meetings. The reason is simply that the presence of the manager can inhibit open discussion of a person's defect and its causes. Such analysis is sensitive enough among one's peers. Furthermore, the information from causal analysis should *not* be used by management for employee evaluation or appraisal.

The causal analysis leader acts as the meeting facilitator, much as the Inspection moderator facilitates the Inspection meeting. Since there is a lot of writing to record the results of the analysis, one or two of the team members act as scribes. The causal analysis format (Figure 17.2) is written on the board. One scribe (or the leader) writes the analysis information on the board and the other scribe copies this on a paper form. For groups with sophisticated meeting facilities, the form can be projected on a screen and filled in by a scribe at a workstation.

In analyzing defects, the team follows a thought process (Figure 17.3) that takes them from something that *exists* and is known (the defect), through something they *derive* through analysis (the causes), to something they *create* (the suggested actions). The causal analysis leader is responsible for keeping the team members' discussion on track as they go across for each defect, from defect description, through cause, to suggested actions.

The focus of the causal analysis meeting is on the 'suggested actions', that is, on improving our processes so that defects do not

Def No.	Defect Abstract	Cause Categ	Cause Abstract	Step Created	Suggested Actions to Prevent

Figure 17.2 Causal analysis format.

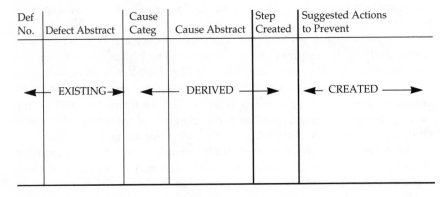

Def No.	Defect Abstract	Cause Categ	Cause Abstract	Step Created	Suggested Actions to Prevent
	◄— EXISTING —►	◄— DERIVED —►		◄— CREATED —►	

Figure 17.3 Defect analysis thought process.

recur. The focus is *not* on placing blame for what has gone wrong. The causal analysis leader needs to be aware of the potential sensitivity that will exist during the discussion of cause and steer the team toward making good preventive suggestions.

The causal analysis meeting is generally conducted for two hours, with the following structure:

- Defect analysis (1.5 hours): look at specific defects, discuss the cause(s), suggest actions to prevent similar defects in the future. Cover as many defects as the time permits.
- Generic analysis (0.5 hour): look more broadly for trends in the defects. Are there additional actions to be taken? Also look at the process as a whole. Are there problems in the development process that should be corrected, even though they may not be causing defects?

In a two-hour meeting, with 1.5 hours devoted to defect analysis, a typical team can cover 10–15 defects. The discussion of each defect is necessarily limited (six to nine minutes each, at this rate), so the team needs to remain focused and not go off on tangents. If the team does not cover all of the defects they had intended, a second causal analysis meeting can be scheduled.

The following discussion covers in more detail the way causal analysis is conducted, in the following sections:

- Defect analysis (1.5 hours)
  - Defect abstract
  - Cause category, cause abstract, process step created
  - Suggested actions.
- Generic analysis (last half hour)
  - Trends and commonalities
  - What went 'right' discussion
  - What went 'wrong' discussion.

Defect Analysis: Defect Abstract

The leader calls for a defect to be analyzed. The person whose defect it is (the 'proposer') explains the defect, perhaps reading some detail from the Inspection report or test record. The leader summarizes the defect, that is, what was incorrect or wrong. The defect abstract is then written on the board. There is little discussion other than for clarification of the defect.

The leader needs to insure that the defect itself has been identified and not a symptom of the defect nor a cause. The defect is what was wrong or incorrect in the work product. A symptom is some outward manifestation of the defect. A cause is some preceding incident that brought about the defect. For example:

- Symptom: the accounting system produced incorrect subtotals in the monthly account summary report (an outward manifestation).
- Defect: the subaccounts were not added into the subtotal variable (what was incorrect in the program).
- Cause: the changes needed for the accounting reports to support subaccounts were overlooked.

In this example, what needs to be written down as the defect abstract is the *defect*, what was wrong in the system (subaccounts not added in), not the symptom (incorrect subtotals in the report). The cause, which may have been brought up by the proposer at this point, should be deferred to the cause section of the analysis.

Defect Analysis: Cause Section

The cause section of the analysis has three parts: cause category, cause abstract and process step where the defect was created. These three pieces of information act together to give a full picture of the cause.

The cause category is used to get the discussion started as to what the cause might have been. Frequently it is easier for the proposer to first identify a general type of cause ('It was a communications problem' or 'I think it was mostly education'). The leader can then (gently) probe for more details ('So what was not communicated?' or 'What was not understood?'). Out of this probing and discussion with other team members, the picture of the cause emerges ('The design changes were not communicated to the developer until after the Inspection' or 'The macro documentation is incomplete and incorrect'). Finally, the process step where the defect was first introduced is recorded ('High level design' or 'Code').

The introduction of additional information may alter the way the team views the cause ('Well if this defect was really injected at the high level design step, it was really a problem that the designers did not include all the information we needed in the design document').

Thus, the causal analysis leader guides the team through (1) cause category, (2) cause abstract and (3) process step where the defect was created:

(1) Cause category: the leader asks the proposer what category of cause this might be. The possible cause categories are:

COMM – Communications failure, for example, incorrect information, lost information, failed to communicate a change in information.

OVER – Oversight, for example, overlooked or forgot something, failed to consider all cases and conditions.

EDUC – Education, for example, lacked knowledge or understanding about something. For software development, we distinguish three kinds of education causes:

EDNF – Education on new function: did not understand the new function being added to the system

EDBC – Education on the base code: did not understand some aspect of the existing function of the system

EDOT – Education other: did not understand some other aspect of the work (for example, the programming language, the compiler, a development tool).

TRAN – Transcription error, for example, transcribed or copied something incorrectly; knew what to do but just made a mistake.

PROC – Process problem, for example, some aspect of the process encouraged the creation of the defect.

Note that the cause category is primarily intended to get the discussion started on the cause of the defect. The danger is that the team will spend much time on just what kind of cause this is. These discussions are a waste of time and should be avoided. If necessary, the leader should skip the cause category and go directly into the discussion of the cause. The cause category is not meant for later analysis, although it may provide some useful information.

(2) When the leader has a tentative cause category, he/she may then ask the proposer follow-on probing questions, such as:

COMM –   What was not communicated, from whom, to whom?
OVER –   What was not considered thoroughly?
EDUC –   What was not understood?
TRAN –   What procedure was being used?
PROC –   What aspect of the process encouraged the defect?

The leader can then probe further as to the specific cause, bringing the other team members into the discussion until general agreement (though not necessarily consensus) is reached as to the cause. This is then written on the board. The other team members can contribute because of their own perspective on what happened during the development step.

Of course, there may be multiple causes which contributed to the defect, either as a chain of causation (C3 was caused by C2 which was caused by C1) or as a set of contributing causes. Each of the relevant causes should be listed on the board. Not all causes will have preventive actions and some causes will be easier to eliminate than others.

The leader should note that this discussion is the most sensitive part of the meeting. The leader should probe for causes gently, for example using the passive voice ('What was not understood?' rather than 'What didn't you understand?'). In asking probing questions, the leader should particularly avoid using 'why' questions ('Why didn't you look at the macro documentation?') because it tends to cause defensiveness.

(3) The leader now asks in which process step the defect was introduced or created. The leader needs to be sure that it is where the defect was created, rather than where it was detected.

Defect Analysis: Suggested Actions

The causal analysis leader can now guide the team in proposing actions that will prevent future defects by eliminating the cause(s) that have been listed. Some of the actions that are typically proposed to eliminate each cause type are:

OVER – Checklists, common error lists, tools to automate checking, process improvements, changes to the software application including improved documentation, design and coding templates, work-in-progress reviews with other team members.

COMM – Assigned liaisons to other groups, on-line forums or discussions, tools to automate notifications, distribution lists, process improvements, newsletters.

EDUC – Technical write-ups, guidelines, classes and seminars, newsletters, new-hire education checklist.

TRAN – Automation of error-prone procedures, automated checking of work, reviews of work by other team members.

PROC – Process improvements and fixes, education on the process, documentation of detailed procedures or methods.

The causal analysis leader now asks for suggestions to prevent the defect under analysis. To stimulate the discussion, the leader may ask the following probing questions:

- If we could change anything, what would we change to prevent this defect in the future?
- Can we automatically eliminate and prevent this defect?
- Can defects similar to this one in the software (or other work product) be removed?

As ideas are proposed, the leader leads the discussion and refinement of the suggestion by the team until there is general agreement (again, full consensus is not necessary). The suggested actions are then written on the board. Since they are 'actions' they are best worded starting with an action verb (for example, create, enhance, document, add to, investigate).

One difficulty frequently encountered in causal analysis is that vague, non-specific actions are proposed (for example, 'Use the common error lists during the process step' or 'Make the reporting tool more flexible'). Such actions are not much help to the action team because they do not give enough details to figure out what to do. The action team may also misinterpret what is being asked and do unnecessary work. It is the causal analysis leader's responsibility to get a specific, concrete action description. This will also have the benefit that the action team will more readily accept the action. Some of the probing questions the leader can use are:

- Is this action implementable?
- Exactly what would you like the action team to do?
- What additional details are needed?

- Would you really use this action if it were implemented?
- What is the justification or rationale for this action?

The actions proposed during causal analysis do not need to be directly related to a specific cause or even to the defect under discussion. During the discussion, if someone gets a good idea ('You know, this is not directly related, but we could really use it'), the leader should include it in the discussion and record it among the other suggested actions to go to the action team.

Generic Analysis (Last Half Hour)

During the last half hour of the causal analysis meeting, the leader shifts the team's focus to a broader view of the defects and of the process which the team just went through. The purpose of this generic analysis discussion is to generate additional suggested actions which will hopefully be more general and broader in scope.

Such issues as trends in the defects, impacts on the developers' productivity and possible improvements to processes, tools and education are brought up. However, this part of the meeting is *not* a general gripe session. The objective is to generate more actions!

There are three parts to the generic analysis portion of the meeting:

(1) Trends and commonalities: do we see any trends or commonalities in the defects, causes or suggestions? What *additional* suggestions can we make to address this broader trend?
(2) What went right in the last stage of work (or in the last 2–3 months)? Can we make that improvement permanent and generally available to everyone in the organization?
(3) What went wrong in the last stage of work (or last 2–3 months)? How can we prevent that problem from recurring?

Generic Analysis: Trends and Commonalities

The causal analysis leader asks the team to consider the defects, causes and actions that have been listed on the board. Are there any 'trends and commonalities' among the defects that have been analyzed? Some examples of commonalities are:

- Common types of defects (for example, registers clobbered, confusion between external references and weak external references, base register definition problems).
- A trend in a cause category, the cause itself or the process step created (for example, education problems, oversights in the design step).
- Common types of suggested actions (for example, tools, documentation).

When a commonality has been identified, the leader directs the team not to discuss it, but to consider 'Is there *anything else* we can do?', for example:

- to prevent this type of defect?
- to eliminate this type of cause?
- to enhance this type of action? (for example, additional tools or documentation).

The leader guides the discussion and any additional actions are recorded.

Generic Analysis: What Went Right?

The leader now asks the team whether anything went 'right' during the last process step of work (or the last 2–3 months). For example, the team might consider:

- things that have enhanced the productivity or effectiveness of the team (for example, new tools);
- new practices that prevented defects (for example, better communications among the team);
- things that are considerably better compared to prior steps.

Again the leader directs the team not to discuss the item but to consider 'What can we do to make this available to everyone?'

- to share the information with everyone;
- to make tools and procedures available to everyone;
- to make improvements to the process permanent.

The leader guides the discussion and any additional actions are recorded.

Generic Analysis: What Went Wrong?

The leader now asks the team whether anything went 'wrong' during the last process step of work (or the last 2–3 months). (Usually there is no hesitancy on this topic.) For example, the team might consider:

- things that have impacted the productivity or effectiveness of the team;
- things that caused problems or created defects;
- things that are considerably worse compared to prior stages.

Here the leader directs the team not to discuss the problem but to consider what the causes were and then to consider 'What can we do to prevent or avoid this problem in the future?' What can we suggest that will:

- improve our procedures and processes;
- remove inhibitors, roadblocks;
- eliminate the cause of problems, prevent more defects.

The leader guides the discussion and any additional actions are recorded.

An Example of an Actual Causal Analysis Meeting

Figure 17.4 depicts the results of an actual causal analysis meeting that was conducted in the IBM RTP Networking Lab in Research Triangle Park, NC. The specific project jargon is explained in the notes and some of the internal program names have been altered. This was a causal analysis of code errors uncovered during code Inspections. Several team members' defects were analyzed.

Take for example defect 2. The developer coded the wrong keyword on a particular macro call. The cause was that the developer did not know how to look up parameters for macros (an 'education other' type of cause). This developer was newly hired into the organization and did not know all of the details of how to find things. The first suggestion was thus to create a New Hire's Guide to resources in the product area. Secondly, since some of the macro descriptions (in the 'prolog' commentary) aren't all that helpful anyway, the suggestion was made to 'clean them up'. (More detail was given here as to which macros should be focused on.) Finally, a more experienced developer suggested that they should have a code reuse library in which to put macros and other reusable components, in order to facilitate finding the code and understanding how to use it.

Some additional comments on this causal analysis meeting are warranted. In the defect analysis portion, the team was able to analyze eight defects. This is somewhat low compared to the 10–15 that are more typical and may have been due to extended discussions of some items.

The action descriptions are quite abbreviated but the causal analysis leader expanded on them and included more information when they were entered into the database before they went to the action team.

During the generic analysis portion (last half hour), the team looked at trends and commonalities among the defects, causes and actions and found two items:

- Education type defects were common, with lack of understanding of the base code and lack of understanding among new hires. In response to the question, 'What other kinds of education is needed?' the team responded 'Provide education on reading listings.'

- Communications problems in the design documentation and in other product documentation (for example, of control blocks) were common. In response to the question, 'What other kinds of documentation are needed?' the team responded 'Precise interface documentation should be required in the design documents'.

The causal analysis leader did ask for items that went well during this code step. There was discussion but no suggestions were made. One item as to 'what went wrong' was proposed, that not enough time had been allotted for the code step. The suggestion proposed was to adjust the 'planning rates' to provide more time for the code step in the future.

The Action Database

Each causal analysis meeting results in perhaps 12–20 suggested actions. With each development team analyzing some portion of its defects at each development step, the number of suggested actions quickly mounts into the hundreds. The action team thus needs a database to keep track of all of the suggestions so that the developers' good ideas aren't lost but rather are acted upon. The action database used in IBM provides a status field that gives the action's current status and who on the action team is currently assigned to work on the action.

The action database also should provide feedback to the developers on the status of their suggestions. The IBM database tool provides notification to the suggester and any other interested parties whenever an action's status has changed.

The action database should also provide statistics to the action team and management on how well the process is doing. Figure 17.5 gives the summary page of a typical status report used within IBM. This report is for a development organization of 200 people. For a given time period (in this case the first half of 1992), the 'activity summary' lists:

- the number of actions that were closed and the total cost to implement them;
- the number of Defect Prevention Process meetings that was conducted and the person time spent on them.

The 'action team work flow' lists:

- the number of actions open at the beginning of the period,
- plus the number of new actions that were created,
- minus the number of actions that were closed,
- equals the number of actions open at the end of the period.

Defect Analysis (first 1.5 hours)

Def No.	Defect Abstract	Cause Categ	Cause Abstract	Step Created	Suggested Actions to Prevent
1	Referenced wrong RU control block	EDBC	Didn't understand router/ sender build interface	CODE	• Create a user's guide for router/sender. • Include descriptions of subcomponent functions used in CLD.
2	Wrong keyword on YYCALL macro	EDOT	Didn't know how to look up parameters for macro	CODE	• Create a New Hire's Guide to resources in the product area. • Clean up macro prologs. • Create a Code Reuse Library.
3	Incorrect use of XXXABORT	COMM	CLD interface document not easily understood	CODE	• Improve utility documentation, especially the description of interfaces.
4	Logic wrong	COMM	Team leader didn't give enough information	CODE	• Team leaders need more time to train new hires and guide them.
5	Invalid condition check	TRAN	Implementing module in phases	CODE	• Write an implementation plan for modules that are developed in phases.
6	XXXXZZ declared on invalid boundary	TRAN	Simple mistake	CODE	• Add control block boundary problems to common error list.
7	XXXXYY CB field was moved that couldn't (boundary)	COMM	No doc for that requirement in the Control Block	CODE	• Create a dissertation on CB boundaries. • See previous actions.
8	XXX call parameter specified incorrectly	EDBC	Didn't read prolog carefully enough.	CODE	• Add error to the common error list.

(continued)

Figure 17.4   Example of a causal analysis meeting.

Generic Analysis (last half hour)

A TRENDS AND COMMONALITIES

Education lacking
(base code, new hires).

What other kinds of education
do we need for the base product
or for new hires?

- Provide education on reading listings.

Communications problems
via CLD documentation,
other documentation.

What other kinds of documentation
do we need for CLDs, what other
kinds of product doc do we need??

- Precise interface documentation should
  be required in CLDs.

B. WHAT WENT RIGHT during this code step? (Some discussion but no suggestions proposed.)

C. WHAT WENT WRONG during this development step?

Not enough time was
allotted for the step

How can we avoid this problem in
the future?

- Provide more time for coding,
  Inspections and for developing the UT
  plan when planning for the code step.

NOTES:

CLD = Component Level Design step (also sometimes called 'high level design'). A 'CLD' is the design document produced during this process step.
UT = Unit Test development step.
RU = Response Unit, a type of data structure used in the software.
CB = Control Block, a data structure used in the software.
Prolog = The prolog comments at the beginning of a module, containing information about the module's interface and parameter requirements.
COMM = Communications failure (cause category).
EDBC = Education lacking on the Base Code (cause category).
EDOT = Education lacking – Other (cause category).
TRAN = Transcription type error (cause category).

Figure 17.4 *Continued*

Defect Prevention Process Summary for 01/01/92 through 06/30/92:

Activity	Number	Person months
Actions closed	98	10.22
Causal analysis sessions	15	1.74
Kickoff meetings	5	0.35
Action team meetings	10	0.78
Classes on Defect Prevention	3	4.50
Total		17.59 person-months
	or	1.47 person-years

Action team work flow:

Actions open at the beginning of the period:	362
+ Actions created during the period:	86
− Actions closed during the period:	(98)
Actions open at the end of the period:	350

Figure 17.5   Defect Prevention Process Status Report.

Action Team Operation

During training sessions for the Defect Prevention Process we ask the students 'What would happen if Defect Prevention consisted just of doing causal analysis and then implementing the actions yourself? What if DP = Causal Analysis + Do It Yourself?' The responses we get are typically:

• We lack the skills to do many of the actions, like tools.
• We lack the authority to change things except just in our area.
• We lack the time to do anything but what we've already been given.
• We don't understand everything that's going on in other areas.
• We wouldn't make these suggestions if we had to implement them ourselves.

The action team is part of this process precisely to address all of these problems. It is staffed with the people in the organization who have the needed skills and knowledge of the entire area. It is given the authority to change the organization's processes and the time to do it. With the action team in place the developers are free to make suggestions that will really improve their work, without the fear that they will have to implement them themselves.

The action team usually has the following set of roles. In smaller action teams, one person may play two or more roles.

• A 'process person' who handles process definition and documentation, including checklists, common error lists, guidelines, and so on.

- An education coordinator who handles education types of actions such as classes and seminars, new hire education.
- A 'tools person' who handles tool requirements for new tools or enhancements to tools, tool acquisition and deployment.
- Representatives from design, development and test to handle actions requiring expertise in those areas, such as technical system write-ups.
- A manager who handles communications and negotiations with other organizations and actions that are specific to management practices.

Action team members typically spend 10–15% of their time on action implementation, action team meetings, and so on. This time is part of their normal work responsibilities. Typically it is the action team member who implements the action. Where a special skill is required for a particular action which is not available among the action team members, someone else in the organization implements it. Even in these cases, however, one of the action team members remains responsible for the action.

The action team meets regularly, usually every two weeks, for 1–2 hours. The team is usually led by the process person, although the manager may lead the team. (The team members generally do not report to this manager.) In a typical action team meeting, the team will:

(1) Review the new actions that have not yet been assigned. There is usually some discussion on whether this is an appropriate action, is there enough information, how should it be implemented and who on the team should be assigned. In some instances the team will modify the action to improve the approach or effectiveness. An action may be rejected for a number of possible reasons and some actions are combined with a similar existing action, as a duplicate.

(2) Review the status of the assigned actions. Usually an action team member will have worked on one or two actions since the prior action team meeting. Any problems or issues with respect to the implementation are raised and discussed.

(3) Review any actions that are ready to be closed or that have recently been closed to insure that all aspects of the suggestion have been addressed and that the action's availability is communicated to the organization.

(4) The action team may also review the overall status of their actions, to set or revise priorities, to develop a case for more funding for specific actions, and so on. They may also look at general trends in defects in the area, plan recognition for suggesters and implementers who have made significant

contributions, plan special communications to the organization about the actions that have been implemented, and so on.

After the meeting, the status of the actions discussed is updated in the action database.

After some time in operation, the action team will have a backlog of suggested actions yet to be implemented. The action team may deal with these actions in a number of ways, for example, negotiating for special resources to get the backlog actions implemented or closing those which are lower priority because it is unlikely they will ever be implemented.

Repositories

The implementation of actions results in numerous items that need to be saved and accessed by the developers, such as process documents, checklists, development guidelines and conventions, design and coding templates, educational materials, tools and tool documentation, common error lists, product or system technical documentation, and so on.

This material is made available in an on-line repository and is maintained and updated by the action team. Usually there is an index to the material by subject area (process, tools, product documentation, education, and so on) and a search capability to allow quick access to the information. The material in the repository is also the basis for the process step Kickoff package.

Process Step Kickoff (Process Review) Meetings

Having an up-to-date, on-line repository of needed technical information does not insure that the developers will actually look at the information during development. We have found that periodic reviews of this information are needed to remind developers of the process details that are critical to their work in a particular process step. It is essential to provide this feedback in a timely way, at the appropriate points in the development process.

The form that this periodic feedback takes is the 'Process step Kickoff meeting'. Process step Kickoffs are held by the team at the beginning of each development step and are conducted by the team's technical leader. They usually last 1–2 hours. The team leader reviews the development process for that step, focusing on areas that have been weak in the past, emphasizing new practices and reviewing other enhancements to the organization's process, methods and tools that have been implemented by the action team.

It is important that Process step Kickoff meetings be integrated into the development process, at the beginning of each development step, and that the developers be directly involved. We have found that simply holding step Kickoffs can achieve significant reductions in defects for that step. Kickoffs thus provide an immediate payback.

In the cases where the developers do not follow a *staged* process, for example, developers who diagnose and fix defects in production software, the team conducts a *periodic process review*, reviewing some aspect of their specific processes, for example, tools, checklists, common errors, Inspection and certification procedures, every two or three months.

The Kickoff package is derived from materials in the repository and tailored by the team leader for that particular team's needs. For example, a team which consisted of new hires would go over the materials in much more detail than a team of experienced developers.

The Kickoff package contains the materials that the team leader feels are useful to help the team prevent defects and get the job done most efficiently. It usually has three sections, for process, quality and technical contacts:

(1) Process
   (a) A description of the process for this step, including specific methodologies, techniques, tools, guidelines, conventions, checklists, and so on. This documentation highlights the information that has changed recently with revision bars.
   (b) The inputs that are available for the step.
   (c) Examples of outputs that should be produced.
(2) Quality
   (a) A brief description of the Defect Prevention Process as it is practiced by the organization.
   (b) A description of the validation methods that will be used for this step (for example, Inspections, reviews).
   (c) The Inspection checklist for this step.
   (d) The common error list for this step.
   (e) A list of error-prone modules or error-prone areas of the work.
(3) Technical contacts
   (a) A list of the external groups supporting the process (for example, information development, test, human factors, other development organizations with whom there are dependencies).
   (b) The specific contacts or liaisons with these other groups.

The Kickoff may also include other topics such as team assignments and development schedules, but these items are not the focus nor emphasis of the meeting.

How Much Does This Cost and What's It Worth To Us?

The experience over almost a decade now in the use of the Defect Prevention Process is that a reduction in defects of the order of two times is achievable with a small investment. The two times improvement is usually achieved in the first one to two years. Subsequent improvements up to a threefold improvement may take an additional two or three years. All of these improvements were observed in organizations that invested between 1% and 2% of their resources in the Defect Prevention Process.

The details of specific defect reductions are contained elsewhere (reference 1) and have now been confirmed in additional products, two within IBM and at least one outside IBM (reference 8), where before and after data were available.

A reduction in defects means that less effort is taken up by the organization to diagnose, fix and re-test defects coming from test and from the field. An analysis we performed of the typical costs of fixing defects from testing and from the field showed that an investment of about 1% of an area's resources in the Defect Prevention Process will return somewhere between 6 and 8 times the cost as savings to the organization (reference 9).

Conclusion

The connection between the Inspection process and the Defect Prevention Process is natural and should be exploited. Whenever Inspections are done, a portion of the defects from each of the developers on the team should be analyzed in a causal analysis meeting. Of course, causal analysis should be continued throughout the development process on defects that are uncovered during testing. The payback for the development organization is substantial but the most significant benefit is higher software quality in production and therefore higher customer satisfaction with the software.

References

1. Mays R.G., Jones C.L., Holloway G.J. and Studinski D.P. (1990). Experiences with Defect Prevention. *IBM Systems Journal*, **29** (1), 4–32
2. Gale J.L., Tirso J.R. and Burchfield C.A. (1990). Implementing the Defect Prevention Process in the MVS Interactive Programming Organization. *IBM Systems Journal*, **29** (1), 33–43

3. Mays R.G. (1990). Applications of Defect Prevention in Software Development. *IEEE Journal on Selected Areas in Communications*, **8** (2), February, 164–168

4. Jones C.L (1985). A Process-integrated Approach to Defect Prevention. *IBM Systems Journal*, **24** (2), 150–167

5. Kolkhorst B.G. and Macina, Anthony J. (1988). Developing Error-Free Software. *IEEE Aerosp. Electron. Syst. Mag.*, **3** (11), November, 25–31

6. Haugh J.M. (1992). Never Make the Same Mistake Twice – Using Configuration Control and Error Analysis to Improve Software Quality. *IEEE Aerosp. Electron. Syst. Mag.*, **7** (1), January, 12–16

7. White A.M. (1988). Modern Practical Methods of Producing High Quality Software. *Quality Assurance*, **14** (3), September, 96–102

8. Dangerfield O., Ambardekar P., Paluzzi P., Card D. and Giblin D. (1992). Defect Causal Analysis: a Report from the Field. *Proc. 2nd Int. Conf. on Software Quality*, October, 109–113, American Society for Quality Control

9. Mays R.G. (1992). Defect Prevention and Total Quality Management. Chapter 15 in *Total Quality Management for Software* eds. Schulmeyer G.G. and McManus J.I. New York: Van Nostrand Reinhold

Appendix A: A One-page Inspection Handbook

> This Handbook shall never be printed on more than a page after updates.
> This note will always be included.

Process Owner: _____   Version/date: _____

(1) The Inspection process is always managed by a trained and certified Inspection leader.

(2) The leader is responsible for managing the process in all respects for productive results.

(3) The first objective of Inspection is to identify and correct major defects.

(4) The second, but most important, objective of Inspection is to identify and remove the source of defects.

(5) The fundamental measure of Inspection success is the quality-to-cost ratio of the total development and service life cycle.

(6) Short-term measures include major issues found per work-hour used (efficiency), and the percentage of defects identified and treated compared to the total defects (effectiveness).

(7) The productivity measure of Inspection is the net hours saved, estimated statistically, due to defects found and removed earlier than they otherwise would be.

(8) **Entry.** The rest of the Inspection process is only entered when a specified set of entry criteria have been met.

(9) **Planning.** The leader selects a set of source documentation, candidate documentation, checklists, rule sets, checking rates, people, roles, and logging meeting rates to ensure maximum productivity.

(10) **Kickoff.** The leader can elect to run a 'kickoff' meeting prior to checking. Team improvement goals and corresponding strategies are adopted. Any necessary instruction is given.

(11) **Checking.** The checking phase has a recommended time or rate, but checkers have instructions to deviate from that whenever individual ability, role or situation dictates, in order to increase productivity.

(12) The objective of individual checking is to identify a maximum of unique major issues which no other checker will bring to the logging meeting. To do this each checker should have at least one special 'role'.

(13) **Logging meeting.** The team concentrates on logging items at a rate of at least one per minute. Items logged include potential defects (issues), improvement suggestions, and questions of intent to the author. The leader permits little other verbal meeting activity. Meetings last a maximum of two hours at the known optimum rate. If necessary, work must be chunked to avoid tiredness. Optimum checking rate for the meeting is determined by the percentage of new issues identified in the logging meeting as well as quantity of documents.

(14) **Edit.** Issue analysis and correction action is undertaken by an editor. Some written action must be taken on all logged issues – if necessary by sending change requests to other authors. The editor makes the final classification of issues into defects, and reports final defect metrics to the leader. Edit also deals with improvements and can deal with 'questions to author.'

(15) **Follow-up.** The leader shall determine that some appropriate written action has been taken on all logged issues. The leader is not responsible for the correctness (the editor is).

(16) **Exit.** The leader determines whether the formal exit criteria have been met before signing off completion of the Inspection. These include follow-up completed, metrics delivered, planned rates kept to, and level of remaining defects within acceptable bounds.

(17) **Process brainstorming.** Immediately after each logging meeting, time is used to brainstorm the process causes of major defects, and to brainstorm improvements to remove these causes. These suggestions are stored in the QA database for the Process Change Management Team. This meeting shall last no more than half an hour. The objective is to maximize production of useful ideas and personal commitment to change within that time.

Appendix B: Procedures – What to Do, by Specialist and by Sub-process

The Purpose of Procedures

- To give individuals on-the-job training in how to do the Inspection process.
- To serve as a record of the best-known practices.
- To serve as a basis for continuous process improvement.
- To help the leader avoid having to remember and repeat to everyone, what is expected.
- To train leaders initially and to upgrade their procedures.

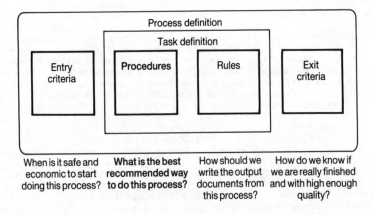

Figure B.1 Procedures are the 'what to do' action part of a process definition. They can be used to teach good practice and to audit whether good practices are really being carried out.

We grant specific permission for the reader to photocopy these procedures for use as handouts when they start doing Inspections. We expect that you will gradually tune the procedures to your terminology, culture and state of maturity in the processes.

A Table Overview of the Procedures

	General	Planning and Entry	Kickoff	Checking	Logging	Brainstorming	Edit	Follow-up
Leader	PSIL	PLPEC	PLK	PLC	PLL	PLB	PLE	PLF PLXC, PLR
Author/ Editor		?	=PCK	=PCC	PAL	?	PEDED	?
Checker		?	PCK	PCC	PCL	PCB	–	–
Scribe	–	–	–	PSL	PSL	–	–
Others	PSRL, PPM, PQAL							

Table B.1 Procedure tags, representing written procedures below. ('–' means not applicable, '?' means maybe a procedure could be written.)

Procedure for Inspection Leader: PSIL

*Owner   Version:
(1) Plan the process:
    (a) assemble a team;
    (b) assign roles to team members;
    (c) identify relevant documents;
    (d) determine optimum rates;
    (e) determine meeting places and times.
(2) Lead meetings.
(3) Collect basic metrics.
(4) Make sure rules and procedures are followed.

---

* You should add 'owner' and 'version' and date to each procedure which you modify and take into use.

Procedure for Leader at Planning and Entry Check: PLPEC

(1) Determine if entry conditions are fulfilled:
    (a) if not, return to author for cleanup;
    (b) or discuss what to do about source documents, rules;
    (c) work to remove failed entry condition.
(2) Determine which documents are to be used:
    (a) procedures;
    (b) master plan;
    (c) checklists;
    (d) rules;
    (e) sources;
    (f) candidate document chunks.
(3) Determine specialist roles to be played:
    (a) get or make role checklists, role procedures, assign individual Inspection procedures.
(4) Determine checking rates for individual checkers (pages/hour).
(5) Determine logging meeting optimum rates (pages/hour and issues logged/minute).
(6) Prepare suggested team objectives (numeric).
(7) Prepare suggested team strategy (to meet objectives).
(8) Book meeting rooms.
(9) Make sure team members agree to timings and location.
(10) Make and distribute copies (physical or electronic).

Procedure for Leader at Kickoff: PLK

(1) Distribute documents.
(2) Ask if any questions as to the master plan.
(3) Train novices on rules, procedures, checklists.
(4) Get team to agree on kickoff objective (numeric).
(5) Get team to agree on kickoff strategy.

Procedure for Leader During Checking: PLC

(1) Check novices after a while to make sure they are finding issues.
(2) Help them to learn to find issues if they have trouble.
(3) Check for issues yourself only if you deem it the best use of your time for the team results, otherwise concentrate on managing the team.
(4) Be available to any team member needing help.
(5) Check that checkers have really had time to check at the optimum rate. If necessary consider delaying the planned logging meeting to allow time for all checkers to do their job.

Procedure for Leader During Logging: PLL

(1) Entry to logging:
   (a) gather individual checking data;
   (b) record it on data summary sheet;
   (c) evaluate if it is worth holding logging meeting;
   (d) cancel meeting if necessary.
(2) Remind team of kickoff objectives and strategy agreed earlier.
(3) Decide and announce a recording sequence and content ('majors only', 'sources first' for example).
(4) Assign scribe task or take it on yourself.
(5) Remind author to validate the written log, and seat accordingly.
(6) Begin logging process.
(7) Make sure that unique majors not in checklist get evaluated for inclusion as a suitable question in an updated checklist whenever rule is not specific enough.
(8) Keep recording pace high (one to four logged per minute).
(9) Stop discussions, defensiveness: focus on logging.
(10) Have fun, joke, help people to learn and enjoy.
(11) Announce results, in relation to kickoff objective, at end.
(12) Decide how to handle lack of time:
   (a) reschedule continuation;
   (b) re-chunk the remainder.
(13) Consult with author. Is this sample enough?

Procedure for Leader During Brainstorming: PLB

(1) Remind team of basic rules (reporting structure, three minutes each, brainstorming mode, purpose).
(2) Suggest a strategy for selecting issues to be discussed ('all supers, first logged majors, for example).
(3) Be the scribe (usually).
(4) Keep rigorous timing three minutes maximum each.
(5) Log issue identification, classify (education, and so on). One minute.
(6) Log team suggestions as to root work process cause: keywords, conflicting views OK. One minute limit.
(7) Log team suggestions as to improvements in work process, keywords, conflicting views OK. Solicit practical, 'we could and would do it ourselves' ideas. One minute.

Procedure for Leader During Editing: PLE

Similar to leader during checking. For a novice editor, the leader must:

(1) Give guidance on issue classification.
(2) Help to deal with issues logged against source documents (for example, via change requests).
(3) Give guidance on dealing with issues that, in the editor's opinion, are not really issues.
(4) Set expectations as to how long the process will take (estimate it and tell editor).
(5) Give advice concerning the next step (follow-up).

Procedure for Leader During Follow-up: PLF

(1) Make sure editor feels properly finished (not pressured by a deadline to give it to you).
(2) Check completeness:
   (a) all logged issues responded to in writing;
   (b) claimed fixes entered in updated version;
   (c) sampled fixes look credible and reasonable (to you). Please note, you do not have to prove each fix is correct.
(3) If the editor is new or novice to editing, then you must sample enough to guarantee that the editing rules have been followed.
(4) If Change Requests (CR) (or other memos to other authors and owners) are issued, then check that they are logged in any configuration management system you have, and that the editor has made appropriate notes in the candidate document about the pending CRs.
(5) Collect and analyze the now final (adjusted by editor) checking/logging/brainstorming/editing metrics in the Data Summary. Put them in the QA database.
(6) Did the team meet their kickoff objectives? Tell them.
(7) Were checking/logging rates close to planned optimum rate? (If not you may fail to exit.) Compute % deviation.
(8) Compute number of probable major defects remaining for the pages you have checked (for exit check).
(9) Compute probable total major defects in entire candidate document, if you have only checked a sample or a chunk to that time.
(10) (for fun) Compute net value (total hours probably saved) of your team work. This is the time saved due to 'major defects corrected now', minus time used for the entire Inspection process needed to eliminate the defects.

Procedure for Leader During Exit Check: PLXC

(1) Check all written exit conditions (generic and specific).
(2) Help others meet exit conditions which have failed.
(3) If all conditions are met, release the document chunk as exited.
(4) If the Inspection was only for sampling purposes, then the computed (estimated) defect pollution per page is put on the front page with the exit signature.

Procedure for Leader During Release: PLR

(1) Document the release (as 'document EXITED') on the latest version of the document (electronically rather than a stamp upon a document).
(2) Include data about remaining issues per page average. Put this in the document under your signature.

Procedure for Chief Inspection Leader: PSRL

(1) Certify new software Inspection leaders after their training course.
(2) Remove certification for software Inspection leaders who persist in practices such as allowing too fast checking rates.
(3) Assist leaders with any difficulties they may have.
(4) Convey updates in the method to their circle of software Inspection leaders.
(5) Keep up to date with new software Inspection methods and the overall metrics for all in company groups.
(6) Represent the interests, experiences and views of Inspection leaders to management and other bodies such as quality assurance and process improvement groups.

Procedure for Quality Assurance Leader with respect to Inspection: PQAL

(1) Plan and work for successful implementations of software Inspection.
(2) Spread Inspection to most areas of your company:
    (a) top management planning;
    (b) engineering;
    (c) product planning;
    (d) software engineering.
(3) Continuously improve the power of the method.
(4) Audit the use of the method in practice.
(5) Provide budgetary support for training, databases, experiments.
(6) Learn from outside organizations about Inspection practices, and evaluate spreading this knowledge to yours.
(7) Establish an Inspection database for metrics, forms, lists, rules and other tools of the Inspection trade.
(8) Monitor benefits of Inspection and report them to top management.
(9) Make sure that the rules for writing documents are upgraded to make identification of issues easier.
(10) Convene practitioners and get their feedback for Inspection process improvement.
(11) Bring in suitable outside consultants, teachers, literature and outside practitioners to make sure the Inspection process is as good as it can be.

Procedure for Project Manager: PPM

(1) Make it clear that you totally support the effective use of Inspection because it contributes to project success.
(2) Promote the spread of Inspection to all project documents, when profitability has been proven in your organization.
(3) Practice Inspection on your own personal level of documents.
(4) Help to determine key exit criteria such as number of allowed probably remaining defects at EXIT.
(5) Help to enforce ENTRY criteria, especially making sure that your project's generated documents are suitably exited before others inside or outside the project make use of them.
(6) Make constructive gestures, then loud noises about source documents for your team which have not exited and show signs of poor quality.
(7) Help make sure the rules used by authors and checkers are strong and updated with regular improvements. Support the rules.
(8) Join your Inspection teams at least once a quarter to see first-hand the current practice, and be visibly interested.
(9) Make sure that brainstorming improvement ideas are followed up by some effective form of Process Change Management Team, either in your project or in your organization.

Procedure for Checker During Kickoff: PCK

(1) Make sure you have all pages of all documents you are supposed to have.
(2) Ask for clarification if you do not understand the master plan or your role.
(3) Adopt quantitative team objectives.
(4) Adopt a suitable strategy to meet the objectives.
(5) Agree to your specialist assigned roles or modify them.
(6) Ask for detailed briefings on rules, checklists, source documents so you can do your checking better.
(7) Ask any questions you like about the Inspection process.
(8) Make any suggestions you like for the team or your role in it.
(9) Make a commitment to spending the necessary checking time before the logging meeting.

Procedure for Checker During Checking: PCC

(1) Try to identify a maximum number of potential issues on behalf of your team, and to help the author.

(2) Your job is to help 'make the author a hero'.

(3) If you get a ridiculously high number of issues:
 (a) consult with the leader;
 (b) generalize and estimate quantity by type.

(4) Play your primary assigned role to the full.

(5) Don't be shy of noting any kind of issue you think you have found (you can later decide whether or not to report it).

(6) You do not have to write a perfectly presented log. It is better to concentrate on finding more issues, but you may write any notes you like, any way you like. They are normally your private notes.

(7) If you have trouble finding issues, consult with the leader or another team member.

(8) If you have any time difficulty, consult with your Inspection leader.

(9) If you believe the assigned rate is too fast for your purposes, slow down. Consider consulting with the leader about this.

(10) Focus on major (and super-major) issues, do not spend a lot of time and effort finding and noting minor issues (classify as you go as S, M, m, ?, I).

(11) Fill in the section called Data Collection at the bottom of your master plan, with your personal checking data, so you can swiftly report your data at the beginning of the Logging Meeting.

Procedure for Checker During Logging: PCL

(1) Contribute your checking data quickly at the beginning to the leader so it can be noted. Use about one minute or less. Be brief. Use the sequence in your master plan.

(2) Follow the agreed logging priority and sequence.

(3) When someone has logged an issue you also had identified, keep silent, and go on to the next one.

(4) Speak clearly, so everyone can hear.

(5) Direct your remarks to the scribe.

(6) Make sure the scribe is following you.

(7) Reports should be in seven words or fewer in total. Think before you speak.

(8) Report document tag, page, line, rule or checklist tag and number, keyword of violation, severity.

(9) Do not discuss anybody else's issue reports. We want them logged whatever the misunderstanding.

(10) Do not justify or explain your report.

(11) If you absolutely must discuss something, make a note and do it later with the appropriate parties.

(12) Do not attack or belittle anybody.

(13) Be supportive and encouraging, especially to novices.

(14) Enjoy yourself! Learn! Joking and laughter are permitted and encouraged.

Procedure for Scribe During Logging: PSL

(1) Make sure the author/editor is sitting so that your writing is visible.

(2) Note down only those words necessary for the editor to understand the issue (let them be the judge).

(3) Insist on a standard reporting sequence (use a table tent card with the sequence on the table).

(4) Don't let checkers go too fast. Ask them to slow down and to wait for your OK signal to report a new issue.

(5) If you are not sure, check it with the leader and the editor before continuing.

(6) If you are exhausted, consider passing the pen to a team-mate.

(7) Report your own issues last, possibly letting another person log them.

(8) When there are many of the same generic error, log multiples by getting a guess as to approximate quantity, and noting it in the right-hand margin.

Procedure for Author During Logging: PAL

(1) Report your own noted issues after giving your team-mates a chance.
(2) Don't say 'I found that too!'
(3) Thank your colleagues for their efforts on your behalf.
(4) Learn as much as possible about avoiding issues as an author.
(5) Respect the opinion of team-mates. Do not justify or defend.
(6) Check the logging for legibility and intelligibility.
(7) Answer any 'questions of intent' logged by checkers at the end of the logging meeting.

Procedure for Checkers During Brainstorming: PCB

(1) When the leader suggests a defect to be analyzed, find it in your documentation as quickly as possible and confirm that you have found it.
(2) Help to brainstorm the defect cause classification (Communication, Oversight, Transmission, Education).
(3) Brainstorm keywords about the root cause. (Do not use more than one minute as a team for this. You can contribute several conflicting ideas.)
(4) Brainstorm keywords about a suggested process cure which would prevent such errors happening in the future. One minute maximum for the team.
(5) Do not try to get to the whole truth. You do not have time. The Process Change Management Team will study this in more depth later.

Procedure for Editor During Editing: PEDED

(1) Correct logged issues according to your sources and rules.

(2) If, in your opinion a logged issue is due to, or first requires correction of a source, rule or checklist – then write a Change Request to the owner of the source document.

(3) Insert a note in your candidate document about the pending CR you sent.

(4) You may, if you wish, make annotation or written answers in your product to any 'questions of intent' which were logged. This will answer questions from future readers for you in advance.

(5) You may change a severity (major, minor) classification to one which you believe is more correct than originally logged. Change the final count appropriately.

(6) Indicate on the log how and where you have edited for each issue, so as to make the leader's follow-up process obvious and easy.

(7) You do not need to respond to an issue in the way indicated by the checkers. Fix the real issue in a responsible way. An issue becomes a defect only when you acknowledge it by making a correction.

(8) You may make corrections to defects which you spot yourself during editing work. Include them in your defect count.

(9) You may make improvements and optimizations to your document without counting them as defects, but take great care as these changes will not have been Inspected. Inform the Inspection leader about any additional changes you have made.

Appendix C: Inspection Metrics and Forms

This appendix is intended as a guide to basic forms to be used during the Inspection process, and to the metrics to be gathered. The forms are the means for gathering the metrics, whether those forms are paper-based or electronic.

The main metrics to be collected are shown on the data summary form, with additional metrics on the process brainstorming log. The master plan is used to plan and initiate and control the Inspection process, and the change request form is used for changes in source documents.

This appendix takes you step by step through the metrics, and the Glossary contains the metric definitions in alphabetical order.

Tailoring Your Own Forms

Everyone needs to make their own variations of these forms, with their own local terminology and content. Inspection is above all tailorable and capable of continuous improvement. What we provide in this appendix is a set of the best currently known basic ideas, a consistent glossary of metrics concepts, and a starting point for beginners.

This appendix contains templates of blank forms which you may copy to use as a starting point for your own Inspection process. You may not want to use every item on every form; just cross out the ones you don't want. After a short time, you will probably design your own form, omitting things you don't want, and adding things which you find you do need. These templates are intended to get you started, and are not final and definitive, so do modify them for your own use.

You may copy the templates to use as handwritten forms, or you may use them to construct a form which you store as a word-processor template or (preferably) a spreadsheet. The advantage of using a spreadsheet is that the metrics can be summed, updated and checked automatically as soon as they are entered.

If you already have your own forms in use, then continue to use them, and use this chapter to get some new ideas to improve your forms.

You will probably want to put on the forms your own company standard headings, format for page numbering, configuration management referencing, form master referencing, and so on. For example, your company reference for printed forms may replace the form owner, and version number or date. One way to start is to take a copy of the template forms in this chapter and 'white-out' the parts you don't want, replacing it with your own standards (hand-written to start with is fine).

This appendix consists of the following: a description and definition of the data collection and metrics terms content, a summary description of the forms, form templates (to copy if desired), samples of filled-in forms (to give you ideas for how they would be used), and example forms from different organizations (to show you some possible variations).

Inspection Metrics and Data Element Definitions

Listed below are a selection of metrics concepts which can be used for Inspection. The list is intended to be comprehensive, but different organizations will have different needs. There may be some categories listed below which you do not need, and there may be other categories which you do find useful which we have not listed.

It is essential that some data is collected, analyzed, and used to control and improve the Inspection process. The most important data items are marked below with an asterisk (*). If you do not collect and analyze any metrics, you are not doing Inspection (with a capital 'I')!

It is not enough simply to collect process data; it must also be used. The Inspection process has a 'feedback loop' which ensures that the process data is used, for example, by determining the optimum standard checking and logging meeting rates, based on previous Inspection effectiveness at various rates.

Neither this appendix nor this book will attempt to describe the organization and use of the QA database.

In the section below, definitions are given for Inspection metrics. These definitions may also be given in the Glossary, sometimes in a condensed form. You should not initially use all of these metrics, but you should use the basic subset marked with an asterisk (*).

Entry, Planning and Kickoff

entry-time: work-hours spent by the Inspection leader to check that entry conditions are met, and to work towards meeting them.

*work-hours: total working hours used per individual or group of individuals for a defined task. Three people in a meeting for two hours would be six work-hours.

*kickoff-time: work-hours spent organizing a kickoff meeting by the Inspection leader, time spent in the kickoff meeting by all who attended, and any kickoff activity by the Inspection leader, such as training new Inspectors alone or in small groups.

*planning-time: work-hours for creating the master plan. This can be done by anyone, but is primarily done by the leader. This time includes any time needed to search for participating documents, create or update them, and copy them. It also includes time to get data such as optimum checking rates.

Individual Checking

*checking-time: total work-hours spent in individual checking of the candidate product document and the associated sources, using checklists, rules and procedures, by all checkers, including the leader's checking time (if any).

page: a unit of work on which Inspection is performed. A page is a document part, containing 600 'non-commentary' words of document text, or 60 non-commentary lines of code or test cases, or your own consistently applied definition.

Practical tip:
Use your word processor's word count facility to get accurate word counts, or use the line-numbering facility in your word processor, or even a paper template with line numbers.

---

*pages-studied: the number of pages which have been closely scrutinized at or near the optimum checking rate by checkers during individual checking. This includes checking related source documents and using rules, checklists, procedures and other relevant documents. This does not include 'pages-scanned'. The purpose of this measure is to help compute the optimum checking rate, which is critical to defect detection effectiveness.

pages-scanned: the number of pages examined in whole or in part for rule violations, but which are read at a rate higher than the optimum rate. These are typically source documents, or the rest (or non-sample part) of a document which was sampled at the optimum rate. This gives an indication of the number of other pages which may contain defects which we missed because they were not studied at the optimum checking rate. It also helps us understand the total volume of documents looked at in any way.

pages-used: the number of pages used in the Inspection cycle. This includes any documents Inspected (studied, scanned or merely referenced), such as product, source documents, rules, checklists and procedures. The purpose of this measure is to get an idea of the volume of checking work.

*major-issues-noted: the number of major issues noted (observed with a view to report during logging) by checkers during individual checking.

minor-issues-noted: the number of minor issues noted by checkers during individual checking.

improvement-suggestions-noted: the number of improvement suggestions noted by an individual checker during individual checking.

questions-of-intent-noted: the number of questions of intent to the author noted by an individual checker during individual checking.

*items-noted: the total number of issues, improvement suggestions and questions of intent to the author noted by an individual checker during individual checking. The sum of major-issues-noted plus minor-issues-noted plus improvement-suggestions-noted plus questions-of-intent-noted.

This (or its components) is one way to analyze individual checking activity. For example, if an individual was finding significantly fewer items than other checkers, it may indicate a need for further training, or it could indicate that that person's role was less effective and should be either eliminated or improved. Major-issues-noted would be a more significant economic indicator of checking productivity. Items-noted gives a fuller picture of all activity.

number of checkers: the number of Inspectors doing checking (including leader if doing checking).

*checking-rate: the number of pages studied intensively per individual work-hour.

*optimum-checking-rate: a rate of pages studied, per hour during individual checking, which gives the best result in terms of effectiveness (percentage of major defects found) or efficiency (major defects found per work-hour). It is usually determined locally by historical observation of Inspection metrics.

The optimum checking rate can, for example, be expressed as pages, words (or K-words), or non-commentary lines of code (or KLOC) per individual work-hour. It is usually in the region of one page per hour for almost any kind of written material (where a page is reasonably full of information, for example, 600 words). One reason for the apparently slow rate is the need to cross-check many other source, rule and checklist documents while studying product pages intensively.

The optimum checking rate is used to guide Inspectors when performing individual checking. It is announced on the master plan and may be reinforced and explained in the kickoff meeting.

Logging Meeting

logging-meeting-duration: the clock time (usually expressed in hours and tenths) of the logging meeting. Logging-meeting-duration includes logging-duration and discussion-duration.

logging-duration: the hours of logging-meeting-duration spent in reporting of items noted by checkers during their individual checking, and in searching for new items to log during the logging meeting. It should not include discussion-duration nor other non-relevant activity.

discussion-duration: the hours of logging-meeting-duration *not* spent in reporting items or checking for new issues. It may include discussion of items, or interruptions to the meeting.

The Inspection leader must keep a note of how much time during the logging meeting has been spent in non-logging activities. If for example there is 15 or 30 seconds of explanation of an issue so that the editor can ensure that the item as logged will make sense when it is edited later on, this is valid logging activity. However, if after a minute Inspectors continue to discuss an issue (possibly with good reason), this time should not be counted as logging time but as discussion time. A reasonable estimate will help keep metrics more honest.

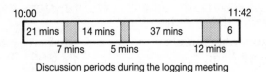

Discussion periods during the logging meeting

Figure C.1 Logging and discussion duration.

In the hypothetical example shown in the Figure C.1, the logging meeting lasted for one hour and 42 minutes, so the logging-meeting-duration is 102 minutes or 1.7 hours. But during that meeting, there were three periods where discussion took place which was not part of the Inspection process. The three discussion periods took seven, five and 12 minutes respectively. The leader should not have allowed this much discussion, but there may have been other considerations which made it necessary. The important thing is that the time taken in the discussion is recorded separately from the time spent in doing Inspection properly, that is, logging issues and looking for new issues in the meeting.

Discussion-duration in this example is therefore 7 + 5 + 12 = 24 minutes, or 0.4 hour. Logging-duration is the sum of the non-discussion time, 21 + 14 + 37 + 6 = 78 minutes = 1.3 hours. This could equally well be calculated by subtracting discussion-duration from logging-meeting-duration.

*logging-time: total work-hours spent in logging activity during a logging meeting. Note that this contains some additional checking time at the logging meeting, simultaneous with the logging activity, but this is counted in with the logging-time. Logging-time excludes discussion-time. Logging-time includes the time the leader spends in the logging meeting. Logging-time is logging-meeting-duration times the number of active meeting participants (checkers, scribe, moderator), not 'observers'.

discussion-time: work-hours spent in the logging meeting on non-logging and non-checking activities. This includes any interruptions to the meeting, any time spent by any members of the team to discuss issues or argue, and time which does not fall into any of the other 'structured discussion' time categories (like kickoff and process brainstorming, or questions of intent).

This is not a direct planned or desired Inspection cost (since such unstructured discussion is actively discouraged within the Inspection framework), but this time should not be 'hidden' in other categories.

Healthy discussion outside the Inspection framework is socially and practically desirable and may even be profitable. However, it is not part of the Inspection process as such, and if not tracked and controlled, can easily make the Inspection process uneconomic.

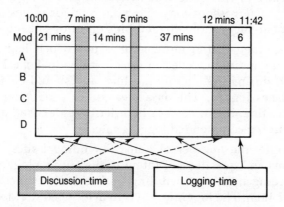

Figure C.2   Discussion and logging time for all Inspectors.

Figure C.2 shows the discussion time spent in the meeting for the Inspection leader as well as for other Inspectors. The discussion-time is the total shaded area above, and the logging-time is the unshaded area above. Discussion-time is equal to discussion-duration times the number of Inspectors (including the leader). Logging-time is equal to logging-duration times the number of Inspectors (including the leader). The time is expressed in work-hours.

*major-issues-logged: the number of major issues reported in the logging meeting and recorded in the issue log, including multiple occurrences.

Multiple occurrences are noted when the same error was made more than once in the document, resulting in several potential defects in different places in the document. For example, if a cost justification was omitted three times, from three different paragraphs in a proposal, this would be three major issues logged, even though it would be recorded as one line item entry in the issue log.

Note that multiple occurrences are *not* when the same issue is found by more than one checker - any single issue is only logged once.

*minor-issues-logged: the number of minor issues reported in the logging meeting and recorded in the issue log, including multiple occurrences.

*improvement-suggestions-logged: the number of improvement suggestions reported in the logging meeting and recorded in the issue log.

*questions-of-intent-logged: the number of questions of intent to the author reported in the logging meeting and recorded in the issue log.

*items-logged: the total number of issues, improvement suggestions and questions of intent to the author reported in the logging meeting and recorded in the issue log, including multiple occurrences. The sum of major-issues-logged plus minor-issues-logged plus improvement-suggestions-logged plus questions-of-intent-logged.

*new-issues-logged: the number of issues which had not yet been noted by any individual checker during individual checking, but were discovered during the logging meeting, and should be approximately 20% of issues logged. This is a measure of productivity during the logging meeting. It is necessary in order to understand and determine the optimum/recommended logging rate.

*logging-rate: the number of items (including issues, improvement suggestions and questions of intent to the author) logged per minute in the logging meeting, including multiple occurrences logged as a single-line item. The logging-rate is items-logged divided by logging-meeting-duration (in minutes). The purpose of this measure is to ensure that the logging meetings are productive, concentrating on recording items and not degenerating into discussion. This measure, therefore, includes the discussion time within the logging meeting (as part of the logging-meeting-duration).

Default: range 0.5–4 items logged per minute, with an average of one item per minute.

logging-meeting-rate: the speed with which pages (or lines or words) are moved through by the logging meeting. Usually product pages per clock hour. This is independent of issue logging activity. The main interest here is how much more checking time is used (and resulting new issues logged). This is the meeting equivalent of 'pages studied'.

*optimum-logging-meeting-rate: the logging-meeting-rate which results in the maximum number of unique major issues logged per work-hour (efficiency) or the maximum percentage of unique major issues logged (effectiveness). A test for finding it is that approximately 20% of new issues should be discovered during the logging meeting, the other 80% having been discovered during individual checking. The optimum-logging-meeting-rate is used by the Inspection leader in controlling or moderating the logging meeting. The rate needs to balance between maximum logging speed and being slow enough to permit additional checking activity to find new issues during logging, but it must be fast enough to discourage wandering discussion.

*leader-time: work-hours spent by the Inspection leader (or anyone else performing leader activities) in entry-time, planning-time, organizing and controlling the individual checking of all checkers, and organizing the logging meeting. The leader's time in kickoff is included in kickoff-time, the leader's time in the logging meeting is included in logging-time, and the leader's time spent in checking is included in checking-time. Leader-time is part of control-time.

*detection-time: Leader-time plus kickoff-time plus checking-time plus logging-time. This is the total work-hours to identify issues, before correcting them and before exploiting them for insights with which to improve the process that created them. Detection-time does not include discussion-time in the logging meeting.

Editing and Exit

defect: an error made in writing, in a document or in code which *may* cause a failure of any kind if the portion containing the defect is used or executed. A logged issue becomes an 'official' defect when the editor classifies it as such during editing. Items may be classified as defects directly from issues, or from analysis of questions of intent or improvement suggestions.

defect-edit-rate: the number of defects analyzed and fixed per hour in editing. This is used by the leader to estimate the time needed for editing the issues which were logged in the logging meeting.

Default: 2 (to 8) minutes per defect, 30 to 7.5 defects per hour.

*edit-time: work-hours spent editing all items by the editor, including time to reclassify issue severity into major and minor defects, to fix defects, and to raise change requests (CRs).

*follow-up-time: total work-hours spent by the Inspection leader to perform follow-up, including the editor's time, if the editor participates during follow-up. Follow-up-time is part of control-time.

*correction-time: edit-time plus follow-up-time. This is the cost of correcting defects and communicating change requests to other authors by the editor, and also the leader's audit that the editing has been completed (follow-up).

*major-defects-detected: the number of defects classified as major during editing. This number is reported by the editor to the leader after edit.

A major defect may be originally logged as major or minor, or may be discovered in any document by the editor during editing possibly as a result of a question to the author or improvement suggestion.

*minor-defects-detected: the number of defects classified as minor defects during editing, and reported by the editor to the leader after edit.

*exit-time: work-hours spent by the Inspection leader to check exit criteria and do exit activities. It includes time to record metrics in the QA database, to initiate action to fix conditions which do not permit exit, and to document the release. Exit-time is part of control-time.

*control-time: total work-hours spent by the leader, or anyone else, doing any form of planning or control of the Inspection process. This includes preparation of the master plan, administration, communication, data-gathering and reporting. It includes entry and exit checking, planning, kickoff and follow-up activities as shown in Figure C.3. It does *not* include any time spent by the leader as a checker, time spent in the logging meeting, or time spent in process brainstorming. It is the sum of leader-time plus kickoff time plus follow-up-time plus exit-time. (See Figure C.4, time terminology diagram.)

correct-fix-rate: the percentage of edit correction attempts which correctly fix a defect and do not introduce any new defects.

Default: 83% – five out of six correction attempts (Fagan, 1986).

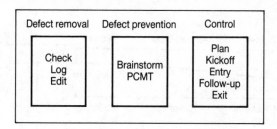

Figure C.3   Inspection activity time–cost areas.

fix-fail-rate: the percentage of edit correction attempts which either fail to correct the defect or introduce a new defect.

Default: 17% – one out of six correction attempts (Fagan, 1986).

undetected defects: defects which are present, but so far undetected (by the Inspection process). They may be discoverable sooner or later, but they have not been found or logged at this stage.

Default (for mature Inspection process): 20% of defects logged for pseudo-code, 12% for module and interface definition, 40% for source code (Lindner, 1992).

Default (for immature Inspection process): 70% in all documents.

defect-removal-time: detection-time plus correction-time. This intentionally excludes discussion-time. It does not include prevention-time. It does include control-time, checking-time, logging-time, edit-time, follow-up-time and exit-time.

*major-time: the average time in work-hours to find, log and edit (fix) a major defect during Inspection, including all related Inspection costs. It is calculated as defect-removal-time divided by the number of major defects found in that time period, for example, one Inspection cycle.

Default: 1 work-hour per major defect (observed by many: ICL, Reeve, JPL).

*estimated effectiveness (or estimated defect-finding effectiveness): the percentage of major defects discovered, compared to the total (estimated) major defects, including undetected defects. This is an estimate of the depth to which the Inspection process is able to penetrate the total defects in an existing document.

The observed range for Inspection effectiveness in mature processes at IBM Rochester Labs in 1991 was 60% of available defects in source code, 80% in pseudo code, and 88% in module and interface definition (Lindner, 1992).

Effectiveness may also be affected by the quality of the products being Inspected. For example, defects are more visible in a more precise and clear document. The percentage of effectiveness can

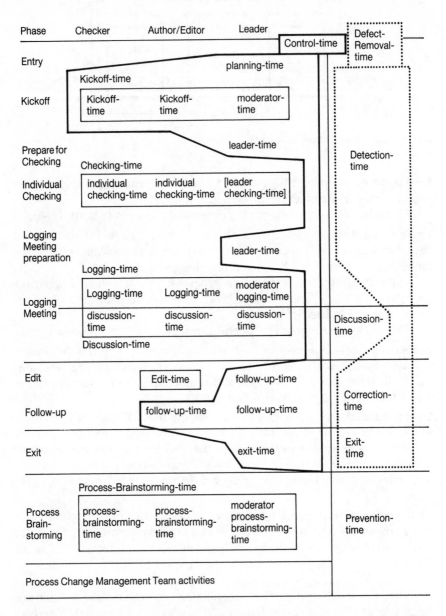

Figure C.4 'Time' terminology diagram: Inspection metrics Time Terminology related to people, sub-processes and cumulative metrics.

change over time, due among other things to process improvements. If there are no defects to find, effectiveness could not be calculated. But how would you know that there were no defects if you didn't Inspect?

*defect-density: number of defects per page in a product. The defect density is an estimate of defects in the product at a defined stage (for example, after edit). The estimate is usually based on the defects found, the known or estimated defect-finding effectiveness, and the correct-fix-rate. It can be expressed as defects per page, defects per thousand lines of code (KLOC) or defects per thousand words (K-words). There are a number of variations of this definition, depending on the defect severity and the scope of the document on which it is based. They are not defined separately, as their meaning should be clear from the above generic definition and the term itself. The specific term intended should be used, or a default specific meaning should be assigned to the generic term, provided it is understood by all who read or write it. For example:

> **major-defect-density-per-page-studied-intensively**
> **minor-defect-density-per-page-studied-intensively**
> **total-defect-density-per-page-studied-intensively**
> **major-defect-density-per-page-used**
> **minor-defect-density-per-page-used**
> **total-defect-density-per-page-used**
> **major-defect-density-per-total-document**
> **minor-defect-density-per-total-document**
> **total-defect-density-per-total-document**

Default expectation: before Inspection, for documents never Inspected, and which have been written by authors without Inspection experience for that document type: 10–20 major defects per page. For mature process documents we would expect fewer than 0.5 majors per page before checking.

*efficiency: major defects found per work-hour, a measure of individual or team ability to exploit their time. It is calculated by the total major defects (after being classified as defects by the editor), divided by defect-removal-time. Efficiency is therefore inversely related to the cost of finding a defect, that is, the less it costs to find a defect, the more efficient you are, and vice versa.

Efficiency is a function of, among other things, how well the Inspection process is designed, organized and carried out. It can be used to help tune the process for improvement and to sense deterioration in the Inspection process. As a rough rule of thumb it seems that it costs about one work-hour to find one major defect, and a few minutes to fix it.

Default: 1 defect found per Inspection work-hour (similar to major-time because fix time is so small).

*development-time-saved: the net savings of time in work-hours, at project delivery time. This is due to defects fixed during editing, instead of during testing. This can only be an estimate, but can be based on detection and correction time in testing, minus major-time for all defects found in Inspection, for all products delivered in the project.

Note: major defects cost about 20 times more to fix at test execution than at editing (IBM, Santa Teresa Labs).

The industrial average savings is observed to vary between 3 (ICL) and 29 (Shell, Applicon) hours saved net per major found, with a useful average of 8 hours (Reeve).

life-cycle-time-saved: the net savings of time in work-hours from defects fixed during editing instead of later, for a measured portion of the software system's total life-time, such as 'to date'. This is also an estimate, but can be based on detection and correction time later, minus major-time, for all defects found in Inspection, for all products in the system.

Post-inspection Measurement

Measurements must be taken after Inspections, in order to get accurate data on effectiveness and the costs saved by doing Inspections. The number of defects found in field or operational use of the software is important, because these are the defects which 'slipped through the net'. In fact they slipped through two nets, Inspection and testing.

It is also important to know how much it costs to fix a major defect found later, because this is what the savings are based on, when the defects are fixed earlier in Inspection.

The defects found and cost to fix should also be recorded during testing, so that future development managers can have accurate data about the costs to balance Inspection and testing effort in the most cost-effective manner. Measuring defects during testing also enables a more accurate estimate of defect-finding effectiveness to be made before the software is released to users.

*effectiveness (or actual defect-finding effectiveness): the percentage of major defects discovered at any one specified stage or cumulation of stages of Inspection or test, compared to the total major defects found so far. Actual effectiveness measurement should be used to improve the estimates of Inspection effectiveness used at exit from an Inspection cycle. Inspection effectiveness would consider only those defects found by Inspection, test effectiveness only those found by test activities, and development effectiveness those defects found by Inspection and testing.

Note that this definition of effectiveness is *Inspection effectiveness*. Test effectiveness should also be measured and stored in the QA database, but this is outside the scope of this book.

The measurement of effectiveness thus improves in accuracy over time, as shown in Table C.1. Suppose there are actually 100 defects, and we have found 60 in Inspection. Our estimated effectiveness now is 75% – we think there are only 80 defects in total. After testing has found a further 24 defects, we now know that Inspection effectiveness can be no higher than 71%, since Inspection revealed only 71% of the total defects found to date, not including those not discovered yet. We have more confidence in our effectiveness measure, and should apply this more realistic figure to Inspections which are currently taking place.

Table C.1   Measuring effectiveness.

Life cycle phase	System construction	Test execution*	Early field use	Later field use	Final use
Where defects found	Inspection	Testing	Use	Use	Use
Defects found	60	24	10	4	2
Estimated effectiveness	75% ±25%	71% ±10%	63% ±5%	61% ±2%	60% exactly

* The two categories of 'System construction' and 'Test execution' together make up the software development life cycle, and are equivalent to the left and right sides of a 'V' diagram.

It may also be useful to look at the costs of Inspecting and not Inspecting, by incorporating the defect-fixing costs at various stages (see Table C.2).

Table C.2   Measuring effectiveness, incorporating defect-fixing costs.

Life cycle phase	System construction	Test execution	Early field use	Later field use	Final use
Where defects found	Inspection	Testing	Use	Use	Use
Defects found	60	24	10	4	2
Estimated effectiveness	75% ±25%	71% ±10%	63% ±5%	61% ±2%	60% exactly
Cost to fix	$10	$100	$1000	$1000	$1000
Cost with Inspection	60×10= $600	24×100 + 600=$3000	$13,000	$17,000	$19,000
Defects found without Inspection	0	60	48	10	2
Cost without Inspection	$0	60×100= $6000	$54,000	$64,000	$66,000

It is clear from the Table C.2 that if we do not do Inspection, we appear to have saved $600 by the time test execution starts. However, it will cost us twice as much in testing (in this hypothetical but conservatively realistic example) as it would have cost for both Inspection and testing. But the real payback comes in operational use. Far more defects would be found, so the total cost over the system's lifetime will be over three times more expensive.

Having the real figures for defect fix costs both in testing and in operation will enable you to quantify the benefits of Inspection. Without quantifying benefits, management will see only the cost and will want to stop them (to save the $600 above).

Process Brainstorming

process-brainstorming-time: total work-hours spent by all Inspectors while brainstorming defect root causes and suggesting process improvements.

process-change-management-team-time: (PCMT-time) work-hours spent by the PCMT. A cost of improving processes.

quality-improvement-team-time: work-hours spent by the quality improvement team.

prevention-time: process-brainstorming-time plus process-change-management-team-time plus quality-improvement-team-time. This is the total time put into improving the software development processes to prevent defects from arising in the future.

Form Descriptions

The Master Plan

The master plan is described in detail in Chapter 8 (Inspection leader), and is given in summary below.

The master plan is used by the Inspection leader to organize the Inspection cycle for a particular candidate document, and all associated activities. The master plan would be distributed to all Inspectors involved in the Inspection cycle to which the plan applies.

Header

Inspection identification tag (Inspection ID)
Inspection leader: name, telephone
Author(s) name(s)

Product title, number of pages, status
Date Inspection requested/initiated
Entry criteria which apply
Current entry status
Kickoff meeting: date, start time, end time, location
Logging meeting: date, start time, end time, location
Process brainstorming meeting: date, start time, end time, location
Exit criteria which will be applied

Documents

Sources: (relevant pages)
Product document(s) or chunk(s)
Rules
Checklists

Participants and Roles

List of Inspectors, with
    Document role assignment(s)
    Checklist or procedure role assignment(s)
    Inspection procedures to use

All of these are identified by tags. The document role is indicated by the tag of the document on which the checker is to concentrate. The checklist or procedure role is indicated by the checklist tag, such as 'C7 contracts' or 'D5 source', or by a procedure tag such as 'CP3 backwards', 'CP6 cross-references', or 'CP2 maths'. The Inspection procedure to use is indicated by the relevant procedure tag, such as 'PAL' – (Procedure for Author in Logging) or 'PCK' – (Procedure for Checker in Kickoff).

Standard Rates and Estimates

Individual checking rate: (pages per hour of product document to be studied intensively) – this is the specified standard checking rate to be used in individual checking by the checkers.

Logging rate: the number of items expected to be logged per minute during the logging meeting – this gives an expectation of the speed of logging for maximum efficiency.

Logging meeting rate: pages treated per hour - this is the specified standard checking rate to be used in the logging meeting. It is the responsibility of the Inspection leader or meeting moderator to ensure that the logging meeting is run at this rate, but this gives the individual checkers an expectation of what that rate will be. Note that this rate overall should aim for 20% new issues to be found in the meeting.

Data from Individual Checking

This section is filled in by the individual Inspectors about their individual checking activity. This data is collected at the beginning of the logging meeting by the Inspection leader.

Work-hours spent (to nearest 10th hour)
Number of pages studied intensively (at specified optimum rate)
Number of pages scanned (looking for potential defects, not at optimum rate)
Number of pages used (total)
Number of major issues identified and noted
Number of minor issues identified and noted
Number of improvement suggestions noted
Number of questions of intent to the author noted

The Inspection Data Summary Form

The data summary form is used by the leader to report the basic cost and benefit data for an Inspection cycle (a chunk or a complete document).

The different parts of the data summary form are filled in at various stages of Inspection, so that the form will only be partially completed while an Inspection cycle is in progress. It is completed fully before the Inspection cycle ends; in fact this is an exit criterion for completing Inspection.

It is important that post-Inspection data is recorded and analyzed, so that the *real* effect of Inspection in testing and field use can be seen.

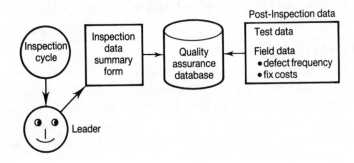

Figure C.5   Use of the data summary form.

Note: the data summary form should always be designed to fit on a single page, both to keep things simple and to avoid the temptation to ask for too much information.

This report is used to follow the status of a single Inspection.

The information in the data summary form is transferred to the QA database, so that the QA database always has an up-to-date 'snapshot' of the current state of all Inspections, including the current rates and Inspection effectiveness. This information is needed as input to new Inspections which are starting, so that they use updated optimum rates, for example.

The format of the data summary form is shown below. This list contains more possible parameters than we have selected for our one-page form. It is given as a starting point. This section gives a fuller list of things you may want to consider in constructing your own forms. We would warn the reader against including 'nice to know' parameters. Each parameter should be cost justified in some sense. The one-page limit is a protection against over-enthusiastic process managers who might over-burden leaders with marginal work!

Heading

Note that those marked with an asterisk (*) are included in the sample forms.

* Date of report
* Software Inspection identification
* Inspection leader
* Document reference tag
* Total pages of full candidate document (may not be part of this Inspection)

Planning and Entry

* Date Inspection requested
List of applicable entry criteria
For each entry criterion
   Date the entry criterion was met, or
   Reason for the criterion not being met, and action to rectify the failed entry condition
* Date of entry completion (authorized by leader)
* Planning-time: work-hours spent in planning activities (by Inspection leader)
* Entry-time: work-hours spent in checking entry criteria (by Inspection leader)

Kickoff

*Kickoff-time: work-hours spent in kickoff activities by all Inspectors, including the leader. Kickoff-time is part of control-time.

If desired, this can be further broken down into:

Training-time: work-hours spent by the leader in training checkers;
Organizing-time: work-hours spent by the leader in organizing the kickoff meeting;

Leader-kickoff-time: work-hours spent by the leader in all kickoff activities;

Checker-kickoff-time: work-hours spent by Inspectors other than the leader in kickoff activities (including being trained).

But be careful of doing this because it is 'interesting', do it if it allows process improvement which justifies the cost and bother to the leader! This remark applies below too.

Checking

For each Inspector doing individual checking, noted anonymously:

* **individual checking time**: (hours checking) work-hours spent in individual checking by each checker (including the leader if participating in checking)
* **pages-studied** (intensively): examined for potential defects at the optimum rate

pages-scanned: examined for potential defects (but not at optimum rate)

pages-used: the total number of pages in documents used in checking, including checklists, sources, rules, procedures, products, and so on (not master plan).

* **major-issues-noted**: during individual checking
* **minor-issues-noted**: during individual checking
* **improvement-suggestions-noted**: during individual checking
* **questions-of-intent-noted**: (to the author) during individual checking

† = **checking-rate**: pages-studied by each individual checker/individual checking time

The following metrics are computed for the individual checking phase as a whole, combining the metrics of the individual checkers into the team metrics.

= **number of checkers**: Inspectors doing individual checking (including leader if doing checking)

= **studied-page-count**: sum of pages-studied for all checkers

* = **checking-time**: total work-hours spent in individual checking, sum of individual-checking-time for all who checked

* = **average checking-rate**: studied-page-count/checking-time, or equivalently, the arithmetical average of all participating checkers' checking-rates

Logging

*logging meeting size: the number of Inspectors (including leader) who attend the logging meeting

† Note: metrics which are derived from data already mentioned are denoted by the ' = ' symbol. A spreadsheet can be set up to derive them automatically.

Date of logging meeting
Start time of logging meeting
Stop time of logging meeting
= **logging-meeting-duration**: meeting stop time minus start time (in hours/tenths)
* **logging-duration**: number of minutes of the meeting spent in logging and checking activities
discussion-duration: number of hours/tenths of the meeting spent in other activities such as discussion or interruptions
= **discussion-time**: work-hours taken in discussion or interruptions, that is, discussion-duration times the logging-meeting-size
* = **logging-time**: work-hours in logging activities: logging-duration times the logging-meeting-size
* **major-issues-logged** (including multiple occurrences)
* **minor-issues-logged** (including multiple occurrences)
* **improvement-suggestions-logged**
* **questions-of-intent-logged**
= **items-logged**: major-issues-logged plus minor-issues-logged plus improvement-suggestions-logged plus questions-of-intent-logged
* **new-items-logged**: items discovered in the meeting, but *not* found in individual checking
new-item-ratio: new-items-logged divided by items-logged – at the optimum logging-meeting-rate, this should be approximately 20%
* = **logging-rate**: items-logged divided by logging-duration – the number of items logged per minute in the logging meeting
specified-logging-rate: as specified for this Inspection on the master plan; would be set to the optimum-logging-rate as computed at the start of the Inspection cycle
leader-time: time spent in planning and control activities by the leader, or by any other Inspector
* = **detection-time**: time taken in defect detection activities in this Inspection cycle – planning-time plus kickoff-time plus checking-time plus logging-time
* **logging-meeting-rate**: pages studied at meeting, divided by logging-duration

Editing

Estimated edit time (estimated by Inspection leader).
* **edit-time**: work-hours taken by editor
* **major-defects-detected**
* **minor-defects-detected**
* Number of change requests raised

Follow-up

* **follow-up-time**: work-hours by leader and editor in auditing edit work
If desired, the follow-up report could contain more detail, such as:

Number of items sampled
Do you believe editing is complete and at least 5/6 correct?
Yes/No
If no: what is necessary action to complete edit?
= **correction-time**: edit-time plus follow-up-time

Exit

List of applicable exit criteria or tags of applicable generic and
specific exit condition sets
For each exit criterion:
    Date the exit criterion was met, or
    Reason for the criterion not being met, and action to rectify the
    failed exit condition
* Date of exit completion (authorized by leader)
Estimated remaining major defects/page
* **exit-time**: work-hours by leader to completion of exit
* = **control-time**: leader-time plus follow-up-time plus exit-time
* = **defect-removal-time**: detection-time plus correction-time plus
exit-time
If desired, information about product release can be included here.

Summary

* Efficiency; major defects per hour of time spent in Inspection
  (defect-removal-time).
* Estimated effectiveness; percentage of defects probably found by
  this Inspection (based on history of similar documents).
* Development time saved; what these defects would have cost to fix
  in testing. Test fix cost (say eight hours) times major defects found.
  Life cycle time saved; what these defects would have cost to fix in
  operation use. Field fix cost (say 80 hours) times major defects
  found.

Issue Log

How the Issue Log is Used

The 'issue log' form is used during the logging meeting to log issues,
improvement suggestions and questions of intent to the author. It
should strictly speaking be called the 'item log,' since 'item' is the
term used to cover all three categories of things logged. However,
since it is the issues which are the main (but not only) source of
potential defects, they are the most important and the things on
which the metrics are based, so it is called the 'issue log.'

The issue log is used by the editor as the main input to the

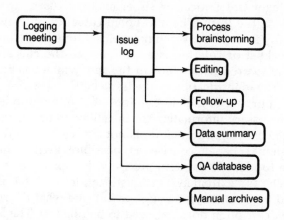

Figure C.6   The Issue Log and its uses.

editing process. Then it is used by the leader to do follow-up, that is, auditing that the edits have been carried out. It is also used to sample defects in the process brainstorming meeting. Finally the leader must get basic metrics for the data summary from this form. The issue log can be filled in manually on paper forms (the most common way to log to date), or electronically (lap-top, palm-top, pen-based computers, meeting display screen).

Issue Log Contents

The number of logging pages depends on how many items are logged during the meeting. The order of the columns in the issue log should correspond to the order in which checkers report them in the meeting.

The document reference gives the unique document 'tag' for the document in which the item is being logged. The document tag is all that should be needed to identify the relevant document. The page number and line number or location (for example, paragraph number, word number in a line) are used to pinpoint the exact location of the item. Multiple document reference tags may be needed and should be used to specify correlation issues. The checker is not asked to identify which one is 'wrong'!

The line number or location is easiest to identify if when you distribute the Inspection materials to the Inspectors, you first number the lines on each document and then copy them. This could be done electronically (most word processors have this facility) or even with a paper template on the copier.

The item category, major issue ('Major'), minor issue ('minor'), improvement suggestion ('Imp') or question of intent to the author ('Q' or '?'), is pre-printed so that when an item is logged, the scribe only has to circle or tick off the correct category. An additional severity category of critical or super-major, if used, would also be pre-printed on the form. The additional category of 'New' would be circled for any issues discovered for the first time in the meeting.

The checklist or rule tag is a reference to the checklist question which was answered with a 'no', or the rule which has been violated, resulting in the identification of the issue being logged.

The sole purpose of the 'description' slot on the form is to give any additional necessary information for the editor to understand the issue logged, if the existing information is not sufficient. The description of the item should be as concise as possible, giving the minimum information to identify the item precisely. For example, a keyword or phrase, such as 'extremely' or 'justification'. If the location/line number and the rule tag are enough to indicate what the rule violation is, then the description does not need to be filled in. The author at the logging meeting is to be used as our judge of what is 'necessary' to understand, what the issue is, the number of occurrences or when it is logged. It is wasteful to write down any more than is needed.

Another column is one for 'multiples' – for a number of occurrences of a type of issue, for example if a word was spelled wrong consistently, it would be logged as a minor issue with multiple instances.

The last column is used by the editor to confirm that action has been taken during editing. It may contain a tick to indicate that the identified issue was classified as a defect and corrected, or it may contain a change request reference, or a reference to an explanation attached (perhaps on the reverse of the sheet).

Issue Log Format

Inspection Identification:_____   Page _____ of _____

Item no.	Document Reference Tag	Doc. Page	Line No./ Location	Type of Item (circle)	Checklist/ Rule Tag	Description (if needed) (key offending words)	Number of occur.	Editor Note
1				Major Imp New minor ?				
2				Major Imp New minor ?				

and so on

Subtotals at the bottom of each logging page are used, if desired, to help in collating the summary information for the data summary form. This is also where a count is made of the new issues which are first discovered in the meeting, that is, an issue was noticed in the meeting by one of the checkers and was not one which any of the checkers had noted during individual checking. It is important to keep track of these, as this has a bearing on the optimum logging-meeting-rate in the meeting.

The Brainstorming Meeting Log Form

The process brainstorming log contains the result of a process brainstorming meeting. It contains usually no more than a sample of ten just-logged defects which are analyzed superficially ('brainstorming mode') by the Inspection team. The brainstorming log data must be put into the quality assurance database for long-term cumulation and reference by the Process Change Management Team and their assistants.

It must be possible to connect specific defects referenced in the brainstorming log to the entries in the issue log relating to that and similar issues.

Although ideally the process brainstorming meeting takes place immediately after each Inspection logging meeting, there may be occasions where this is not possible. In that case, the process brainstorming log may refer to the issues from more than one logging meeting.

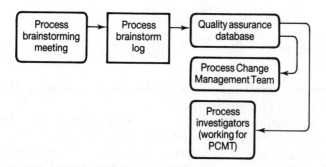

Figure C.7   Brainstorm log uses.

Heading Information

Date of the process brainstorming meeting
Inspection leader's name
Software Inspection identification(s)
Product document references
Other document references (if required)
The start time of the brainstorming meeting.

In addition, a few items of summary information are filled in by the Inspection leader at the conclusion of the process brainstorming meeting.

Summary Information

The stop time of the brainstorming meeting
The total brainstorming meeting time in minutes (usually maximum 30)
The number of people in the meeting (including the leader)
The work-hours spent on process brainstorming by all involved (including leader).

Main body

Brainstorm Item No.	Issue Ref.	Classification of Cause (tick)	Root Cause (keywords)	Improvement Suggestions (keywords)
1		Communication Oversight Transcription Education		
2		Communication Oversight Transcription Education		

and so on.

The brainstorm item number is simply used to refer to the items discussed in this process brainstorm meeting.

The issue reference should be a reference to the issue or issues in the issue log, either by sequential issue number, or by page and line number on the issue log. If desired, it can also include a reference to the product document in which the issue was raised, possibly as a separate column. The severity of the issue can be noted (critical, major), or an assumption can be made that the issue is major unless otherwise stated. Minors should never be discussed.

The classification of the cause of the error is the suggested probable basic process reason why the error was made:

- communications failure (information required not received, incorrect information received);
- oversight (didn't include something, not enough time to do the job thoroughly, or simply forgot something);
- transcription error (knew and understood what to do, but a 'slip of the finger' resulted in an unintended outcome);
- education (didn't realize that something else or something different should have been done, didn't understand the problem, the solution, the context, the job).

Change Request Form

The change request form is used when a logged issue is identified as a defect in a document other than the product document which is currently being Inspected. Editors do not have authority to make changes in any document which they do not own. Changes in that document must be done by the owner.

Change requests are sent when defects or issues are found in source, rule, checklist or procedure documents. A standard (rule, checklist, procedure, forms and so on) can also be changed using improvement suggestions. A change request is a more formal responsible way of asking for a necessary change.

Heading Information

Date of change request
To: document owner: (the person the change request is sent to)
From: sender: (the editor, requesting the change)
Change request identification.

Change Description

Document in which the change is requested
Details of the requested change
Details of action required from document owner – reply required by date
Authorization of change requested (if required).

Response from Document Owner

- Change accepted
  - Date change scheduled
  - Date change performed.

- Change not accepted
  - Detail of reasons why it was not accepted
  - Recipient is not the document owner
  - Document owner's name and contact details
  - Whether this form was forwarded to new document owner or not.
- Work-hours spent on processing change request, including making any changes.

Rules for Forms: Specific Rules (see also Generic Rules)

Owner: TG   Version 0.2   9 January 1993
Application: Inspection forms on paper.

F1. (One page): No form shall ever exceed a single page.

F2. (Consistent): Forms shall use terminology consistent with procedures, rules, exit and entry criteria and any other written material used by those who use the forms.

F3. (Self-instruction): Forms shall contain as much instruction for correct use of the form as is practical and useful. The back of the page might be used for additional information if necessary (but try to avoid this!).

F4. (Codes): Whenever possible, codes, or at least the most frequent ones, shall be on the form so that a tick or circle shall be all that is necessary. The decoding of an abbreviation shall be given if possible (for example, 'Imp(rovement suggestion)').

F5. (User): The forms shall be optimized for ease of learning and use by all users (readers as well as writers), as well as for correct and meaningful information.

F6. (Improvement): Forms will be subject to continuous improvement through improvement suggestions. The form owner shall upgrade the master copy of the form when valid improvements are suggested.

Form Templates

The form templates are given in this section in the same order in which they were described in the previous section.

The forms themselves are each on a full page.

Inspection Master Plan

Inspection ID _____ Inspection Leader: _____ Tel: _____

Author(s) _____ Date Inspection requested: _____

Product _____ No. pages _____ Status _____

Entry Criteria which apply _____

Current Entry Status _____

Exit Criteria which will be applied _____

Meetings
Kickoff: Date _____ Location _____ Start Time _____ End time _____

Logging: Date _____ Location _____ Start Time _____ End time _____

Process Br: Date _____ Location _____ Start Time _____ End time _____

Documents
Sources (relevant pages) _____

Product document(s) samples or chunk(s) _____

Rules _____

Checklists: For Task Product: _____ For other Documents: _____

Participants: Name/tel.	Document Role Tags	Checklist or Procedure Role Tags	Inspection Procedure Tags

Standard Rates and Estimates

Individual checking rate: _____ pages per hour of product document

Logging rate: _____ items to be logged per minute

Logging meeting rate: _____ pages per hour reviewed

Estimated effort in individual checking: _____ work-hours (to nearest tenth)

Data Collection (by you the Checker)

Actual work-hours spent _____ Number of pages studied (at optimum rate) _____

Number of pages scanned (not at optimum rate) ____ No. pages used ___ (excl. this page)

Major Issues _____ minor Issues _____ Improvements _____ Questions _____

Form Owner____*G+G*_____ Version_*8 Jan, 1993*_

Inspection Data Summary

Date _____   Inspection ID: _____   Inspection Leader _____

Product Document Reference _____   Total Pages _____

Date Inspection Requested _____   Date Entry Criteria passed _____

Planning-time ____   Entry-time ____   Kick-off time_____ (wk-hrs)

Individual Checking Results (to be reported during the entry process of the logging meeting)

Inspector	Hours checking	Pages studied	Major Issues	minor Issues	Improve-ments	Questions noted	Checking rate
1							
2							
3							
4							
5							
6							
Totals							

Totals for all Inspectors:
Checking-time _____ (wk-hrs) Average checking rate _____

Logging

No. of people ____ Logging-duration (hours) ____ Logging-time ____ (wk-hrs)

Major issues logged	Minor issues logged	Improvement suggestions	Questions of intent	New items found in the meeting

Logging-rate _____ (items/min) Detection-time _____ (wk-hrs) Logging-meeting-rate____

Editing, Follow-up and Exit

No. major defects_____ No. minor defects _____ No. Change Requests _____

Edit-time _____ Follow-up-time _____ Exit-time _____ Exit date _____

Control-time ____ Defect-removal-time ___ Estimated remaining defects/page _____

Estimated effectiveness (maj defects found/total) _____Efficiency (maj/wk-hr)_____

Development time probably saved by this Inspection ____ (based on 8 or ___ hrs/major)

Form Owner *DRG*   Version *Aug 28, 1993*

Inspection Data Summary (annotated version for metrics calculation)

Date _____   Inspection ID: _____   Inspection Leader _____

Product Document Reference _____   Total logical (600 words) Inspected Pages _____

Date Inspection Requested _____   Date Entry criteria passed _____

(1) Planning-time ____   (2) Entry-time ____ hours (tenths) The time to check that entry
criteria is met
(3) Kickoff Meet Work Hours_____

Individual Checking Results (to be reported during the entry process for Logging meeting)

Inspector	Checking hours (t)	Pages studied (P)	Major issues	minor issues	Improve-ments	Questions noted	Checking rate
1							
2							
3							
4							
5							
Totals	(4)						

Checking-rate _____ -average P/t

Logging
No. of people ____   Logging-duration (hrs) ____(5) Logging-time ____ (work-hours)

Major issues logged	minor issues logged	Improvement suggestions	Questions of intent	New items found in the meeting

Item-Logging rate __ (items/minute). Logging-meeting-rate __ (pages per hour reviewed)

(11) Detection-time (Plan+Kickoff+Check+Log) _____ -(wk.hours)
            (1+2   +3 + 4 + 5)

Editing, Follow-up, Exit and Final Summaries

No. Major defects:_____   No. minor defects _____   No. Change Requests _____

(6) Edit-time _____   (7) Follow up time _____   (8) Exit-time _____   Exit date _____

(9) Control-time __   (10) Defect-removal-time ___   Est remaining Maj defects/page ____
    1+2+3+7+8   11+6+7+8

Est.effectiveness (% maj defects found/page) _____%   Efficiency (maj/wk-hr)_____
                        assumption or history

Development time probably saved by this Inspection ____ (based on 8 or ___ hrs/major)

Form Owner <u>TG&KTG</u>   Version <u>Aug 28 1993</u>   Status_____

Inspection Issue Log

Inspection Identification _____ Page _____ of _____

Item no.	Document Reference Tag	Doc. Page	Line No. Location	Type of Item (circle)	Checklist or Rule Tag	Description (key offending words)	Number of occur.	Editor Note
1				Major Imp New minor ?				
2				Major Imp New minor ?				
3				Major Imp New minor ?				
4				Major Imp New minor ?				
5				Major Imp New minor ?				
6				Major Imp New minor ?				
7				Major Imp New minor ?				
8				Major Imp New minor ?				
9				Major Imp New minor ?				
10				Major Imp New minor ?				

Subtotals:

New issues found in meeting _____ (among items logged on *this* page)

Major issues logged _____ minor issues logged _____

Improvement suggestions logged _____ Questions of intent logged _____

Form Owner _G+G_   Version _20 Jan, 1993_

Process Brainstorming Meeting Log

Date of process brainstorming meeting _____ Start time _____

Software Inspection Identification(s) _____ Inspection Leader _____

Product Document Reference _____

Other Document References _____

Brainstorm Item No.	Issue Ref.	Classification of Cause (tick)	Root Cause (keywords)	Improvement Suggestions (keywords)
1		Communication Oversight Transcription Education		
2		Communication Oversight Transcription Education		
3		Communication Oversight Transcription Education		
4		Communication Oversight Transcription Education		
5		Communication Oversight Transcription Education		
6		Communication Oversight Transcription Education		
7		Communication Oversight Transcription Education		
8		Communication Oversight Transcription Education		
9		Communication Oversight Transcription Education		
10		Communication Oversight Transcription Education		

Stop time _____ Brainstorming meeting duration _____ (minutes) No. of people ____

Total Brainstorming time (in work-hours for all) _____

Form Owner _G+G_ Version _20 Jan, 1993_

Change Request

Date of Change Request _____   Change Request Identification _____

To: Name _____

Location _____

From: Name _____   Tel: _____

Location _____

Details of action required from document owner – reply required by (date) _____

Change Description
Document in which the change is requested _____

Details of the requested change

```



```

Authorized by _____   on (date) _____

Response (please tick)

☐   Change accepted. Date scheduled _____   Date performed _____
☐   Change not accepted. Detail of reasons why it was not accepted.

```


```

☐   I am not the document owner. Document owner is Name _____

Location _____   Tel: _____

☐   I have forwarded a copy of this Change Request to the actual owner.

Time spent
I have spent _____ work-hours on this Change Request. Date _____

Form Owner _DG_ , Version _6 Jan, 1993_

Sample Filled-in Forms

This section contains sample copies of the templates shown in the previous section, but filled in to show how the forms could be used.

The forms are in the same order as in the previous sections. The following forms are shown:

Master plan
Inspection data summary
    after kickoff
    at the end of the logging meeting
    at exit
Issue log
Process brainstorming meeting log
Change request form.

Following each filled-in form, there are comments on the contents of the form for any field which may not be immediately obvious.

These examples may not be identical in every respect to the blank ones shown earlier.

The rest of this page is intentionally left blank, so that the forms are on pages in their entirety.

Inspection Master Plan

Inspection ID _____42_____ Inspection Leader: _Rod O'Mator_ _____ Tel : ___6279___

Author(s) ____ _Ginny Pigg_ ____ Date Inspection requested: ___11 June 93___

Product _Graphical Obj Module Des GD.MAINSYS.GRMOD V2.0_ No. pages ___15___ Status _Not Inspected_

Entry Criteria which apply _Vol. Prod Mini-Inspected, Sys. Des Insp'd Waived: Leader cert. Test Plan Insp'd_

Current Entry Status _____ _Passed 13 June 93_ _____

Exit Criteria which will be applied _Edit complete, CR raised, rates ±10% Std. est. rem. defects <= 1/pg_

Meetings
Kickoff: Date ___16 June 93___ Location __Conference Room C9__ Start Time _10:30_ End time _11:00_

Logging: Date _22 June 93_ Location _Conference Room C4_ Start Time _10:00_ End time _12:00_

Process Br: Date _22 June 93_ Location _Conference Room C4_ Start Time _12:00_ End time _12:30_

Documents
Sources (relevant pages) _____ _GSD: Graphic System Design (pp 24–26), GSD: System Test Plan (3.7–3.12)_

Product document(s) samples or chunk(s) _Graphic Object Module Design, Vers. 1.3, 11 June 93, CHUNK pp 1–4_

Rules _GIS: Graphic Interface Standard, MDRS: Module Design Rule Set_

Checklists: Products: _GDC: Graphic Des Chlst_ Other Docs: _DC: Des Chlst, SDC: Sys. Des Chlst_

Participants: Name / tel.	Document Role Tags	Checklist or Procedure Role Tags	Inspection Procedure Tags
1 Ginny Pigg	MDRS: Rule Set	CI: Interfaces, PC3	PAK, PAC, PAL
2 Penny Lane	GSD: Source	CT: Tester	PCK, PCC, PCL
3 Ivor Heddaicke	GDC: Graphic Des Ch	CC: Coder	PCK, PCC, PCL
4 Francis French	GDT: Test Plan	CU: User	PCK, PCC, PCL
5 Alex Shufflebottom	GIS: Rule Set	CMA: Accuracy	PCK, PCC, PCL
6			

Standard Rates and Estimates

Individual checking rate: ___1___ pages per hour of product document

Logging rate: ___1.5___ items to be logged per minute

Logging meeting rate: ___2___ pages per hour reviewed

Estimated effort in individual checking: ___4___ work-hours (to nearest tenth)

Data Collection (by you the Checker)

Actual work-hours spent _3.6_ Number of pages studied (at optimum rate) ___4___

Number of pages scanned (not at optimum rate) _6_ No. pages used _19_ (excl. this page)

Major issues _16_ Minor issues _25_ Improvements _3_ Questions _8_

Form Owner _G + G_ Version _8 Jan, 1993_

Inspection Master Plan: comments on filled-in example

Entry criteria which apply:

- The normal entry criterion of the Inspection leader having to be certified is waived in this example, because a certification system for leaders is being brought into effect a few months from now.

- The normal entry criterion of the test plan having to be Inspected is waived because test plans are not yet Inspected here. We plan to start Inspecting test plans in a few months' time.

Meeting dates:

- The Inspection was requested on the 11th of June, a Friday. The kickoff meeting is scheduled for the following week, on Wednesday 16th. The logging meeting is scheduled for the week after that, on Tuesday 22nd.

- Another statistic which could be gathered is the time between Inspection requests and final exit, to get an idea of how long a single Inspection cycle normally takes.

Product document:

- Note that the 15-page document is Inspected in chunks, the first of which is the first four pages.

Standard rates and estimates:

- Note that a checking rate of one page per hour has been specified, a logging rate of 1.5 items a minute, and a logging meeting rate of two pages reviewed per hour. Will they be achieved?

Data collection:

- As this master plan would have been received by each individual checker, each one can record their own individual checking data here on the bottom of the form. They can then bring their copy of this form to the logging meeting, to give the information to the Inspection leader at the beginning of the meeting (which will be the first thing the leader will ask for in the meeting).

Inspection Data Summary

After kickoff Example

Date ___21 June 93___ Inspection ID: ___GD5___ Inspection Leader ___Rod O'Mator___

Product Document Reference ___GD.MAINSYS.GRMOD   V 2.0___ Total Pages ___15___

Date Inspection Requested ___11 June 93___ Date Entry Criteria passed ___15 June 93___

Planning-time ___0.7___ Entry-time ___0.3___ Kickoff-time ___1.0___ (wk-hrs)

Individual Checking Results (to be reported during the entry process for Logging meeting)

Inspector	Hours Checking	Pages Studied	Major Issues	Minor Issues	Improve-ments	Questions noted	Checking rate
1							
2							
3							
4							
5							
6							

Totals for all Inspectors:

Checking-time _____ (wk-hrs)   Average Checking rate _____

Logging

No. of people _____ Logging-duration (hrs) _____ Logging-time _____ (wk-hrs)

Major Issues Logged	Minor Issues Logged	Improvement suggestions	Questions of intent	New Items found in the meeting

Logging-rate ____ (items/min) Detection-time ____ (wk-hrs) Logging-meeting-rate ____

Editing, Follow-up and Exit

No. Major defects_____ No. minor defects _____ No. Change Requests _____

Edit-time _____ Follow-up-time _____ Exit-time _____ Exit date _____

Control-time _2.0_ Defect-removal-time _2.0_ Estimated remaining maj defects/page ____

Estimated effectiveness (maj defects found/total) _____ Efficiency (Maj/wk-hr) _____

Development time probably saved by this Inspection ____ (based on 8 or ____ hrs/Major)

Form Owner ___DRG___ Version ___Aug 28 1993___

Inspection Data Summary: comments on filled-in example: After Kickoff

Date:

- The date of this initial data collection is the 21st of June, the day before the logging meeting. Most of the information in the heading comes from the master plan.

Leader planning time:

- Note that the leader has spent 42 minutes (0.7 hours) in planning activities so far. This would include organizing the kickoff meeting, distributing the documents, and planning for the logging meeting tomorrow.

Entry time:

- The leader has spent 18 minutes (0.3 hours) in entry activities, checking the entry criteria.

Control time:

- The control time includes planning time and entry time. The kickoff meeting was held as scheduled on the 16th, and lasted for 10 minutes. Since 6 people attended (including the Leader), this was one work-hour.

Defect removal time:

- Defect removal time is currently the same as control time, since all Inspection activities so far have been control activities.

Inspection Data Summary

'After checking and logging' Example

Date ___22 June 93___   Inspection ID: ___GD5___   Inspection Leader ___Rod O'Mator___

Product Document Reference ___GD.MAINSYS.GRMOD   V 2.0___   Total Pages ___15___

Date Inspection Requested ___11 June 93___   Date Entry Criteria passed ___15 June 93___

Planning-time ___1.2___   Entry-time ___0.3___   Kickoff-time ___1.0___ (wk-hrs)

Individual Checking Results (to be reported during the entry process for logging meeting)

Inspector	Hours Checking	Pages Studied	Major Issues	Minor Issues	Improve-ments	Questions noted	Checking rate
1	3.6	4	16	25	3	8	1.11
2	1.9	4	7	23	0	2	2.11
3	2.8	3.5	20	14	5	0	1.25
4	4.2	5	9	44	1	12	1.19
5	2.4	2.6	15	21	1	19	1.08
6							

Totals for all Inspectors:

Checking-time ___14.9___ (wk-hrs)   Average Checking rate ___1.35___

Logging

No. of people ___6___ Logging-duration (hrs) ___1.72___ Logging-time ___10.3___ (wk-hrs)

Major Issues Logged	Minor Issues Logged	Improvement suggestions	Questions of intent	New Items found in the meeting
27	30	8	22	3

Logging-rate _0.84_ (items/min) Detection-time _27.7_ (wk-hrs) Logging-meeting-rate _2.33_

Editing, Follow-up and Exit

No. Major defects: _____ No. minor defects _____ No. Change Requests _____

Edit-time _____ Follow-up-time _____ Exit-time _____ Exit date _____

Control-time _2.5_ Defect-removal-time _27.7_ Estimated remaining maj defects/page _____

Estimated effectiveness (maj defects found/total) _____ Efficiency (Maj/wk-hr) _____

Development time probably saved by this Inspection ____ (based on 8 or ____ hrs/Major)

Form Owner ___DRG___ Version ___Aug 28 1993___

Inspection Data Summary: comments on filled-in example: At End of Logging Meeting

- The date of this added data is the 22nd of June, after the logging meeting has taken place.

Individual checking:

- Each individual checker's data has been entered on the data summary form. Inspector Number 1 is the one who filled in the bottom of the sample master plan. Notice that the amount of time spent checking, which was estimated to be four hours, varies quite a bit between the Inspectors. Inspector 2 only spent 1.9 hours in checking – perhaps this Inspector should be scribe for this meeting. Note that Inspector 2's checking rate is also over twice as high as was specified, and this Inspector found the fewest number of major issues.

Logging:

- In this example, the meeting duration is 103 minutes (1.72 hours), and the logging time is 10.3 work-hours.

- Note that only 30 minor issues were logged, even though one Inspector found 44. Although it would have been better to log all the minor issues, it is more important to log all the major issues, and to look for new major issues in the meeting. There were three new items discovered in the meeting, which is lower than it should be. For 27 major issues, we should be finding 5 or 6 new major issues in the meeting, but the Inspection process here is relatively immature, and we still have room for improvement.

Logging rate:

- The logging rate was 0.84 items logged per minute, although we had specified a rate of 1.5.

Detection time and defect removal time:

- The total time taken so far is the cost of detecting the issues which have now been logged, and includes the leader's time as well as all time spent by all Inspectors. This total is now at 27.7 hours.

Inspection Data Summary

At 'Exit' Example

Date *1 July 93*   Inspection ID: *GD5*   Inspection Leader *Rod O'Mator*

Product Document Reference *GD.MAINSYS.GRMOD   V 2.0*   Total Pages *15*

Date Inspection Requested   *11 June 93*   Date Entry Criteria passed   *15 June 93*

Planning-time   *1.2*   Entry-time   *0.3*   Kickoff-time   *1.0* (wk-hrs)

Individual Checking Results (to be reported during the entry process for logging meeting)

Inspector	Hours Checking	Pages Studied	Major Issues	Minor Issues	Improve-ments	Questions noted	Checking rate
1	3.6	4	16	25	3	8	1.11
2	1.9	4	7	23	0	2	2.11
3	2.8	3.5	20	14	5	0	1.25
4	4.2	5	9	44	1	12	1.19
5	2.4	2.6	15	21	1	19	1.08
6							

Totals for all Inspectors:

Checking-time   *14.9*   (wk-hrs)   Average Checking rate   *1.35*

Logging

No. of people *6* Logging-duration (hrs) *1.72* Logging-time *10.3* (wk-hrs)

Major Issues Logged	Minor Issues Logged	Improvement suggestions	Questions of intent	New Items found in the meeting
27	30	8	22	3

Item logging-rate *0.84* (items/min) Detection-time *27.7* (wk-hrs)Logging-meeting-rate *2.33*

Editing, Follow-up and Exit

No. Major defects   *29*   No. minor defects   *54*   No. Change Requests   *3*

Edit-time   *16.6*   Follow-up-time   *1.5*   Exit-time   *0.6*   Exit date *1 July 93*

Control-time *4.6* Defect-removal-time   *46.4* Estimated remaining maj defects/page *6.04*

Estimated effectiveness (maj defects found/total)   *60%*   Efficiency (Maj/wk-hr)   *0.63*

Development time probably saved by this Inspection *134.6hrs* (based on 8 or *6.4* hrs/Major)

Form Owner *DRG*   Version *Aug 28 1993*

Inspection Data Summary: comments on filled-in example: At Exit

Date:

- The date of this report is the 1st of July, when exit conditions are achieved for the first chunk, and the first chunk of the product has completed its Inspection cycle.

Major and minor defects, change requests:

- Note that after editing, the number of major defects is 29, whereas 27 were logged as major issues. There were 54 minor defects corrected, although only 30 were logged as minor issues. Three change requests have been raised in documents which the editor does not 'own', that is, does not have direct control over.

Edit time, follow-up-time, exit time and exit date:

- The editor spent 16.6 hours in re-classifying issues, correcting defects and raising change requests. The leader then spent half an hour checking the editing, and found a few issues which had been forgotten, or had not been seen through. For example, a note was made to raise a change request, but it had not been raised. The editor then spent another half hour with the leader in completing the editing. This gives 1.5 hours for follow-up-time.

- The leader spent 36 minutes (0.6 of an hour) in checking that all chunk exit criteria had been met, including entering all the metrics in the QA database. On July 1, the leader confirmed that the chunk had completed its Inspection cycle.

Control time and defect removal time:

- Control time now includes follow-up and exit time, and defect removal time includes all of control time plus edit time.

Estimated remaining defects and effectiveness, efficiency:

- We can assume we find 60% of all defects during one Inspection (effectiveness). We corrected 29 major defects on four (4) pages. Then there are approximately six (6) remaining defects per page after editing.
  We find this by dividing 29 major defects by 4 pages = 7.24 major defects corrected per page. With 60% effectiveness there are 4.83 major defects per page we did not find. If we assume 1 out of 6 defects were not corrected correctly (Fagan, 1986) we can add 1.21 defects per page to the 4.83 defects we did not find, and now we have our estimate of six (6.04) major defects per page remaining after editing. Note that our efficiency is the number of major defects found (29), divided by defect-removal-time, giving 0.63 majors per Inspection work-hour.

Development time saved:

- The total Inspection cycle has taken 46.4 hours. It took 1.6 work hours to find and fix one major defect (+ some minor ones). If it would have taken 6.4 work hours to find it later (at test, or in the field), then we have saved 139.2 work hours for our organization. This is found by taking the number of major defects corrected (29), times the time it would have taken to find and fix them if we did not use Inspection (6.4), minus the time we used to find and fix the major defects through the use of Inspection (46.4).

Inspection Issue Log

Inspection Identification ____GD5____   Page: ___1___ of ___9___

Item No.	Document Reference Tag	Doc. Page	Line No. Location	Type of Item (circle)	Checklist Rule Tag	Description (if needed) (key offending words)	Number of occur.	Editor Note
1	GRMOD 2.0	1	4	**Major** Imp / New / minor ?	CI4	'interface spec'		
2	"	"	7	**Major** Imp / New / minor ?	CT3			
3	"	"	15–17	**Major** Imp / New / minor ?	CU2	New standard User Guidelines not followed		
4	"	"	6	Major Imp / New / **minor** ?	GDC5			
5	GDT	"	–	Major **Imp** / New / minor ?	GDT	Test Plan format would be better corresponding with GDC		
6	STP	2	3.7–12	**Major** Imp / **New** / minor ?	CHK-7	Test missing		
7	GRMOD 2.0	2	5	**Major** Imp / New / minor ?	CMA 7	' response time'		
8	"	"	13	Major Imp / New / **minor** ?	SDC 1	Wrong format	12	
9	"	"	44–46	Major Imp / New / minor _?_		Meaning unclear		
10	"	3	25	**Major** Imp / New / minor ?	GDC 6			

Subtotals:

New issues found in meeting: _____1_____ (among items logged on *this* page)

Major issues logged____6____   minor issues logged ____13____

Improvement suggestions logged ____1____   Questions of intent logged____1____

Form Owner _G+G_   Version _20 Jan, 1993_

Process Brainstorming Meeting Log

Date of process brainstorming meeting ___22 June 93___ Start time ___12:30___

Software Inspection Identification(s): ___GD5___ Inspection Leader ___Rod O'Mater___

Candidate Document Reference GD.MAINSYS.GRMOD Graphical Object Module Design V2.0

Other Document References Graphic System Design (pp 24–26), System Test Plan (3.7–3.12)

Brainstorm Item No.	Issue Ref.	Classification of Cause (tick)	Root Cause (keywords)	Improvement Suggestions (keywords)
1	6	Communication -> Oversight Transcription Education	*Different type of test only needed for graphic design*	*Add checklist question to GDC*
2	3	Communication Oversight Transcription -> Education	*New User guidelines not widely known*	*Publicize in newsletter Memo to all graphic designers*
3	7	-> Communication Oversight Transcription Education	*Old interface conventions not updated in current manual.* *Interface names very similar*	*Audit status of manual before beginning task* *Update project leader* *Add checklist question CRS*
4		Communication Oversight Transcription Education		
5		Communication Oversight Transcription Education		
6		Communication Oversight Transcription Education		
7		Communication Oversight Transcription Education		
8		Communication Oversight Transcription Education		
9		Communication Oversight Transcription Education		
10		Communication Oversight Transcription Education		

Stop time _12:45_ Brainstorming meeting duration ___15___ (min.) No. of people __6__

Total Brainstorming time (in work-hours for all) ___1.5 hrs___

Form Owner _G+G_   Version _20 Jan, 1993_

Change Request

Date of Change Request ___24 June 93___ Change Request Identification ___GDI.54___

To: Name _____Peter Principal_____

Location _____Room 1106,   Copse Building_____

From: Name ___Alex Shufflebottom___ Tel: ___Ext 485___

Location _____Room 46B,   HQ Building_____

Details of action required from document owner – reply required by (date) ___2 July 93___

Change Description
Document in which the change is requested ___GD.STP V3.2 System Test Plan___

Details of the requested change

> Add tests for the graphic objects being overlaid,
>
> with combinations as in Section 3.8 for movement.

Authorized by ___Thea Stickler, Test Manager___ on (date) ___24 June 93___

Response (please tick)

☐   Change accepted. Date scheduled _____ Date performed _____

☐   Change not accepted. Detail of reasons why it was not accepted.

>

☐   I am not the document owner. Document owner is Name _____

Location _____ Tel. _____

☐   I have forwarded a copy of this Change Request to the actual owner.

Time spent
I have spent _____ work-hours on this Change Request. Date _____

Form Owner _G+G_ , Version _6 Jan, 1993_

Example Forms

Example Change Request

Here is an example of a Design Change Request from a client's handbook:[†]

TO: From:
                                                             Date:

DESIGN CHANGE REQUEST (DCR) REFERENCE NO. DCR /   /   –
        (this ref. no. is embedded in our documentation now.)

Our Inspection sometimes finds apparent defects in others' documents. As a result this form is completed and sent to the owner concerned.
May we ask you to fill out the form below, as indicated, and to return either all of it or just the bottom to:

Alan F. Brown, Mgr. Q&BP, OASIS, BRA01
The document concerned is:

The requested change is:

Please tick the appropriate box.

[ ] 1. The document is no longer our responsibility. The current responsible party
is _____. We have forwarded the material to them, while returning a copy of this page to you for your information.
[ ] 2. The change is not required for the reason given in the space below.
[ ] 3. We have handled the DCR as explained in the space below.
(Space for reply to 2. and 3. above)

Signed: Date:

---------------------------- tear along here -------------------

[ ] 4. Regarding DCR/   /   – , we will complete the action by week _____ and return the rest of the form to A. F. Brown then.
Signed: Date:

† ICL–85. *Appendix A4-1* modified by the authors.

The following is a sample Inspection Report and Inspection Statistics from Racal Redac.

INSPECTION REPORT

Inspection Ref: 0   Moderator: 0   Project No.: 0

Document

       Ref no.:   0   chunk: 0
       Issue: 0   pages: 0
       Title:

       Type: 0

Costs

Insp'n cost: 0.00   hours   Rework
Rework cost: 0.00   hours   completed: 1 Jan 04

Defects

       Majors: 0   DCRs raised: 0
       Minors: 0
       Majors/page: #NUM!

Disposition

       ACCEPT   REJECT

       Moderator certification   Date:

       comments

Distribution:

       Project Leader
       Author
       Facilitation

PLANNING

Insp. Ref		Doc type:		Submitted:	
Doc. Ref		Issue:		pages:	
Proj. no		chunk:		Pages insp.	
Moderator		Plan time:		minutes	

KICK-OFF MEETING

#people:
duration: minutes
Total meeting effort   0.00 work-hours

PREPARATION   # inspectors:

Role	minutes	majors	minors	questions	pages

Prep. cost   0.00 work-hours   Avg. pages:

MAIN MEETING   # people: Date:

			Low level	High level
scheduled start				
actual start		majors:		
logging start		minors:		
Questions start		others:		
Analysis start			0	0
AOB start		new defects		
Meeting end		found in Mtg:		#NUM!

Total Meeting effort   0.00 work-hours
Logging time   0 minutes
Logging rate   #NUM!   defects/min.   Maj/ page: #NUM!

FOLLOW-UP   Adjusted defects

Moderator time:		minutes	Fixed majors:	
Estimated rework:	3 x #defects	minutes	Fixed minors:	
Actual rework:		minutes	DCRs:	

Competition date:
Folow up cycle: 0 days

Tick List	
Follow up:	Stats:
Log:	People:
Report:	Defects:

INSPECTION COST
          0.00 work-hours   0 days elapsed

Figure C.8   RACAL REDAC data summary form (terminology may differ from this book). Filling this spreadsheet will automatically feed the data into the Inspection database.

MLog.Mac

	A	B
1	Enter_data	command-option-d
2	=SELECT(!log_input)	
3	=RETURN()	
4		
5	Print_log	command-option-l
6	=SELECT(!log_sheet)	
7	=SET.PRINT.AREA()	
8	=PRINT()	
9	=RETURN()	
10		
11	Print_report	command-option-r
12	=SELECT (!insp_report)	
13	=SET.PRINT.AREA()	
14	=PRINT()	
15	=RETURN()	
16		
17	Update_stats	command-option-s
18	=ECHO(FALSE)	
19	=FORMULA.GOTO("mtg_stats")	
20	=SELECT("RC1")	select the first field
21	=COPY()	get the insp. ref.
22	=ACTIVATE("Meeting Statistics")	
23	=SELECT("C1")	use column 1
24	=FORMULA.FIND("",1,2,1)	find a blank record
25	=SELECT ("R")	select the row
26	=INSERT(2)	insert a new row
27	=SELECT("RC1")	select the first field
28	=ACTIVATE("Meeting log")	
29	=FORMULA.GOTO("mtg_stats")	
30	=COPY()	copy Meeting Stats record
31	=ACTIVATE("Meeting Statistics")	
32	=PASTE.SPECIAL(3,1)	and paste in the values
33	=RETURN()	

Figure C.9 RACAL REDAC. Some of the spreadsheet commands for Inspection metrics.

Appendix D: Rule Sets

The Concept of a Rule Set

'Rules', as used here, is short for 'software engineering rules'. Groups of software engineering rules we call 'rule sets'. Sometimes we feel they should be called guidelines – but it amounts to the same thing.

A rule set:

- defines acceptable behavior when doing software engineering;
- recommends the best known practices;
- is improved on a regular basis as experience provides insight;
- can be used during Inspection as the basic standard for judging the content of a software engineering work product;
- is a procedure for writing a document.

'Standards should be:
Attainable ... Economic ... Applicable ... Consistent ...
All-inclusive ... Understandable ... Stable ... Maintainable ...
Legitimate ... and Equitable'. He explains these concepts in more depth.
J. M. Juran in *Management Breakthrough*, p.235.

Specific Examples

Rule sets are conveniently classified as 'generic' – meaning they can be used in most task types, and 'specific' – meaning they can be used in one well defined single task type.

It would be wasteful to have many separate rule sets for various types of plans which related to things they have in common such as clarity, grammar, spelling, headings and the like. On the next few pages we have some examples of rule sets. These are not specific recommendations of 'best practice'. They are included only to give realistic examples of real rule sets which some people find useful. They can also serve as a starter kit.

A Rule Set for Rules

Version 2.0 February 1992 TG. Tag=RULE.S

> S1 (PAGE). No rule set shall ever exceed a single page of text (about 60 lines).
> S2 (EXIT). All rule sets shall have successfully exited from an Inspection against this rule set and the generic software engineering document rule set before being taken into use.
> S3 (REF). All rules shall have a unique code for reference. For example this is 'S3'.
> S4 (GEN). All rule sets shall follow the Generic Software engineering document rule set (RULE.G).
> S5 (NEW). When old rules are deleted, their reference code (like 'S5' here) shall not be reused by essentially different rules. Mark 'deleted and code not to be reused'. (Suggested by Los Alamos Labs 1992.) This is to permit long-term analysis of the usefulness of particular rules which cause reporting of issues.

A Generic Software Engineering Document Rule Set

Version 2.1 July 1992 TG. Tag=RULE.G

> G1 (DEF).[†] A 'Software engineering document' is the product of any software engineering-related task. It includes code, test cases, requirements, contracts and user manuals.
> G2 (ONE). All documents shall be unambiguous to the intended readership, unless clearly marked (for example, using the <angle parentheses>).
> G3 (NOTE). All form of comment, note, suggestion, idea which does not form an official part of the document shall be clearly distinguished as such (for example, by 'quotes', *italics*, footnotes,[‡] for example, prefacing words.)

[†] The notion of separating the mnemonic part of the tag (we originally used the format 'G1-DEF') is due to Ed Barnard, Cray Research, 1992. The tag itself ('G3') is declared and logged at the logging meeting. The key word in parentheses is also declared aloud to remind other checkers what the issue is. But the keyword does not get logged.

[‡] This is a footnote example. Problems in it are not likely to be major.

G4 (EXTRA). All documents shall be as brief as possible, to support their purpose.

G5 (CLEAR). All documents shall be crystal clear to all possible readers as to intent. The burden is on the producer, not the reader.

G6 (HEAD). All documents shall contain producer, date, source document codes, rule set codes, quality status (exited or not), identification tag, revision code.

G7 (UNIQUE). Ideas shall be stated once only in documents and thereafter referred to by their unique tag. Use comments (") to paraphrase ideas elsewhere.

G8 (SOURCE). Statements shall contain information about their exact and detailed sources. Normally use the '<–' source arrow, but also 'evidence' and comments.

G9 (EL). Statements shall be broken up into their most elementary form (to permit separate analysis, costing, implementation).

G10 (TAG). All elementary statements shall have their own identity tag for direct reference from other parts of any larger document set. Parameter name and qualifiers can be used as sub-tags, for example, USABILITY.PAST[1991].

G11 (HIER). Documents shall be organized into clear hierarchical structures, with tagging reflecting the structure.

G12 (CHANGE). Date and unique author initials (or employee code) of any change shall be indicated at the level of change, for example, PLAN 60%<–{REQT-R, TG, FEB-15-91} Inspection rework.

G13 (RISK). Any known or suspected uncertainty or risk shall be clearly indicated using devices such as { <vaguely defined>, ?, ??, 60->70, 70%± 20 } and suitable comments.

G14 (STATUS). A document shall show its Inspection status clearly. In particular EXITED (from the Inspection process), NOT EXITED. Not exited shall be assumed until other status is claimed. The number of maximum major issues probably remaining per non-commentary full page shall be noted next to the exit declaration.

Generic Rule Set for Source Code

Owner: Ed Barnard, Cray Research, Inc.   January 1993

The generic rule set for all documents (RULE.G) is assumed to be at the base of this rule set.

Note: the term 'mod' below refers to any change to an existing module, including documentation and commentary.

If allowing a violation of the rule set to remain in the document could have dangerous consequences, classify the violation as major. Otherwise, the violation is minor.

Rule	Violation	Description of Rule
GC1	(project)	The document (code) must meet all relevant project requirements.
GC2	(unconfined)	The code should confine itself to the problem at hand, as defined in the mod header, problem report or design document.
GC3	(regression)	The code should introduce no regressions in performance, functionality, or other qualities, except as noted in the mod header or other accompanying documentation.
GC4	(incompatible)	The code should not introduce incompatibilities with other systems, e.g., create a library dependency. Where this is unavoidable, the situation must be clearly documented in the mod header or other accompanying documentation.
GC5	(hard-coded)	The code should use symbolic constraints, instead of hard-coded values, whenever appropriate.
GC6	(interface)	Module preambles should describe the interface between the module and the 'outside world'. The preamble should describe entry and exit conditions and a statement of the module's purpose. The preamble should include any orientation necessary for understanding the module as a whole.
GC7	(complexity)	The level of commentary should match the complexity of the code. Explanatory text should be complete and relevant.
GC8	(style)	For mods, the coding style should match that of the surrounding code. The author may use differing styles where he or she deems appropriate.

Source References
Version 2.1, Not Exited. 60 predicted remaining Major defects per page.
Last update 7/14/92 by ewb; no Inspection reference.
File name /home/cherry5/ewb/PI/ewb.latest/Rule.GC.
Must comply with rule set(s): Rule.S,Rule.G
Relevant policy document(s): Pol.RS.

Requirements Specification Rule Set

Version 2.1   20 July, 1992 TG. Tag=RULE.R.
The generic software engineering rule set RULE.G is assumed to be at the base of this Rule set.

> R1 (SEP). Functional requirements (those without SCALE) shall be clearly separated from attribute requirements (those with SCALE).
> R2 (NUM). Attribute requirements (benefit and costs) shall be specified measurably and testably (SCALE and TEST).
> R3 (PLANGUAGE). The parameters for describing attributes are SCALE, TEST, PAST, RECORD, MUST, PLAN and other language elements described in the 'Quality Planning'[†] book.
> R4 (RESULT). Requirements must be stated in terms of final need, not perceived means (these means are solutions and must be stated separately).

Solution Specification Rule Set

(For designs or strategies to meet requirements)
Version 2.1   20 July, 1992 TG. Tag=RULE.SS. The generic software engineering rule set RULE.G is assumed to be at the base of this rule set.

> SS1 (JUST). The *requirement justification* for each solution or hierarchical set of solutions must always be indicated, with the solution specification itself using tags of requirements (this is the specific equivalent of G8 (SOURCE) in RULE.G).
> For example: Strategy-X: Hire a new chairman <- {PROFIT-1, GROWTH-2}.
> SS2 (IMPACT): A numeric quality estimation table with evidence shall accompany all solution specifications, so that we have the designer's opinion of how all attributes are impacted by all solutions.

[†] At this stage, Quality Planning is a manuscript, and is freely available. The reader can also refer to Gilb: *Principles of Software Engineering Management* (Gilb, 1988) for an understanding of the principles involved.

Quality Estimation Rule Set

Version 2.1   20 July, 1992 TG. Tag=RULE.I.
The generic software engineering rule set RULE.G is assumed to be at the base of this rule set.

I1 (ALL). All critical attributes of benefit and cost shall be included on the table.

I2 (SOLS). All solution concepts which are needed to ultimately meet planned levels shall be included in one or more quality estimation tables.

I3 (EST). All intersections between attribute requirements and solutions shall be estimated.

I4 (RISK). All estimates shall have plus/minus uncertainty (in detail or overall for each table) specified for each estimate.

I5 (SAFE). A safety factor of at least TWO shall be used. For example, at least 200% total for benefits and no more than 50% total for costs.

I6 (NET). The ratio of benefit to costs for each solution or solution group shall be computed.

I7 (PROOF). Each significant (10% or more) estimate (at least) shall have a corresponding evidence statement (see RULE.E).

Evidence Rule Set

Version 2.1   20 July, 1992 TG. Tag=RULE.E.
The generic software engineering rule set RULE.G is assumed to be at the base of this rule set.

E1 (CHECK). Evidence shall permit the reader to further investigate the claim by going to written or oral sources for confirmation.

E2 (FACT). Evidence shall be based on historical evidence. This means dates, places, projects, people and measures of effect shall be given. Otherwise 'no facts available' shall be stated.

E3 (MINUS). Negative evidence – facts which do not support the estimate – shall be given if known. Exceptional circumstances (that is, why we do not believe these are relevant) can be explained.

E4 (CREDIBLE). Credibility of the evidence shall be classified on a scale of 1.0 (perfect) to 0.0 (worthless).

Rules for Forms: Specific Rules (see also Generic Rules)

Version 0.1   29 July, 1992 TG. Tag = RULE.F.
Application: Inspection forms on paper.

F1 (ONE PAGE). No form shall ever exceed a single page.

F2 (CONSISTENT). Forms shall use terminology consistent with procedures, rules, exit, and entry criteria, and any other written material used by those who use the forms.

F3 (SELF-INSTRUCTION). Forms shall contain as many instructions as necessary for correct use on the form itself. The back of the page might be used for additional information if necessary.

F4 (CODES). Whenever possible, codes (or at least the most frequent ones) shall be on the form so that a tick or circle shall be all that is necessary. The decoding of an abbreviation shall be given if possible (for example, 'M(ajor)').

F5 (USER). The forms shall be optimized for ease of learning and use by all users (readers as well as writers), then for correct and meaningful information.

Rules for Document Type: Test Plan[†]
Document Tag: 'TP'

Version 1.0   13 April, 1993 DG. Tag = RULE.TP.

TP1 (ID). Specify test plan identifier as SYS.TP.n, where SYS is the system name, and n is the sequential test plan number.

TP2 (INTRO). Introduction: summarize software items to be tested with references to project plan, quality plan and test design documents.

TP3 (ITEM). Identify test items including version level, hardware and software requirements, and references to requirements specifications and design documentation.

TP4 (FEAT). List features to be tested and features not to be tested (with reasons).

TP5 (APPRO). Describe test approach to be used, including techniques and level of comprehensiveness.

TP6 (PASS). Specify item pass/fail criteria, and person responsible for the decision.

TP7 (SUSPEND). Specify test suspension and resumption criteria.

TP8 (ENVIRON). Specify test environment, including tools required, user involvement and special equipment.

TP9 (SCHED). Specify schedule, resources required, responsibilities and contingencies.

[†]Adapted from *ANSI/IEEE Standard for Software Test Documentation*, Std 829 – 1983.

Appendix E: Policies

Inspection Policy

Version 1.0   4 Nov, 1992 TG. Tag=POL.IP.

IP1. All 'documents' costing over one work-hour to produce, or which affect more than one work-week of cost, shall be 'exited' correctly from Inspection before further use.

IP2. All paperwork processes shall be defined by written 'owned' rules and procedures, entry criteria and exit criteria.

IP3. Default exit condition for maximum remaining major defects per page is three (for this year) and 0.3 (three years from now).

IP4. Optimum checking and logging meeting (including further checking) rates shall be determined and used.

IP5. Inspection team leaders will be trained (5 days) and 'certified', to permit them to take responsibility for Inspections. They shall then be continuously monitored for reasonable performance by their metrics.

IP6. Quality Assurance will provide all support functions for Inspection (training, database, audit, certification, forms, ownership of standards by default).

IP7. Defect prevention through process improvement will be given priority (kickoff objectives and strategies, Quality Assurance database, process brainstorming, Process Change Management Teams).

IP8. Inspection will be applied 'upstream' first in development, and to maintenance and change control.

IP9. Inspection will be subject to regular, no less than annual, process audit.

IP10. Managers will lead by using Inspection on all their important documents (objectives, budgets, strategies, policies, presentations to the board and the like).

A Policy for Continuous Quality Improvement

Version 1.0   24 Nov, 1992 TG. Tag=POL.CQI.

CQI1. The full Inspection process will be exploited (especially Mays and Jones, Improvement Logging and so on).

CQI2. Return on Investment shall be continuously monitored (time spent versus time saved).

CQI3. All quality improvement shall be planned and monitored using agreed measures of it.

CQI4. Entry and exit controls shall be established for all work processes under continuous improvement.

CQI5. All work processes shall have 'owners' of the processes, through ownership of their corresponding standards (rules, procedures, exit criteria, entry criteria, forms, codes, optimum work rates).

CQI6. The overall continuous improvement rate shall be at least 40% per year unless other specific rates are needed for individual measures of improvement.

CQI7. Documents shall not exit unless they have fewer than three (note this policy within two years should be less than 0.3) major defects per page (600 words, non-commentary) estimated remaining after correct editing of logged issues.

CQI8. Management is responsible for quality and the changes needed to improve it.

CQI9. Staff must have daily-use practical mechanisms for suggesting process improvements.

CQI10. We will give priority to effort and mechanisms for learning to avoid mistakes (time, training, tools for the staff).

Glossary

Audit an independent investigation to find out whether written process descriptions (procedures, rules, entry, exit criteria) are being properly applied in practice.

Author a person or team who has written something (product) using a set of source documents, in accordance with a set of rules.

When referring to a specific type of author, a specific function title may be used, for example coder, test planner, software architect, designer, technical writer.

Bug colloquial term for major defect or fault in software code.
Synonyms: defect, fault, issue, problem.

Candidate a product document submitted for Inspection.

Category a subdivision of issues or defects whose occurrences can be tracked statistically. For example, defects may be listed as occurring in the categories of something missing, wrong, extra, and ambiguous. Defects can also be categorized into types such as spelling/grammatical errors, logic errors, interface errors, performance errors, usability errors, and so on. Categories are not used much in the Inspection process described in this book, but older inspection processes use them.

Champion a person who has taken the responsibility for implementing the Inspection process within an organization.
Synonyms: change agent, facilitator.

Change Request a formal record of an issue raised for a document not under the direct control of the editor, and requiring resolution or change by the owner of the document. Responsibility for document update is always with the document owner.
Synonyms: design change request.

Checker a person who examines a set of related (source and product) documents with the primary objective of finding major potential defects as defined by written rules and checklists. All checkers are part of the larger process of Inspection and are also 'Inspectors'.
Related term: Inspector.

Checking   the act of looking for potential defects in a set of related (source and product) documents.

Individual checking is done by each individual checker before the logging meeting. During the individual checking process, the checker finds any issues to be raised at the meeting.

Checking is also done during the logging meeting when Inspectors also try to identify issues which were not already identified during the individual checking. The leader may perform checking superficially during the entry process on a small sample to determine if the documents are good enough for the Inspection to go ahead. The leader will also perform some checking during follow-up.

Synonyms: Inspecting, (traditional term) 'preparation'.

Checking-rate   the number of pages studied intensively per individual work hour.

Checking-time   total work-hours spent in individual checking of the candidate product document and the associated sources, using checklists, rules and procedures. This includes all checkers' checking time and any time spent in individual checking by the leader. Checking performed in the logging meeting is counted in logging time.

Checklist   A specialized set of questions designed to help checkers find more defects, and in particular, more significant defects. Checklists concentrate on major defects. A checklist should be no more than a single page per subject area. Checklist questions interpret specified rules.

Classifying   during the logging meeting, the act of determining the type of logged item – deciding whether an item should be logged as an issue, an improvement suggestion, or a question to the author, and whether the issues logged are major or minor.

During the editing process, the act of determining the type of logged issues: whether the issue should be finally classified as a defect, an improvement suggestion, a question to the author, or a 'change request' (CR). The final defect severity classification into major or minor is also made by the editor during editing.

Control-time   total work-hours spent by the leader or anyone else involved in any form of planning or control of the Inspection process, including preparation of the master plan, administration, communication, data gathering and reporting. It includes entry and exit checking, planning, kickoff and follow-up activities. It does *not* include any other time spent by the leader as a checker, time spent in the logging meeting, or in process brainstorming. It is the sum of leader-time plus kickoff-time plus follow-up-time plus exit-time.

Correct-fix-rate   the percentage of edit correction attempts which correctly fix a defect and do not introduce any new defects. See also *Fix-fail-rate*.
Default: 83% – five out of six correction attempts (Fagan, 1986).

Correction-time   edit-time plus follow-up time. This is the cost of correcting defects or communicating change requests to other authors by the editor, and also the leader's audit that the editing has been completed (follow-up).

Critical   a defect classification more severe than major.
See also Synonym: super-major.

Cycle   a portion of the Inspection process which is complete for the whole or for a prescribed part of a product. A cycle will consist of a minimum of checking, logging and editing. Multiple cycles are needed when the product documents are too large to inspect at once. Only when all cycles are successfully exited can the product document be said to be exited. A cycle may need to be repeated due to failure to exit.
Related / traditional term: chunk.

Default estimate   a number you can use, until you have your own data, to give some idea of the order of magnitude to expect.
Here are some default estimates:
time-to-fix-later:	8 work-hours per major defect
major-time:	1 work-hour per major defect to find and fix
undetected defects:	50% of defects logged
fix-fail-rate:	1 in 6 fixes attempted – 17%
defect-edit-rate:	12 defects per hour – 5 minutes per defect
logging-rate:	1 per minute

Defect   an error made in writing in a document or code which violates a rule. A logged issue becomes an 'official' defect when the editor classifies it as such during editing. Items may be classified as defects directly from issues, or from questions of intent or from improvement suggestions.
Informal synonyms: bug, fault, issue, problem.

Defect density   number of defects per page in a product. The defect density is an estimate of defects in the product at a defined stage (for example, after edit). The estimate is usually based on the defects found, the known or estimated defect-finding effectiveness, and the correct fix-rate. It can, for example, be expressed as defects per page, defects per thousand lines of code (KLOC) or defects per thousand words (Kwords). This generic definition also applies to specific applications such as major defect density per page used and so on.
See also *Effectiveness*.

Defect-edit-rate: the number of defects fixed per hour in editing. This is used by the leader to estimate the time needed for editing the issues which were logged in the logging meeting.
Default: 3.0 to 7.5 defects per hour – 2 to 8 minutes per defect.

Defect prevention   activities directed at improving a process so that defects tend not to occur. In Inspection it is things like process brainstorming and Process Change Management Team activity which are directed towards defect prevention.

Defect removal   identification and removal of defects. In Inspection it is particularly the sub-processes of checking, logging and editing which make up the defect removal part of the process.

Defect-removal-time   Detection-time plus correction-time plus exit-time. This intentionally excludes discussion-time.

Defects-detected   the total number of defects as classified by the editor during editing. The sum of major-defects-detected and minor-defects-detected. Final metrics should be based on the former since minor defects give minimal pay-back.

Detection-time   the total work-hours to identify issues, before correcting them or before exploiting them for insights in order to improve the process that gave rise to them. Detection-time is the sum of leader-time plus kickoff-time plus checking-time plus logging-time. It does not include discussion-time.

Development-time-saved   the net savings of time in work-hours, at project delivery time, due to defects fixed during editing, instead of during testing for a software activity. This can only be an estimate, but can be based on detection and correction time in testing, minus major-time.

Discussion-time   work-hours spent in the logging meeting on non-logging and non-checking activities (by all parties).

Discussion-duration   the hours of logging-meeting-duration which are *not* spent in reporting items or checking for new issues. This may include discussion of items or interruptions to the meeting.

Document   a written set of information – which can be the subject for Inspection. Referred to in this book as a product – to link it with a particular author and process.
Synonym: product.

Downstream   the work processes which take place after a particular reference point (usually *this* Inspection). Downstream activities are impacted by current activities. Particular types of activities may sometimes be downstream and at other times upstream from each other. For example, requirements analysis is initially upstream to both architectural design and acceptance test design.

However, acceptance test design may impact the requirements, which is *then* downstream to that acceptance test design version.

Edit the process of working through the issue log to give each issue a final classification, to correct any defects in the documents for which the editor is currently responsible, and to raise any change requests (CR) required. Edit work includes 'improvement' suggestions for voluntary implementation on the current product, 'questions' for voluntary written answers in the current product and other associated tasks as defined by the current edit procedure.
Synonyms: fix, correct.
Traditional term: 'rework'.

Edit-time work-hours spent editing all items by the editor, including time to reclassify issue severity into major and minor defects, to fix defects, and to raise change requests (CRs).

Editor the person or group who reads the issue log, determines what is to be done about each issue, and does it. The editor is normally the author of the product document being Inspected. The editor also raises and cross-references change requests where appropriate, decides on the final classification, computes the final metrics on defects, and ensures that all improvement suggestions are given to the appropriate owner.
Synonym: re-worker.

Effectiveness (or actual defect-finding effectiveness) the percentage of major defects discovered at any one specified stage or cumulation of stages of Inspection or test, compared to the total major defects found so far. Actual effectiveness measurement should be used to improve the estimates of Inspection effectiveness made at exit from an Inspection cycle. Inspection effectiveness would consider only those defects found by Inspection, test effectiveness only those found by test activities, and development effectiveness those defects found by Inspection and testing.
See also *Defect density*.

Efficiency (Major) defects found per work-hour. A measure of individual or team ability to exploit their time. It is therefore also a measure of the cost of finding defects. It is calculated by the total major defects (after being classified as defects by the editor), divided by defect-removal-time. Efficiency is therefore inversely related to the cost of finding a defect; that is, the less it costs to find a defect, the more efficient you are, and vice versa.
Default: 1 defect found per Inspection work-hour (similar to major-time because fix time is so small).

Entry criteria the set of generic and specific conditions for permitting a process to go forward with the defined task. The purpose of entry criteria is to prevent a task from being done which would entail more (wasted) effort compared to the effort needed to remove the failed entry criteria. The entry criteria are a part of the process definition.

Entry-time   work-hours spent by the Inspection leader to check that entry conditions are met, and to work towards meeting them.

Error   an act by a person which violates applicable written rules for a process, and which may result in a defect in a document, because the product document does not conform to what is expected. Errors can be classified as slips or mistakes. Slips are inadvertent acts in spite of correct knowledge. Mistakes are errors committed in good faith based on faulty knowledge (for example, wrong source data) or a faulty model of reality. Errors are not intentional.

An error made in the product Inspected, when identified as a potential defect by a checker, would be reported in the logging meeting as an issue, which the editor may classify as a defect and may then correct so that a failure (associated with that particular defect) cannot occur.

Estimated effectiveness   the percentage of major defects discovered compared to the total (estimated) major defects, including undetected defects. This is an estimate of the depth to which the Inspection process is able to penetrate the total defects in the document.

Exit criteria   the set of generic and specific conditions for permitting a process to be officially completed. The purpose of exit criteria is to prevent a task from being considered completed when there are still outstanding parts of the task which have not been finished. The exit criteria are part of the process definition. There can be exit criteria for each development process, and also for the Inspection process and any of its sub-tasks. Exit criteria are part of process standards. They are changed as required, as part of continuous process improvement.

The primary effect of Inspection exit criteria is to ensure that the exited documents are of sufficient quality for use by others. This does not imply zero defects or perfection, but rather an economically defensible quality; it would no longer be worth looking for further corrections *at this stage*.

Exit-time   work-hours spent by the Inspection leader to check exit criteria and do exit activities. It includes time to record metrics in the QA database, to initiate action to fix conditions which do not permit exit, and to document the release. Exit-time is part of control-time.

Exited Product   a product document which successfully exits Inspection.

Failure   a failure in a product document is an undesired result on use of the document, due to a defect in the document itself. A failure which occurs in software code may cause a system crash or simply a wrong message to appear. A failure which occurs in a human-readable document may cause a misunderstanding or an incorrect action.

Fault   see *Defect*.

Final classification   the ultimate classification of logged items into major or minor defect, improvement suggestion, question of intent to the author, or change request (CR).

Fix-fail-rate   the percentage of edit correction attempts which fail to correct the defect.
Default: 17% – one out of six correction attempts (Fagan, 1986).

Follow-up   the process of checking that all editing has been completed, by the editor, according to the current edit procedure. The leader does not check the content of the edits, he or she only checks that the edit process has been carried out for all items in the issue log. Successful completion of follow-up is an exit requirement for the Inspection process to exit.
Synonym: edit check.

Follow-up-time   total work-hours spent by the Inspection leader to perform follow-up. It includes the editor's time if the editor participates during follow-up. Follow-up-time is part of control-time.

Generic checklist   a checklist which applies to all documents (or to many of a defined class, for example 'requirements and design documents'). It may contain generic questions such as: 'GC8: is the source of any estimate specified in detail?<- Rule G8'.

Improvement champion   a person who is given the responsibility of ensuring that a specific improvement to the software development process or task is carried out by all those performing that process or task. The improvement champion may be a quality improvement team rather than a single individual. See also *Process improvement* and *Quality improvement team*.

Improvement suggestion   a proposal recorded during the process brainstorming meeting, or in the logging meeting, regarding a change to any software engineering process. They differ from issues in that issues are logged against a *document*, but improvement suggestions are logged against a process (which produces the product), or against the Inspection process itself.

Improvement-suggestions-logged   the number of improvement suggestions logged in the logging meeting.

Improvement-suggestions-noted the number of improvement suggestions noted by an individual checker during individual checking.

Individual checking the checking performed by an individual on the product and source documents, using rules, procedures and checklists before the logging meeting (which *itself* permits further checking).
Synonym: (traditional term) 'preparation'.

Inspection a quality improvement process for written material. It consists of two dominant components; product (document itself) improvement and process improvement (of both document production and Inspection).

Inspector a person participating on an Inspection team, including authors, Inspection leaders, checkers, editors, process brainstorming participants, and scribes.

Issue an item which a checker suspects may be a defect is reported during the logging meeting as an issue, which must be resolved. A valid issue must contain a reference to the possible violation of a specific written rule (or to a checklist question which itself is an interpretation of a specified rule).
A logged issue must be resolved. It becomes recognized as a defect only by the editor (who is usually also the author).
Synonyms: problem, item, defect, error, fault.

Issues-logged the number of issues reported in the logging meeting and recorded in the issue log, including multiple occurrences.

Issues-noted the number of issues noted (observed with a view to report during logging) by checkers during individual checking.

Items the set of things written down at the logging meeting. This consists of issues, improvement suggestions and questions of intent to the author.

Items-logged the total number of issues, improvement suggestions, and questions of intent to the author reported in the logging meeting and recorded in the issue log, including multiple occurrences. The sum of major-issues-logged plus minor-issues-logged plus improvement-suggestions-logged plus questions-of-intent-logged.

Items-noted the total number of issues, improvement suggestions, and questions of intent to the author noted by a checker during individual checking. The sum of major-issues-noted plus minor-issues-noted plus improvement-suggestions-noted plus questions-of-intent-noted.

Kickoff a team meeting, prior to the individual checking activity. It has several components: to ensure that checkers know what to do

and how to do it (are trained in what they need to do including feedback on recent process improvements). Team objectives for improved checking and logging results, and strategies to achieve those objectives through experimental improvements in the checking and/or logging process are agreed.
Traditional term: 'kickoff meeting'.

Kickoff-time   work-hours spent organizing (leader) or attending a kickoff meeting, and time spent on any other kickoff activities, such as additional 'getting started' time for new Inspectors.

Leader/Inspection Leader   an Inspector who is trained and certified to coordinate and control all Inspection team activities. The Leader is responsible for planning, motivation, meeting management, capturing data, approving entry and exit criteria, checking the editing of issues, training of checkers, and in all possible ways supervising the Inspection process so that it succeeds. The Leader may also be an author, checker or scribe.
Synonyms: (traditional term) 'moderator'. The Inspection leader does much more than just moderate the logging meetings.

Leader-time   work-hours spent by the Inspection leader (or anyone else performing leader activities) in entry-time, planning-time, organizing and controlling the individual checking of all checkers, and organizing the logging meeting. The leader's time in kickoff is included in kickoff-time, the leader's time in the logging meeting is included in logging-time, and the leader's time spent in checking is included in checking-time. Leader-time is part of control-time.

Life-cycle time-saved   the savings of time in work-hours from defects fixed during editing instead of during testing or in field use, for a measured portion of the software's total life-time, such as 'to date'.

Logger   see *scribe*.

Logging   the act of writing or recording items at a logging meeting or process brainstorming meeting.

Logging-duration   the hours of logging-meeting-duration spent in reporting of items noted by checkers during their individual checking, and in searching for new items to log during the logging meeting. It should not include discussion-duration nor other non-relevant activity.

Logging meeting   the gathering at which checkers who have completed their individual checking meet to record or log their suspicions as issues, and to discover new issues. Improvement suggestions to standards, rules, procedures and forms, and questions of intent to the author are also logged at the logging meeting.

Traditional term: 'meeting'.

Logging-meeting-duration the clock time (usually expressed in hours and tenths) of the logging meeting.

Logging-meeting-rate the speed with which pages (or lines or words) are moved through by the logging meeting, usually product pages per hour. This is independent of issue logging activity. This is to monitor how much more checking time is used in the logging meeting, a meeting checking rate.

Logging-rate the number of items logged per minute in the logging meeting, including multiple occurrences logged as a single-line item.
Default: range 0.5–4.0 items logged per minute, with an average of one item per minute.

Logging-time total work-hours spent in logging activity during a logging meeting, including checking time at the logging meeting by all participants.

Major a severity classification for issues and defects. It is used when the defect would probably have significantly increased costs to find and fix later in the development process, for example in testing or in use. The primary purpose of this classification is to help ensure that the Inspection process is directed towards economically useful work. An additional classification of 'super-major' or 'critical' can also be used to indicate particularly serious majors – 'project/product threatening'.

Major-defects-detected see *Defects-detected*.

Major-issues-logged see *Issues-logged*.

Major-issues-noted see *Issues-noted*.

Major-time the average time in work-hours to find, log and edit (fix) a major defect during Inspection, including all related Inspection costs, calculated as defect-removal-time divided by the number of major defects found in one Inspection cycle.
Default: one work-hour per major defect.

Master Plan the one-page plan made by the leader during the planning process and given to the checkers. It contains the selection of documents to be used, the list of people on the Inspection team and their special checking roles, recommended optimum checking rates, notice of agreed meeting places and times, and a request for the checker to note certain information such as time used, issues found, pages studied, scanned and read, and other related data.
Synonyms: (traditional term) 'invitation'. This is too narrow for

the present content and function of the document.

Minor   an issue or defect which is not major. The cost of fixing this type of defect is not of the same order of magnitude as for major defects. However, they are still logged and fixed, since what first appears to be minor may turn out to be major, and there is no point in leaving even minor defects in software products.

Minor-defects-detected   see *Defects-detected.*

Minor-issues-logged   see *Issues-logged.*

Minor-issues-noted   see *Issues-noted.*

Moderator   the person who leads a meeting (kickoff, logging, process brainstorming) usually the Inspection leader.

Multiple occurrences   more than one instance of the same issue or defect, logged as a single description but with an estimated or actual count of instances in the documents to be dealt with by the editor. For example, if the same word is mis-spelled or mis-used many times, or if the same mistake is made in every error message, a multiple issue would be logged. Multiples are counted in the Inspection metrics as if each single occurrence was logged separately.

New-issues-logged   see *Issues-logged.*

New-issues-noted   see *Issues-noted.*

Non-commentary   non-commentary statements are ones where defects can be major. In commentary statements, defects will not normally result in major defects.

Number of checkers   the number of Inspectors doing checking (including leader if doing checking).

Optimum-checking-rate   the number of pages studied per hour during individual checking per unit of time, which gives the best result in terms of effectiveness (percentage of major defects found) or efficiency (major defects found per work-hour). The optimum checking rate is usually in the region of one non-commentary full page per hour and this should be used as a default rate.

Optimum-logging-meeting-rate   the logging-meeting-rate which results in the maximum number of major new issues logged per work-hour or per page. A guideline for finding the optimum-logging-meeting-rate is that approximately 20% of new issues should be discovered during the logging meeting, the other 80% having been discovered during individual checking.

Owner   the person, group or organizational unit which is designated as responsible for the maintenance of a document.

Page   a unit of work on which Inspection is performed. A page should be defined as a quantity of non-commentary words (e.g. 600).

Pages-scanned   the number of pages examined in whole or in part for rule violations, but which are read at a rate higher than the optimum rate.

Pages-studied   the number of pages which have been closely scrutinized at or near the optimum checking rate by checkers in individual checking, checking all source documents, using rules, procedures, checklists and other relevant documents. The purpose of this measure is to help compute the optimum checking rate.

Pages-used   the number of pages used in the Inspection cycle. This includes any documents Inspected (studied, scanned or merely referenced), such as product, source documents, rules, checklists and procedures. The purpose of this measure is to get an idea of the volume of checking work.

PCMT   see *Process Change Management Team.*

Phase   see *Stage.*

Planning-time   work-hours for creating the master plan. This can be done by anyone, but is primarily done by the leader. This time includes any time needed to search for participating documents, create or update them, and copy them. It also includes time to get data such as optimum checking rates.

Prevention-time   process-brainstorming-time plus Process-Change-Management-Team-time plus quality-improvement-team-time. This is the total time put into improving the software development processes to prevent defects from arising in the future.

Procedure   a standard which describes what to do to perform a specific task. A procedure must be written for auditing, teaching and continuous improvement. Rules are specific procedures for carrying out the task of writing a document.

Process   an activity defined by (1) entry criteria, (2) a task with associated procedures and rules, and (3) exit criteria. A process normally produces some output, which may be called deliverables or products.

Process Brainstorming   a meeting held after a logging meeting to speculate about the root causes of major issues logged, and to generate ideas for improving the software development process or the Inspection process. The improvement suggestions are logged and the Process Change Management Team (PCMT) has the responsibility of following up all suggestions.
Traditional term: 'causal analysis' (Jones, 1985).

Process-brainstorming-time   total   work-hours   spent   by   all

Inspectors while brainstorming defect root causes, and suggesting process improvements.

Process Change Management Team (PCMT)   a team of people with the responsibility for monitoring the quality assurance database, for identifying opportunities for process improvements, for getting someone to investigate the opportunity in detail (process investigators), for evaluating the investigators' work, for making recommendations for spreading useful improvements, and for actively promoting the improvements throughout the organization. Traditional term: 'Action Team'.

Process Change Management Team time (PCMT-time)   work-hours spent by the PCMT. A cost of improving processes.

Process improvement   the quality improvement process which uses Inspection (and other) metrics. It includes the following: process brainstorming meetings, Process Change Management Teams, stage kickoff library, process change feedback at kickoff meetings, quality assurance database.

Process investigator   someone working for the Process Change Management Team who is specifically charged with investigating in depth why a process produces defects, with finding process improvements to reduce the frequency of such defects, and with performing a cost–benefit analysis for implementing the suggested improvements within the organization.

Product   a document or set of documents produced by a task done by an author. If the document successfully exits Inspection it becomes an 'exited' product.
A 'candidate' document is not limited to the product of a particular single task. For example, a maintenance change may entail multiple documents such as code, pseudo code, test plans, test cases, user manuals, requirements, and interface design specifications as part of the product group.
Synonyms: work-product, product document, (traditional term) 'low-level document'.

Quality Assurance (QA) the function of ensuring that the organization and its processes provide the required levels of quality within required or competitive constraints.

QA database   a database with all data related to defects and process improvements, their costs, types and status.

Quality Improvement the removal of defects not only from products but also from the process which produced a faulty product, by analyzing the root cause of individual product defects. Inspection as described in this book is a quality improvement method.

Quality improvement team a group of people who have responsibility for implementing improvements to quality. See also *Improvement champion*.

Quality-improvement-team-time work-hours spent by the quality improvement team.

Question of intent an item logged at the logging meeting, which is not classed as an issue or as an improvement suggestion, but which requires some oral reply or explanation from the author at the end of the logging meeting. When the document is actually edited, the editor may voluntarily on their own initiative decide that the question does indicate a defect and re-classify it as a defect. For example, if something is not intelligible to novices, they may not be confident enough to raise it as an issue, when in fact it is a defect. Questions of intent are not included in the issue or defect Inspection metrics.

Questions-of-intent-logged the number of questions of intent to the author reported in the logging meeting and recorded in the issue log.

Questions-of-intent-noted the number of questions of intent to the author noted by an individual checker during individual checking.

Release the act of officially certifying that a particular document has met its exit criteria, and can therefore be safely and economically given to its 'customers'.

Reported defects reported issues which are classified as defects during editing, and reported by the editor to the leader after edit.

Role a specialized checking responsibility assigned to an individual checker when doing individual checking, or during the logging meeting. The role objective is to increase the Inspection team's productivity. Productivity is measured by major suspicions or issues found per hour and per page. Effective roles permit each checker to find a relatively large number of unique issues (issues found by that individual only and not by the other checkers). Checklists for individual roles help the checker to search effectively for a specified class of major defects. Examples of checklist roles are user, tester, designer, maintainer, legal advisor, and marketing. A document role is a responsibility to concentrate checking on a particular document.

Role checklist a checklist to help an Inspector to fulfill a specific role. For example, a checklist question for a legal role might be: CLG 'Are we safe from being sued if anything goes wrong? <– Rule G16'.

Rule a procedure for writing a product document using the task source document implied or specified in the rules. A rule specifies the content and format of the task product documents. A rule specifies how source data is translated into product by a task.

Traditional term: 'standard'. A standard is anything which guides an activity, whereas a rule is a specific type of standard procedure related only to documents, and states what must be written.

Scribe   the person who records or logs items at a meeting. Issues, improvement suggestions, and questions of intent to the author are logged at the logging meeting. Causes and improvement suggestions are logged at the process brainstorming meeting. The scribe can be the meeting moderator (by default – though it is not recommended), a checker, an outside assistant or visitor, or even the author (not recommended). Several people may take it in turns to be the scribe at a single meeting.

Synonym: recorder, logger.

Severity   a classification of an issue based on the estimated future cost to find and fix a defect at a later stage, if not fixed at this stage. The alternatives are minor (about the same), major (substantially greater), critical (product or project threatening later).

Software Inspection Plan   see *Master Plan*.

Source   any document which contains information which is a necessary prerequisite for the correct production of the product document using the pertinent rules.

Traditional term: 'high-level document'.

Specific checklist   a checklist relating to a particular type of document. For example, a requirements specification checklist question may be: 'CRQ6: Is sufficient information given for all error handling to be designed? <– Rule RQ23'.

Stage   a development or change task (for example, coding, requirement specification).

Standard   guidance in the way processes are performed. A standard guides people to do something in a particular way.

Super-major   an optional additional classification for a major issue or defect which is extremely serious or critical, that is, potentially project threatening or which is at least two orders of magnitude more damaging than an average major issue or defect.

Super-major is counted as a major unless reported separately.

The purpose of this category is political; to highlight, especially for management, the 'show stoppers' caught by a particular Inspection cycle.

Synonym: 'critical'.

Task an activity defined by written procedures, rules, and other standards. A task start and completion is controlled by entry and exit criteria.

Undetected defects defects which are present but so far undetected by the Inspection process. They may be discoverable sooner or later, but they have not been found or logged at this stage.

Default (for mature Inspection processes): 20% of defects logged for pseudocode, 12% for module and interface definition, 40% for source code.

Default (for immature Inspection process): 70% in all documents.

Upstream the work processes which occur before some specified reference point.

Work-hours total hours used by an individual or a group in doing a defined task.

Synonyms: man-hours, person-hours.

Relationship to Traditional Terminology

A number of terms and concepts have been adopted in this book which are different from those used in conventional software inspections, including the Inspection terms used in Gilb's previous books.

The novice reader with no knowledge of such things may safely skip this section, although they may need to reference it when communicating with people who know the older methods.

Below is a basic list of Inspection terms and the equivalent traditional terms.

New Inspection Term	Traditional Term(s)
Checker	Inspector
Checker roles	Inspector roles
Individual Checking	Preparation
Defect (after editing)	Defect (at all Inspection stages)
Edit	Re-work
Editor	Re-worker
Exited Product	Low-level document after Inspection
Improvement Suggestion	(no formal previous term)
Inspection Library	Stage (Kickoff) Library
Issue (as logged)	Defect (in logging)
Item (issue, improvement, question)	Defect (in logging)
Kickoff	Kickoff meeting, overview
Leader, Inspection Leader	Moderator
Moderator (leading logging meeting)	Moderator
Master plan	Invitation
Logging (meeting)	The meeting, defect logging meeting
Procedure	Standard (for doing things)
Process brainstorming	Causal analysis
Process brainstorming meeting log	Action item log
Process Change Management Team, (PCMT)	Action team
Product (of task)	Low-level document
Question of intent to author	(no previous term)
Rules (rule sets)	Standards (for writing documents)
Senior Inspection leader	Chief moderator
Software Inspection	Software (Fagan's) Inspection
Source documents	High-level documents

Bibliography

Ackermann A. F., Fowler P. and Ebenau R. (1984). Software Inspections and the Industrial Production of Software. In *Software Validation* (Hausen, Hans-Ludwig, ed.), pp. 13–40, North-Holland

Ackermann A. F., Buchward L. S. and Lewski F. H. (1989). Software Inspections: An Effective Verification Process. *IEEE Software*, May 1989, 31–36

Arksey, Cindy (1989). *Fagan method pilot, final report*. Internal Technical Report, Boeing, Seattle WA, 1–8

Barnard, H. Jack and Price, Arthur (1991). Managing Inspection Information. *Proc. 8th Int. Test Conf.*, June 1991, 189–198

Bisant, David B. and Lyle, James R. (1989). A Two-Person Inspection Method to Improve Programming Productivity. *IEEE Trans. on SW Eng.*, **SE-15**(10), October 1989, 1294–1304

Boehm, Barry W. (1981). *Software Engineering Economics*. Englewood Cliffs, NJ: Prentice-Hall

Bouldin, Barbara M. (1989). *Agents of Change*. Prentice-Hall

Britcher, Robert N. (1988). Using Inspections to Investigate Program Correctness. *Computer*, November 1988, 38–44

Brothers L., Sembugamoorthy V. and Muller M. (1990). ICICLE: Groupware for Code Inspection. *CSCW 90: Proceedings of the ACM Conf. on Computer Supported Cooperative Work*, October 1990, 169–181

Buck F. O. (1980). *Indicators of Quality Inspections*. IBM Technical Report, Kingston NY, 6 April 1980, 19pp. A study of optimum rates, numbers on team

Buck, Robert D. and Dobbins, James H. (1984). Application of Software Inspection Methodology in Design and Code. In *Software Validation* (Hausen, Hans-Ludwig, ed.), pp. 41–56. North-Holland

Buckle J. (1990). *Software Inspection Handbook*. London: Institute of Electrical Engineers

Bush M. (1990). Improving Software Quality; the use of formal Inspections at the Jet Propulsion Laboratory. *Proc. of 12th Int. Conf. on Software Engineering*, Nice, March 1990, 196–199

Bush M. and Kelly J. (1989). The Jet Propulsion Laboratory's

Experience with Formal Inspections. *Proceedings of the 14th Annual Software Engineering Workshop.* NASA Goddard Space Flight Center, Software Engineering Laboratory

Christenson D. A. and Huang S. T. (1987). Code Inspection Management Using Statistical Control Limits. *Proc. National Communications Forum*, **41**(2), 1095–1100

Christenson D. A. and Huang S. T. (1988). Code Inspection Model for Software Quality Management and Prediction. *Proc. IEEE Global Telecommunications Conf.*, **1**, 1988, 468–472

Christenson D. A., Huang S. T. and Lamperez A. J. (1990). Statistical Quality Control Applied to Code Inspections. *IEEE Journal on Selected Areas in Communications*, **8**(2), Feb. 1990, pp. 196–200

Christenson D. A., Huang S. T. and Lamperez A. J. (1991). A Code Inspection Model For Software Quality Management. *Proc. 8th Int. Test Con.*, June 1991, 245–257

De Bono E. (1971). *Lateral Thinking for Management.* London: Penguin Books

DeMarco T. and Lister T. (1987). *Peopleware.* New York: Dorset House

Deming W. Edwards (1986). *Out of the Crisis.* Cambridge, MA: MIT Center for Advanced Engineering Study

Dion R. (1993). Process Improvement and the Corporate Balance Sheet. *IEEE Software*, July, pp. 28–35

Dobbins J. H. (1987). Inspections as an Up-Front Quality Technique. In *Handbook of Software Quality Assurance* (Schulmeyer G. G. and McManus J. I., eds) pp. 137–177. Van Nostrand Reinhold

Doolan E.P. (1992). Experience with Fagan's Inspection Method. *Software Practice and Experience*, February, 173–182

Dyer M. (1991). Error Prevention and Detection During Software Development. *Proc. of 8th International Testing Conf.*, June 1991, 173–180

Fagan M. E. (1976). Design and Code Inspections to Reduce Errors in Program Development. *IBM Systems Journal*, **15**(3), 182–211

Fagan M. E. (1977). Inspecting Software Design and Code. *Datamation*, Oct. 1977, 133–144

Fagan M. E. (1986). Advances in Software Inspections. *IEEE Transactions on Software Engineering.*, **SE-12** (7), July, 744–751

Fowler P. J. (1986). In-Process Inspections of Workproducts at AT&T. *AT&T Technical Journal*, **65**(2), March–April, 102–112

Frank A., Buchwald L.S. and Lewski F. (1989). Software Inspections: An Effective Verification Process. *IEEE Software*, May, 31–36

Freedman D. P. and Weinberg G. M. (1982). *Handbook of Walkthroughs, Inspections, and Technical Reviews*, 3rd edn. Little, Brown, 1982. Reprinted New York: Dorset House, 1990

Gale J.L., Tirso J.R. and Burchfield C.A. (1990). Implementing the Defect Prevention Process in the MVS Interactive programming organization. *IBM Systems Journal,* **29**(1), 33–43

Garcia S. (1991). Inspections as a First Step in a Measurement Program, paper (pp. 5.28 to 5.43), and foils (pp. 3.47 to 3.57). *Proc. of Applications of Software Measurement Conf.,* Orlando, 1991

Gilb T. (1976). *Software Metrics.* Sweden: Studentlitteratur and USA: Winthrop (out of print)

Gilb T. (1988). *Principles of Software Engineering Management,* pp. 205–226 and pp. 403–422. Wokingham: Addison-Wesley

Gilb T. (1991). Advanced Defect Prevention Using Inspection, Testing, and Field Data as a Base. *American Programmer,* May 1991, 38–45

Gilb T. (1992). *Document Quality Control: The case for quality control in written products and processes.* Computer Task Group's PEOPLEWARE, August 1992, 800 Delaware Ave., Buffalo NY 14209, USA, 12–15

Godfrey (1986). *AT & T Technical Journal,* **65**(2), March–April

Graden M. E. and Horsley P. S. (1986). The Effects of Software Inspections on a Major Telecommunications Project. *AT&T Technical Journal,* **65**(3), May/June, 32–40

Hankinson T. *et al.* (1991). *Software Quality: An Executive Guide to Software Testing – the key to quality computer applications.* Performance Software Ltd

Hetzel W. (1984). *The Complete Guide to Software Testing.* QED Information Sciences

Hollocker C.P. (1990). *Software Reviews and Audits Handbook.* John Wiley & Sons

Humphrey W. S. (1989). *Managing the Software Process.* Addison-Wesley

Imai M. (1986). *Kaizen: The Key to Japan's Competitive Success.* New York: Random House

Jones C. L. (1985). A Process-Integrated Approach to Defect Prevention. *IBM Systems Journal,* **24**(2), 150–167

Juran J. M. (ed.) (1985). *Quality Control Handbook,* 4th edn. New York: McGraw-Hill

Kitchenham B. A., Kitchenham A. and Fellows J. P. (1986). The Effects of Inspections on Software Quality and Productivity. *ICL Technical Journal,* May 1986, 112–122

Knight J.C. and Meyers E.A. (1991). Phased Inspections and their Implementation. *ACM SIGSOFT, Software Engineering Notes,* **16**(3) July, 29–35

Larson R. R. (1975). *Test Plan and Test Case Inspection Specification.* IBM Report TR 21.586, 4 April 1975

Lindner R. J. (1992) Rochester Programming Center, Application System/400™ software development life cycle, 'Lecture notes', 45pp.

Martin J. and Tsai W. T. (1990). N-Fold Inspection: A Requirements

Analysis Technique. *Communications of the ACM,* **33**(2), Feb., 225–232

Mays R. G., Jones C. L., Holloway G. J. and Studinski D. P. (1990). Experiences with Defect Prevention. *IBM Systems Journal,* **29**(1), 4–32

Mays, Robert G. (IBM Networking Systems Labs) (1992). Defect Prevention and Total Quality Management. In *Total Quality Management for Software* (Schulmeyer G. and McManus, eds.), pp. 389–402 Van Nostrand Reinhold

Modelling a Software Quality Handbook (1991). 91 pages, ISBN 9979-9004-0-7. Icelandic Council for Standardization, Keldnaholti, IS-112 Reykjavîk, Iceland. Fax +354–1–687409

Myers W. (1988). Shuttle Code Achieves Very Low Error Rate. *IEEE Software,* Sept., 93–95

O'Neill D. (1991). What is the Standard of Excellence? *IEEE Software,* May, 109–111

Parnas D. L. and Weiss D. M. (1987). Active Design Reviews: Principles and Practices. *Journal of Systems and Software,* No. 7, 259–265

Pressman Roger S. (1988). *Making Software Engineering Happen.* Prentice-Hall

Radice R. *et al.* (1985). A Programming Process Study (pp. 91–101). A Programming Process Architecture (pp. 79–90). *IBM Systems Journal,* No. 2, 1985

Radice R. and Phillips R. W. (1988). *Software Engineering, An Industrial Approach.* Prentice-Hall

Redmill F. J., Johnson E. A. and Runge B. A. (1988). Document Quality – Inspection. *British Telecom Telecommunications Engineering,* Vol. 6, Jan., 250–256

Reeve J.T. (1991). Applying the Fagan Inspection Technique. *Quality Forum,* **17**(1), March

Remus H. (1978). *Directions for the Applications of Structured Methodologies.* IBM Report TR 03.050, July 1978 (updated numbers appear in Christensen K., Processing Management in Programming. *Proc. of SHARE 53,* New York, 29 August, 1979)

Runge B. (1992). The Inspection Method Applied to Small Projects. In *Proceedings of 6th Int. Conf. on Software Engineering,* 416–417. Computer Society Press

Russell G. W. (1991). Experience with Inspection in Ultra-large-scale Developments. *IEEE Software,* January, 25–31

Schulmeyer G. C. and McManus J. I. (eds.) (1987). *Handbook of Software Quality Assurance.* New York: Van Nostrand Reinhold

Shirey G.C. (1992). How Inspections Fail. *Proc. 1st International*

Software Testing Analysis & Review Conf. (STAR'92), 4–7 May 1992, Las Vegas NV,1.205–1.234

Sutton K. (1992). Independent Test Teams – an Experience. *The British Computer Society Specialist Interest Group in Software Testing,* 24 January, 1992

Svendsen F. (1990). Experience with the use of Inspection in the maintenance of software. *Proc. of EOQC/SQA Second European Conf. on Software Quality Assurance,* Oslo, May 1990

Ulmer D. (1991). Life After Testing: A Unisys Experience. *Proc. 8th International Conf. on Testing Computer Software,* 17-20 June 1991, Washington DC

Weinberg G. M. and Freedman D. P. (1984). Reviews, Walkthroughs, and Inspections. *IEEE Trans. on Software Engineering,* **SE-10**(1), Jan., 68–72

Weller Edward F. (1993). Lessons Learned from Three Years of Inspection Data. *IEEE Software,* September

Yourdon E. (1989). *Structured Walkthroughs.* New York, Yourdon Press

Index